Sephardi Jewry

JEWISH COMMUNITIES IN
THE MODERN WORLD

David Sorkin, Editor

1. *The Jews of Modern France,*
   by Paula Hyman

2. *Sephardi Jewry: A History of the Judeo-Spanish Community,*
   14th–20th Centuries,
   by Esther Benbassa and Aron Rodrigue

Sephardi Jewry

A History of the Judeo-Spanish Community,
14th–20th Centuries

Esther Benbassa and Aron Rodrigue

University of California Press
Berkeley • Los Angeles • London

University of California Press
Berkeley and Los Angeles, California

University of California Press, Ltd.
London, England

First California Paperback Edition, 2000
©1993, 1995 by Esther Benbassa and Aron Rodrigue

First published in English as *Jews of the Balkans: The Judeo-Spanish Community, 14th to 20th Centuries* by Blackwell Publishers, Oxford, England and Cambridge, Massachusetts

Library of Congress Cataloging–in–Publication Data
Benbassa, Esther.
[Jews of the Balkans]
Sephardi Jewry: a history of the Judeo-Spanish community, 14th—20th centuries/Esther Benbassa and Aron Rodrigue.
   p. cm. — (Jewish communities in the modern world; 2)
"First California printing"—T.p. verso.
"Parts of this publication were first published as Juifs des Balkans . . . by Editions la Découverte, 1993"—T.p. verso.
Originally published: The Jews of the Balkans. Oxford; Cambridge, Mass.: Blackwell, 1995. With new prologue.
Includes bibliographical references and index.
ISBN 0-520-21822-1 (pbk.: alk. paper)
   1. Jews—Balkan Peninsula—History.   2. Sephardim—Balkan Peninsula—History.
3. Balkan Peninsula—Ethnic relations.   I. Rodrigue, Aron.   II. Benbassa, Esther. Juifs des Balkans.   III. Title.   IV. Series.
DS135.B3 B44 1999
949.6'004924046—dc21   99-035111
                                                                   CIP

08   07   06   05   04   03   02

10   9   8   7   6   5   4   3   2

The paper used in this publication meets the minimum requirements of
ANSI/NISO Z39.48-1992 (R 1997) (*Permanence of Paper*). ⊗

Contents

List of Maps		vi
Note on Translation		vii
Note on Transliteration and Place Names		viii
Series Editor's Preface		ix
Acknowledgments		xi
Preface		xvi
Introduction		xviii
Prologue		xxv
Notes to the Prologue		lv
1	Community and Society	1
2	Economy and Culture	36
3	Eastern Sephardi Jewry in the Era of Westernization	65
4	Paths of Politicization	116
5	The End of the Judeo-Spanish Balkans: The Holocaust and Migrations	159
	Conclusion	192
	Notes	199
	Archival Sources	267
	Newspapers and Periodicals	268
	Select Bibliography	271
	Index of Names and Places	299
	Subject Index	306

Maps

Map 1 The Ottoman Empire in Europe, 1574   xiii

Map 2 The Ottoman Empire in Europe, 1815   xiv

Map 3 The Balkans after World War I   xv

Note on Translation

The translation of the sections of this book written originally in French was made possible by a grant from the *Ministère français chargé de la culture*. A first draft of this translation was done by Miriam Kochan.

Note on Transliteration and Place Names

All titles in non-Western European languages have been translated into English in the notes and in the bibliography. Most diacritical marks have been eliminated from the text, and a simplified transliteration system, based on the *Encyclopaedia Judaica* usage, has been adopted for Hebrew. Personal names have been cited according to common English usage. Given the multi-ethnic, multilingual nature of the area which is the subject of study here, it is impossible to give all the renditions of place names. The ones most commonly accepted in English have been used throughout.

Series Editor's Preface

JEWISH COMMUNITIES IN THE MODERN WORLD

This series represents the first attempt to provide a systematic overview of the major Jewries of the modern world. Such an overview is a fundamental enterprise for any branch of historical scholarship. That it has not previously been undertaken for Jewish history is hardly surprising. While Jews struggled to gain equal rights in the Diaspora or to build their own state, scholarship had more pressing concerns. Now that emancipation appears secure and the State of Israel has passed its fiftieth anniversary, the central issues of the modern period can be approached as historical processes to be interpreted rather than struggles to be waged.

The volumes in this series offer the general reader interpretive histories that address the central issues of the modern period: emancipation and assimilation, nationalism and anti-Semitism, secularization and migration. And they strive to investigate how all Jews experienced those issues: rich and poor, female and male, religious and secular, rural and urban.

Each volume presents a synthesis of the current state of knowledge about the history of the Jews in one country or region. In the past three decades there has been an explosion of scholarship in Jewish history. These volumes utilize that scholarship to offer a broadly-based history that analyzes a community's social structure and political situation to illuminate its cultural and religious self-understanding.

The series examines with impassioned disinterest the experiences that have shaped the contemporary Jewish world. By helping us to understand how we have become what we are, they empower us to imagine what we might wish to be.

SEPHARDI JEWRY: A HISTORY OF THE JUDEO-SPANISH COMMUNITY, 14TH – 20TH CENTURIES

It is appropriate that a study of Sephardi Jewry appear as the second volume in this series since modern Jewish historians have long neglected the two "easts"—Eastern Europe on the one side, North Africa and the Middle East on the other. The authors of this volume use the extant scholarship and the results of their own research to offer an engaging synthesis of the Judeo-Iberian experience with a focus on five centuries of Jewish life in the Balkans.

The volume focuses on a region since this is a part of the world in which national politics were belated, and not necessarily welcome, arrivals. From their immigration after the expulsion from Spain (1492) until late in the nineteenth century, the Sephardi Jews constituted a unified "cultural sphere" in the multi-ethnic, polyglot Balkans that long remained the possession of the Ottoman Empire. The demise of that empire and the rise of nation-states spelled the decline of this cultural sphere. The resulting isolated and diminished Jewish communities lurched along until they, like their Ashkenazi counterparts, were destroyed or dislocated during the Second World War.

The authors have revealed a largely unknown world whose history had much in common with that of Ashkenazi Jewry. The major themes of modern Jewish history were sounded here: emancipation and acculturation, nationalism, and anti-Semitism. Yet they were sounded in a different key from the original events in Western and Central Europe; and they were sounded under the influence of those events, though often a generation or two later. Thanks to Esther Benbassa and Aron Rodrigue, we are now able to grasp the important comparative dimension that the Judeo-Iberian experience in general, and that of the Sephardi Jews of the Balkans in particular, represent for our understanding of modern Jewish history.

David Sorkin

Acknowledgments

This work is a somewhat modified and updated version of a book that first appeared in Paris in 1993 under the title *Juifs des Balkans: espaces judéo-ibériques, XIVe–XXe siècles* (Editions La Découverte). It is the culmination of research and reflection over a period of a decade and closes a cycle of publications by both of us on the history and culture of the Judeo-Spanish community.

Our thanks go to David Sorkin for encouraging us to write this book and whose editorial input has been invaluable. We are deeply appreciative of the help provided to us by the following institutions who responded positively to our requests to use their holdings. In France, the library and archives of the *Alliance israélite universelle*, the archives of the *Ministère des Affaires étrangères*, the archives of the *Ministère de la Guerre*, the *Archives de la Marine*, the *Bibliothèque nationale*, the *Bibliothèque de documentation internationale contemporaine* (BDIC). In the United States, the Harvard University Library, the Indiana University Library, the Stanford University Library, the Archives of the American Joint Distribution Committee, the United States National Archives (for microfilms of the archives of the US Department of State and of the German *Auswärtiges Amt*). In Germany, the archives of the *Auswärtiges Amt* (Bonn). In Israel, the National and University Library in Jerusalem, the Central Zionist archives, the Central archives of the History of the Jewish People, the Israel State Archives, the Library of the Ben Zvi Institute, the archives of the *Haganah*, the Lavon Institute, the archives of the *Makabi* organization, the Diaspora Institute (University of Tel-Aviv), the archives of the Jabotinsky Institute, the Research Center of the *Hashomer Hazair* (Givat Haviva). In Turkey, the archives of the Italian Jewish Community of Istanbul, the Atatürk Library, the *Institut français d'études anatoliennes*, and the Library of Istanbul University.

We would like to thank the Maurice Amado Foundation (USA) and the *Ministère de la Recherche et de l'Espace* (*Délégation à l'information scientifique et technique*) (France) for their financial support of this project. Many organizations and institutions have helped us over the years. Esther Benbassa thanks the Lady Davis Fellowship Trust (Canada/Israel), the *Yad Hanadiv/Barecha* Foundation (Great Britain/Israel), the Memorial Foundation for Jewish Culture (New York), the Department of Jewish History at the Hebrew University of Jerusalem, the *Institut d'études turques* and the UA 041057 of the CNRS (while they were under the directorship of Louis Bazin and James Hamilton), and the *Centre de recherches sur la civilisation de l'Europe moderne* and the *Institut de recherches sur les civilisations de l'Occident moderne* of the Université de Paris IV – Sorbonne. Aron Rodrigue thanks Indiana University, Stanford University, the Institute for Advanced Study at the Hebrew University of Jerusalem, the American Council of Learned Societies, and the Memorial Foundation for Jewish Culture. He would like to thank his colleagues in the Jewish Studies Programs and History Departments at Indiana and Stanford Universities for providing intellectually stimulating and congenial environments for pursuing his academic work. He would also like to thank Joan Clinefelter at Indiana and David Rechter at Stanford for their research and editing help.

We cannot finish without mentioning here our deepest gratitude to Jean-Christophe Attias, who followed this work step by step since its inception and who provided inestimable scholarly, linguistic, and moral support.

Map 1   The Ottoman Empire in Europe, 1574

Map 2   The Ottoman Empire in Europe, 1815

Map 3   The Balkans after World War I

In memory of our fathers
Jacques Benbassa, Joseph Rodrigue

Preface

This is an updated English translation of our book that appeared initially in French under the title *Juifs des Balkans: Espaces judéo-ibériques, XIVe-XXe siècles* (Paris: La Découverte, 1993). A shortened version was published in English under the title *The Jews of the Balkans: The Judeo-Spanish Community, 15th to 20th Centuries* (Oxford: Basil Blackwell, 1995).

This new edition of our book provides us with another opportunity to reiterate the basic principles and assumptions that guided us in the conceptualization and execution of our project. The history of the descendants of the Jews who left the Iberian peninsula en masse after the expulsions at the end of the fifteenth century is one that has been told in a fragmentary and piecemeal fashion, with the specificity and distinctiveness of this group usually lost in broad frameworks such as "Jews in the lands of Islam" or "Jews of the Ottoman Empire," or in narrower approaches which limit themselves to the history of the Jews in one nation-state or another. We have preferred always to keep the group at the center of our attention, with its core area of settlement after the expulsion in the Ottoman Balkans and Asia Minor, focusing on the communities that formed a specific Judeo-Spanish culture area. This study traces the rise, evolution, fragmentation, and dissolution of this entity, which was an integral part of Jewish, European, Balkan, and Middle Eastern realities. The history of the Sephardi Jews of the Levant continues to be marginalized in the standard narratives that dominate each of these respective fields, at best to be given cursory and exoticized treatments that obscure, rather than enlighten.

The neglect or distortion of this history is also intimately linked to the dominance of nationalist paradigms that held or continue to hold sway in modern Jewish and non-Jewish historiographies. The Eastern Sephardi communities were at home in what was above all a "Levantine" world that was destroyed by the rise of the nation-state in the Balkans and in the Eastern Mediterranean. The term "Levantine" could not but be pejorative for the nationalisms that triumphed. In terms of representation, coming to incarnate hybrid, half-Europeanized, half-Eastern "rootlessness" that was the product of the encounter of East and West in the modern period, the "Levantine" was deeply unsettling to the nationalist desperately seeking to impose a putatively "authentic" "national" essence onto a refractory cultural reality composed of a bewildering array of ethnic and religious groups. The "Levantine" was an equally disturbing figure for the European observer by his or her threatening mimicry of European ways that upset the stereotypical image of the exotic "native."

Multilingual, multicultural, Westernizing Sephardim, with diverse cultural repertoires in different social settings, were, together with the Greek, Armenian, and other diasporas, an indispensable element in the making of the cosmopolitan tenor of life in the major cities and towns of the Levant in modern times. Negotiating with multiple local and international influences, and yet maintaining their identities as Jews within the framework of plural cultures, the Sephardim were the quintessential "Levantines." Of course, the classic diasporic "Levantine" has disappeared, swept away by forces that dissolved the Ottoman Empire, only to haunt the perfervid nationalist imagination in its successor states, to be excised as "foreign" from the historical narrative of the "nation." And in the state of Israel, the gathering place of the bulk of the exiled Sephardi and Eastern Jewries, the mixture of East and West in the cultural domain, dubbed "Levantinism," continues to be a threat to the purveyors and guardians of a "Western" elite culture. The history and culture of these groups can hardly receive equal status in such a setting. Outside the state of Israel, Jewish historiography, reflecting its origins that lie at the heart of the Europeanization and Westernization projects of European Jewries at the period of emancipation, and engaged profoundly with Jewish nationalism after the trauma of the Holocaust, remains largely sealed off from attempts to integrate the story of groups which would complicate the reigning teleologies. And this, paradoxically, for groups whose multiple hybrid cultural stances were the norm rather than the exception for much of the Jewish diaspora throughout history.

The Levantine Judeo-Spanish community, now on the verge of extinction as a culturally specific group, neither subaltern nor nationalist victor, has not managed to have its voice heard in all its complexity. This book attempts to begin to redress the balance and to restore that voice.

Esther Benbassa
Aron Rodrigue

Introduction

Deshame entrar
Yo me hare lugar
["Let me enter, I will make a place for myself"]
Judeo-Spanish proverb

The year 1492 represents a major turning point in the history of the Jewish people. In that year the most populous, distinguished, and important of all medieval Jewries was expelled from Spain, an event, followed by forced mass conversions in Portugal five years later, which brought to an end the more than millennial Jewish presence in the Iberian peninsula. The Sephardim, the "Spaniards" according to their Hebrew appellation, spread in their overwhelming majority to the countries around the Mediterranean basin in the half century that followed the Expulsion. In the course of the sixteenth century, small groups of converted Jews or their descendants who retained a Jewish identity, the Marranos, also left the Iberian peninsula and either rejoined their brethren in the East or established new communities in Western Europe, in cities such as Bordeaux, Amsterdam, Hamburg, and London, and eventually in the New World. A major displacement, decentering, and dissolution of an old established center in the Jewish universe hence took place, bearing within it the seeds of reconstruction, renewal, and revival.

This book begins with this rupture in Jewish history. It follows the Sephardim along the paths of their exile to the East, and recounts the history of the constitution of new Judeo-Spanish centers. It concentrates on the Balkans where the great majority of the exiles gathered. A Sephardi presence continued long into the modern period in many other parts of the world. Western Sephardim in Europe and the Americas continued to be a significant part of Jewish communal existence in their localities. Sephardim arriving in North Africa altered irrevocably Maghrebi Jewish civilization. Nevertheless, in none of these areas did the Sephardim survive as a distinctive majority group that numerically dominated the surrounding Jewish communities. Ashkenazi migrations eventually swamped the Western Sephardim who then lost their Judeo-Hispanic specificity. The Sephardi Portuguese "nation" did not have the same longevity as the Judeo-Spanish culture area in the East. The history of Western Sephardim – more dispersed and fewer in numbers than their Eastern counterparts – eventually merged with the history of their Ashkenazi fellow Jews, even if some Western Sephardi islands in places such as Bordeaux, Amsterdam, London, and New York survived into the modern period.

Likewise, while the encounter between the Sephardi and Judeo-Arab culture in North Africa proved to be extraordinarily fructifying, the new Maghrebi Jewish culture that it created was distinctive. With the exception of a few communities such as Tetuan and Tangier in the North, most of the Sephardim of the Maghreb assimilated into this "Sephardized" Judeo-Arabic culture. Uniquely Judeo-Hispanic groups remained a tiny part of a much larger North African Jewry.

The situation in the Levant was very different. In the Ottoman lands of the Balkans, from the Adriatic coast, through Bosnia, Serbia, Macedonia, Bulgaria, Greece, Thrace, and in Asia Minor, a new Sephardi *Kulturbereich* (culture area), an Eastern Sephardi heartland, came into being that lasted as a distinct Judeo-Hispanic unit well into the twentieth century. The fact that it remained under Ottoman rule for almost four centuries promoted its specific unity despite slight regional variations in dialect and popular traditions. An important factor was the pattern of communal organization prevalent in the lands of Islam which contributed to the Jews' maintenance of their ethnic–religious identity.

Unlike their counterparts in the West and in North Africa, the Sephardim in these regions overwhelmed local Greek-speaking Romaniot ex-Byzantine Jews, as well as the few Ashkenazim that migrated over the centuries from Central and Eastern Europe. While the process lasted well into the seventeenth century, it was the local Romaniots who assimilated to the newcomers and not the reverse. The Sephardim Judeo-Hispanicized the Jewish world of the Ottoman Balkans and the Aegean littoral, and in cities such as Istanbul, Edirne (Adrianople), Izmir (Smyrna), Salonika, and Sarajevo, reconstituted a transplanted *Sepharad*. Of course, further south in the Fertile Crescent, in the communities of Aleppo, Damascus, Safed, Jerusalem, Alexandria, Cairo, and Tripoli, numerous enduring Sephardi communities took root from the end of the fifteenth century onwards. However, while in some of these communities such as Safed and Jerusalem the Sephardim outnumbered other Jews in certain periods, in none of them did they remain dominant majorities into contemporary times. And none of these communities were rooted in a large Sephardi hinterland. The situation in the Fertile Crescent remained complex and fragmented, with Mustarabim (Arab Jews), Judeo-Spanish speaking Sephardim, and by the end of the nineteenth century, Ashkenazim in Palestine all coexisting within a multifaceted Jewish context.

It is the history of the new Judeo-Spanish heartland in the Ottoman Balkans and Asia Minor and its fate in modern times that is the central object of our study. We do not treat here areas which became Rumania in the nineteenth century, usually considered part of the Balkans, since the Sephardi group remained demographically tiny in the midst of a very large Ashkenazi population whose culture and history diverged from their Judeo-Spanish neighbors south of the Danube river. Developments in other Sephardi communities of the Levant are, of course, examined as they influenced this central area. But our focus is this Judeo-Spanish unit as a compact, specific entity that transcended individual communities. Our approach is not structured by geography or twentieth-century political borders. We follow the inner continuities that overdetermined the dialectic between unity and diversity that was the hallmark of this group which came to form a distinct, internally cohesive part of the Jewish people.

Modern Jewish historiography has been remarkably silent about the Eastern Judeo-Spanish world. Obsessed with the Spanish Golden Age, it has only deigned to study the Eastern Sephardim from the perspective of high intellectual history, tracing the problematics of Expulsion and the themes associated with it as they reverberated in the following two centuries, until the denouement of Sabbatean messianism. And even this history is narrated incidentally, to provide the background for the depiction of a famous personality, a movement, or intellectual work.

The Eastern Sephardim have been exoticized, placed into the "Middle Eastern" slot and hence ignored or denigrated, or have been romanticized for their preservation of the Iberian past through language and song. The Judeo-Spanish community in the modern period has been unseen and unheard of except in "folklore." Jewish historiography has been blind to the lessons that could be drawn from the Eastern Sephardi experience to offer comparisons and contrasts with trends and developments that have shaped modern Jewish history. Other Jewries considered "peripheral," mostly of the Islamic world, not all of them stemming from the Iberian peninsula, have suffered the same treatment.

Most of Jewish history of the last few decades has been written in Israel. The majority of the makers of the new state were Ashkenazim and the part played by non-Ashkenazi elements in its building was either neglected or simply ignored: they do not have a place alongside the founders, nor in the general history of Zionism. Non-Ashkenazim are absent from the project and from the history of the heroes. For ideological reasons, the voice of so-called "oriental" Jews had been silenced. Only in recent years has the Israeli establishment taken steps to create scholarly institutions charged with writing the history of almost half the Jews in the country, namely, these same "Eastern Jews." Despite such praiseworthy efforts, much remains to be done. This history has yet to become academically respectable; it has often been confined to a sphere of exoticism, and for a long time left in the hands of amateurs. Modern Jewish historians have also been influenced, sometimes even despite themselves, by an academic elitism and Eurocentrism which construes the history of the "European" Ashkenazim as more central. We are therefore still far from a global history of the Jews which is unbiased, and from a more complete – beyond "important" and "unimportant" – history.

The historiography of the Eastern Sephardim has suffered as a result of all these trends, even though copious literature – which stops largely at the seventeenth century – has been devoted to it in recent years. Curiously enough, the Sabbatean crisis is the breaking-off point. Looking at the state of the field, one would think that the post-Sabbatean, modern period was of no interest. The second "golden age" comes to a resounding halt. Furthermore, this historiography is fragmented, written in fits and starts, from different angles, without any attempt at an overall synthesis. Here again, there is a hierarchy: more thorough and more numerous studies deal with the area of the Ottoman Empire within the frontiers of present-day Turkey, and with Salonika; Bulgaria and Yugoslavia have been condemned to semi-oblivion.

Yet the history of the Judeo-Spanish culture area constitutes a challenge for modern Jewish historiography. It offers new avenues of study and interpretation. It can bring fresh perspectives, especially in the field of modern Jewish history, now mainly devoted to the European world and tending to rehearse major themes such as emancipation, assimilation, acculturation, and nationalism on an exclusively European stage. The Eastern Sephardi culture area in the Balkans offers an important alternative and also supplies a significant comparative angle. Great historical currents, such as the French Revolution or Western-style emancipation, passed through a number of filters and their repercussions only came late and in a modified form to the Sephardim. Many local factors played an important and decisive role in the transformation of the community. At the crossroads of East and West, having followed its own particular route, with its own organizational model, culturally "colonized" by the Jewish West, neither assimilated nor acculturated, indeed barely integrated, the Judeo-Spanish culture area opens onto another history.

It has been mostly Ottomanists or Middle Eastern specialists who have dealt with these communities, and mostly in the last few years during the countdown to the unseemly commemoration/celebration of the Expulsion and the Sephardi experience that took place in 1992. Much has been learnt through their efforts. Insofar as these Judeo-Spanish communities were under Ottoman rule for approximately four centuries, studies of the history and culture of the Jews of the Ottoman Empire cover many aspects of Judeo-Spanish existence in the Levant. And indeed, these Jews were an integral part of the Ottoman mosaic of ethnic and religious groups that made up the Balkans and the Middle East. The Eastern Sephardi heartland came into being as part of an Ottoman reality.

However, there is as yet no unified history of the Judeo-Spanish culture area that covers its complete history. The Ottoman framework as an organizational structure of study collapses with the age of nationalism in the nineteenth century when the area fragmented into different nation-states. Historians of the Jewish communities that fell under the rule of the latter have uniformly chosen the nineteenth and twentieth-century borders of these states to tell the story of the Jews living within their boundaries. However, "Greek" or "Bulgarian" Jewry as concepts are meaningless for the period prior to the emergence of the Greek or Bulgarian nation-states. And even in the case of "Ottoman" or "Turkish" Jewry where the tie with the Ottoman past is much more evident, the history inevitably becomes slanted as one approaches the twentieth century in a manner that ignores major Jewish communities such as Salonika that were no longer under Turkish Ottoman rule after 1912/1913. The comparative dimension, the essence of all good history, and doubly important in the case of dispersed Jewish groups such as the Eastern Sephardim, is inevitably lost.

While both the Ottomanist and the nation-state perspectives have their merit and use in particular contexts, they implicitly transform the Eastern Sephardim into objects whose history is mediated through schemas that displace the unity and specificity of the group and miss crucial perspectives. Fragmentary approaches chase after an ever elusive object whose history is never grasped as a whole, and provide an incomplete or deformed picture. We have chosen to begin in reverse, with the Judeo-Spanish group as the constitutive subject of the study irrespective of the political regime under which it found itself in different periods. The inner life and dynamic of the Eastern Sephardim together with their dealings with the outside world, whether Ottoman or nation-state, form the twin poles of our narrative. This book is, then, the history of the evolving Judeo-Spanish collectivity with a vertical relation to its past and horizontal dialectic with the surrounding societies, cultures, and political systems. Our frame of reference remains throughout the Sephardi unit and not an outside reality. We contextualize the latter in the Jewish, Ottoman, Balkan, and modern nation-state settings in a comparative framework with Jewish and non-Jewish developments that we hope provides fresh insights.

Above all, this is a history of a world that has come to an end. Most people are aware of the destruction of the Ashkenazi heartland in the middle of the twentieth century. Its Judeo-Spanish counterpart, reconstituted in the East at the same period at the end of the Middle Ages, also disappeared at approximately the same time. The process of radical change began long before. By the eighteenth century, declining economic conditions in the Levant had sapped the Eastern Sephardi community of its vitality. The age of reform and Westernization affected it profoundly, within and without. New challenges were posed, and the community as a whole underwent an uneven transformation. New élites rose, while older ones declined. The changing economy provided intermittent but sometimes significant prosperity in certain locales such as Salonika. Both the reforming Ottoman state and successor states in the Balkans fundamentally altered the political system under which the Judeo-Spanish communities had lived for centuries. The age of the nation-state caught up with the Eastern Sephardim with a vengeance. The Sephardi unit was forcibly fragmented by the destruction of the Ottoman Levant. The Eastern Sephardim were forced to adapt to many new masters who replaced the old single Ottoman ruler. In the process, new political ideologies, especially Jewish nationalism, made their appearance. Just like the Ashkenazim, the modern Judeo-Spanish communities had to grapple with issues of identity, community, loyalty to the collectivity versus the local state, and with the larger question of how to be a Jew, indeed a *Sephardi* Jew, in the modern world. They offered answers that were sometimes similar, and sometimes very different, to those provided by their Ashkenazi counterparts.

The exploded Eastern Sephardi *Kulturbereich*, now under nation-state systems singularly ill-adapted to the complex realities of the Balkans, lurched from one crisis to another until the arrival of the Nazis. The Holocaust dealt a death blow to the Judeo-Spanish world. Whole communities were destroyed, while those that escaped the Nazi onslaught chose the route of emigration, mostly to Israel. While a few remnant communities survive in the area today, the Judeo-Spanish collectivity as a distinct Jewish entity is, for all intents and purposes, dead.

This book, then, tells the story of the constitution, evolution, fragmentation, and death of a specific Judeo-Spanish civilization that existed in the Levant for four and a half centuries. It is both an interpretative synthesizing essay and also the result of original research in numerous archives for the sections dealing with the modern period. We are well aware that it is impossible to do justice to all aspects of a rich history that spans half a millennium. There are huge lacunae in many parts of the history and culture of the Eastern Sephardim. We are encouraged by recent developments that promise freer access to local archives, and also by growing awareness of the importance of studying this part of Jewish history. Multiple partial accounts, individual studies, communal histories, discussions of particular trends in the history and culture of the Eastern Sephardim pullulate in an uneven way without an overarching framework to give this history cohesion. We have attempted to provide such cohesion through an overview of the whole, offering one particular interpretation, and at the same time have focused on certain themes which have appeared to us especially significant. We are as interested in raising questions, in identifying and crystallizing the very problematics of the history of the Eastern Sephardi unit, as in providing answers. The field as a whole is still in its infancy, and we very much hope that this essay will provide the stimulus and impetus for more research. We will be content if, above all, in this very first general history of Eastern Sephardi Jewry from its constitution as an entity at the end of the fifteenth century through its dissolution in the twentieth, we have succeeded in restoring the voice of a collectivity that did not survive and in putting the spotlight on a world that we have lost.

PROLOGUE

JUDEO-IBERIAN ORIGINS

In January 1492, the victorious armies of the Catholic monarchs entered Granada. This heralded the end of the *Reconquista*, the rolling back of Muslim power by the Christian forces of the north that had been continuing since the beginning of Arab Muslim rule in the eighth century. Three months later, on 31 March 1492, the Catholic monarchs signed the edict of expulsion of the Jews in the same city of Granada. Promulgated and made public between 29 April and 1 May, the edict gave the Jews the choice of either converting to Christianity or else leaving Spain by the end of July 1492. Many opted for conversion, having decided not to risk the perils of traveling long distances, by sea or on land. The exodus of those who chose to remain true to their faith began in May. By 31 July 1492, the last openly practicing Jew had left Spain.[1]

The fall of Muslim Granada, and the expulsion of the Jews, represented symbolically the definite triumph of Christianity and the culmination of the spirit of intolerance that had been gaining strength for the last century. However, while the clouds had increasingly darkened in the decades preceding the event, the Expulsion had come as a complete surprise for the majority of the Jews. The myth that had constituted the dominant ideology of Spanish Jewry, stressing its great success, its rootedness in Iberian soil, and its indispensability, had made the Jewish elite and society completely unprepared for this final act of intolerance that closed the curtain on the Iberian stage of Jewish history. But the myth was a particularly strong one that had its origins in the past, in the days of Muslim Spain and in the first period of the *Reconquista* itself.

JEWS IN CHRISTIAN SPAIN

Jews had had a continuous existence in the Iberian peninsula since Roman times. Undergoing many travails at the time of the Visigothic kingdom, Jewish life had flourished under Muslim rule, which had begun with the Arab invasion of 711. Jewish culture and civilization in the Middle Ages had some of their greatest advances on Iberian soil, achievements that were later to be characterized with the term "the golden age." Jews in Muslim Spain had been active in all areas of life. Particularly significant, however, was the emergence of a self-assured Jewish courtier class that was important in finance, in administration, and in governance. This class had really come into its own with the collapse of united Al-Andalus in the beginning of the eleventh century and its replacement by numerous Arab and Berber kingdoms which had multiplied the possibilities of employment and success at the various courts. Perfectly attuned to Arabic culture, familiar with the great accomplishments of Arab literature, and with rationalist and other philosophical thought that had made its appearance in Arabic, individual members of this courtier elite had been active in the Judeo-Arab symbiosis that had underpinned so many of Sephardi achievements in culture and in politics.[2]

The fanatical and intolerant Almohade (1130–1269) invasion from Morocco in 1146 spelled the end of meaningful Jewish life in the south. The *Reconquista* with its Christian mission also appeared foreboding, equally threatening to end Jewish existence in Spain. However, paradoxically, the very opposite happened. The Jews together with their leadership made a relatively smooth transition from the Muslim environment to the Christian kingdoms that were now expanding southward. Precisely the same circumstances that had made the Jews indispensable for many Muslim kingdoms also became significant in the new *Reconquista* kingdoms. The Jews with their specialization in trade and commerce were a particularly important element in the colonization plans of the latter, and the Jewish courtier class brought with it many skills that were crucial for the smooth functioning of the new, fledgling administrations. Hence the transition from Muslim to Christian Spain, while perilous, was completed successfully by the majority of the Jews. With the fall of Seville in 1248, all of the Iberian peninsula, with the exception of the Kingdom of Granada at the very south, had entered Christian rule, and the bulk of the Jewish population was now living under new masters.[3]

The fundamentals of Jewish existence in Christian Spain were to be governed, as elsewhere in the Diaspora, by what can be called the "royal alliance."[4] Christian Spain was far from being a united country; Castile, Aragon, Catalonia, Valencia, Navarre all had different laws and customs, and different configurations of power among the aristocracies, the city elites, and the royal rule. Elements of German law, Visigothic law, canon law, the king's law, *fueros* (local customary law) all coexisted uneasily. Nevertheless, the place of the Jews in society was determined by a remarkably similar constellation of circumstances. The Jewish community, sidestepping other loci of power, stood in a direct, one-to-one relationship to the king. The Jews, in fact, belonged juridically to the king; they were his "serfs." They paid taxes directly to him, in return for which he protected them, and gave them extensive communal autonomy.

This was, of course, the classic pattern of Jewish existence in the Diaspora in the premodern period. The Jews felt secure in the protection afforded them by a strong centralized power. The latter also imposed a certain uniformity with regard to the legal place of the Jews in society, which in turn facilitated the governance of the community and the administration of its internal affairs. Both sides perceived this as a mutually beneficial relationship. The Jews obtained protection and privileges, in return for which the king was assured a steady source of revenue in the form of taxes from them. Furthermore, he could rely on the Jews as an element which had no direct power base in the locality. Hence, Jewish administrators and financiers could represent the royal interest and could be put to work to expand the power of the center against local forces.

Since Carolingian times, the Jews had been used for these very purposes by centralizing authorities throughout Europe. Whether in Spain or, later, in Poland, especially in earlier periods of expansion, the Jews were seen as useful for purposes of settlement, colonization, tax collection, and centralization. The activities of the Jews in these fields were especially remarkable in *Reconquista* Spain, and gave a very special intensity to the "royal alliance," exercising a hypnotic effect on the courtier elite that set the tone for the rest of Jewish society. Nowhere else in medieval Europe did so many Jews reach the uppermost echelons of royal administration, and nowhere else did they become as important, and as useful to the kings.

These very achievements, however, hid some central facts that were built into the "royal alliance" itself. The strong identification of the Jews with central power meant that the local elements with which they were obliged to live were inevitably driven to a position of hostility toward them. The local aristocracy, or the local bourgeois forces in cities, as well as the peasantry which frequently had to pay taxes to the Jewish tax collector, all were continuously brought into a position of friction with the Jews by the very fact that the latter had become buffers between the crown and the locality. In many ways, the very seeds of disaster were implicit in the dialectic of the "royal alliance" itself. Its very nature bred hostility with all the other forces in society. And all that could protect the Jews were the power and will of the kings or of central authorities. Hence any abandonment of the Jews by the center, or a vacuum of power or a weakening of authority, could spell disaster. This particular development was, of course, to have fateful consequences for the Jews of Christian Spain.

Most of the history of the Jews in Christian Spain can be seen within the perspective of the unfolding of this "royal alliance." The high points corresponded to the periods of the greatest need for the Jews by centralized authority. The nadir was reached with deteriorating circumstances associated with momentary losses of royal power or with the abandonment of the Jews by the center upon finding itself obliged to yield to pressures coming from other forces in society. The thirteenth century can be seen as the apogee of the "royal alliance," when the Jews received the best treatment which underlay much of the successful transition from Muslim to Christian rule. The Jewish elite knew Arabic and were in touch with Arabic learning in all fields, and thus could act as intermediaries between Muslims and Christians. Furthermore, the extensive administrative experience of this courtier class was particularly useful in the frontier society that was in the process of being conquered and settled. Finally, traditionally concentrated in commercial occupations, the Jews supplied a ready-made middle class to Christian Spain, especially in certain areas of Castile and of Valencia that were now entering Christian rule.[5]

The *Reconquista* was, hence, accompanied by the confirmation of the privileges of the Jews and in fact by their extension. The *aljama* (the Jewish community) could live according to its own internal laws based on Jewish religious law and was granted extensive autonomy covering all areas of life, including civil and criminal jurisdiction—the latter representing an unparalleled development.[6] At the same time, many individual Jews rose to positions of prominence. Alfonso VI (r. 1072–1109) of Castile was served by Josef Ferruziel (d. 1145), also known as Cidellus, who occupied the position of physician to the crown.[7] In the thirteenth century in Aragon the Jews occupied the position of *baile* (bailiff).[8] With the southward expansion of the *Reconquista*, James I (r. 1213–76) of Aragon invited the Jews to Valencia, to Aragon, and to Majorca, and gave them exceptional tax exemption for settling in abandoned or sparsely populated cities and towns.[9] The Alconstantini and the de la Caballeria families in Aragon were active in the civil service and were utilized extensively by the king as a counterweight against the nobility and the clergy.[10] Apart from the importance of the Jews as administrators and financiers, the place of their community in the finances of the treasuries is well illustrated by the fact that in 1294 the Jews paid 22 percent of all direct taxes in Aragon and in 1323 paid 35 percent of all Catalonian taxes.[11] Hence, the Jews represented an extraordinarily useful population for the kings not only for collecting the taxes owed by his subjects but also because of their substantial contribution to the royal coffers. They were represented in all areas of the economy.[12]

While the dynamics of the "royal alliance" and the concomitant utilization of the Jewish courtier elite for the administration and financing of royal activities were constants in all the Christian kingdoms of Spain, notable differences can be observed between Castile and the areas under the rule of the crown of Aragon. Castile was very late in developing an urban middle class, while Aragon, especially in Catalonia, saw the flourishing of such a class as the thirteenth century progressed. As a result, the role of the Jews in the economy and in the royal administrations began to decline in Aragon, whereas in Castile the Jewish communities continued to be perceived as very important and useful populations. The nobility and the clergy also opposed strongly the role of the Jews in the royal administration. While the crown continued to protect the Jewish communities against riots and attacks in Aragon, it is clear that after 1283 it had to yield to public pressure, and the place of the Jews in public service became severely circumscribed after this date.[13] There were no counterparts in fourteenth-century Aragon to Don Samuel Halevi, the chief treasurer of Pedro the Cruel of Castile (r. 1350–69) and the builder of the famous Toledo synagogue *El Transito* in 1357.[14]

However, to illustrate the one-sided nature of the "royal alliance," and the powerlessness of the Jews deeply embedded in Diaspora existence, it is important to note that the same Halevi died in the king's prison. Whether because of the whim of a ruler or because of a tactical necessity to yield to the demands of local forces or to heed public opinion, the position of the Jewish courtier and of the Jewish community was never secure or guaranteed, and it was often perilous.

The extensive privileges granted to the Jews, the achievements of Jewish courtiers, and the positive aspects of the "royal alliance" in general should not obscure the fact that even in the positive circumstances of the thirteenth century, the Jews were never on an equal footing with the rest of society. Much has been made of *convivencia*, the relatively harmonious coexistence of the members of the three monotheistic faiths in Spain.[15] This situation was unusual in medieval Europe. Spain was the only place where Muslims, Jews, and Christians were found living in the same land, and where the cultures of the three groups had deeply influenced each other. Yet the "royal alliance" and *convivencia* pointed not to a pluralist society, but to a relatively plural one. Ultimately the place of the non-Christian as well as the Christian was firmly fixed in a hierarchical social and ideological system. The Jews and Judaism constituted a minority and a religion that were despised, and in spite of privileges still suffered severe social disabilities. The position of the Jews in Christian Spain in the early *Reconquista* period can appear in a positive light only in comparison with other Jewish communities of the time in Europe. But even under the best circumstances, the Jews in Christian Spain were a clearly defined caste whose traditional pariah status in a medieval

Christian setting was obscured thanks to an exceptional configuration.[16] Their continued existence and well-being were tied to their perceived "utility" and to the will and power of the rulers. The latter continued the "royal alliance" relationship until the end, even in an attenuated form. Hence, Jewish civil servants like Isaac Abravanel (1437–1508) and Abraham Seneor (1412–93) continued to act in important positions as financiers and administrators up to the very period of the Expulsion in 1492 in Castile, and the "royal alliance" would still, even in periods of decline, carry a semblance of power and reality to satisfy the expectations of the Jews, especially of their intellectual and societal elite, and to offer them the mirage of security.

The same thirteenth century which witnessed the flourishing of Jewish life in Christian Spain and the strong involvement of individual Jews of the courtier class in the affairs of the state also saw the beginnings of change that would eventually undo all these developments. It is instructive to look across the Pyrenees to developments in Western Europe as a whole. This period emerged as one of great intolerance and persecution of the Jews. The Fourth Lateran Council, in 1215, promulgated a series of discriminatory measures against Jews, limiting the areas where they could live, defining the kind of clothing they could wear, and restricting their place in the economy. Indeed, by the end of the thirteenth century the economic activities of most of the Jews had been limited to moneylending. The extensive missionizing by the friars that began in this period, the burning of the Talmud, and the squeezing of Jews from their hitherto accepted positions in society all pointed in one direction—the end of Jewish existence in Western Europe. The Jews were expelled in 1290 from England, and in 1306 from France; they were briefly readmitted to France again in the following decades, only to be finally expelled in 1394.[17]

There were only faint echoes of these developments in Spain. By the end of the thirteenth century, the intermediate stage of the *Reconquista* was over, with a hiatus of two centuries before Granada was to be conquered at the end of the fifteenth century. The role of the Jews in colonization lost its great importance to the Spanish authorities as the century progressed and as the new *Reconquista* societies took firm shape. The increased zeal to re-Christianize Europe which was so significant north of the Pyrenees—epitomized by the Albigensian Crusade against the Cathars, and the establishment of the papal Inquisition against heretics[18]—also spilled south and began to affect public life in the Iberian peninsula. The same Inquisition against heretics soon also appeared in Aragon.[19]

The zeal for re-Christianization slowly reset the place of the Jews of Spain into that of the classic pariah caste. Already in the 1240s James I of Aragon allowed Dominican friars to preach and missionize among the Jews.[20] This period also saw the beginnings of disputations between leading Jewish thinkers and Christian missionaries such as the famous one that took place in Barcelona between Moses Nachmanides (1194–1270) and Pablo Christiani (d. 1274) in 1263.[21] These were elaborately staged events which set the scene for the renewal of pressure on the Jews to convert. Indeed, even the crown, the strongest protector of the Jews, often supported efforts to missionize among them. Several polemical works, such as Raymundus Martini's *Pugio Fidei* ("The Dagger of Faith"), emerged as particularly influential in the struggle against the Jews and in fanning the flames of anti-Judaism.[22] Even the noted mystic Ramon Lull (1235?–1315), who had extensive knowledge of Judaism and Islam and occasionally appeared sympathetic to the Jews, began to preach to them in 1299 with the express purpose of bringing about mass conversions.[23] The middle of the thirteenth century also began to see the occurrence of blood-libel accusations, the most notable of which took place in Saragossa in 1250.[24]

Nevertheless, on the whole, the Spanish monarchs acted as a brake against increasing demands coming from the papacy for the implementation of new restrictions. The many papal bulls that followed in rapid succession after 1215 trying to impose the wearing of a distinctive badge by all Jews, and calling for their dismissal from administrations where they exercised authority over Christians, were all effectively resisted.[25] The Jews were still important and useful to the kings, who continued in their traditional task of protecting them.

The fourteenth century saw a steady deterioration of the situation. In 1320 the Shepherds' Crusade (the Pastoureaux) from France caused disturbances in Aragon with numerous attacks against the Jews. They were eventually put down by King James II (r. 1291–1327). The Black Death of 1348 was accompanied by anti-Jewish riots which threatened Jewish communities throughout the Iberian peninsula.[26] Although the authorities strongly opposed this violence, the attacks against the Jews illustrated the depth of hostility that had been gaining strength over the past decades. The period also witnessed the conversion of some leading Jewish personalities. In the early fourteenth century, Abner of Burgos (ca. 1270–1340), a Jewish physician and thinker, was baptized and emerged as Alfonso of Valladolid to polemicize against Judaism. His work served as important source material for future attacks on the Jews.[27] The role played by apostates in fanning the flames of intolerance against their previous coreligionists is a sorry feature of Jewish life in Spain in the fourteenth and fifteenth centuries.

The polemics of Christian missionizing were also accompanied by the beginning of the erosion of certain aspects of Jewish communal autonomy. The Jews of Castile saw the end of the right of criminal jurisdiction which they had enjoyed since the beginning of the *Reconquista*, during the reign of John I (r. 1379–90). The same development took place in Aragon in 1377.[28] The *aljamas* themselves were also disintegrating internally, with increased class conflict brought about by friction between the mass of the Jewish population and the strong oligarchic leadership that held power and had close links with the Jewish courtier class. Even though these conflicts never saw a firm resolution, they sapped morale and threw communal institutions into disarray.[29]

The economic crisis of the 1380s and sharpening class conflict added fuel to the growing hostility of the population toward the Jews. Accusations of desecrating the Host gained in frequency. The archdeacon of Ecija, Ferrant Martínez, engaged in a fierce campaign against the Jews in 1378. When Martínez became the administrator of the archdiocese of Seville in 1390, the scene was set for the most important turning point in Jewish history in the Iberian peninsula. Economic crisis, increased social frictions, the rise to prominence of a fierce anti-Jewish polemicist, and an unfortunate power vacuum brought about by the death of King John I and the succession of a minor, Henry III (r. 1390–1406), to the throne all provided context for an outbreak of mass attacks and rioting and pogroms against the Jews. On 4 June 1391, pogroms began in Seville and spread rapidly throughout the Iberian peninsula. Thousands were killed, hundreds of urban Jewish quarters were attacked and burned, and many Jews either were forced to convert or else converted of their own free will in the prevailing atmosphere of threat and crisis. While there were many instances of noblemen or royal soldiery protecting the Jews in some areas, the traditional protectors proved to be ineffective.[30]

In Castile the power vacuum at the throne very clearly demonstrated the Achilles' heel of the "royal alliance." With the traditional strong centralized leadership not in place, there was no alternative power base that could safeguard the Jews. But even in areas under the crown of Aragon, where the king was still very much in control, the Jewish communities were not spared. When the population rose with great force against the Jews, and animosity had reached a critical level, action by royal authority would have imperiled its own power and strength and hence was not particularly effective as an agent of protection. Many famous Jewish communities were hit hard; those of Toledo and Cordoba were laid waste, and the historic community of Barcelona disappeared forever when the rioting reached northwards from Valencia into Catalonia. Some of the leading members of the Jewish community, especially the upper echelon of society, were among the first to convert. It is conceivable that for many, the fall from high position was too hard to endure. Many others were forcibly baptized and could escape only later. The pogroms of 1391 and the accompanying mass conversions changed the Iberian scene dramatically. Even though the Jews of the Iberian peninsula were not then expelled from its various kingdoms, unlike the situation in England and in France, their social position was now considerably more circumscribed. The re-Christianization that had been taking place in Spain as a result of the increased activities of the friars, as well as of religious polemicists, converged with social unrest in a particular political context to deal Jewish society a mortal blow. After 1391, the remnant of the Jewish community in Spain much more closely resembled the rest of post-1215 medieval European Jewry than had been the case in the previous two centuries.

The place of the Jews continued to decline considerably after this period. In the fifteenth century, most Iberian Jews were to be found not in the large cities, but in small towns dotted across Spain, engaged in small-scale trade, in artisanal occupations, and in local small-scale financial operations. Indeed, it is estimated that while some Jews continued to be used as tax farmers and tax collectors by the crown in Castile, there were no more than seventy-five Jewish tax farmers between 1440 and 1469, who collected between 0.3 percent and 25 percent of the crown revenues.[31] This was in marked contrast to the situation that had prevailed prior to 1391, and especially to the thirteenth century. The financial role of the Jews, hence, had declined considerably, in spite of the fact that personalities such as Abraham Benveniste (1406–54), Abraham Seneor, and Isaac Abravanel would still be active and continue as tax collectors in the old tradition of the court Jews.[32] But the community as a whole was a pale shadow of its former self.

The pressure on the Jews continued intermittently throughout the fifteenth century. The friar Vicente Ferrer (1350–1419) was active preaching in Castile between 1411 and 1412 against the Jews and asking for even further restrictions, which were in fact adopted in Castile in 1412. New regulations took effect banning Jews from holding public office and from acting as physicians to Christians and restricting them to distinct, separate areas in cities. The same rules were adopted in Aragon.[33]

In 1413–14 the famous Disputation of Tortosa took place. This was an elaborately staged event to bring even further pressure on the Jews to convert. The Jewish rabbis and thinkers Zerahiah ha-Levi and Joseph Albo faced Jerónimo de Santa Fé (a Jewish convert formerly named Joshua Lorki; d. 1419) in a disputation over Scripture that ended in an open declaration of the defeat of the Jewish position. In the dark atmosphere that surrounded the event, thousands of Jews further converted.[34]

This disastrous disputation, which shook the very foundations of Jewish communities already reeling after the pogroms of 1391, was followed by a relative calm under most of the reigns of the kings Alfonso V of Aragon (r. 1416–58) and John II of Castile (r. 1406–54). There were internal attempts to restructure the communities; particularly important among them was the Convention of Valladolid in 1432, which tried to reorganize Jewish communal activities and to develop a standard, uniform administrative system.[35] Nevertheless, even though the communities were slowly reestablished and started to function again, the basis of Jewish existence in the fifteenth century remained fragile.

The year 1391, with the great number of Jewish converts to Christianity, saw the emergence of a "New Christian" problem in Spain. The new converts, representing some of the most dynamic elements of Jewish society, began a massive entry into those areas of public life from which Jews had been excluded. The examples were numerous in all domains of life, from city and municipal administration, to corporations, and indeed to the Church itself, with such figures as Salomon Halevi of Burgos, who became a bishop after converting under the name Pablo de Santa María (1350–1435), or his son Alonso de Cartagena. Members of the courtier class now reappeared after conversion, and they and their descendants held important positions of power and authority: Fernand Díaz of Toledo, for example, who was of "New Christian" origin and became the secretary of John II of Castile.[36]

This entry by "New Christians" into the public life of the country elicited great jealousy and hatred. Since most of the conversions happened en masse, many converts kept together because of family links, intermarried among themselves, and often kept a close relationship with their relatives who had remained Jewish. The "New Christians" remained a distinct group. Their very adherence to their new faith remained in doubt. It is undoubtedly true that many of the converts took their new religion very seriously. But for others, conversion had been nothing but an act of convenience. Many had long since developed a fairly relativistic view of religion and had switched allegiance in order to save their lives and to advance in society. Still others had been obliged to convert under duress, with death as the only alternative. Hence, the "New Christian" class contained devout Christians, relativistic agnostics, and devout crypto-Jews. Nevertheless, in spite of the wide range of behavior and belief among them, the old Christians soon began to perceive their whole group as suspect and projected onto "New Christians" the accusation of crypto-Judaism to limit their social ascent and to brake their achievements in society. Every "New Christian" could be accused of being a Marrano ("Swine")—to use the pejorative given them to denote their being crypto-Jews—despite the fact that any one of them might be a genuine and devout *converso* to Christianity.[37]

An economic downturn in the 1440s added fuel to the growing resentment of the "New Christians" among the population, and in 1449 riots broke out in Toledo in which they were attacked. In that same year, in the aftermath of the riots, Pedro Sarmiento (1400–64), a municipal leader, passed a statute in Toledo denying "New Christians" access to ecclesiastical or municipal office. This was opposed by leading "New Christians" such as Fernand Díaz, the secretary of the king, and the bishop of Cuenca, Fray Lope de Barrientos. In keeping with their views, Alonso de Cartagena, while severely attacking those "New Christians" who might be crypto-Jews, maintained that the majority were now devout Christians and should be allowed to integrate into society.[38] Although this statute was not implemented, such *limpieza de san-*

gre decrees were eventually adopted as the decades passed, and became especially important in the sixteenth century, emerging as a major concern for those of "New Christian" origin.

However, the problem did not go away. The period between 1449 and 1492 saw the deterioration of the situation, and the economic crisis of 1465–73 made attacks on the "New Christians" worse. The fact that they were important in the economy made them easy targets, and they were attacked in riots in 1465 in Seville, in 1467 in Toledo, and in 1473–74 in Valladolid and Segovia.[39] Leading theologians also, in direct continuation of the great missionizing efforts of the past century, made a particular point of casting doubt on the sincerity of the faith of the "New Christians." Once baptism had taken place, any least relapse into Judaism emerged as heresy and called into question the very unity of Christendom. In 1460, the leading theologian of the day, Alonso d'Espina, called in his very influential and important book *Fortalitium Fidei* for the establishment of an Inquisition to look into such heretical Judaizing. This book, which set the scene for the Spanish Inquisition, went through six editions before 1500.[40]

Many believed the Inquisition was the only way to deal with the problem, since—whether through innuendo, appearance, or reality—there did seem to exist a Judaizing heresy, and this heresy had to be extirpated. Even though many like Fray Hernando de Talavera, the confessor of Queen Isabella, opposed the establishment of the Inquisition,[41] the argument for it appeared overwhelming. The institution of the Inquisition already had well-established antecedents in the investigation of heresy by the Church. As mentioned above, the Inquisition had already been established during the Albigensian Crusade in southern France, and by the fourteenth century it had already made its appearance in Aragon, across the Pyrenees. However, this was a very different institution from what would follow in Spain: it was a papal Inquisition, under the jurisdiction of local bishops, and was engaged in the elimination of heresy among Christians.[42] However, the task set for it after the middle of the fifteenth century in the Iberian peninsula became principally the putting down of the Judaizing heresy that had emerged among the "New Christians." Hence, the Inquisition as it appeared in Spain began crystallized as a specific means to combat the problem of Marranism. Already in 1461 King Henry IV of Castile had appealed for an Inquisition to be established for this task, without much result.[43] After the situation became worse, however, with increasing conflict and friction around the "New Christian" issue, the call for an Inquisition gained strength. This was accompanied by an increasing harshness shown to the Jews and increasing problems in various local communities. Blood-libel cases appeared in Sepúlveda in 1468; in 1472 riots took place against the Jews in Valladolid, and in 1473 the Jews were expelled from Cordoba, with troubles continuing in Seville.[44]

The marriage of Ferdinand of Aragon (r. 1479–1516) and Isabella of Castile

(r. 1474–1504) in 1469 led to the unification of the two crowns ten years later. However, their countries were not really united; this was nothing more than a union of crowns, with each area maintaining local customs, privileges, systems of laws, and so forth. Their union did, however, coordinate certain levels of political activity, and it is undoubtedly true that there was, from this period onwards, a stronger push for centralization, which would evolve many centuries later. In this context of centralization, friction around the issue of Marranism increasingly appeared intolerable. The crown threw its weight behind the establishment of an Inquisition in Spain, envisioning the creation of a royal institution under the monarchy and not directly subject to the papacy. After many petitions this was finally granted by the pope in 1478, and the Inquisition began to function in 1481 in Seville. Tomás de Torquemada (1420?–98), the confessor of the queen, became the Inquisitor General in 1483.[45] The Catholic monarchs were motivated by a genuine religious concern about the extirpation of what they saw as heresy, but also by the will to extend royal power through the Inquisition.

The Inquisition launched upon its task with great zeal. Thousands of "New Christians" were judged by the Inquisitorial tribunals and had their properties confiscated; hundreds were burned at the stake for the Judaizing heresy.[46] The attempt to grapple seriously with the issue of Marranism had very major repercussions for the Jews. The fight against "Judaizing" put an increased spotlight on living Judaism in the Iberian peninsula.

While the Catholic monarchs were embarked upon the elimination of the Judaizing heresy, they continued to behave vis-à-vis the Jews within the paradigm of the age-old "royal alliance." Jews were employed as tax farmers and tax collectors. Abraham Seneor and Isaac Abravanel were particularly important in this regard; in fact, Isaac Abravanel was involved in raising funds for the conquest of Granada.[47] So the act expelling the Jews that would follow came as quite a surprise to the Jewish community. Furthermore, it seems evident from a variety of sources that the monarchs themselves had not long prepared and premeditated the Expulsion, as they had granted several long-term concessions to various Jewish tax collectors in the few months that preceded the event.

Nevertheless, pressure from the Inquisition had been building for some time to segregate the Jews. The expulsion of the Jews from Andalusia in 1483 appeared as a straw in the wind. The blood-libel accusation at La Guardia in 1490–91 brought anti-Jewish feeling to a fever pitch. While many attempts were made to annul the Decree of Expulsion, they were all to no avail. By the end of July 1492, the last openly practicing Jews had left Spain.

It is very hard to reach a consensus as to how many Jews were expelled and how many converted. The figures seem to vary widely, ranging from as high as 400,000 departures to as low as 50,000 in a recent argument.[48] It is likely that 100,000 Jews converted between 1391 and 1412.[49] The latest archival research about the number of Jews entering Portugal (which absorbed the largest number of refugees) in 1492 gives the figure 23,320.[50] However, this appears quite low judging by accounts of the Portuguese situation a few decades later. Ottoman sources put the number of arrivals between 1492 and the middle of the sixteenth century at 12,000 families.[51] Assuming the standard coefficient of 5 per household, this represents 60,000 people. However, the latter figure is for the total number of arrivals and includes families originating outside the Iberian peninsula, as well as later departures from Portugal. So it is impossible to work back from Ottoman statistics. Taking all these factors into account, a reasonable guess, but a guess nevertheless, could put the number who left Spain in 1492 at between 100,000 and 150,000.[52]

Much has been written about the motivation of the Catholic monarchs to explain the momentous event of 1492. While no deterministic causality can be attributed to the Expulsion, several factors emerge as particularly significant. The most important one, which has sometimes been easy for historians to discount but which in many ways provides the best clue to their reasoning, was given by the monarchs themselves in the Decree of Expulsion. As the decree itself stated, it was the Jews who were seen as aiding and abetting the "New Christians" to lapse back into Judaizing and, hence, to continue in heretical behavior in the Iberian peninsula. One "elegant" solution was to remove the Jews as a presence from society, which would also remove the temptation and the means for any lapse among the "New Christians." Hence both the establishment of the Inquisition and the expulsion of the Jews can be seen as addressing the same problem, which was perceived to have reached crisis proportions in Spain and was giving rise to increased social conflict. It can be stated that the direct causal chain that led to the Expulsion in 1492 really began in 1391 with the mass conversions themselves.[53] At the same time, it was indubitably true that the fall of Granada represented the end of an independent non-Christian presence in Spain and heralded the end of the much-touted *convivencia* that had at least ostensibly characterized the relationship between members of the three faiths in the Iberian peninsula. The scene appeared set to bring to a logical conclusion the Christianization and missionizing efforts that had been gathering momentum since the thirteenth century and to begin the construction of a religiously united Spain under an increasingly centralizing monarchy. The presence of the Jews in this respect was becoming increasingly undesirable. Furthermore, the Jews appeared to have lost whatever utility they might have had. It is quite clear that the "royal alliance" that had characterized the relationship between the Jews and the monarchs in the Iberian peninsula as well as elsewhere was a one-way affair. Its continuation was strictly dependent upon the will of the rulers, with the Jews having no choice in the matter. As the utility of the Jews seemed to have faded in the eyes of the crown, Spain began to follow the same path as the rest of medieval Europe. Severe limitations there on the place of Jews in society from the thirteenth century onwards had also been followed by the expulsions from England and France.

In this respect, 1391 also supplies one of the keys to the causes of the Expulsion. Very large numbers of Jews had converted and were engaged in all the occupations in society that had been the specialty of the Jews. "New Christians" were to be found in all areas of commerce and also in royal administrations. This meant that in fact the Jews as a group were no longer needed for their particular skills, as the "New Christian" class itself supplied those very same skills. The one problem that remained with the "New Christians" appeared to be the issue of Judaizing, and once the Jews had been expelled and the Inquisition set to work trying to impose religious orthodoxy by eliminating heresy, it was hoped that the problem would disappear and the "New Christians" would integrate totally. Hence, the very existence of the "New Christians" rendered the Jews dispensable.

THE "NEW CHRISTIANS" OF PORTUGAL

While many Jews leaving Spain managed to depart by ship for Italy or on the dangerous trip to Muslim lands to the south and in the East, large numbers chose the most logical step and moved overland across the border into Portugal. Portugal had a Jewish community which had been present there since Roman times. In 1492 there was still no persecution of the Jews in Portugal, and nothing like the Spanish pogroms of 1391 had occurred. In 1492 King John II (r. 1481–95) allowed wealthy Jewish families from Spain to purchase the right to reside permanently in Portugal. The same privilege was granted to economically useful craftsmen. The rest, the great majority of the incoming Jewish refugees, were allowed to stay for eight months and then were supposed to leave on ships to other countries. However, as the eight months passed, most of the necessary ships were not made available for the Jews, who as a result mostly remained in Portugal. The attitude of the king and the authorities hardened considerably, and the Jews were declared to be slaves once the initial time period had passed. The last years of the reign of John II were extraordinarily difficult ones for the Jewish community, with considerable economic hardship, and constant harassment and persecution. Many Jewish children were taken forcibly from their families and shipped to the São Thomé islands to be raised as Christians.[54]

The situation improved for a short period upon the accession to the throne of King Manuel I (r. 1495–1521), who ended the slavery of the Jews. They could now look forward to a more tolerant rule in Portugal and expected to be able to continue to live unharmed in their new land. However, the marriage of the king to Isabella, the daughter of the Catholic monarchs of Spain, complicated the situation: part of the marriage bargain included the express wish of the Catholic monarchs that the Jews be expelled from Portugal. The king after some prevarication yielded to this request and on 5 December 1496 signed the Edict of Expulsion of the Jews with only a few months' notice given them to leave the kingdom. It does appear, however, that the king was not happy to have this new and useful population depart from his realm. Portugal did not have a middle class, and the new skills brought by the Jews were proving to be of great benefit. As a result, the Jews of Portugal were all forcibly converted en masse in 1497, with no alternative offered them.[55]

The issue of Marranism posed itself with even greater acuity in Portugal than in Spain. It was the normative Jewish community itself which had been converted in Portugal. Furthermore these were the very Jews who had been unprepared to make compromises and convert in order to stay in their original homeland in Spain and had chosen the risks of exile over conversion to Christianity. Their faithfulness to the religion of their forebears was an already proven fact. Their mass conversion without being given a choice simply transformed them overnight from Jews into Christians, without altering their deeply held allegiances. It is not surprising, therefore, that crypto-Judaism became particularly rife in Portugal.

The Jews were promised upon conversion that for twenty years there was to be no examination of their religious practices in Portugal. Nevertheless, many chose the first opportunity to leave the country in order to revert back to Judaism. This alarmed the king, who, acting from the same motives as in the initial decree of conversion, chose to forbid emigration in 1499 in order to keep this population in Portugal. The sixteenth century saw various bans on the emigration of "New Christians," interspersed with their occasional relaxation, which gave rise to increased departures from the Lusitanian kingdom.[56]

Once the initial shock had passed, the "New Christians" became active in the life of the country and as in Spain were to be found in all areas of the economy and in the administrative system. The old Christian population, also behaving as had their counterparts in Spain, did not look kindly upon "New Christian" success. Jealousy and hatred eventually erupted in a pogrom in 1506, when two thousand "New Christians" were massacred in a riot in Lisbon.[57] Although the king eventually managed to quell the disturbance and to protect the "New Christians," conditions remained explosive. Emigration was allowed in 1507, when many managed to avail themselves of the opportunity to leave. However, this emigration was soon stopped, and the situation reverted back to what it had been prior to 1507.

Marranism appeared particularly intense and acute in Portugal, and soon brought calls for the establishment of an Inquisition. In fact, the crown had already in 1516 started to make tentative moves to establish the dreaded institution. The Judaizing heresy that Marranism represented, which seemed to be widespread among the "New Christians" of the Lusitanian kingdom, called for extreme measures. The Inquisition had gone from strength to strength across the border and seemed to be reaching its desired goal of eliminating the heresy. As the movement toward the establishment of the Inquisition began to gather strength, many "New Christian" leaders, now economically powerful and also well represented in the administrations of the country, managed to block it by appealing directly to the papacy, and through politicking and bribery delayed the arrival of the Inquisition. Finally, after many appeals on the part of the crown, the papacy authorized the establishment of the Portuguese Inquisition in 1535. The institution was established for a trial period of three years, and the first auto-da-fé took place soon thereafter. However, the "New Christians" managed to delay the full functioning of the Inquisition, which managed to implant itself definitively only in 1547. After this date, the Portuguese Inquisition pursued its goal with great ferocity, and thousands of "New Christians" became objects of its zeal.[58]

In Portugal, as in Spain, the "New Christians" performed the same function in society as the Jews had. In both countries, a primarily religious motivation had led to the Decree of Expulsion by the monarchs. However, in contrast to Spain, Portugal could not afford to let the Jews go once the particular benefits they brought had become evident. In Spain the "New Christian" class was already in existence since 1391 and had become, in spite of posing problems from the point of religious orthodoxy, a fixture in the economy of the state. The only solution available to the king of Portugal, hence, was to oblige the Jews to stay, but make them conform to the desired religious uniformity in the country by forcibly converting them.

The phenomenon of crypto-Judaism denoted by the term "Marranism" assumed many forms. The one in Portugal was similar to that in Spain. While some converts took their newly acquired faith seriously, dropped all allegiance to Judaism, and became sincere and devout Catholics, others simply adopted an opportunistic attitude toward both religions and paid only lip service to their new faith. For yet another group, perhaps the majority of "New Christians" in Portugal in the first decades after the conversion, the adherence to the faith of their forebears remained paramount in importance. However, it would be wrong to think of the crypto-Judaism of the Marranos as the secret practice of Judaism. This would imply the observation of the laws of normative rabbinical Judaism. With the passage of time and with the stopping of the transmission of this rabbinical Judaism, the decline in the knowledge of Hebrew, and the impossibility of fulfilling many of the religious commandments in extraordinarily hostile surroundings, the crypto-Judaism of the Marranos evolved into a particular form of behavior, practice, and belief. It might have had normative Judaism as its referent, but now—in a situation utterly unlike that in Spain before 1492—it was cut off from direct contact with any Jews, and was obliged to evolve independently, on the basis of memory, tradition, and a shared vision of belonging together as a group. Hence certain Jewish practices were maintained, whereas others were dropped. Certain dietary laws were obviously easier to keep than others, and many of the more difficult commandments were abandoned altogether. The Old Testament was the only Jewish holy text that Marranos had available to them, and in time they developed their own rites and rituals, prayers, and forms of belief, using this as their basic text and embroidering upon it.[59]

Marrano religion, based on secret, individual-family transmission, eventually developed a subculture of its own, which explains its extraordinary longevity and resilience. The depth of allegiance to Judaism and the hope for better days to come were evident in the strong messianism among sixteenth-century Marranos in Portugal. When the curious figure David Reubeni (d. 1538), claiming to represent the lost ten tribes, arrived in Portugal in 1525, he found himself the center of the attention of thousands of Marranos who saw in him the harbinger of messianic times. The messianic career of the Portuguese Marrano Diego Pires (ca. 1500–1532), who managed to leave Portugal and returned to Judaism under the name Solomon Molho, and eventually declared himself the Messiah, is also instructive in this respect, as representing the extraordinary aspirations and hopes of a whole class of people who had undergone a terribly traumatic transformation in the recent past.[60]

In spite of considerable debate among rabbinical figures in the Jewish world as to the Jewishness of the Marranos (discussions which mainly ended in their acceptance as Jews), what really counted from the point of view of the internal life of this particular group was in fact its own self-definition as belonging to the Jewish people and its adherence to forms of ritual, practice, and belief which for it represented true Judaism. So while the Inquisition, both in Spain and in Portugal, caught many who were not guilty of Judaizing, but who under torture and the threat of death were obliged to confess heresy, many others who fell prey to it were, from the perspective of Catholic Christianity, engaged in a form of Judaizing heresy. The Inquisition tracked down the so-called heretic, but became itself, by its very existence, and by the very pressure it brought upon the "New Christians" as a class, a very strong factor in the maintenance and heightening of their group identity. In Spain this was only strengthened by the statutes of *limpieza de sangre*, which after the middle of the sixteenth century came to restrict many areas of economic and political life to "Old" Christians.[61] Hence discrimination and persecution, in a classic situation, contributed to the perpetuation of the original problem, without altering its dimensions. This group identity was so strong that especially in Portugal the "New Christians" were called "men of the nation" (*homens da nação*). The "New Christians" appeared to be a particular nation within the nation.

The Portuguese "New Christians" were soon to be found throughout Europe, primarily in Spain. The union of Portugal with Spain between 1580 and 1640 opened the border and allowed the possibility for departure from Portugal to those who feared persecution and who were increasingly chafing at growing restrictions. While Marranism in Spain proper seems to have slowly begun to disappear by the middle of the sixteenth century, it was replaced by a much more vibrant, stronger Marrano phenomenon coming directly from Portugal, which gave it an additional life for at least another century and kept the Inquisition busy. The fact that the whole Jewish community had been forcibly converted in Portugal, and the reentry into Spain of the descendants of these converts—who themselves had been expelled in 1492—brought the problem back onto Spanish soil to become a thorn in the side of the Church and royal authority until the late eighteenth century. In fact, the very word "Portuguese" became associated with "New Christian" and often became synonymous with "Marrano." Marranism remained active in the Iberian peninsula for two centuries after the Spanish Decree of Expulsion, fed periodic departures to the Jewish world, and led to the reenactment and the revival of the memory of the most tragic episodes in Iberian Jewish history among Sephardim far-flung in the world Diaspora.

THE MARRANO DIASPORA IN WESTERN EUROPE

With the establishment of the Inquisition in all parts of the Iberian peninsula, there was no alternative but emigration for many "New Christians." This emigration continued throughout the sixteenth century, depending on bans periodically imposed and lifted by the crown. The first destinations early in the century were southern France, Antwerp, and the Ottoman Empire, as well as Portuguese colonies overseas. Soon, large families had members in all the major trade centers of the world. The quest for religious freedom and economic opportunity together fueled their desire to leave as they felt increasingly threatened by the Inquisition.

The "New Christians," sharing a corporate identity and in many cases a subterranean religion, formed a veritable social class, one that was mercantile in economic orientation and was set apart, by both external persecution and inner resistance, from the rest of society. At a time when the whole of the Western world was shifting from a Mediterranean to an Atlantic economy, their Iberian background and connections rendered them ideally suited to take full advantage of new economic opportunities. Family relationships were extraordinarily important, and the settlement of members of "New Christian" families in the new centers of the emergent Atlantic economy gave them the international contacts vital for carrying out trade in this period. It was this fact which would make them particularly welcome in major ports such as Bordeaux, Amsterdam, Hamburg, and London. The Portuguese for "merchants," *homens de negócios*, soon became synonymous with "New Christians," *Cristãos Novos*.

"New Christians" departing from the Iberian peninsula were often attracted to already existing Jewish communities, especially the ones in the East which had been established by Sephardi Jews of similar origins in the previous half-century. Many eventually emigrated to the new Jewish centers of the Ottoman Empire. (See below.) But for commercial reasons as well as for other family considerations, many also emigrated to various Italian cities which had established Jewish communities.

It is a paradox of Jewish history that one of the great protectors of the Jews until the middle of the sixteenth century was the papacy, which did not necessarily share the more extreme attitudes toward the Jews that the national Inquisitions in Spain and Portugal exhibited. In 1547, for example, Pope Paul III (r. 1534–49) issued a liberal bull inviting Levantine as well as other Jews, among whom were to be found many an ex-Marrano, to come to his port city of Ancona.[62] The extraordinary efflorescence of trade with which Jews were involved between Italy and the Ottoman Empire, as well as farther afield, had made the Jewish presence lucrative for those rulers who wanted to expand their economic activities in their own realms, and the papacy was no exception. By 1552 over a hundred Portuguese Jewish families were present in Ancona. Other families also established themselves in various Tuscan cities, in Mantua, in Ferrara, and in Urbino.[63] Duke Ercole II of Ferrara issued a safe-conduct to the so-called Portuguese in 1550, and it was in this city in 1553 that the famous translation of the Hebrew Bible known throughout the world as the Ferrara Bible was published by the printer Abraham Usque, a Portuguese Jew.[64]

However, the Counter-Reformation proved to be extremely problematic for the Jews in Catholic Italy. The attitude of the papacy hardened considerably and came to converge with that of the national Inquisitions of the Iberian peninsula. The Portuguese families in the city of Ancona were arrested by Pope Paul IV (r. 1555–59) on charges of Judaizing and for having abandoned their original status as Christians, and many were burned in the city in 1555, giving rise to great outrage across the Jewish world. The papacy launched a campaign to put great pressure on dukedoms, principalities, and cities throughout Italy for the expulsion of ex–"New Christians" now living openly as Jews, and for the imposition of increased restrictions on the latter.[65] While this was successful in many areas, some rulers resolutely refused these requests, seeing in the loss of the Jewish and Portuguese communities a grievous blow to the financial well-being of their lands. Economic calculations often won the day. While Venice earlier in the century had been particularly harsh toward the Marranos and the Jews, it became much more tolerant in the 1570s, and "New Christians" emigrated to Venice in considerable numbers from 1573–74 onwards. Indeed, the 1589 charter regulating Jewish existence in the *Serenissima* made explicit references to the "Ponentine" (a euphemism for Iberian Marranos) and "Levantine" Jews in the granting of privileges.[66] By 1600, there were 2,500 Jews in Venice.[67]

Many "New Christians" hence rejoined Jewish communities in the course of the sixteenth and seventeenth centuries in Italy.[68] However, Jewish settlements in Italy remained for the most part composed of Jews who had not previously converted; these settlements were dominated by autochthonous Italian Jews, Ashkenazim, and Sephardim who had arrived after 1492. "New Christians" joined these already existing communities and made up a fraction of the total Jewish population. While these immigrants were to contribute significantly to Jewish life in these communities, and would provide a great ferment in literature and culture and in the economy, they did not necessarily set their stamp on them.

The situation was quite different in new settlements in France, the Netherlands, and northern Germany. These were areas without any particular Jewish presence at the end of the fifteenth century, because of previous expulsions of Jews or because of a previously very limited Jewish presence. In the course of the sixteenth century, in a great irony of history, it was the "New Christians" who had been forcibly converted in the Iberian peninsula that were to establish the nucleus communities which would relaunch organized Jewish existence in areas which had not seen an active Jewish life for many centuries. Such cities as Bordeaux and Bayonne in southwestern France, Amsterdam in the Netherlands, and Hamburg and the surrounding area in northern Germany became important Jewish centers and heralded the renewed age of Jewish activity in mercantilist early modern Western Europe.

Some "New Christian" families made their way north over the Pyrenees into southwestern France after the establishment of the Inquisition in Portugal in 1536. In 1550 the French king Henry II (r. 1547–59) passed a decree naturalizing the Portuguese merchants and promising them royal protection, and allowed them freedom of trade. This decree was reissued in 1574, with an additional ordinance indicating that no maltreatment of this group would be tolerated and furthermore that no inquiry would be made "whatsoever into their lives."[69] This guarantee already indicates a fairly accurate knowledge on the part of the crown of the origins of these Portuguese merchants and the existence among them of elements that did not exhibit Catholic

Christian behavior. The union of Portugal with Spain in 1580 which saw the mass arrival of Portuguese "New Christians" into Spain also saw many taking this opportunity to leave the Iberian peninsula. This increased the numbers of Marranos in southwestern France. The period saw extensive immigration not only to Bordeaux but also to Bayonne, St. Jean de Luz, and from the 1590s onwards to Nantes, Rouen, and Paris. Not all the "New Christians" who arrived in this area were in fact Marranos. Many were genuine *conversos* who remained faithful to their new religion. Nevertheless a substantial number among them were indeed lapsed Catholics who used the opportunities of the removal of the threat of the Inquisition to continue to practice Judaism to a lesser or greater extent, secretly or openly.

It is estimated in a 1633 report that there were forty Jewish families in Bordeaux, sixty in Bayonne, eighty at Labastide-Clairence, forty at Peyrehorade, ten at Dax, twenty at Rouen, and twelve in Paris.[70] This settlement increased further during the contraband trade that followed the trade embargo on Holland that Spain imposed from 1621 to 1647. The economic activity of the *marchands portugais* was especially valuable for the crown and explains the relatively tolerant attitude toward this group evident throughout the seventeenth century, especially under Richelieu, for whom economic and political calculations overrode purely religious considerations. The families that had established themselves in southwestern France had constant commercial relations with the Iberian peninsula, exporting and importing merchandise such as wine and spices and other colonial products coming from the New World. Most such trade was carried out by members of the same families on both sides of the border; some of them made very large fortunes out of it. Members of such wealthy families as the Fernandes, the Lopes de Villeneuve, the d'Espinosa, and the Lopes d'Oliveira were particularly important figures in the city of Bordeaux.[71]

Nevertheless, in spite of the toleration shown by the crown, there were many episodes in the course of the seventeenth century which put the continuation of Jewish settlements in southwestern France in danger. Ironically, they were threatened numerous times both for their Iberian background and for being Jewish. The many wars with Spain in which France was engaged throughout this period posed grave threats to them both from a xenophobic populace and from the crown. They were considered potential traitors and were treated quite severely during wartime. In 1597, at the height of the hostilities with Spain, they were made to leave their houses near the city walls and reside near the center.[72] In 1625, when the king of Spain confiscated the property of the French merchants in his kingdom, the king of France issued a decree demanding that an inventory be made of the "Spanish and Portuguese" of Bordeaux prior to a retaliatory confiscation. This was stayed with great difficulty by the intervention of the *Parlement* of Bordeaux.[73] In

1636, during the war with Spain, they were again made to leave their houses near the city walls, and a census of their numbers was taken—tallying 260 "Portuguese" residents of Bordeaux[74]—to assess their potential threat: all this at a time when it had become known that the Spanish army "wanted to throw itself on the Portuguese and Moors" and therefore was not likely to be in league with them.[75] Finally, in 1684, ninety-three "Portuguese" families in Bordeaux, Dax, Bayonne, and other French cities were ordered to leave the kingdom because of their extensive trade and family links with the Jews of the Netherlands, with which France was then at war.[76] However, because of numerous protests from merchants, this order was annulled after a few months.

This strange amalgam of policies, of on the one hand considering the "Portuguese" merchants economically beneficial to the country and on the other viewing them as potential allies of France's enemies in time of war, appears even more curious given the fact that the crown had a more or less clear idea of the Jewish identity of these "Portuguese" and "Spaniards" and therefore knew of their experience in Spain. To some extent, this ambiguity in the crown's relationship with the Jews was an expression of the tension that existed between religious and economic considerations in its policies. For a very long time, although fully aware of the Jewish origins and practices of the "Portuguese," the crown refused to face this fact squarely. In spite of the Expulsion Decree of 1394, the Jews of Alsace could be allowed to remain after the conquest of the territory at the end of the Thirty Years War in the seventeenth century because of the special status of the area, which was not administratively united to the rest of France. Therefore it was possible to tolerate the Jews there without necessarily reversing the medieval policy of expulsion.[77] The cases of Bordeaux and other parts of France which sheltered Marranos, such as Bayonne and Rouen, were very different. Once it was openly admitted that these Iberian merchants were Jewish, the crown would have had to come to a decision whether to expel them or to let it be known that the medieval statutes of expulsion no longer applied.

Intimations of the former course of action were in evidence in the decree passed by Marie de Medici in 1615, expelling the Jews, "disguised or otherwise" from the kingdom.[78] This decree, which was the last of its kind in France in modern times, was never implemented in Bordeaux, the *Parlement* and the *Jurade* taking the necessary steps of proclaiming the religious orthodoxy of their "Portuguese." One hears of Louis XIV's expressing the desire to expel the Jews from his kingdom. This was in fact done in the French American islands, where local circumstances permitted such an expulsion, since the Jews were few and had not yet managed to obtain a real foothold.[79] But in France, nothing more came of such sentiments.

Raison d'état dictated to the absolutist state that Sephardic Jews, with their numerous international trading contacts, had to be tolerated. As the seventeenth century progressed, religious considerations with respect to this problem dimmed with great rapidity. It was Colbert's (1662–83) voice which triumphed in the end. Writing to an *intendant* at Aix over the question of protecting the Sephardim of Marseilles against hostile attacks by their competitors, he made it quite clear that commerce was the only issue at stake, and since the Jews were good for the economy, their presence had to be maintained.[80] Shortly after his death, his brother, Colbert de Croissy, who was then the foreign minister, issued two decrees in 1686 and 1687 inviting all foreigners, of whatever quality, condition, or religion that they might be, to trade in France. It was this decree which most likely finally encouraged the Jews of Bordeaux to drop all pretense and stop their purely external observance of Catholicism in the eighteenth century, as it appeared to be an open invitation by the crown to Christians and Jews alike to trade in France.[81]

The same economic calculations were to underpin the Jewish settlements in the Low Countries. Antwerp under Hapsburg rule already had Marranos settled there in the course of the early sixteenth century. However, the wars with the Dutch and the sacking of the city by the Spaniards in 1576, as well as its blockade by the Dutch in 1595, effectively put an end to the importance of Antwerp as a linchpin of economic activity in northwestern Europe.[82] The center of gravity of this economy eventually shifted to Amsterdam. Marranos fleeing the renewed zeal shown by the Inquisition in the 1590s began to arrive in large numbers in the new Calvinist state. The local middle-class groups did not object to the arrival of the "New Christians" from the Iberian peninsula, as they were correctly seen as bringing new trade and skills to the economy. The relatively more tolerant attitude of the Calvinists toward self-avowed Jews also encouraged the settlement.

This tolerant attitude should not, however, be equated with the granting of formal equality, as even so liberal a thinker as Hugo Grotius was of the opinion in 1615 that as a religion Judaism could not hold an equal position to Christianity in Amsterdam and had to operate under restrictions.[83] For long periods of time, for example, Jews were excluded from all the major artisanal guilds and were restricted to particular new trades. The open practice of Judaism was not concomitant with the initial Jewish presence in the 1590s: the right to practice Judaism was granted in Haarlem and Rotterdam in 1605 and 1610, respectively; in Amsterdam, three Jewish congregations united into one recognized Jewish community in 1639.[84] The Jews were an economically important segment of the population, but their economic importance took some time to eclipse Christian arguments for restrictions upon them.[85]

The Jewish place in the local economy was particularly significant in trade with Portugal. Many Jews kept extensive trade relationships with their families, and were in control of the commerce with Portugal and with the Portuguese colonies, most notably in the importing of colonial products such as wood and sugar from Brazil, diamonds from India, and cinnamon from Ceylon. The economic embargoes that Spain imposed on Dutch shipping in 1621—which lasted until midcentury because of the war between Holland and the Hapsburgs—put a serious dent in this trade and diverted part of the Jewish population of Amsterdam toward Hamburg, which began to assume a great degree of importance. However, after the end of hostilities in 1648, Amsterdam soon reached its former economic glory, and Jews began to be particularly significant again in trade with the Spanish and Portuguese territories in the New World and the reexport trade via the Iberian peninsula. Jews were important in the Dutch West India Company, which traded with northern Brazil.[86] In 1644, there were 1,450 Jews living in this area.[87] The Jewish population of Amsterdam increased from 200 in 1610 to 1,800 in 1655, and to 2,500 in 1675.[88]

Amsterdam was also to occupy an important place in the Jewish world because of the extraordinary function it fulfilled in reintroducing the Marranos into normative rabbinical Jewish practice. This was a mostly Marrano community, and most of its members were of Marrano descent. Furthermore, the community was continuously replenished by new arrivals from the Iberian peninsula whose knowledge of normative Judaism was sketchy at best. The task at hand was to integrate the newly arrived into the Jewish world. No effort was spared to make them adopt and accept the faith of their forefathers. The missionizing effort that took place was significant especially in the realm of printing, with scores of books in Spanish and Portuguese produced to explain the elements of Jewish faith to a Marrano audience in need of instruction. Such figures as Orobio de Castro and Menasseh ben Israel were active as popularizers and defenders of the faith. Nevertheless the return to rabbinical Judaism was no longer easy for many Marranos. This Judaism was not at all what it had been projected to be in the Iberian peninsula, where the practice and knowledge of the religion had been patchy and were very often constructed out of remnants of tradition and an intensive study of the Old Testament. In this context there could arise great conflict when an inquisitive mind that had not accepted many elements of Christianity would, under the shock of the introduction to rabbinical Judaism, also rebel and reject normative Judaism as well. The cases of Uriel da Costa (1585–1640) and Baruch Spinoza (1632–77), both with Marrano backgrounds, are illustrative of the kind of religious ferment that could exist within a community composed of ex-Marranos or descendants of Marranos.[89]

Nevertheless, most "New Christians" who arrived in places like Amsterdam eventually made a successful transition to rabbinical Judaism. On the other hand, many remained as *conversos* to Christianity in other places, most notably in Bordeaux and in some Italian cities, in Catholic environments. Once freed from the threat of the Inquisition, they did not express any great interest or willingness to go back to a normative Jewish existence. The kaleidoscope of motivations that had been behind the original decision to convert in the Spain of the fifteenth century was still in operation. Radical relativism, the acceptance of the new faith, and return to Judaism were all evident in the "New Christian" Diaspora. Out of this ferment arose some of the great achievements of early modern European Jewish civilization.

"New Christians" started to arrive in Hamburg in the late sixteenth century, at first from Antwerp (after its blockade by the Dutch, which stopped trade with the Iberian peninsula), and then from Amsterdam. Although initially they tried to lead an outwardly Catholic life, it soon became clear to them that this was not a viable option in a devoutly Protestant city. By 1605, it had become obvious that the "Portuguese" were in reality Jewish, and in 1612, after great deliberation, a contract was signed between them and the senate, stipulating the conditions they had to abide by to remain.[90] Open religious practice was severely limited, and no synagogues were allowed.

As far as trade and commerce were concerned, Hamburg enjoyed a golden age in the seventeenth century, fully participating in the great development of trade between northwestern Europe and the Iberian peninsula, the major entrepôt for transatlantic goods such as sugar, spices, and other luxuries. Amsterdam and Hamburg were the two main ports at the receiving end of this flow of goods from south to north, and it is hardly surprising that the Sephardim of both cities, with extensive family contacts in the Iberian peninsula, played a very active and significant role in the development of this commerce.

In Hamburg, the Iberian trade saw from the beginning a very heavy involvement by the Sephardim. According to the statistics available for the year 1612, eighteen of the forty-one merchants doing business with Spain were Sephardim, closely followed by the Dutch, with ten merchants.[91] Of these eighteen, all but one were importers of unrefined sugar, a trade which would remain almost exclusively in the hands of the Jews until the second half of the century. Their specialty long remained the importation of unrefined sugar and spices, especially pepper—goods from the Iberian colonies in America which had to pass through Spain and Portugal first, since direct trade with non-Iberian merchants was not permitted.

Hostilities between the Netherlands and Spain, especially between 1621 and 1648, reinforced the position of the Sephardim in Hamburg, with Iberian trade with Amsterdam shifting elsewhere (mostly to Hamburg) as a result of Spain's economic embargo on the Netherlands. The Spanish-Hanseatic commerce expanded dramatically, Hamburg becoming Spain's principal supplier of Baltic products as well as a major importer of colonial goods.[92] The Jews of Amsterdam were hard hit by this embargo on the trade in which they had specialized, only recovering after Portugal gained its independence in 1640. The Jews of Hamburg, on the other hand, profited enormously, and many Jews from the Netherlands emigrated there, attracted by the numerous opportunities offered by this bustling port. During this period the Sephardi population of Hamburg increased rapidly. In 1612, at the time of the first contract between the Sephardim and the city, their population was limited to 150 people. By 1646, this number had reached 500, or about 100 families.[93]

Important families were often interrelated and had correspondents all over the world. In the spice trade, names such as the Ximenes, the Rodrigues d'Evora, and the Mendes were responsible for the bulk of the imports. The Cardosos, the Falerios, the Dinis–Millão–de Lima group, and the de Britos were the major figures in the sugar trade.[94]

The economic activities of the Sephardim of Hamburg were not, however, limited only to overseas trade. They were among the founders of the Hamburg Bank in 1619, a major financial institution of northern Europe, maintaining forty-six different accounts there by 1623.[95] The number of Sephardic brokers in the city was, percentagewise, even higher than in Amsterdam. They were also very active in maritime insurance and in the stock exchange. The Teixeiras, the Nunes de Costas, the Abensurs, and the Mussaphias were major figures not only in Hamburg but also in the larger European financial scene. There was even a momentary panic at the European stock exchanges when Duarte de Silva, the head of a very important Hamburg family dealing in securities and brokerage, was arrested by the Inquisition on a visit to Spain as the result of a denunciation.[96]

As the century progressed, Amsterdam and London far outstripped Hamburg in economic activity and prosperity. Because of this economic decline, and because of political conflicts within the city, which created an unfavorable situation for trade, most of the major Sephardi merchants and financiers left it for these more attractive centers. The Sephardi population decreased rapidly, being replaced by the much poorer and largely artisanal German Ashkenazi Jews. As the Iberian economy collapsed and other powers such as the Dutch and the English started dealing directly with the New World, Sephardi connections in the Iberian peninsula became superfluous, and their lead in this trade was lost forever.

It was mainly their economic activities which opened many doors to the Jews in their new homes. In an age when a new Atlantic economy revolving around the Iberian colonies in the New World and northwestern Europe was coming into being, the core of their structure as a group, the family, put them in a very advantageous position to exploit the new opportunities to the full. With many relatives in the far-flung territories of the Iberian empires as well as in Portugal and Spain and northwestern Europe, they could and did play a very significant role in the development of the mercantile capitalism of the age. They did not create this new economy, as some have assumed, but followed its fortunes. In this respect, they were very similar to other closed "in groups," such as the Huguenots, who played important roles in the economy of Europe. Their fate in these societies was intimately connected with their economic function, with their potential and actual value to the outside world.

The medieval world's reaction to the Jews had been governed by similar economic and political considerations. But religion had played the most important role, and all arguments had been expressed within that medium. In the aftermath of the Reformation and the development of mercantile capitalism, this unitary religious medium was slowly disintegrating, while economics and politics began to emerge as forces in their own right. The ambiguity that characterized the history and the position of the "New Christians" in early modern Europe fully reflects the uneven nature of these developments.

The "New Christian" experience, by a curious twist of fate converging with the emergence of an Atlantic world economy and the rise of new capitalist commercial centers in northwestern Europe, encouraged not only the reestablishment of a Jewish presence in Western Europe, where it had been excluded since the Middle Ages, but also eventually led to the emergence of new Jewish centers in the New World and elsewhere. The Jews in the English-speaking world reappeared in the middle of the seventeenth century as "New Christian" emigrants from Amsterdam to London, and from Dutch Brazil to what were eventually to become English colonies in the New World. These and other spin-off western Sephardi communities pointed in new directions, to areas where some of the great events of modern Jewish history were to take place. The expulsion of the Jews and the events that led to the end of open Jewish life in the Iberian peninsula bore the seeds of Jewish renewal in Western Europe.

However, in the sixteenth and seventeenth centuries, numerically speaking, the western Sephardi communities were small and remained so. Nowhere did they number more than a couple of thousand souls. In the eighteenth and nineteenth centuries, these communities declined, assimilated into the non-Jewish world, or fused with larger Ashkenazi groups which swamped them in size. Iberian cultural traits survived only in attenuated form. Portuguese and Spanish disappeared from everyday use, and were preserved only in a few prayers and expressions. By and large, the fortunes of the western Sephardim followed those of their compatriot Ashkenazi fellow Jews from the end of the eighteenth century onwards.

In the early modern period, the demographic weight of the Jewish world lay in the East. The series of expulsions from medieval Europe which eventually culminated with the expulsion from the Iberian peninsula at the end of the fifteenth century shifted the center of gravity of world Jewry. The Spanish expulsion had a domino effect, with Jewish communities being expelled from Sicily in 1492, from Navarre and Provence in 1498, and from Naples in 1510. Except for a few imperial cities in Germany and a few areas in Italy, by the early sixteenth century most of Western and Central Europe had been emptied of Jews with the end of openly Jewish existence in those areas.

New areas of Jewish concentration emerged in the East. Most Ashkenazi Jews were now concentrated in the new Kingdom of Poland, which had allowed them free access and the promise of toleration, and the possibility of a new life. The majority of Sephardi Jews had established themselves in the emergent Ottoman Empire, which had come to dominate the eastern Mediterranean and the Balkans. The overwhelming majority of Sephardim shifted their areas of settlement back once again to the lands of Islam, which had seen the original efflorescence of Sephardi life in the early Middle Ages.

NORTH AFRICA

Many Sephardim found their way to North Africa. The links between the Jewish communities of the Maghreb and those of the Iberian peninsula had always been strong. North African Jews had migrated to Muslim and Christian Spain in the centuries that preceded the Expulsion. The close economic links between the two regions had fostered extensive contacts, with Jews often acting as intermediaries. Some Jews of the Tunisian, Algerian, and Moroccan kingdoms, as well as those of Aragon and Majorca, had received privileges from rulers on both sides to conduct trade and commerce in the thirteenth and fourteenth centuries. There were particularly close contacts between the Jews of Catalonia and Tunisia in the fourteenth century.[97] Furthermore, the flourishing of rabbinical learning in the Iberian peninsula attracted North African scholars and led to close links in the intellectual realm. Some of the leading groups among the Jews of Fez, such as the Ibn Danan and Gagin families, had moved to Spain, to the Muslim kingdom of Granada, in the course of the fifteenth century because of local difficulties. They returned with other Sephardi exiles in 1492.[98]

Many Jewish refugees arrived in North Africa after the pogroms of 1391 in Spain. Because of internal crises in Merinid (1196–1470) Morocco, they seem to have bypassed this country. Most went to various cities in Algeria— Tlemcen and Algiers, for example—settling in many towns of the littoral all the way to Tunisia.[99] Two towering Spanish rabbinical figures, Rabbi Isaac bar Sheshet Perfet (1326–1408) and Rabbi Simon ben Semah Duran (1361–1444), were the most famous personalities among the refugees, settling in Algiers under Ziyanid rule (1235–1393).[100] The latter rulers treated the Jews well, and some of the arrivals and their descendants occupied important positions in the country.

In contrast to the events of 1391, the majority of the exiles of 1492 who arrived in North Africa seem to have gone to Morocco. The Wattasid dynasty, in power since 1472, was favorably disposed toward the refugees, who were quickly perceived as bringing much-needed skills. Most of the exiles arrived in the Portuguese-held ports on the northern coast, and many eventually made their way to centers farther south. Their presence eventually emerged as significant in the cities of Fez, Debdou, Tetuan, Meknes, Salé, Larrache, Arzilla, Rabat, and Safi in Morocco, and in western Algerian cities such as Tlemcen and Oran.[101] Very few appear to have gone to Tunisia. The earliest immigrants were followed by many Marranos, who arrived in the course of the sixteenth century, with the cities of Meknes, Fez, and Tetuan becoming important centers for their reintegration into Judaism.

Paradoxically, except for a few episodes, many Sephardim who settled in the Portuguese-held towns such as Safi and Azemmour were tolerated, and were able to create important communities. Until the establishment of the Portuguese Inquisition in these areas in the middle of the sixteenth century, Marranos openly returned to Judaism there.[102] The Spaniards who occupied Oran and Bougie in Algeria also tolerated the existence of Jewish communities, largely because of the utility of important Sephardi families such as the Sasportas and the Cansinos.[103]

Nevertheless, most Sephardim settled under Muslim rule, usually in Morocco. It is impossible to reach a firm conclusion as to the numbers that arrived in North Africa after 1492. While one account mentions twenty thousand arriving in Fez alone,[104] another indicates that there were four thousand Jews (local and immigrant) in the city in 1541.[105] Inflated numbers are also in evidence in the accounts of arrivals in Tlemcen, one source indicating twelve thousand while another puts the figure at two hundred.[106] The difficulty is compounded by the fact that information about the number of Jews prior to the arrival of the Sephardim is also lacking. The arrivals were certainly in the thousands, but the paucity of documentation allows no more than guesses as to the true number.

It was the links between the Sephardim and the Iberian peninsula that rendered them useful in the eyes of the Muslim rulers. In the first half of the sixteenth century, some were employed as diplomats and intermediaries. Two Sephardim, Jacob Rosales and Jacob Roti, were responsible for peace treaties between the Wattasid sultan in Fez and the Portuguese in this period.[107] While many Sephardim were important as purveyors, administrators, and diplomats, many others emerged as traders in grain, in sugar processing, as artisans, and as shopkeepers.[108]

Relations between the exiles, the *Megorashim*, and the local Jews, the *Toshavim*, remained tense in many areas. Iberian Jews had a long-established tradition of intellectual leadership, and they were not often prepared to compromise under new conditions. Wherever they arrived in significant numbers, *Megorashim* founded separate synagogues and congregations,[109] maintained their particularism in religious customs and rites, and remained socially separate for a very long time. The Sephardi rabbinical families soon came to occupy center stage in Jewish communities such as that of Fez.

Nevertheless, eventually, these distinctions faded in most areas. While religious customs continued to differ slightly, most congregations ceased to be separate according to place of origin. The descendants of the Sephardim became acclimated and adapted to the local context, while the local Jews remained deeply influenced by the imprint of the Sephardim in cultural and economic life. The two cultures borrowed from each other, and fused to create a unique North African Jewish civilization.[110] In cities such as Fez, Meknes, Mazagan, Tlemcen, and Algiers, while Spanish surnames and customs survived, the descendants of the Sephardim gradually lost their Hispanicity, and became full-fledged participants in a Sephardized Judeo-Arabic culture.

It was only in the north, the area closest to the Iberian peninsula, in cities such as Tetuan and Tangier, that the Sephardi presence managed to maintain its separate specificity. Here the Sephardim, relatively few in number compared to the bulk of Maghreb Jewry, eventually absorbed local elements, and kept steadfast to their customs and mores. Their language, called *Haketia*, while borrowing extensively from Hebrew and Arabic, remained essentially Spanish, and survived until the twentieth century, when it was thoroughly re-Castilianized under new Spanish rule.

While North Africa was an important refuge for the exiles, it is quite understandable why this region, though nearest to Spain, did not become the destination for the majority. The multiplicity of kingdoms, dynastic and tribal wars, and continuing Portuguese and Spanish conquests on the coast created a volatile situation. While the Islam of the Maghreb was more tolerant than the Christianity of the Iberian peninsula, the lack of any long-lasting centralized authority frequently allowed for more restrictive interpretations vis-à-vis the Jews to emerge on the local level. Political stability was not to emerge for a long time. The situation did not change substantially when Algeria and Tunisia fell under Ottoman rule in the sixteenth century. These areas remained largely autonomous from Istanbul, and the plurality of local centers of power survived the veneer of Ottoman control, which became yet another complicating factor in the local configuration.

Political stability, a relatively tolerant rule, and attractive new socioeconomic conditions drew most of the Sephardi exiles farther east in the half-century that followed the Expulsion, to another Muslim-controlled area, the Ottoman Levant. There a new Judeo-Spanish presence was reconstituted and would endure as a distinct entity until the twentieth century.

NOTES TO THE PROLOGUE

1   For details of the expulsion, see Yitshak Baer, *A History of the Jews in Christian Spain*, tr. L. Schoffman (Philadelphia: The Jewish Publication Society of America, 1978), vol. II, pp. 424–39.

2   For a history of the Jews in Muslim Spain, see Eliyahu Ashtor, *The Jews of Moslem Spain*, 3 vols. (Philadelphia: The Jewish Publication Society of America, 1973–79).

3   For the early stages of the *Reconquista*, see Baer, *A History*, vol. I, pp. 39–110.

4   For a discussion and illustration of the "royal alliance," see Yosef Hayim Yerushalmi, *The Lisbon Massacre of 1506 and the Royal Image in the Shebet Yehudah* (Cincinnati: Hebrew Union College, Jewish Institute of Religion, 1976).

5   See the overview of the relationship of the Jews with the rulers and the rest of society in J. N. Hillgarth, *The Spanish Kingdoms*, 2 vols. (Oxford: Clarendon Press, 1976–78), vol. I, pp. 167–78; and Maurice Kriegel, *Les Juifs à la fin du Moyen Age dans l'Europe méditerranéenne* (Paris: Hachette, 1979), pp. 59–69.

6   On the structure and autonomy of the Jewish community, see Baer, *A History*, vol. I, pp. 212–36. See also Kriegel, *Les Juifs*, pp. 111–43.

7   Baer, *A History*, vol. I, pp. 50–51.

8   J. L. Shneidman, "Jews as Royal Bailiffs in Thirteenth-Century Aragon," *Historia Judaica*, 19 (1957), pp. 55–56.

9   Baer, *A History*, vol. I, pp. 138–44.

10   Ibid., pp. 138–40, 144–46.

11   Hillgarth, *The Spanish Kingdoms*, vol. I, p. 240.

12   Angus MacKay, "The Jews in Spain during the Middle Ages," in Elie Kedourie, ed., *Spain and the Jews: The Sephardi Experience, 1492 and After* (London: Thames and Hudson, 1992), p. 34.

13   Baer, *A History*, vol. I, pp. 171–77.

14   Ibid., pp. 362–64; Hillgarth, *The Spanish Kingdoms*, vol. II, pp. 132–33.

15   For the classic exposition of *convivencia*, see Americo Castro, *La Realidad histórica de España* (Mexico, D.F.: Biblioteca Porrúa, 1954).

16   See Kriegel, *Les Juifs*, pp. 39–69.

17   For the changes in the position of the Jews in the Middle Ages, some of the latest works are Robert Chazan, *Church, State, and Jew in the Middle Ages* (New York: Behrman House, 1980); idem, *Daggers of Faith: Thirteenth-Century Christian Missionizing and Jewish Response* (Berkeley and Los Angeles: University of California Press, 1989); and Jeremy Cohen, *The Friars and the Jews: The Evolution of Medieval Anti-Judaism* (Ithaca: Cornell University Press, 1982).

18   See, *inter alia*, Edward Peters, *Heresy and Authority in Medieval Europe* (Philadelphia: University of Pennsylvania Press, 1980); idem, *Inquisition* (New York: The Free Press, 1988); and Elie Griffe, *Le Languedoc cathare et l'Inquisition (1229–1329)* (Paris: Letouzey et Ané, 1980).

19   Hillgarth, *The Spanish Kingdoms*, vol. I, p. 135.

20   Ibid., pp. 210–11.

21   See Baer, *A History*, vol. I, pp. 152–57; R. Chazan, "The Barcelona

'Disputation' of 1263: Christian Missionizing and Jewish Response," *Speculum*, 52 (1977), pp. 824–42.

22 Baer, *A History*, vol. I, p. 185.

23 Ibid., p. 417.

24 Hillgarth, *The Spanish Kingdoms*, vol. I, pp. 212–13.

25 See Yom Tov Assis, "The Papal Inquisition and Aragonese Jewry in the Early Fourteenth Century," *Medieval Studies*, 49 (1987), pp. 391–410.

26 Baer, *A History*, vol. II, pp. 15–28.

27 Ibid., vol. I, pp. 327–54.

28 Ibid., vol. I, pp. 375–76; vol. II, pp. 64–69.

29 Ibid., vol. I, pp. 222–31 and *passim*; vol. II, 21 and *passim*; Kriegel, *Les Juifs*, pp. 111–44.

30 On the pogroms of 1391, see Baer, *A History*, vol. II, pp. 95–169; Hillgarth, *The Spanish Kingdoms*, vol. II, pp. 137–42; P. Wolff, "The 1391 Pogroms in Spain: Social Crisis or Not?" *Past and Present*, 50 (1971), pp. 4–18; and A. MacKay, "Popular Movements and Pogroms in Fifteenth-Century Castile," *Past and Present*, 55 (1972), pp. 33–67; Kriegel, *Les Juifs*, pp. 206–15.

31 Maurice Kriegel, "La Prise d'une décision: L'Expulsion des Juifs d'Espagne en 1492," *Revue Historique*, 260, no. 527 (1978), p. 63.

32 On these figures, see Baer, *A History*, vol. II, *passim*. On Abravanel, see Benzion Netanyahu, *Don Isaac Abravanel, Statesman and Philosopher*, 3d ed. (Philadelphia: The Jewish Publication Society of America, 1972); and Jean-Christophe Attias, *Isaac Abravanel, la mémoire et l'espérance* (Paris: Cerf, 1992).

33 Hillgarth, *The Spanish Kingdoms*, vol. II, pp. 142–43.

34 Baer, *A History*, vol. II, pp. 170–243.

35 Ibid., pp. 259–70. See also Elazar Gutwirth, "Towards Expulsion: 1391–1492," in Kedourie, ed., *Spain and the Jews*, pp. 62–65.

36 There is a large literature on the "New Christians." For some of the famous figures in the fifteenth century, see Roger Highfield, "Christians, Jews, and Muslims in the Same Society: The Fall of *Convivencia* in Medieval Spain," in *Religious Motivation: Biographical and Sociological Problems for the Church Historian*, ed. Derek Baker (Oxford: Basil Blackwell, 1978), pp. 121–46. See also Haim Beinart, "The *Conversos* and Their Fate," in Kedourie, ed., *Spain and the Jews*, p. 94.

37 For the *converso* problem, see *inter alia* B. Netanyahu, *The Marranos of Spain from the Late XIVth to the Late XVIth Century according to Contemporary Hebrew Sources* (New York: American Academy for Jewish Research, 1966), and the reviews by A. A. Sicroff, "The Marranos—Forced Converts or Apostates?" *Midstream*, 12 (1966), pp. 71–75, and Gerson D. Cohen, *Jewish Social Studies*, 29 (1967), pp. 178–84. See also Haim Beinart, "The *Converso* Community in Fifteenth-Century Spain," in *The Sephardi Heritage*, vol. I, ed. R. D. Barnett (London: Vallentine Mitchell, 1971), pp. 425–56; idem, *Conversos on Trial: The Inquisition in Ciudad Real* (Jerusalem: Magnes Press, 1981); and B. Netanyahu, *The Origins of the Inquisition in Fifteenth-Century Spain* (New York: Random House, 1995). On *conversa* religiosity, see Renée Levine Melammed, *Heretics or Daughters of Israel? The Crypto-Jewish Women of Castile* (Oxford: Oxford University Press, 1999).

38 Highfield, "Christians, Jews," pp. 125–28.

39 Hillgarth, *The Spanish Kingdoms*, vol. II, p. 155.

40 Ibid., p. 156.

41 Highfield, "Christians, Jews," p. 129.

42 For a discussion of this Inquisition and the Jews, see Yosef Hayim Yerushalmi, "The Inquisition and the Jews of France in the Time of Bernard Gui," *Harvard Theological Review*, 63 (1970), pp. 317–76.

43 Hillgarth, *The Spanish Kingdoms*, vol. II, pp. 422–23.

44 Highfield, "Christians, Jews," p. 128.

45 Hillgarth, *The Spanish Kingdoms*, vol. II, pp. 422–25.

46 Ibid., pp. 434–35.

47 Highfield, "Christians, Jews," p. 130.

48 See Henry Kamen, "The Mediterranean and the Expulsion of Spanish Jews in 1492," *Past and Present*, 119 (1988), p. 44. He repeats this argument in "The Expulsion: Purpose and Consequence," in Kedourie, ed., *Spain and the Jews*, pp. 74–91.

49 Jonathan I. Israel, *European Jewry in the Age of Mercantilism, 1550–1750*, 2d ed. (Oxford: Clarendon Press, 1989), p. 6. See also John Edwards, *The Jews in Christian Europe, 1400–1700* (London: Routledge, 1991), p. 29.

50 M. J. Pimenta Ferro Tavares, *Os Judeus em Portugal no século xv*, 2 vols. (Lisbon: Universidad Nova de Lisboa, 1982–84), vol. I, pp. 253–56.

51 See the discussion in Halil İnalcık, "Jews in the Ottoman Economy and Finances," in *Essays in Honor of Bernard Lewis: The Islamic World*, ed. C. E. Bosworth et al. (Princeton: Darwin Press, 1989), p. 515.

52 See also the discussion in Hillgarth, *The Spanish Kingdoms*, vol. II, p. 449; and in Edwards, *The Jews*, pp. 34–36.

53 See *inter alia* the discussion of the causes of the Expulsion in S. Haliczer, "The Castilian Urban Patriciate and the Jewish Expulsion of 1480–1492," *American Historical Review*, 78 (1973), pp. 35–58; Maurice Kriegel, "La Prise d'une décision"; and Hillgarth, *The Spanish Kingdoms*, vol. II, pp. 440–83.

54 For the latest overview, see Yosef Hayim Yerushalmi, *A Jewish Classic in the Portuguese Language*, vol. I (Lisbon: Fundaçao Calouste Gulbenkian, 1989), pp. 11–12.

55 Ibid., 13–14.

56 Ibid., p. 17.

57 For the discussion of the incident, see Yerushalmi, *The Lisbon Massacre*.

58 See A. Herculano, *History of the Origin and Establishment of the Inquisition in Portugal*, tr. J. C. Branner (New York: Ktav, 1972). See also the discussion in Beinart, "The *Conversos*," p. 118.

59 For a discussion of Marranism, see I. S. Révah, "Les Marranes," *Revue des Etudes Juives*, 118 (1959–60), pp. 29–77; and Yosef Hayim Yerushalmi, *From*

Spanish Court to Italian Ghetto: Isaac Cardoso, a Study in Seventeenth-Century Marranism and Jewish Apologetics, 2d ed. (Seattle: University of Washington Press, 1981), pp. 1–50.

60   For a summary of the Reubeni-Molho episode, see Yerushalmi, *A Jewish Classic*, vol. I, pp. 31–34.

61   See Albert A. Sicroff, *Les Controverses des statuts de pureté de sang en Espagne du XVe au XVIIe siècle* (Paris: Didier, 1960).

62   Israel, *European Jewry*, p. 17.

63   Ibid., pp. 20–21.

64   See the discussion of this press in Yerushalmi, *A Jewish Classic*, vol. I, pp. 75–91.

65   For a general overview of the Counter-Reformation and the Jews, see Salo W. Baron, *A Social and Religious History of the Jews*, 18 vols. (New York and Philadelphia: Columbia University Press and The Jewish Publication Society of America, 1957–83), vol. XIV, chaps. 59, 60.

66   For the situation in Venice, see Benjamin Ravid, "The Socioeconomic Background of the Expulsion and Readmission of the Venetian Jews, 1571–1573," in *Essays in Modern Jewish History: A Tribute to Ben Halpern*, ed. P. Albert and F. Malino (Rutherford: Fairleigh Dickinson University Press, 1982), pp. 27–55; and Israel, *European Jewry*, p. 47.

67   Edwards, *The Jews*, p. 90. For a discussion of "New Christians" in Venice, see Brian Pullan, *The Jews of Europe and the Inquisition of Venice, 1560–1670*, (Oxford: Basil Blackwell, 1983).

68   The latest overview is in Joseph Kaplan, "L'Impact social et économique de la diaspora judéo-hispanique sur l'Europe occidentale au début de la période moderne," in Shmuel Trigano, ed., *La Société juive à travers l'histoire* (Paris: Fayard, 1993), vol. III, pp. 240–65.

69   Gérard Nahon, "The Sephardim in France," in *The Sephardi Heritage*, vol. II, ed. R. D. Barnett and W. M. Schwab (Grendon, Northants: Gibraltar Books, 1989), pp. 47–48. See also Gérard Nahon, *Les "Nations" juives portugaises du sud-ouest de la France (1648–1791): Documents* (Paris: Fondation C. Gulbenkian, 1981).

70   Israel, *European Jewry*, p. 116.

71   See T. Malvezin, *Histoire des Juifs à Bordeaux* (Bordeaux: Lefebvre, 1875), pp. 137–38; Z. Szajkowski, "Trade Relations of the Marranos in France with the Iberian Peninsula in the Sixteenth and Seventeenth Centuries," *Jewish Quarterly Review*, 50 (1959–60), pp. 75–78. For the numbers of Jews in this period, see A. Detcheverry, *Histoire des Israélites de Bordeaux* (Bordeaux: Balarac Jeune, 1850), pp. 62–66.

72   Malvezin, *Histoire*, p. 113.

73   Archives Municipales de Bordeaux, *Inventaire*, 8 (1913), p. 244.

74   Ibid., 4 (1909), p. 231.

75   Ibid., 8 (1913), p. 245.

76   Detcheverry, *Histoire*, p. 65.

77   Arthur Hertzberg, *The French Enlightenment and the Jews* (New York: Columbia University Press, 1968), pp. 20–21.

78   Malvezin, *Histoire*, p. 122.

79   Hertzberg, *The French Enlightenment*, p. 24.

80   J.-B. Colbert, *Lettres, Instructions et Mémoires*, 7 vols., ed. P. Clément (Paris: Imprimerie Impériale, 1861–73), vol. II, p. 679.

81   Hertzberg, *The French Enlightenment*, pp. 24–26. However, long before this, Richelieu's *politique* stance had made it clear to the Jews that they could be more open. See Israel, *European Jewry*, p. 117. This is indicated by Jewish names appearing on gravestones in places like Peyrehorade as early as 1641. See Gérard Nahon, "Inscriptions funéraires hébraïques et juives à Bidache, Labastide-Clairence (Basses-Pyrénées) et Peyrehorade (Landes)," *Revue des Etudes Juives*, 127–28 (1968–69), pp. 347–65, 349–75.

82   Israel, *European Jewry*, pp. 50–51.

83   Ibid., p. 65.

84 Wilhelmina C. Pieterse, "The Sephardi Jews of Amsterdam," in Barnett and Schwab, eds., *The Sephardi Heritage*, vol. II, p. 78.

85 For a discussion of the general context in Amsterdam, see Simon Schama, *The Embarrassment of Riches* (New York: Knopf, 1987); Henry Méchoulan, *Amsterdam au temps de Spinoza: Argent et liberté* (Paris: PUF, 1990); idem, *Etre Juif à Amsterdam au temps de Spinoza* (Paris: Albin Michel, 1991); idem, "The Jewish Community of Amsterdam in the Seventeenth Century," *Peamim*, 48 (1991), pp. 104–16 (in Hebrew).

86 For a discussion of the economic activities of the Sephardim of the Netherlands, see Jonathan I. Israel, "The Economic Contribution of Dutch Sephardi Jewry to Holland's Golden Age, 1595–1713," *Tijdschrift voor Geschiedenis*, 96 (1983), pp. 505–36.

87 Jonathan Israel, "The Sephardim in the Netherlands," in Kedourie, ed., *Spain and the Jews*, p. 203.

88 Pieterse, "The Sephardi Jews," p. 96.

89 For a study of the intellectual and cultural ferment among the Dutch Sephardim, see Yosef Kaplan, *From Christianity to Judaism: The Story of Isaac Orobio de Castro*, tr. R. Loewe (Oxford: Oxford University Press, 1989). The identity of the Dutch Sephardim is studied by Miriam Bodian, *Hebrews of the Portuguese Nation: Conversos and Community in Early Modern Amsterdam* (Bloomington: Indiana University Press, 1997).

90 A. Feilchenfeld, "Anfang und Blütezeit der Portugiesengemeinde in Hamburg," *Zeitschrift des Vereins für Hamburgische Geschichte*, 10 (1899), p. 206.

91 H. Kellenbenz, *Sephardim an der unteren Elbe* (Wiesbaden: F. Steiner, 1958), p. 111.

92 Jonathan I. Israel, "A Conflict of Empires: Spain and the Netherlands, 1618–1648," *Past and Present*, 76 (1977), pp. 34–47.

93 Kellenbenz, *Sephardim*, p. 41.

94 Ibid., pp. 113–26.

95 Ibid., pp. 40, 201.

96 C. Roth, "Neue Kunde von der Marranen-Gemeinde in Hamburg," *Zeitschrift für die Geschichte der Juden in Deutschland*, 2 (1930), p. 235.

97 H. Z. Hirschberg, *A History of the Jews in North Africa*, vol. I (Leiden: E. J. Brill, 1974), pp. 372–83.

98 Jane S. Gerber, *Jewish Society in Fez, 1450–1700: Studies in Communal and Economic Life* (Leiden: E. J. Brill, 1980), pp. 43–44.

99 Hirschberg, *A History*, vol. I, pp. 387–88.

100 Ibid., p. 387.

101 André Chouraqui, *Histoire des Juifs en Afrique du Nord* (Paris: Hachette, 1985), pp. 128–29.

102 Hirschberg, *A History*, vol. I, pp. 436–39.

103 Ibid., vol. II, pp. 58–68. See also Gerber, *Jewish Society*, pp. 27–28.

104 Ibid., p.47.

105 Ibid., p. 48.

106 Hirschberg, *A History*, vol. I, pp. 406–7.

107 Gerber, *Jewish Society*, p. 28.

108 Ibid., pp. 161–83.

109 For a study of this situation in Fez, see Gerber, *Jewish Society*, p. 55. See also Haim Zafrani, *Mille ans de vie juive au Maroc: Histoire et culture, religion et magie* (Paris: Maisonneuve et Larose, 1983), p. 13.

110 Chouraqui, *Histoire*, p. 192.

1

Community and Society

The power of the Ottomans grew constantly during the fourteenth and fifteenth centuries. What had been no more than a small tribal outpost on the Anatolian frontier of Byzantium, had become an empire in the process of securing control of the major part of the Balkans, ultimately conquering Constantinople itself in 1453. The Ottomans put an end to Mameluk rule in the Holy Land and Egypt in 1516–17 and, by the mid-sixteenth century, had overwhelmed the greater part of the Near East and North Africa. The rest of the world now saw them as a menacing and invincible force.

Developing from its initial status as a frontier principality into a sophisticated bureaucratic state, deriving its legitimacy from both Islam and pre-Muslim imperial traditions of the Middle East and Asia, the Empire succeeded for several centuries in mobilizing all the dynamic forces of the societies it governed. Separation between religion and the state did not exist: the sultan, as caliph, was responsible for implementing Muslim religious law (*sharia*), in the exercise of justice. He was also theoretically the owner of the whole country and its subjects. The strongly centralized bureaucracy, the army, with the janissaries – a corps of slave soldiers – at its heart, and the clergy formed the three pillars of the ruling élite. These were the only groups that escaped taxation. The rest of the population, tax-paying subjects or *reaya* (the flock), remained strictly separate from the ruling class. However, access to this class was not hereditary; it was open to all Muslims or converts who gained renown for knowledge or military prowess.[1]

The ruling élite, whose economic survival depended on the continuation of tax gathering from the *reaya*, attempted systematically to eliminate any concentration of economic and social power which might challenge its authority. It was consequently difficult for horizontal bonds to be forged capable of creating autonomous forms of authority and legitimacy. All power and all status depended on a vertical relationship with the center.

Most of the Jews came to live in large towns or in zones which were closely controlled by the center. They had relatively little to fear from a periphery which, at least during the first centuries of the Empire, was rendered harmless from the outset. For this reason, when they did become the objects of local incidents, such as accusations of ritual murder, the Jews usually succeeded in securing the protection of the Ottoman sultan and the central authorities and in obtaining redress. Such a *de facto* alliance with the center functioned in the Ottoman imperial state for several centuries, the Jews initially rendering many services to the government in return for its protection. And although the importance of the Jewish role declined over time, the model was nonetheless perpetuated until the end of the Empire. The Jewish communities continued to identify strongly with the central authorities and regarded the appearance of new national options in the modern period with mistrust.

From the start, the Ottoman attitude to the Jews was naturally dictated by considerations of self-interest. In a society where the dominant Ottoman Turkish element, formed of soldiers and peasants, was abandoning other sectors of activity, especially international trade, to conquered Christians or foreigners, the Jews could appear as a reliable force. Their skills could be useful and they were not suspected of harboring anti-Ottoman sentiment. The Ottoman policy of tolerance and protection in regard to the Jews had thus already taken on the dimensions of an established tradition from the first centuries of the Empire, well before the arrival of the Sephardim from the Iberian peninsula.

The important role the Jews played in the Empire in the fifteenth and sixteenth centuries was therefore closely linked to the Ottoman perception of their usefulness for craft and trade and for their administrative talents. Here, as elsewhere, was the real basis of the Judeo–Ottoman coexistence. Its justification in legal theory was, however, couched in the vocabulary of traditional Islamic discourse. In fact, the Ottoman attitude to the Jews followed the classic model of the *dhimma*[2] in Muslim lands.

The Muslim tradition (*sunna*) made express provision for the presence of non-Muslims in the land of Islam, so long as they could claim kinship with the Book, that is, the Bible. It forbade their conversion by force, and prescribed the details of their status in a series of stipulations developed in the first centuries that followed the rise of Islam. A hierarchy existed among non-Muslims which determined their status. Pagans had the choice of death or conversion; Jews and Christians, followers of a revealed religion, and Sabaeans and Zoroastrians had a third possibility: submission. This was governed by a pact (*dhimma*) whereby their new masters guaranteed the public and private rights of these categories of non-Muslims, the people of the Book (*ahl-al kitab*),[3] living in territories conquered by Muslims. Those subject to the pact came to be called *dhimmis* (*zimmi* in Turkish).

The *dhimma* conferred a legal status on the *dhimmis*, who were to be protected and tolerated, even if it transformed them into second-class subjects in Muslim society. The origin of this type of contract, or at least of some of its prescriptions, is said to originate with the treaties the prophet Muhammad concluded with conquered populations. These prescriptions were said to be developed and written in the form of a pact under the caliph Umar, though they were probably actually formulated in their final form in the Abbasid period (750–1258). Moreover, several versions of this apocryphal pact exist. Its implementation varied with regime and period. In fact, it is difficult to speak of a consensus on this subject in the Muslim world. According to Muslim jurists, the *dhimma* was a bilateral, permanent contract, and each of the contracting parties was bound to respect its terms.

The restrictions which affected the *dhimmis* had social implications, symbolic as well as practical. They were there in order to indicate the supremacy of Islam and the superiority of the Muslims. The major penalty affecting the *dhimmis* was the payment of a poll tax (*cizye*). In return, they obtained the guarantee of life and property as well as the free practice of their religion. The *dhimmis* also paid a series of other regular or *ad hoc* taxes.

These restrictions were counterbalanced by concessions. The personal status of the non-Muslim was governed by the *jus religionis*. Thus, the protected communities enjoyed a large degree of freedom as far as their internal affairs were concerned. The *dhimmis* were subject to the authority of their own leaders and judges and could lead their personal, family, and religious lives in accordance with their own laws and customs.

The restrictions were more apparent in daily life. The inferiority of the *dhimmis* was defined in social and religious terms. The place assigned them in civil society underpinned their inferiority. Inequality pervaded their relationships with the outside Muslim world. Their clothing, headgear, and even names marked them off from Muslims. Their homes and buildings had to be lower than those of the dominant faith. They were forbidden to carry weapons and did not have the right to ride "noble" animals such as horses and camels. A *dhimmi* could not marry a Muslim woman nor take a Muslim slave. His testimony was inadmissible in a lawsuit involving a Muslim.

What must not be lost sight of is that, however numerous these restrictions affecting Jews in Ottoman lands, they were insignificant compared with what Jews had recently experienced in Spain or elsewhere in medieval Europe. The legal tradition concerning non-Muslims was never a fixed, immutable entity that remained static over the centuries, but was constantly interpreted and reinterpreted in the light of current political and social realities. Hence, the implementation of restrictions varied in severity from place to place, from one regime to another.

A new and triumphant force, offering a safe refuge, the Ottoman Empire attracted many Jews even before the Expulsion. Edirne (Adrianople), for example, the capital of the Empire before the conquest of Constantinople, saw the arrival of Jews expelled from Hungary in 1376. Jews driven out of France are also known to have reached this city after 1394.[4] The existence of this community, as well as the immigrants' attitude towards their new masters, were expressed in the famous letter in which Rabbi Isaac Zarfati invited his fellow Jews in Europe to settle in Ottoman lands:

I have heard of the afflictions, more bitter than death, that have befallen our brethren in Germany – of the tyrannical laws, the compulsory baptisms and the banishments, which are of daily occurrence. I am told that when they flee from one place a yet harder fate befalls them in another . . . on all sides I learn of anguish of soul and torment of body; of daily exactions levied by merciless oppressors. The clergy and the monks, false priests that they are, rise up against the unhappy people of God . . . for this reason they have made a law that every Jew found upon a Christian ship bound for the East shall be flung into the sea. Alas! How evil are the people of God in Germany entreated; how sad is their strength departed! They are driven hither and thither, and they are pursued even unto death . . . Brothers and teachers, friends and acquaintances! I, Isaac Zarfati, though I spring from a French stock, yet I was born in Germany, and sat there at the feet of my esteemed teachers. I proclaim to you that Turkey is a land wherein nothing is lacking, and where, if you will, all shall yet be well with you. The way to the Holy Land lies open to you through Turkey. Is it not better for you to live under Muslims than under Christians? Here every man may dwell at peace under his own vine and fig tree. Here, you are allowed to wear the most precious garments. In Christendom, on the contrary, you dare not even venture to clothe your children in red or in blue, according to our taste, without exposing them to the insult of being beaten black and blue, or kicked green and red, and therefore are ye condemned to go about meanly clad in sad colored raiment . . . and now, seeing all these things, O Israel! Wherefore sleepest thou? Arise! And leave this accursed land forever![5]

Some Spanish Jews, fleeing the massacres of 1391, also eventually reached Ottoman lands. They were followed by some Jews expelled from France in 1394, some of whom settled in Edirne. Names such as Zarfati and Fransez (Frenchman), Yarhi (Lunel), Harari (Montpellier) bear witness to this immigration.[6] They were followed in the course of the fifteenth century by small waves of immigrants from other European areas, such as Bavaria for example, after the expulsion in 1470.[7] Most of the immigrants settled in Balkan lands controlled by the Ottomans, in Edirne, as well as in areas covered by present-day Bulgaria. This explains why there was a synagogue in Sofia in the fifteenth century, placed under the authority of Rabbi Benjamin Meir Halevi of Nuremberg. The Jewish district of La Baviera in Sofia is proof of the presence of German Jews, corroborated also by family names such as Zalman, Calman, Aciman, Tadjer (Deutscher-Taytscher), Eskenazi, and Zvi (Hirsch), to be found in all the Ottoman Balkans.[8] Some East European and Italian Jews also made their home in this expanding empire. The names of the synagogues, as well as onomastics, are evidence of these diverse waves of migration.

Nevertheless, the great majority of Jews settled in Ottoman territory before 1492 was formed of Greek-speaking elements, the Romaniots.[9] As the Ottoman state expanded and gained ascendency over initially Byzantine areas, so the number of Jewish communities under its jurisdiction increased. Most of the Rabbanite and Karaite (Jews who did not recognize the authority of the Oral Law) Romaniots remained in the Balkans and Asia Minor.[10] Arabophone Jewish communities were to be found to the South and East of Anatolia, spread over the major part of the Fertile Crescent.

The sultan Mehmed II (1451–81), who conquered Constantinople, used Jews to populate the city, deserted by its Greek inhabitants, and to revive its economic life, which had formerly been dominated by Venetians and Genoese. The population of the capital after the conquest approximated between 50,000 and 60,000 inhabitants.[11] As there was insufficient voluntary immigration, Mehmed II resorted to deportations. The motives for this policy of population transfer, called *sürgün* in Turkish, were primarily economic, a means of implementing settlement. Many different ethnic–religious groups, including Muslims, as well as Jews, were affected by deportations during the fifteenth to sixteenth centuries.[12] For example, a number of Romaniots, sometimes entire communities, were moved from places such as Edirne, Salonika, Philippopolis, Nicopolis, and Lamia to be settled in the old Venetian sector of Istanbul.[13] They subsequently moved on to the Istanbul quarter of Hasköy, which remained a Jewish district until the contemporary period. Even though they were not intended as punitive measures, these forced removals were indeed a harsh trial to many communities. The Karaites also suffered deportation en masse to the new Ottoman capital. If the Romaniot Jews had suffered persecutions under the Byzantines, the arrival of the Ottomans did not signal an immediate improvement in their lot, as it was often accompanied by similar forced uprootings.

The policy of *sürgün* was pursued into the sixteenth century. It is known, for example, that 150 of the richest Jewish families of Salonika were exiled to Rhodes in 1523. In 1526, large numbers of Jews from Buda were transplanted to Istanbul, Edirne, and Sofia, where they founded new congregations. In 1576–7 an attempt was made to move hundreds of Jewish families from Safed to Cyprus.[14] While this practice of transferring populations eventually lapsed, it nevertheless had noticeable repercussions on the distribution of populations in the Empire. Its impact on the Jewish community was particularly severe, with demographic and organizational consequences, in addition to the anguish of uprooting and the difficulties of starting a new life. Jewish groups, who did not form part of the mass of the conquerors but rather were of the subject populations, faced particular hardships. In the sixteenth century, the Jews tried various means to have these transfer decrees annulled. The deportations, principally from the Balkans and Anatolia, led to the disappearance of entire communities from some regions and to the creation of new ones in places where previously there had been no Jews. Indeed, this was how Edirne and Istanbul became the two greatest cities of the Empire with a marked concentration of Jews, even before the arrival of the Spanish expellees, while other cities remained devoid of Jews until the massive wave of Sephardi immigration. According to the 1477 census, the Ottoman capital contained 1,647 Jewish households, which represented about 11 percent of its population,[15] a very high proportion for the time.

The large Jewish population of Istanbul indicates the importance of the Romaniot community, comprising Rabbanites and Karaites, well before the arrival of the Sephardim. The Romaniots of the city mainly worked in trade, and their role was particularly important in farming taxes, the collection of customs dues, and in the mint.[16] They controlled all major tax farming in the Istanbul region in 1470–80.[17] Jews engaging in this type of activity in Ottoman lands before 1492 sometimes went into partnership with non-Jews. But very often, Jewish tax farming was based on the community of the region, which became the guarantor for its collection.[18] Jews continued to play an important role in this sector in the sixteenth century when the Romaniots were joined by a number of Sephardim who had already proved their ability in this field in the Iberian peninsula.

The Jews' relatively high economic profile in Istanbul and other Ottoman towns in the Balkans naturally inclined the sultans to favor Jewish immigration into the Empire. This economically useful population arrived at a propitious moment. The Jews had already proven their usefulness to the sultans' demographic and economic policies, and the state had much to gain from welcoming the post-1492 immigrants, who could add to the wealth of the country without posing a political problem. Consequently, they were not merely authorized to come; they were actively encouraged. Some settled in the harbor towns where they landed, while others were guided to specific localities. The new communities were exempted from certain taxes, although the poll tax (*cizye*, or later, *haraç*, in Turkish) was regularly paid. The story is told that when the sultan Bayezid II (1491–1512) learned of the expulsion of the Jews from Spain, he tried to attract the exiles to his territories for political purposes:

So the sultan Bayezid, king of Turkey, heard all the evil that the Spanish king had brought upon the Jews, and heard that they were seeking a refuge and a resting place. He took pity on them, and wrote letters and sent emisaries to proclaim throughout his kingdom that none of his city rulers may be wicked enough to refuse entry to Jews or expel them. Instead, they were to be given a gracious welcome.[19]

Bayezid is also said to have voiced the following sentiments concerning the rulers of Spain: "Can you call such a king wise and intelligent? He is impoverishing his country and enriching my kingdom."[20]

All these quotations are taken from Jewish sources; nothing equivalent can be found in Ottoman documentation. The Ottomans welcomed the Sephardim as a useful population. However, these apocryphal sentences throw more light on the state of mind of the Jews of the period than on formal Ottoman policy. They also express deep-seated Jewish expectations, in the face of the terrible shock of the Expulsion, which would continue to foster a strong submerged messianic current, already present in the Iberian peninsula and destined to surface a century and a half later with Sabbateanism.[21]

Elijah Capsali (1450–1523), a Romaniot, himself descended from those who had suffered from the Ottoman conquest, was one of the first to formulate this new perception of the Ottomans in his chronicle, *Seder Eliyahu Zuta* ("The Lesser Order of Elijah"), written in 1523. He linked gratitude to an empire which had been so good as to offer safe haven to the expellees with the model of the good king, which the new arrivals had projected onto an Ottoman context of which they had no experience, in a sort of continuity that attached them to the "lost paradise" of Spain where "good kings" had once been their protectors. This was another myth, magnified by exile and the difficulties of adjustment which are the lot of all immigrants. Yet the Romaniots who had been major objects of the settlement and of the repopulation policy of the new masters and who had not had a smooth transition to Ottoman rule in the first decades after the fall of Constantinople, could not have left the new arrivals in the dark about the local situation.[22] Nothing, it seems, could stem this strong projection of goodwill onto a sovereign who could be the source of no evil and whose help would always be forthcoming. It should be recalled that under this same Bayezid II, whom Capsali extolled, the Jews were subjected to major restrictions stemming from the particularly devout concerns of the sultan.[23] But could the lost *Sefarad* not be recreated on Ottoman soil, and thus make the transplantation easier by the rediscovery of an already familiar terrain? Was Capsali influenced by the hopes cherished by the Spanish immigrants? Was there also perhaps a desire to please the Ottoman authorities? In any case, these myths remain alive today and have received new currency in the celebrations of the 500th anniversary of the arrival of the Sephardim in Turkey.

Depictions similar to Capsali's can be found in other testimonies. For example, the letter which Jews from Provence, living in Salonika, sent to their coreligionists expelled from Provence in the beginning of the Sixteenth century, contains the words: "Come and join us in Turkey and you will live in peace and freedom as we do."[24] In about the same period, the poet Samuel Usque describes Salonika in the following terms:

It is the mother of Israel which has grown stronger on the foundations of the religion, which yields excellent plants and fruit trees, unequalled the world over. Its fruits are delicious, because watered by rivers. Jews of Europe and other countries, persecuted and banished, have come to seek refuge there, and this town has received them with love and cordiality, as if it were our revered mother Jerusalem.[25]

The picture the immigrants held of their new "homeland" could not fail to be positive in comparison with the sufferings previously endured. The fact remains that all Jewish historiography would be influenced by this idyllic vision, putting the Ottoman sovereigns on a pedestal and mythifying the welcome given the Sephardim, without identifying the larger political and economic picture.

Two major waves of Sephardi migration to the Empire can be distinguished. The first was formed of the Spanish expellees of 1492 and those who succeeded in leaving Portugal after the mass, forced conversions of 1497. Of course, many did not arrive on Ottoman soil immediately. They stayed in various regions of Italy for a few years before moving east, either by land from the Adriatic, across the Balkans and Asia Minor, or by sea towards the main Ottoman ports. The second wave, much more fragmented and numerically smaller, brought the Marrano immigration, principally from Portugal after the definitive establishment of the Inquisition in the mid-sixteenth century.[26] This immigration continued in spurts into the seventeenth century. While many followed their predecessors' Mediterranean itinerary, the Marranos also took more circuitous routes, via the Low Countries in the North.

Ottoman statistics provide ample evidence of the increased Jewish presence in certain large centers of the Empire at the beginning of the sixteenth century which resulted from these migratory movements, with hundreds of Jewish households in cities such as Istanbul, Salonika, Bursa, and Edirne.[27] The contours of the Jewish population of the Ottoman capital emerge clearly from censuses taken at the beginning of the seventeenth century. In 1603, 973 "new" Jewish households were reported, principally formed by post-1492 immigrants. The 1608 census recorded 1,222 "old" Romaniot households, which brings the total to 2,195. Overall therefore, the Sephardi newcomers did not yet dominate numerically the Jewish community of the city.[28]

The 1478 census does not record the presence of a single Jew in Salonika.[29] The Judeo-Byzantine community of that town had been transferred to Istanbul after its conquest by the Turks. The registers for subsequent decades point to a strong increase in the Jewish population, the overwhelming majority Sephardic. In 1529, Salonika contained 2,645 Jewish households against 1,229 Muslim and 989 Greek households.[30] This community continued to expand as a result of natural growth and arrivals from various European countries, as well as of Marranos from the Iberian peninsula. Salonika thus became one of the most important Jewish centers in the world in the sixteenth century and the leading Jewish city on the Mediterranean, its 2,933 Jewish households in 1613 representing more than 68 percent of its total population.[31]

The important commercial city of Valona, in Albania, contained 609 Jewish households in the sixteenth century; in Bulgaria, Nicopolis possessed 186, Sofia 21, Vidin 31, Philippopolis 41.[32] These latter cities gradually expanded into fairly important Sephardi centers. Other Bulgarian and Anatolian towns and the Aegean islands also housed Jewish settlements of variable size. In the mid-sixteenth century, Sephardim settled in Uskub (Skopje) and Monastir (Bitola) in Macedonia, and in Belgrade and Sarajevo. The Sephardim took up residence in Belgrade after the Turkish conquest in 1521; near the end of the seventeenth century, the community numbered some 800 persons.[33] At that time it was reputed to be the third center of Jewish learning in the Balkans, after Istanbul and Salonika. As for Sarajevo, 15 families of Salonikan merchants settled there in 1565; 16 years later, there is mention of 60 families, and the estimate for the eighteenth century is of about 1,000 Jews.[34] The Jewish community of the city grew uninterruptedly. It was referred to as the little Jerusalem. In Venetian Dalmatia, the republic of Ragusa (Dubrovnik), a vassal state of the Ottoman sultan, and Spalato (Split), where the port owes its birth to a Sephardi, also had Judeo-Iberian communities that played an important role in trade between the Empire, Venice, and Ancona.[35]

The conquest of Mameluk Palestine in 1516–17 cleared the path for a revival of Jewish settlement in the region. In this way many Sephardim reached the Holy Land, although their presence remained limited compared with the Jewish populations of the Balkans and the Ottoman capital. Gaza contained 115 Jewish households in 1548–9, and Jerusalem 324 in 1553–4.[36] Safed had 719 in 1553–6 and as many as 977 in 1596–7, after reaching a total of 1,700 Jewish households in 1568, which corresponded to the period of the town's growth.[37] The demographic fall apparent at the end of the sixteenth century was the direct result of the economic problems experienced by the city, which had been, with Salonika, an important center of the textile industry. These problems caused Jews to emigrate to other areas.

Internal economic developments also contributed to the redistribution of the Jewish populations. They explain the presence of an important Jewish community in Izmir in the seventeenth century, following the arrival of the Marranos and of large numbers of Jews from Salonika in particular, on account of the commercial boom Izmir experienced from the second half of the sixteenth century, which was linked to the activities of the Levant Companies.[38]

The overall total of Jewish families that arrived in the Ottoman Empire after 1492 is estimated at 12,000, which represents approximately 60,000 persons.[39] Some estimates suggest a figure of 50,000 for the whole Jewish population of the Empire at the end of the first quarter of the sixteenth century,[40] and others put this at 150,000, making the Ottoman Jewish community one of the largest in Europe.[41] Variations in demographic assessments are a constant factor as far as the Ottoman Empire is concerned, even in the nineteenth century. It is important to note that the Ottoman statistics were used for levying taxes, and that it was always very much in the interests of the Jewish community, which was taxed as a group, to underestimate its size, so that the real figures could well have been higher than the official count. In any case, and even on the basis of the data supplied by official censuses, 12,000 families represented a very considerable group for the time. The Mediterranean cities were relatively underpopulated in that period. Venice, for example, had 100,000 people in 1509 rising to 175,000 in 1575; Naples and Milan each contained 100,000 souls at the end of the fifteenth century.[42] None of the large European cities of the day sheltered more than a few thousand Jews. By comparison, Istanbul and Salonika, as well as the Empire as a whole, appeared to have very large Jewish agglomerations, thus illustrating the eastward movement of the Jewish world's center of gravity in the course of the previous two or three centuries.

COMMUNAL CONFLICTS

Relations between the Sephardim and the autochthonous Jews remained strained and stormy for decades. Differences in interpretation of Jewish religious law (*halakhah*), customs, and culture divided the communities, whether Sephardi, Ashkenazi, or Romaniot. Nevertheless, the real issue was the battle between Sephardim and Romaniots. Istanbul, where the bulk of Romaniot Jewry was concentrated, paid the heaviest price for these endemic frictions.

Most of the Romaniots in the conquered city had been transferred from other regions of the Empire. In Istanbul, they reorganized themselves according to their native town or region. The new Sephardi arrivals would later adopt the same model.[43] It is not known whether the Ottomans imposed this type of organization or if the Jews themselves preferred it, since they had been deported in groups from one place or one region. This geographic mode of community restructuring was conducive to the formation of self-identifying units, thus strengthening their sense of Romaniot identity. In the early days, this identification was helpful in overcoming the difficulties of adjusting to an unknown environment. The uprooting they had suffered was partially alleviated by the attachment to the place of origin, while the shared experience of uprooting and common origins welded the community together.

It should not be forgotten that the deportees and their descendants were not allowed to leave their new city without express permission.[44] In some cases they were even forbidden to contract marriages with outsiders. For economic reasons, the deportee was required to continue with the trade he had practiced prior to being transferred. These restrictions were aimed at implanting the exiles by force into their new context, if only by compulsory restrictions.

Added to this was the fact that, despite everything, the Romaniots, even displaced, were autochthonous Jews when compared with the Sephardi immigrants. The Romaniots had experienced the Ottoman regime in their native region and this familiarity eased their relationship with it. It must also be taken into account that the Ottomans had offered some benefits, such as exemption from certain taxes, to Romaniots who were deported or came of their own free will, in order initially to attract them and subsequently make it easier for them to settle. They did the same for the Sephardim in the early days. The new masters of the country needed this population, as well as others, in order to rebuild Istanbul.

In the beginning, when they were slightly more numerous than the Sephardim, quite naturally, the Romaniots appeared as the stronger group in Istanbul, anxious to defend their identity in the face of another group of exiles who had chosen departure rather than conversion to Christianity and enjoyed a high cultural reputation in the Jewish world. To a certain extent, the Romaniots and the expellees from the Iberian peninsula shared the same fate; nonetheless, the expellees disembarked in an area which was totally foreign to them and, in theory, should only have disadvantaged them as the most recent arrivals. However, in the long run the restrictions imposed on the Romaniots as a result of the *sürgün* process proved particularly disadvantageous. The Jews expelled from the Iberian peninsula, for their part, had to get acquainted not only with their new land and new rulers but also with the Jews who were already there.

The Romaniot congregations who had been transferred to the capital, as well as those already in existence when the town was conquered, came under the heading of *sürgün* or *sürgünlü* (from "deportees"), while congregations formed by the new arrivals were called *kendi gelen* ("came of their own free will"), names which are still found in the seventeenth century.[45] The last category did not only include the expellees from the Iberian peninsula, but also Italian, German, and Hungarian Jews. The Italian and Ashkenazi congregations in Istanbul and Salonika gradually joined the dominant Sephardi community. Although this Ottoman distinction was a fiscal measure, leading to the formation of two separate communities, each with its own system of collecting taxes, it is still a good indication of the margin for maneuver left to those who voluntarily chose to settle in the Empire. They were not put into the same structure as the Romaniots. The "welcomed" (to adopt their own self-image), beyond the gratitude they pledged to their "welcomers," were conscious of having made a choice, first in leaving the Iberian peninsula, then in directing their steps towards the Empire rather than other destinations, such as Italy.

The Sephardim formed a group which was confident of its strength, endowed with great self-esteem, equipped with a stratum of creative intellectuals, and proud of its skills.[46] The Romaniots themselves, like other Jewish communities around the Mediterranean, had consulted the Jewish thinkers of Spain over a long period. The Sephardim therefore arrived with a glorious cultural and social reputation, or at least such a reputation in the Jewish world. Magnified by the vagaries of exile, this past was mythified and glorified. Judeo-Spanish identity had its roots in this past, in a collective historical experience, and in a fate of shared suffering resulting from the wrenching from a land that the Iberian Jews considered their own – in accordance with a myth that their presence dated back to the destruction of the first Temple (568 BCE). This perception was linked to the right they claimed over Iberian soil. The idealization of the homeland and the value placed on the cultural heritage were embedded in this context. It was again this attachment to Spain which impelled the expellees to emphasize their links with the city or region whence they came. By perpetuating their customs and traditions in their new host country, they would be able to recreate the "paradise lost" and their sufferings would assume some meaning. If they had made sacrifices in order to remain Jews, they also had the sacred duty to hand on this Hispanicity which was inseparable from their Jewishness.

How acute this problem of transmission was becomes clear when the experiences of the expellees are examined over several generations. Each generation was obsessed with the question of continuity.[47] The experience of exile had literally destroyed families, separated couples, and left many parents without their children. Forced conversions, disease, abductions, and exhaustion shattered the family nucleus. Some had remained in the peninsula, preferring conversion to departure. This explains why many arrived in the Empire alone, without a family to support them in confronting the new reality. Various calamities such as epidemics and the high death rate which ensued weighed heavily for several generations over the newcomers' perception of their lives. In this period, when the Jew remained attached to the faith, when, furthermore, the notion of "individual" as we know it did not yet exist, the destruction of families meant above all a break in the continuity of the lineage and a challenge to the survival of the Jewish people itself.

In their host countries therefore, the Sephardim organized themselves into separate communities. They did not adopt the *halakhic* rulings (religious law) and the *minhag* (customs) of the autochthonous communities, thereby infringing an accepted rule in the Jewish world, that the newcomer must bow to the customs of the place. This did not fail to provoke serious conflicts between the communities: in this case, it was the new arrivals who wanted to impose their law on the locals, and who rejected, scorned, or disdained local customs. The synagogue liturgy, the decisions based on religious law which regulated the daily life of the group, traditions, cultural activity – all became grounds for confrontation. The expellees placed their past teachers on a pedestal and their inherited culture above anything in their new surroundings. Not to betray this heritage was not only to keep faith with the past but also to trust in the future, through the maintenance of a tradition.

In places where the Sephardim found well established communities, such as the Romaniots in Istanbul or Edirne, or the Mustarabim (Arab-speaking Jews) in Safed or other Jewish centers in North Africa, the general assimilation to Judeo-Iberian practices did not take place overnight. At first, it met opposition, which varied with the size of the local non-Sephardi community and with its own self-image. It took time for the Sephardim to impose their authority when confronted with the Romaniots, whose scholars fought to safeguard their customs and traditions and prevent the newcomers from speaking for the whole Jewish population. Nevertheless, the Sephardim eventually emerged triumphant, succeeding in imposing their will around the turn of the seventeenth century. The Romaniots underwent a gradual process of Judeo-Hispanicization and, except for a few isolated centers, such as Ioannina in Epirus, Arta, or Corfu (outside the Empire), completely assimilated into the Sephardi group.[48]

Their growing numbers do not explain why the Sephardim succeeded in dominating the Romaniots in a city such as Istanbul, since even by 1623 they did not yet constitute a majority.[49] It was the weight of their scholars, their culture, and the dynamism of their many rabbis which tipped the scales. In this Jewish world still inseparably bound up with the religious, in the framework of an autonomy itself based on religion, power was in the hands of religious leaders. There are other ways of explaining the Romaniots' decline. The Sephardim disembarked with a network of relationships outside the Empire which could not fail to be of service to them, since it represented a window on to the world of the Infidels for the Ottomans. This asset worked in favor of the expellees, not only for economic reasons, but also by facilitating their relationships with the authorities.

The arrival of the Marranos in the sixteenth century widened this link with the outside and breathed a certain new dynamism into local Sephardim, even though conflicts occurred between the Marranos, who were regarded as newcomers, and the previous settlers.[50] What is more, these Marranos brought capital and skills born of experience in Christian lands. In this period some lay leaders became privileged intermediaries between the Jewish communities and the Ottomans, because of the place they held in the intricate machinery of the Palace. Their number included such personalities as Shealtiel, a Sephardi; Joseph Nasi, the famous Duke of Naxos, a Marrano from Portugal, and his aunt, Doña Gracia Mendes; the Marrano diplomat the Duke of Mytilene, Salomon Abenaish; and the doctors Moses and Joseph Hamon, probably natives of Granada. Provincial communities were also obliged to go through these intercessors to settle delicate problems. These men helped to advance the cause of the Sephardim at the Court, and by so doing strengthened their position in the capital.

When they arrived, the Sephardim found Moses Capsali (1420–96/7), the spiritual leader of the Jews of Istanbul and the surrounding area, apparently appointed to the position of "Chief Rabbi" by Mehmed II after the conquest of Constantinople. He was succeeded in 1498 by Elijah Mizrahi (although the precise nature and importance of his responsibilities remain unconfirmed).[51] Both were Romaniots. There was no successor when Mizrahi died because of the power struggles between Romaniots and Sephardim. Responsibility for collecting the taxes, formerly entrusted to the holder of this office, was henceforth assumed by a Sephardi lay leader.[52] The presence of people like Capsali and Mizrahi was initially an advantage for the Romaniots. The subsequent dissolution of a unified leadership at the head of Istanbul Jewry and the rise of Sephardi lay personalities as intermediaries was a factor in changing the balance of forces.

At the outset, the Romaniots had also been a group of exiles, and had needed to respond to new challenges in the same way as those who would later join them. They now began to lose both economic and political ground *vis-à-vis* the Ottoman central power. The restrictions which had been imposed on them deepened their isolation from the outside world at a time when the centers of European international economy were moving from the Mediterranean towards the Atlantic. Family connections enabled the Sephardim to continue to play a part in the new economic configuration, even though they, too, gradually became isolated, losing their economic power in the Empire to Christian groups who were more closely linked to the West. Other conjunctural factors, specific to the seventeenth century, relating to structural and taxation issues, helped to weaken the Romaniots' position.

In towns such as Salonika, where the Sephardim did not find local communities, the question of a balance of forces between them and the Romaniots did not even arise. The Sephardim also exercised power over the Italian and Ashkenazi communities who were numerically weak. As a result, in Istanbul there were three principal Jewish communities at the end of the sixteenth century: the Sephardi, the Romaniot, and the Karaite.[53] The latter, which was also Byzantine, was not directly involved in the struggle for hegemony, because it was regarded as separate from the stuggling Rabbanite communities.

In Safed, the Sephardim did not integrate into the existing *Mustarabi* community. Instead, they established a parallel system of communal organization without any real opposition from local scholars or from the population as a whole.[54] These local Jews did not have the self-confidence to confront the newcomers as the Romaniots had done. Subsequently, the Sephardim used their prestige, numbers, and strength to impose their own norms. In Jerusalem and other towns in Palestine, they gained the upper hand over the other communities, though they did not necessarily Judeo-Hispanicize them as in the case of the Romaniots in the North.[55] In Cairo, Damascus, and Aleppo, the Sephardim retained their specific character for a long time because of their economic supremacy.[56] However, in these populous Arabophone sectors of the Empire, they were gradually absorbed by the autochthonous communities, who maintained longstanding relations with the authorities and were familiar with local practices.

The same trends can also be observed in North Africa, where disputes between *megorashim* (the expelled) and *toshavim* (local residents) were not rare. In some regions, the expellees were forced to assimilate into existing groups; elsewhere, they founded parallel communities, in Tangier, Tetuan, and Fez, for example, or took over the leadership of an existing community.[57] They rapidly became dominant in the economy as well as in rabbinic learning.[58] The so-called "Castilian" law, for example, was eventually imposed on all of Moroccan Jewry. In addition, at the end of the sixteenth and the beginning of the seventeenth centuries, Jewish merchants from Italy, mostly descendants of Portuguese Marranos, settled in the Mediterranean towns, particularly Tunis. They organized themselves as a separate "nation," and eventually founded a separate community in 1710, the Leghorn community of *grana*. From then on, friction between the autochthonous Jews, the *touansa*, and the new arrivals was endemic to Tunisian life until the twentieth century.[59]

COMMUNITY STRUCTURES AND AUTONOMY

The Sephardim who arrived on Ottoman soil found in cities with a concentration of Jews an extant community organization. They adapted to it, grouping according to their place of origin, as had the deported Romaniots. They called these congregations by specifically Iberian names of towns or regions (Catalonia, Toledo, Cordova), by countries (Portugal), by families (Hamon, *Seniora* – for Doña Gracia Mendes, the great benefactress of Marrano origin), or by status (*Gerush*, in Hebrew, "Expulsion"). These existed alongside those adopted by the Romaniots: (*Poli Yashan*: old town, Ohri), the Hungarians (*Budun*: Buda), the Ashkenazim (*Alman*: German), the Karaites (*Edirne*: Adrianople), or the Italians (Sicily, Calabria).[60] Dozens of congregations were formed, their numbers varying from town to town. If Istanbul and Salonika contained between 30 and 100, other smaller places only had six or ten.[61] The purpose of people from the same place of origin banding together was to ensure that their specific rites, traditions, customs, languages, or dialects were preserved and the bonds of Jewishness and the specific ethnic–regional character protected.

This is a regular phenomenon among immigrant populations and a constant feature of the Jewish world (Ashkenazim and Sephardim alike) into the contemporary period. The *landsmanshaftn* created by the East European Jews in Western Europe and on the American continent are a contemporary example. Likewise, the Jewish emigrants from the Maghreb in the 1950s and 1960s founded similar societies where they settled anew. This also applied in Israel where, *a priori*, the Jewishness of the immigrant does not need to be affirmed in order to be safeguarded. In actual fact, ethnic–religious identity can be confused with Jewishness – as is normally the case when Jews are transplanted into new non-Jewish environments. But it can also mark a distinction within it – as, for example, in Israel today. It is a typical characteristic of displaced populations, who not only bring the lost country with them, but also the town, village, or region they lived in, with everything this suggests about customs and traditions.

In this manner, an ethnic and regional Jewish mosaic emerged on the territory of the Ottoman Empire. This diversity did not fail to generate specifically ethnic conflicts. The Spaniards and the Portuguese were in conflict in Monastir, Valona, and elsewhere in the sixteenth century. Differences even arose among the many, varied elements inside the Spanish group itself.[62]

In communities which were founded later, such as Izmir, secondary distinctions between immigrants from elsewhere in the country were superimposed onto these initial differences. For example, the divergent opinions that appeared among Salonikan and Istanbul Jews on questions relating to the conduct of community life, religious law, and customs, show that each of these communities had gone its own way since leaving the Iberian peninsula.[63]

The organization into congregations also corresponded to the requirements of the Ottomans who preferred to deal with groups or corporations rather than with individuals.[64] Ottoman society itself was structured in this way. The congregation (*kahal* in Hebrew) was a collection of individuals or families around a synagogue. From the seventeenth century, there are signs of a gradual movement from organization by congregations of immigrants from the same place of origin towards organization by district. This was more in accordance with the realities of an urban life structured around districts (*mahalle*), whose leaders were interlocutors with the authorities.[65] Remnants of the earlier organization continued to exist, but it was the new model which predominated, a congregation henceforth comprising the inhabitants of one street or one district. Although congregations retained their old names, their composition no longer corresponded to the places of origin. They now formed on the basis of residential area.

The entire organization of Ottoman society was based on religion, as had indeed been the case in the Byzantine Empire. Non-Muslim communities, as was the custom in the lands of Islam, enjoyed a relative autonomy. In fact, in a noncentralized, multi-ethnic, and multireligious empire, the Ottomans had no choice but to leave these groups a certain degree of freedom in the conduct of their internal affairs. The *cemaat* or *taife*, later called the *millet*, or ethnic–religious community, was the most advanced form of this type of self-government, to which the Jews had already become accustomed in

Christian Europe and elsewhere in the Islamic world.[66] With its privileges and restrictions, it closely resembled the medieval "nation" in Europe.

Under the terms of the *dhimma* (or *zimmet* in Turkish), the Jews grouped into religious communities on Ottoman lands were *zimmis*, with the same status as the Greeks and Armenians. However, their communal relationships with the Ottomans conformed more to an adaptable model of *de facto* local arrangements than to the actual centralized *system* so long portrayed, based on nineteenth-century realities when the different ethnic–religious groups were granted organic statutes which made their status official.[67] The "*millet* system" is a myth, projected onto an earlier and entirely different situation. The non-Muslim communities enjoyed relative autonomy in return for payment of a poll tax and other taxes. They formed theocratic "microstates," where the temporal and spiritual merged,[68] and which the Ottomans left more or less alone, according to prevailing circumstances.

The leaders of these "states" had to place the people they administered into social, cultural, economic, and juridical frameworks, though without possessing the real power they would *a priori* have required to procure compliance with laws and regulations. The external authority only intervened at the request of parties directly involved, such as communal leaders who only appealed to it as a last resort, preferring to avoid all interference in internal conflicts.[69] However, it was not rare, depending on the period, for the Ottoman authorities to intervene in the appointment of communal leaders. In addition, Jewish law and Jewish judges did not enjoy official recognition.[70] Nor did the verdicts of non-Muslim courts have real legal status, even if the state did not force non-Muslims to appeal to a Muslim judge (*kadı*) to settle their internal disputes. The only law officially recognized was Muslim law. Nevertheless, the judgments of the Jewish courts, in principle, had the force of law for Jews.[71] There were prisons inside the communities to punish recalcitrant elements.[72] The Jewish courts, however, were impotent when faced with Muslim ones who might reject their authority.[73] On the whole, Jews tended to appeal to their own courts in all questions concerning their internal affairs, and the Jewish authorities preserved a certain degree of discretion *vis-à-vis* the Ottoman power in this sphere. Jewish juridical autonomy was therefore not established as a formalized system, even if the Jews benefited from a certain official goodwill in this domain.

Many legal cases involving Jews alone often came to be tried under Muslim jurisdiction. In view of the limited power of their own courts, Jews sometimes preferred to appeal to the *kadı* in matters relating to inheritance or commercial litigation.[74] The rabbis regularly issued prohibitions in an attempt to check this practice. The increasingly fragmented state of Jewish society weakened Jewish juridical power and this, in turn, helped to make

Jewish society even more fragile by reducing juridical autonomy with respect to the outside world. Hence, Jewish juridical autonomy was entirely relative. Jewish society could not enforce total compliance with its laws within the community when this same law was not considered absolutely binding by the dominant ruling non-Jewish authority.

A good part of the group's strength derived from the position its members or leaders occupied in the service of the Ottoman officials at a provincial level, or at the Palace in the capital. As already noted, when the Romaniots succeeded initially in holding their own against the Sephardim, this was also the result of the privileged relationships that the spiritual leaders of the community, themselves Romaniots, maintained with the Ottoman power. This was later true also of the Sephardim, when they could rely on their own "lay" leaders, doctors, businessmen, army contractors, etc. In fact, up to the contemporary period, the Jewish community of the Empire benefited from a greater or lesser degree of protection depending on the stature of these personalities. Sometimes the Chief Rabbi played an important role in this respect. The outstanding twentieth-century personality Haim Nahum (1873–1960) is a case in point.[75] Conversely, those privileged with access to the Ottomans often derived their power within the community itself from their relationships with the Ottomans. This was clearly not the sort of situation which would permit a single strong authority to emerge.

In the sixteenth century, authority gradually concentrated in the hands of powerful lay leaders who ruled the communities in tandem with the religious leadership which was not itself in contact with the centers of Ottoman power. This evolution occurred within a Jewish society which still had religion as its basis, which was governed by religious law, and which owed its semiautonomous organization to its status as a religious group. In spite of constant friction the system held together because the Jews had no real place outside their community, even though relationships with the non-Jewish world were not uncommon and social interchanges did occur. It also held because of strong individual and collective discipline, experienced in everyday life within the religious framework. The Jews lived within their group, worked with other Jews, depended on Jewish mutual aid societies, attended the synagogue; their existence, from birth to death, was not conceivable outside this structure. Rebels who dared to oppose the authority which administered this Jewish society were subject to a whole gamut of punishments. These ranged from fines, public rebukes, suspension of religious rights, to excommunication (*herem*), pronounced amidst great solemnity in the synagogue – the most serious punishment for a Jew at that time.

The effectiveness of the *herem* (or the threat of the *herem*) was the best reflection of the Jew's dependence on his or her group in a context such as the Ottoman. To be excluded from the group was to cease to be a Jew and, quite simply, to cease to be (at least, socially speaking). No longer could the bread, wine, or books of the excluded person be used. A man could not form part of the quorum of ten men required for religious prayer, nor be buried in a Jewish cemetery. He was isolated from other Jews who were forbidden to visit him. Even the material life of those excommunicated was affected since they were deprived of "civil rights."[76] They were *apartado de la juderia* (cut off from the community). Excommunication was obviously only effective when the surrounding society did not present a feasible alternative. In some cases, the Muslim authorities were appealed to for help in bringing the rebels back to the community. This is another indication of the constitutive weakness of the Jewish authority in the framework of an autonomy which can definitely be described as relative and circumscribed.

The "state" within the state which the Jewish community (*kehilah*) constituted, like the other non-Muslim groups, was itself made up of "microstates" in the form of congregations. Thus, different reference circles can be drawn at many levels: the Empire, the Jewish community, the Sephardim and the Romaniots, and the congregations by origin. Although this mode of organization certainly encouraged a degree of insularity, it institutionalized at the same time a plurality (if not a pluralism) far removed from the unifying structures of the modern nation-states.

Two types of communal organization seem to have dominated the Ottoman Jewish world in the sixteenth century: those of Salonika and of Istanbul.[77] The first was adopted by the communities of the Balkans and the European part of the Empire; the second, by the Jews of Anatolia and the Eastern provinces. In Istanbul, the Sephardim established themselves as an independent body; the Romaniots did likewise. When it came to revising the regulations concerning all the Jews in the locality, the two groups met to reach a decision. An interplay of crossing solidarities was thus set up between multiple circles, which touched but never penetrated each other. The congregations were ruled by a supracommunal organization, which had authority over them, the majority deciding for the minority, a system which restricted the autonomy of each. In Salonika, on the other hand, no such higher authority was formed, each congregation remaining an autonomous unit. In the sixteenth century attempts were made to form a federation of congregations, and then towards the end of the century, to create a body similar to that in the capital.

The type of organization adopted was partly inspired by the Regulations of the Jews of Castile determined in 1432 by the synod of Valladolid which formulated the status of the *aljamas* in Spain.[78] This imported model could be adapted to the new circumstances. Each congregation possessed its own administrative structures, since it formed a mini-society, which had to be managed and was also regarded as a fiscal unit. There, too, authority was indispensable in order to ensure that it functioned well, not only internally, but also *vis-à-vis* the Ottoman authorities, since the congregation was responsible for the collection of taxes. It raised these taxes from its members, and the sums levied were paid by it or by the whole Jewish population of the town to the state. In the latter case, therefore, the congregation was also responsible to the community of the locality for the payment of taxes.

The general assembly of taxpayers took decisions by a majority of votes and delegated its powers to an executive council (*maamad*) in which every stratum of society was proportionately represented in accordance with categories fixed by the Ottomans. The members of each social group elected only their own representatives.[79] In theory, therefore, the whole male Jewish population of the town or locality participated in the conduct of the public life of its mini-society, i.e. the congregation, which denotes a certain initial concern for democracy. However, in times of trouble, when the Ottomans increased the tax burden in order to meet expenditure on war, when economic crises impoverished the Jewish population and raised the number of unemployed, and when the rich had to take on much of the internal costs of the community and the payment of taxes to the authorities, or simply when exceptional events dictated the need for a strong authority, leadership of the community became concentrated in the hands of a rich minority. Then, the members of the new leadership were very often chosen by the outgoing leaders, a procedure which encouraged the hegemony of a limited number of families. We know that the rich formed a small minority within the communities. Eventually, leadership fell into the hands of the wealthy middle class at the expense of the poor, who increasingly lacked representation.[80] A ruling oligarchy was thus formed – still to be found in the nineteenth and twentieth centuries – with the reins of power in the hands of a few notables.

The executive council was composed of six to eight members, elected for one or two years at the most. Administrators or wardens (*manhigim, parnasim*) were elected as leaders from within this council. Also elected were the treasurer (*gizbar*), tax collector (*gabay* or *goveh*), and other officials supervising the morals and religious conduct of the rank and file, as well as the burial associations (*hevrah kadisha*). In addition, the general assembly of taxpayers chose a body of tax assessors (*maarikhim*), who, as the years went by, acted independently of the council, with total freedom. Sometimes, however, the council itself appointed tax assessors from within the assembly. Their role consisted of distributing the fiscal burden among

the members of the congregation. The executive council generally dealt
with matters concerning taxes, education, religious requirements, the
distribution of aid to the needy, the provision of funds to redeem prisoners
who had fallen into the hands of pirates (*pidyon shevuyim*), the regulation
of competition, the implementation of rules and laws governing the
congregation, etc. The council of each congregation or its representatives
participated in the general meetings of delegates from the different councils
in the city, and thus kept a watchful eye on the life of the whole
community. In localities which functioned in accordance with the Istanbul
model, a general council of the city's congregations (*maamad kolelet*) met
regularly and took decisions for all the congregations. In Salonika, on the
other hand, an *ad hoc* council was called to settle serious matters, but it did
not have the power to impose its decisions on all the congregations, as its
rulings needed to be unanimous. This situation continued until the end of
the sixteenth century.

The lay leadership, that is to say the leaders of the executive, existed side
by side with the religious authority concentrated in the hands of the rabbis.
It took charge of the fiscal and organizational conduct of the communities,
as well as their representation before the constitutive bodies of the Ottoman
Empire.[81] In fact, the lay leaders were held responsible for the communities' fulfillment of the obligations the government imposed upon
them, financially guaranteeing its debts. They were backed up in their task
by the rabbinical courts and community regulations. The establishment of
this sort of leadership was an old practice in the Jewish world and in no
way peculiar to the Sephardim of the Empire. These lay leaders received
no payment and took office as a religious obligation and an act of charity.
They interceded with local governors and bureaucrats in the provinces.
Only in cases of serious litigation did they appeal to the Sublime Porte
through the intermediary of highly placed Jews.[82] In their negotiations, they
tried to obtain authorization for building, renovating, or reconstructing
synagogues or cemeteries, the settlement of disputes concerning individuals, the freeing of coreligionists imprisoned for failing to pay their taxes
to the government or their debts to private persons, etc. They were at the
same time responsible for relations with other congregations.

There was actually a hierarchy even inside this lay leadership, whose
power depended on its privileged relationships with the Ottomans and
other influential Jewish personalities in the capital. When problems arose,
presidents of congregations, in the provinces or in Istanbul itself, could not
dispense with the services of powerful men in Palace circles. Moreover, it
was this multiplicity of power centers, in the absence of centralization,
which sometimes made this organization seem chaotic, even though there
was a logic of interdependent relationships. These Istanbul leaders were in

contact with the vizir, the commander of the Palace police, the chief eunuch, or the *Şyhülislam* (the top Muslim religious official). Over the centuries and into the modern period, these lay leaders were invested with increasing power at the center, with the progressive erosion of rabbinic authority in a society which was gradually emerging from its traditional framework. Moreover, when the Ottomans granted the *millets* formal statutes in the nineteenth century, they gave official sanction to these leaders, forcing them to take on the role of reformers charged with the modernization of their community. Istanbul thus became a sort of political capital of the Jews because of the importance of its lay leaders to the provincial communities and because provincial rabbis were accustomed to consult their colleagues in Istanbul on religious matters.[83] This situation introduced a hierarchy among the communities themselves.

In theory, every congregation had its rabbi (*rav, hakham,* or *marbiz torah*) or rabbis if it was wealthy. The rabbi was paid by the congregation and chosen by the executive council with the supposed consent of the people. Not infrequently, his appointment was the subject of dispute between rival factions. He was not only responsible for religious education but also possessed legislative power. In that capacity, he issued ordinances (*haskamot, takanot*) and adjudicated lawsuits between Jews. He assumed religious leadership, gave sermons in the synagogue, and represented his congregation when all the rabbis of the town met to legislate. Some were renowned for their great learning, which added weight to their authority as well as to their ordinances. The rabbi presided at the religious court (*bet din*) with two assessors (*dayanim*).[84] He was supported by officiating ministers, ritual slaughterers (*shohatim*), the teacher (*melamed*) employed by the religious school (the *talmud torah* or *meldar*), as well as by other minor officials carrying out various functions within the congregation.

In the sixteenth to eighteenth centuries, attempts were made to centralize these communities, with a view to meeting the new circumstances of an empire in crisis and of increasingly heavy taxation. However, the congregations did their utmost to retain independence,[85] which allowed their organization to remain freer and less bureaucratic. Nevertheless, in time there came about the transition from the system of congregations to the system of communities, which corresponded better to the new profile of the Jewish populations, rendering grouping according to town or region of origin increasingly archaic. Internal and external migrations, the evolution of districts, and mixed marriages between people from different places had complicated this first type of structure, though without causing its complete disappearance. In a town like Izmir,[86] where the community was founded late, the new arrivals no longer organized themselves as in the past, but according to wave of migration, residential area, or common interests.[87]

It was the Portuguese Marranos, relatively recent arrivals from the peninsula, who continued to group themselves according to town of origin. From the outset, Izmir also opted for centralized leadership, which was more suited to the needs of the time.

In the seventeenth to eighteenth centuries, the rabbi of the congregation was gradually supplanted by a Chief Rabbinate (*rabanut kolelet*) of the town or region.[88] This favored the formation of pressure groups around an institution encompassing several congregations or districts. Some towns did not even succeed in electing a Chief Rabbi; the office was then shared between two or even three rabbis, among whom a hierarchy was established.

The legal office of titular Chief Rabbi (*hahambaşı*) was not officially introduced until 1835. The absence of religious hierarchy in the Jewish world meant that the office of a Chief Rabbi supervising the community throughout the Empire did not emerge as a necessity. This position came as a result of the Ottomans' efforts at centralization. After 1835, the Chief Rabbi had to be elected by the community and his appointment ratified by the sultan, on the model of the Greek and Armenian Patriarchs. Interference by the authorities in the appointment of community leaders had not been uncommon in the past. Nevertheless, except during the reign of Haim Nahum (1908–20), who made several such attempts, the Chief Rabbi of the Empire was never able to achieve centralization which would affect all the communities. Every local Chief Rabbi guarded his own ability to maneuver *vis-à-vis* the capital. The Jewish communities continued to mistrust centralization. The Chief Rabbi of the Empire was in theory the leader of all the Jews in the land and the executive agent of the Ottoman government. From the time when the Jewish community was granted an organic statute in 1865 until the advent of the Republic in 1923, only one Chief Rabbi of the Empire – Haim Nahum – was elected according to the new rules. The others were formally only acting Chief Rabbis. In fact this high office was never able to function effectively.

The congregation, which was always formed around a synagogue, owed its members certain services. In traditional society, the synagogue was not only a place of worship but also an area of socialization, with an internal hierarchy. It was equally a public forum, since decisions there were generally taken on a majority vote with only taxpayers having the vote. The life of the Jew was inconceivable outside the congregation, which was responsible for education and welfare. The mini-society it formed evinced a great deal of dynamism, despite its inherent conflicts.[89]

Rich congregations endowed with great scholars also had their own higher institute of Jewish education (*yeshivah*).[90] It could happen that all the congregations maintained one educational institution or charitable foundation; the great *Talmud Torah* in Salonika is a case in point.[91] This came into being as the result of a merger of all the major educational institutes in the area two generations after the arrivals of the expellees. It emerged as the center of Jewish public life, and remained so for four centuries. Its management was under the control of the different congregations' representatives. This institution had the right to levy special taxes on cheese, oil, etc., or to collect money to provide for the needs of poor children. It offered a whole series of charitable services and owned business undertakings, such as a press, printing prayerbooks for the students. The *Talmud Torah* of Salonika trained generations of spiritual leaders. Fathers of families all over the Mediterranean sent their children to be educated at this institution which continued to exist, despite many transformations, till modern times. At the beginning of the twentieth century, it became a center of Jewish nationalism. It survived until the Second World War when the Nazis destroyed Salonika Jewry.

The institution of *hevrot* (associations) was imported into the Empire by the expellees.[92] In the seventeenth and eighteenth centuries, the *hevrot* underwent an extensive development similar to that of parallel institutions in the Jewish communities of Italy, Holland, and Eastern Europe.[93]

The Committee of Officials of *Erez Yisrael* in Istanbul (*Pekidei Kushta*) was founded in 1726, on the initiative of the Jews of Istanbul, in order to help the Jews of Palestine who had been subsisting from Diaspora assistance since the seventeenth century.[94] Its aim was to rescue the Jerusalem community from its severe problems. Demographic imbalance caused by the advanced age of its inhabitants, who had in many cases gone there to die, epidemics, and emigration to other towns in the Empire deprived this community of long-term stability. Istanbul was then transformed into an international conduit for help for the Jews of the Holy Land, and the Committee took an increasingly prominent role in the administration of the Palestinian communities, deciding the appointment of their rabbis and leaders, as well as their financial management. This mutual aid system served as a model for the *halukah* (financial assistance) which was set up in Europe in the modern period to aid the Jews of Palestine. By then, leadership in this area had passed from Istanbul to European Jewry. In fact, the activities of the Committee of Officials show early signs of the formalized Jewish solidarity institutionalized on an international scale in Europe in the nineteenth century.

The organizational models described here were valid, with some variations, for all the Jewish communities in Ottoman lands. They disappeared when Jewish centers changed masters, as happened with Belgrade, occupied on several occasions by the Austrians, who imposed certain restrictions, and Sarajevo, which lost its original structure after the Austro-Hungarian occupation in 1878 and became a centralized *Kultusgemeinde* subject to state control.[95]

COMMUNAL FINANCES

Congregations had duties towards their members, and, if necessary, towards other groups of Jews in the Empire or outside. But their members also had duties towards them, towards the larger Jewish community as a whole, as well as towards the Ottoman state.

As the price of autonomy was payment of the poll tax, the congregations were responsible for its division and levying, after the Jewish community of the city had first apportioned the total sum due among its members according to their respective capacity, as was the practice at Salonika, for example.[96] The *dhimma* was specifically based on payment of this tax. It was natural that it should be at the center of relationships between the members of the congregation and its leadership. On another count, living, as it essentially did, from direct and indirect taxes levied on its worshippers, plus gifts and legacies, having practically no financial autonomy, nor means of coercion comparable to those that the state could employ, the congregation administered this aspect of Jewish public life with determination.

Taxpayers were clearly listed on an official register, but the authorities only levied taxes on congregations, even groups of congregations, not on individuals. This practice also applied to Christians. The state, therefore, did not intervene directly with individuals; responsibility for the levy was left to the congregation, which, unlike the state, only possessed a moral and religious authority. Jewish religious law regarded each congregation as a town in its own right.[97] The Jews themselves decided who was or who was not taxable. Matters were arranged so that the poor, scholars who did not practice another trade, and rabbis were exempt. Exempted categories varied with time and place.[98] The communities took care to keep their own registers, ensuring that the Ottomans did not learn the names of those who did not pay tax.

In the first quarter of the sixteenth century, the rich paid 200 aspres as the poll tax, members of the middle class 100, and the poor 20 aspres.[99] The central power in theory required every male aged 15 or over to pay the tax, but in the sixteenth century only heads of families were taxed, regardless of the number of adults in the family. Bachelors who had no family also had to pay. At the same period, Suleiman the Magnificent (1520–66) excused the Jews of Salonika from payment of poll tax against a levy of cloth for the manufacture of uniforms for janissaries.[100]

In addition to the poll tax, Jews, like other non-Muslims, were obliged to pay various other taxes in certain parts of the Empire.[101] The right to have a Chief Rabbi involved payment of a specific fee (*rav akçesi* or *cizyei rav*). It is conceivable that this tax, as in the case of Christian churches, was aimed at marking dependence *vis-à-vis* the Ottomans.[102] Not only the Jews of Istanbul were affected, even if the powers of the Chief Rabbi did not extend beyond the capital; it was also paid by the Jews of Salonika.[103] The Jews continued to pay it even when there was no Chief Rabbi after the death of Elijah Mizrahi in 1525. On the other hand, no evidence of such a levy is found in the communities of Palestine, Syria, and Egypt. Still other taxes were imposed during crisis years, for the upkeep of the navy, soldiers, mounted constabulary, imperial couriers, palaces, and slaves; for the construction and repair of trenches and fortifications; for the housing of Ottoman officers and employees in transit through the region; and for exemption from various corvées. These obligations included the provision of a certain number of specialists to the Ottoman army in wartime to attend to logistical matters.[104] Exceptional taxes could not be levied more than once, concurrent with the others levied regularly. Sometimes, depending on circumstances, communities were obliged to pay large sums to officials to avoid persecution.[105]

The tax each Jewish household paid could vary considerably from one town to another. For example, in Istanbul, it rose to 660 aspres in the mid-sixteenth century, whereas in Salonika it did not exceed 180.[106] As the Empire declined, principally as a result of territorial losses in the eighteenth century, the Jews faced a considerable increase in taxation designed to cover the costs of war. A number of communities fell into debt and were no longer in a position to pay the interest on their loans. It was inevitable that under such circumstances disputes between rich and poor on the question of taxation should increase.[107] A community such as Jerusalem, which at the time numbered 2,000 souls and represented 15 percent of the total population of the city, began to witness an exodus of Jews in the eighteenth century, as they fled the pressure exerted by governors and other inhabitants to pay their dues.[108] Community levies and taxes destined for the Ottomans were henceforth beyond the financial capacity of the members of the congregations.[109] A large number of fires, earthquakes, economic crises, and waves of internal migration destabilized the communities in the seventeenth to eighteenth centuries, depriving the congregations of their members and resulting in their impoverishment. In addition, the effects of the Sabbatean crisis which had shaken the Jews of the Empire in the seventeenth century also had reverberations in this domain.[110]

Istanbul remained relatively stable in the eighteenth century; not so the provincial Jewish communities. Even in Istanbul, the 1772 budget clearly reflects the economic difficulties and the communal problems that resulted. Receipts of only 49,000 aspres appear against expenses of 65,000 aspres.[111] In addition, the community had debts of 325,000 aspres. The arsenal tax alone, for the manufacture of warships which the Jews paid in this particular period, came to 18,000 aspres. The poll tax and many others must of course be added to this tax.[112] In the same period as well, Jewish economic activity was showing serious decline compared to non-Muslim communities supported by the European powers increasingly present in the Empire. Poverty was rampant, even if certain Jews profited from the army's activities. The communities became trapped in a vicious circle: external crisis caused internal crisis and, as individuals were unable to pay their dues to the congregation, communal budgets showed a growing deficit.

Members of the congregations also paid direct taxes to cover internal costs, such as the upkeep of the synagogue, ritual bath, and cemetery, wages of community employees and the rabbi, donations to the Jews of the Holy Land, redemption of prisoners, etc. These taxes do not appear in the budgets.[113] A contribution was also levied for circumcisions, marriages, and funerals, in proportion to the financial position of the parties concerned.[114] Indirect taxes were also levied on goods sold to Jews and food products such as meat, wine, etc. If the "gabelle" (salt tax, *gabela*) on these products had not been paid, they were considered impure and therefore forbidden. They were sold at a higher price than outside the Jewish community, which was an additional expense for Jewish consumers.

There were also other ways for the communities to raise money. In Rhodes, for example, occupied by the Ottomans since 1525, commercial documents were drafted and approved by the community, and business owners paid the community a sum for every document drawn.[115] In addition to this revenue, communities could also own concessions. The Rhodes community held the concession on sulphur. The communities received rent from properties which they owned as a result of donations, legacies, or investments made in a period of prosperity. When it came to building a synagogue, initiating a new philanthropic or educational enterprise, or a special event, exceptional duties were levied on the imports and exports made by Jewish merchants in the city, as was the case in Istanbul and Salonika.[116]

Regulations relating to taxation were far from unified. Each congregation provided for its own needs, and tried to attract the greatest number of rich Jews. Members of the congregation were taxed on their wealth. Those who had little were almost or completely exempt from tax. The assessors valued the taxpayers' wealth, and the latter could challenge the decision, as had been the custom in Spain.[117] In Salonika, the party concerned could assess his property himself under oath or leave this task to the assessors. The evaluation included jewellery, gold and silver articles, precious stones, books, and livestock, assessed at half their value. Money owed was not included in the assessment; the property of widows and orphans was not taxable. In Salonika, rabbis and their widows, as well as printers, were excused from communal taxation.[118] In Rhodes, Jewish translators to the consul and foreign protégés, did not pay state taxes but were still liable for community taxes.[119] There were cases when the rich refused to pay the community tax on their wealth. The distribution and levying of taxes were often the subject of conflict in the communities. Nonpayment of community tax was punishable by excommunication and heads of families who were delinquent were deprived of religious services for circumcisions, marriages, and burials. The congregations did everything in their power to prevent their members leaving, as a departure occasioned increased expense for those who remained. No member could leave a congregation without paying a considerable sum.[120] A congregant was someone who was permanently settled in the locality; this was not the case with traders passing through. There were numerous cases of people trying to evade payment by changing congregation or settling in other cities. Of course, this primarily applied to the rich who could afford to be mobile. At the time of the great waves of immigration, the arrivals were distributed equally between the different congregations. The question of taxes thus did not fail to generate a certain dynamism, even if only by the coming and going it occasioned. In any case, it always remained central to the life of the congregations, since it guaranteed their existence as a separate unit.

COMMUNAL LEGISLATION

The congregation as a microsociety needed to ensure that it was administered by appropriate regulations and ordinances. These internal measures were superimposed on the legislation of the state, which already enforced rules of conduct for the peoples under its administration in general, and on non-Muslims in particular (in the framework of the *dhimma*). The application of the law passed through the filter of each ethnic–religious group: what was valid for Muslims could not be applied to Christians and Jews, except in criminal matters and in other areas which involved Ottoman society as a whole. This superimposition of legislation posed the same problem as the administration of justice. In fact, the regulations and ordinances decreed by the Jewish group only had the force of law within the community itself and, in order to be applied, required an authority which *a priori* the Jewish legislator did not possess. So long as Jewish society remained traditional and the legislator could count on both the solidarity of the group and its religious belief, there was still the chance that this internal legislation would be more or less strictly observed.

The legal texts produced were tailored initially for a special audience. First and foremost, whether Sephardim or Ashkenazim, these were transplanted Jews who had been forced to leave their countries of origin. The Sephardim were traumatized, obsessed with the threat of a break in their history, living with the fear of having no future. They needed a framework in which to recreate a Judeo-Hispanic society elsewhere. The collection of regulations and ordinances put into practice drew directly from the immigrants' recent past, but were adapted to the new context. This type of arrangement was possible within the skeleton of organization the Empire offered. At the same time, it ensured a certain continuity for the uprooted Eastern Sephardi world. A sort of equilibrium was established in the attachment to the known, making social praxis, and therefore integration, quicker and smoother.

The ordinances and regulations were generally written in Hebrew, or in Judeo-Spanish. Their style is reminiscent of the Regulations of Castile in 1432, on which they were based.[121] Most of them were composed by the first generation of exiles; qualifications and variations were added by subsequent generations. Over time certain regulations fell into disuse and new ones emerged. Evolution is visible at the level of language, since later regulations were studded with words borrowed from the non-Jewish environment – a good indication of interrelationships in certain areas of social activity.

The whole life of the group, in both its religious and its secular aspects, was meticulously maintained. A rigid framework, controlled from inside, made it possible both to escape the anarchy of a nascent society and to ensure autonomy in respect of the outside world, any visible disorder being liable to attract its intervention. It was also feared that deviation by an individual might lead to the punishment of the group and the restriction of its already constrained autonomy. This was the typical organized society, with its subtle interpenetration of the religious and the secular, of the individual and the collective, as found throughout the premodern Jewish world.

The corps of *berurei averot* (inspectors responsible for combating transgressions) was an institution imported directly from Spain, and did not exist in other Jewish communities. Headed by scholars, its task was to punish moral and religious transgressions, particularly adultery.[122] This body was sometimes instructed to intervene in order to ensure the safety and harmony of the community, to suppress certain developments which were damaging its image, or to punish counterfeiters. It did not exist in every community and, in some, it functioned in conjunction with the executive council. Even publications were subject to censorship. According to an ordinance of 1529 published in Salonika, anyone who published a text, or bought such a text in published form, which had not been approved by an *ad hoc* commission formed of six rabbis, was liable to excommunication.[123] These supervisory powers of religious authorities tightened in times of crisis, such as the messianic excitement in the seventeenth century. As they were not subject to any independent control, these powers were sometimes prone to stifle independent intellectual activity. Such supervision was not sufficiently effective to eliminate all risk of transgression, as is proven by the frequent renewal of ordinances.

Clothing poor children, accommodating the sick, collecting money for specific purposes, distributing scholarships to pupils and students, investing the revenues of an educational or charitable foundation, collecting taxes, appointing the leading members of congregations and guards for the defense of the town, dress, marriages, the remarriage of widows, divorce, property law, rentals, the wearing of jewellery, leisure, the enforcement of monogamy, business exchanges, speculation, competition between business rivals: these and many other sectors of community life were subject to regulations and ordinances.[124] Decreed in a town, these had the force of law in neighboring localities as well. In Salonika, they had to be signed by the majority of rabbis at the head of congregations; the only exceptions to this rule were decrees governing the internal administration of one specific congregation.

One of the regulations written by the first generation of exiles concerned the usufruct of real estate (*hazakah*). It was an attempt to solve the problem of accommodation caused by the continuous immigration of Jews to Salonika over a period of a hundred and fifty years,[125] to prevent anarchy and speculation, and to defend the most deprived members of the community. Landlords were raising rents incessantly; the consequence was that many people might be evicted. The *hazakah* regulated this market tightly. This type of regulation on accommodation already existed in the Ashkenazi world in the Middle Ages. It was actually proclaimed in the Empire the year following the Expulsion and underwent regular revision with changing circumstances in the East.

Other regulations were born directly of the vicissitudes of the new exile. For example, some ruling was necessary in the case of women who found themselves separated from their husbands without a writ of divorce (*agunot*). There was also the problem of childless widows whose deceased husbands were without descendants, and who were theoretically bound by Jewish law to marry their brothers-in-law (*yevamot*). What happened if this brother-in-law was not reachable, or was living elsewhere as a Christian, and could not release her from this obligation by the ceremony of "un-shoeing" (*halizah*)?

The patriarchal family was in fact the base on which the exiles rebuilt their social and religious life around the synagogue, in their congregation, in a given district. Monogamy was the rule in Castile and Aragon.[126] A very early ordinance reminded the Jews of this provision. Girls married when they were between eight and 12 years old; boys between 13 and 16.[127] In view of the couple's early age, the marriage was consummated later. The family took charge of the young couple; the son worked with the father or the son-in-law with the wife's family, both families playing an important role at all levels of the couple's life. There were alliances between powerful families who even reserved a separate place in the cemetery.

Families also dominated the life of the congregations and communities, with the most affluent wielding power. Their preeminence was directly linked to the size of their financial contributions to the various communal bodies. As the economic crisis deepened, the gap between rich and poor widened. In Istanbul in the seventeenth century, the social composition of the community was as follows: 15 percent very poor; 15 percent rich or members of the upper middle class; the remainder consisted of small shopkeepers and therefore people of modest means.[128]

Even so, certain strata of this society were able to indulge in luxury, as they had done in their country of origin.[129] The sixteenth-century sumptuary regulations, which were regularly renewed, show that the restrictions on dress, recommended by the authorities for non-Muslims, were not followed.[130] According to these regulations, the Jews had been led astray by their love of music and festivities. Their extravagant habits in apparel had given rise to complaints by non-Jews. The women wore jewellery in the street, and danced with men. The men liked gambling games, particularly with dice. Measures were taken to stem the growing number of divorces. Nocturnal wedding processions were held in the streets. The rabbis issued regulations to control these activities, in order to ensure that the community did not attract too much attention.

This is very far from the ideal and moralistic "traditional" society that has frequently been depicted. Rather, it was, purely and simply, a society like others, with margins for transgression which the religious authorities closely watched, responsible as they were for their community's internal morality as well as for its relations with the outside world.

Where did the Jews live? Even if the *dhimma* actually contained some restrictions on this point, for example forbidding non-Muslims to live near mosques or in Muslim districts, ghettos did not exist in Ottoman lands.[131] In various localities, Jews lived in quarters adjacent to Muslim ones. Eventually, as a result of greater mobility inside the towns, mixed quarters became increasingly common. The Jews probably had a tendency to group together into what eventually became Jewish quarters, but they were never compelled to do so.

The emergence of a specific type of Jewish dwelling can also be observed. Built around a courtyard, it housed a number of families. In Sarajevo in 1581, the Ottoman governor constructed a building of 2,000 square meters to house 60 Jewish families, on the basis of one or two rooms per family. This building was situated on the edge of the Muslim quarter, east of the *Kal Grandi* (The Great Synagogue) and near the central market. It was called *Il Kurtijo* ("The Court") by the Jews, *Çifut Han* ("The Jews' Block") by the Muslims.[132] There again, Jews were not forced to live in the building. It gradually became the dwelling of the poor, the rich preferring to live elsewhere. In the first half of the nineteenth century, there were several Jewish quarters close to one another in Sarajevo, all situated in predominantly Muslim areas. The Jewish district in Belgrade, *Jevrejski Mala*, was also near the Muslim district. In Monastir (Bitola), many Jews were concentrated in a large building complex also called "The Great Court" – a typical Jewish dwelling in certain Balkan towns.[133] The fact that the quarters were mixed encouraged some intercommunity relations. Ottoman society did not integrate its members into a unitary culture but social interchanges were not absent from daily life. They were found in music, clothing, and cooking.[134] Relations between Jews and Christians, competitors in the economic arena, posed some problems. Tension between Greeks and Jews was particularly apparent: Jews had to some extent supplanted Greeks in power in the Ottoman capital in the fifteenth century when transferred to the city to repopulate it.[135] These relationships eventually became more acrimonious, particularly in the nineteenth century, when the European powers appeared on the scene, and set non-Muslim groups against each other as a means of establishing their influence.

It cannot be claimed that the Jews' relations with the non-Jewish exterior were close, but they certainly existed, mostly in the economic sphere,[136] and in the realm of law (if only when Jews attended Muslim court hearings). The Sephardim came to the Empire with a tradition of openness to the surrounding society. It was their economic activities that prevented isolation; they were sometimes even obliged to break the Jewish dietary laws, to drink forbidden wine, to frequent cafes, or even to transgress the Sabbath laws.[137] The mixed guilds in towns such as Bursa or Istanbul in the seventeenth century were an important setting for contact. The richest Jews owned slaves, another mode of daily contact with non-Jews.[138] Jewish women also worked in Muslim houses. Prostitution too, rare but present, linked the two worlds, if only temporarily. Jews in many towns served as intermediaries between the European Levant Companies and the Turks and Arabs, and were thus influenced in their way of life and dress. The Jews' relations with the European consuls in the seventeenth century, and their association with Christian companies, expanded the range of contacts even further. The arrival of the Francos, Jews from Christian Europe, particularly Italy, in the eighteenth century, also reintroduced certain European customs into Jewish society.

Nor were Jews completely absent from Ottoman political life before the nineteenth century. Doctors, translators, contractors, and financiers, gravitated to the Palace, where they played a role. A similar phenomenon can be noted in the provinces, where influential Jewish families in Damascus, Acre, or elsewhere, held positions as economic or political advisors to local pashas.[139] Connections were thus established between the Muslim and Jewish communities. However, intercommunity relations were more developed in ports or market towns, which were more open to outside influences.

The after-effects of the cataclysm of the Expulsion and exile did not turn these Jews into an apathetic or discouraged population. The new country presented them with a number of challenges: heads of household had to continue to provide for the daily existence of their families; the many men who had lost wives or children had to build a new life, sometimes at an advanced age. These challenges seem to have inspired them with the dynamism specific to the first generations of immigrants. However, it is impossible to describe this as a happy and contented society, savoring its success and resting on its laurels by the mid-sixteenth century. Alongside its self-glorification and an assessment of its own worth at times verging on arrogance, there also existed an existential anguish, sorrow, and a sense of defeat, a feeling of impotence and a desperate and unfulfilled yearning for the simple joys of family life. Alongside the drive for achievement, of intense activity in economic, social, and cultural life, there were also traces of abdication – remoteness from public life, hopelessness, a feeling of abandonment, and even the fear of having been "irremediably cursed."[140] This was a complex society whose trauma and trajectory played itself out in ways that are somewhat reminiscent of the after effects of the great catastrophe of the Jewish people in the twentieth century, the Holocaust. Time has helped to make banal the Expulsion from Spain and consign it to a drawer of history, from which it was brought out during the commemoration of its 500th anniversary with trumpets and fanfares. But it should not be forgotten that it left deep marks on the Sephardi world for several generations and influenced its future evolution.

This society of exiles came to form a Judeo-Spanish community in the Levant which over the centuries acquired a separate identity from other much smaller Sephardi groupings in Western Europe and North Africa. It maintained its unity and individuality in spite of changes of masters and frontiers. For centuries, it remained the living memory of the Iberian peninsula in Balkan lands.

2

Economy and Culture

Sephardi Jews were found in most domains of Ottoman economic life in the centuries that followed the expulsions from Spain. Several factors converged to encourage Sephardi economic activity, especially in the sixteenth century. The ever-expanding Ottoman Empire needed elements that could be useful in the economic and administrative consolidation of the lands it occupied. The Empire also controlled major trade routes from Asia to Europe and could provide, at the height of its power, relative security that aided trade and commerce. It controlled regions that supplied in abundance several commodities needed in Europe while constituting in itself an important market for European products. Furthermore, the overarching importance of religious communities in the Ottoman social hierarchy had important economic consequences, providing for a great deal of ethnic/religious-specific economic activity that relied on ethnic-based networks of trade and production.

The Sephardim, while never dominating the Ottoman economy in any period as has been claimed in some of the breathless accounts of European travelers, became an important group that played an especially active role in certain domains. The sixteenth century saw the heyday of this role, which went into a relative decline in the following century until the modern period, without ever being effaced completely. While the great majority of the Sephardim were involved in small-scale trade, artisanal and craft occupations, and in shopkeeping, and were integrated into local economies, a smaller élite emerged that became significant in often interlinked areas such as finance, international commerce and brokerage, and the manufacture and marketing of textiles.

Sephardim joined the ranks of Romaniots as tax farmers after 1492. The latter had been in leading positions in this field in Istanbul in the 1470s and 1480s. The Jewish élite in Spain had been active in this domain over the centuries, and managed to transfer its skills to the Levant. The Sephardim became involved in tax farming in many areas of the Empire, especially in the Danubian provinces, and also controlled customs collection in the Danubian, Adriatic, and Aegean ports.[1] Jewish tax collectors were important in most of the major Ottoman cities, from Bursa,[2] to Egypt,[3] to Izmir. In the latter city, which emerged as an important economic center by the early seventeenth century, two Jews administered the tax farms of Western Asia Minor as a whole in 1604 and 1607, and by 1620, most of the tax farmers and customs officials of the area were Jews.[4] The wealthy Marrano financier Don Joseph Nasi or João Mendes brought not only his wealth but also his administrative and financial skills to the Empire, and among other activities he headed a major tax farming network in the middle of the sixteenth century.[5] His economic success made him a powerful personality at the imperial Court, and his intimate knowledge of European affairs led to his active involvement in Ottoman and European diplomacy concerning relations with Poland, Italy, and Spain during the latter part of the reign of Suleiman the Magnificent, and during that of his successor, Selim II (1566–74).[6]

Jews were also involved with the administration of the mint in Istanbul and elsewhere.[7] Unlike in medieval Europe, Jewish moneylenders were not present in significant numbers in many locales due to the relatively free availability of credit through the pious foundations (*vakıf*).[8] Nevertheless, in different periods, Jewish *sarrafs* (bankers) played important roles as purveyors, contractors, and bankers of the janissaries, and often supervised the finances of highly placed Ottoman officials. A Jew usually held the position of *bezirgan* the banker of the janissary corps.[9] This financial link between Jewish *sarrafs* and the janissaries was to last until the latter's downfall in 1826.

However, the Jews were not the only ones involved in finance and did not dominate it. Muslim Turks, Armenians, and especially Greeks were also active in customs and tax collection, and often outshone the Jews. The renowned Greek tax farmer, financier, and trader Michael Cantacuzenus reached an extraordinarily influential position in the middle of the sixteenth century, and his example was followed by many other non-Jews in the following centuries.[10]

Nevertheless, the close linkage between some Jews and Ottoman officialdom and indeed royalty evident in the domain of finance, while not exclusive, did constitute an important feature of Jewish life in the Empire and had its counterpart in other areas. For example, physicians at the imperial Court often rose to significant positions of power and influence. Already before 1492, an Italian Jew, Jacobo of Gaeta, was the chief physician of Sultan Mehmed II and became one of his principal political advisors, and either before or after his conversion to Islam held important positions in the Ottoman administration.[11] The number of Jewish physicians at the Court rose with the arrival of the Sephardim. Doctors among the latter had been significant in the various courts in Spain and in Europe, and many either came directly after 1492 or made their way to the Empire in the course of the following decades.

Joseph Hamon, physician at the court of the last sultan of Granada, moved to Istanbul after 1492 and continued his family's distinguished medical tradition by becoming one of the physicians of Selim I (1512–20). His son Moses Hamon followed in his father's footsteps and was one of the leading physicians of Suleiman the Magnificent. Jewish physicians continued to be present at Court and elsewhere, though their numbers declined by the eighteenth century. More often than not, their diplomatic and political skills were as much in demand as their medical prowess. Familiar with European ways, they made good advisors and diplomats. Physicians such as the Hamons, Salomon Ashkenazi, and others were linked to European Jewish communities, and supplied much needed information about events in Europe. Often, as in the case of Salomon Ashkenazi in the sixteenth century, and Daniel de Fonseca in the early eighteenth century, they became involved in diplomacy between the Ottomans and European powers. Further, they were important in intervening on behalf of Ottoman and foreign Jewish personalities and communities as the need arose.[12] Again, it is important to note that the Jews, while very much present in the medical retinues of the sultans, did not monopolize or dominate these positions over the centuries. However, certain influential figures among them did periodically enjoy great power.

Some Jewish women were significant as intermediaries between the imperial *harem* and the outside world. Known under the Greek name of *kyra* (lady), figures such as Esther Handali and Esperanza Malchi at the end of the sixteenth century became purveyors of goods to the *harem*, supplying it with items such as jewellery and clothing, and formed close friendships with the sultans' wives and mothers. They reached influential positions and took part in many a Court intrigue, for which they often paid with their lives.[13]

The roles played by many Jews in the sixteenth century as purveyors and contractors to the Court and the army, as advisors to and negotiators on behalf of the sultans and other leading officials such as governors and military leaders, as tax and customs collectors, all point to their relatively successful insertion as intermediaries and middlemen between the Ottoman ruling class and the rest of society. However, unlike in Spain, the Jews, with rare exceptions, did not dominate these positions. Other groups, whether Muslim or non-Muslim, often vied successfully with them for the best slots. While Jews were present at the Court and in intermediary positions surrounding the administrative/military apparatus, the Ottoman counterpart of the Jewish courtier élite of Spain did not develop.

On the other hand, Sephardim became extraordinarily significant in two domains in the Ottoman economy in the sixteenth century, the manufacture of textiles, and international commerce, far surpassing their previous achievements in these areas in the Iberian peninsula.

In the early sixteenth century, the Sephardi community of Salonika emerged as an important center of weaving and the manufacture of woolen broadcloth. By 1540, the city produced 40,000 pieces of cloth.[14] The Judeo-Spanish communities of the Balkans such as Edirne, Larissa, Pleven, Trikkala, with offshoots in Rhodes and Safed, manufactured over 60,000 pieces of cloth a year, with a production and technology comparable to that of Spain and England.[15] The communal base of the cities of Salonika and Safed, with flourishing economies and increasing populations, relied to a large extent on this industry. The availability of a plentiful supply of fine wool in the Balkans, the existence of nearby water springs that facilitated the finishing process of the cloth manufacture, the presence of a large Ottoman market, as well as other markets in Italy, provided the necessary incentives for the development of the Salonika textile economy.

While there had existed a small Ottoman textile industry in Salonika before the arrival of the Sephardim, this was concentrated on the weaving of a rough woolen product. The Sephardi exiles, in all likelihood experienced in the weaving techniques of mechanical fulling mills in the Iberian small towns,[16] utilized their skills in the new environment. These skills were enriched by those the Jewish weavers of Sicily brought, who also began to arrive in the Empire after their expulsion in 1493.[17] A wide range of economic activities revolved around this manufacture. Jewish merchants bought the raw wool from the peasants in the Balkans and brought it to Salonika or sent it to other manufacturing centers such as Safed. Jewish weavers, dyers, pressers, driers, brushers, etc. were involved in the various stages of cloth production.[18] In the absence of factories, contractors arranged for the completion of the various stages of the manufacturing process, with whole families – men, women, and children – engaged in a putting out system that depended on an elaborate division of labor. Large-scale manufacturers provided the capital and investment, and traders marketed the product in local, regional, and international markets.[19]

In the meantime, finer textile products from Italy and elsewhere continued to be imported, often by Jewish traders. The Salonika broadcloth, though frequently exported, was essentially geared to the Ottoman market. The rising Ottoman population, especially the increasing janissary army, emerged as the principal consumers. Indeed, the Ottoman government, ever vigilant about its internal economic needs, soon tied the Salonika textile industry to the military's economic nexus. From the middle of the sixteenth century onwards, the poll tax of the Jewish community of Salonika was paid in cloth to provide for the needs of the janissary corps.[20] This tax, known as "the king's cloth," eventually became a major problem for the Salonika community. It constrained its economic activities, kept the industry limping along in unprofitable circumstances long after it ceased to be economically viable, and led to strict control by the janissaries of all stages of the manufacturing process.[21] It even resulted in harsh punishment after disagreements between the government and the community. In 1637, Judah Covo, a leading rabbi in charge of a delegation of Salonika Jews to Istanbul to plead for the improvement of the terms of the cloth tax, was executed after being charged with supplying the janissaries with cloth of unsatisfactory quality.[22]

While there is some debate about timing, the Sephardi textile industry began to face serious problems as the sixteenth century progressed. The price of raw wool began to rise and continued to do so in response to increased demand from both the local and international markets. Given the lucrative nature of the sale of raw wool abroad, the rabbinical leadership of the Salonika and Edirne communities banned Jews from being involved with its export around 1540.[23] They also regulated the importation of indigo, which was necessary for the completion of the manufacturing process. These measures are indications of shortages that had begun to create difficulties for the industry. The latter were further compounded by the entry into the Ottoman market towards the end of the century of superior quality finished English cloth sold by the English Levant Company at much cheaper prices.[24] Safed, which relied on the importation of expensive raw wool, suffered most directly and its textile industry which had supported its flourishing Jewish community collapsed.[25]

Salonika held out longer, though its Jewish textile manufacturing had also gone into definitive decline by the early seventeenth century. Raw wool continued to be expensive, and contributed to making the finished product uncompetitive with English cloth. The cloth levy for the janissaries took its toll, as the price used to calculate the amount of cloth was fixed uneconomically low by the Ottoman authorities. On the other hand, the bans forbidding exports of raw wool were increasingly circumvented and the Jews continued to be involved with this trade as well as with the export of hides. They were in an advantageous position in this respect since the Ottoman authorities had given them the first right of purchase of raw wool in connection with the cloth tax for the janissaries.[26] However, the economic foundations of the community based on the textile industry were seriously shaken, compounded by numerous fires and epidemics in the early seventeenth century that ravaged it even further. The economic crisis affected the thousands that had made a living from the manufacturing process. Many Jews, unable to survive economically in Salonika, began to emigrate in this period, most notably to the newly ascendant port city of Izmir.

While Jews had been and were to continue to be involved in other industries and crafts such as exploiting silver mines around Salonika, sulphur in Rhodes, and alum in Corinth, and were engaged in food processing, soapmaking, tanning, and a host of other artisanal occupations,[27] they no longer dominated any particular sector of major economic importance to the extent that they had with the Salonika textile industry. The decline of the latter also precipitated a crisis in the important Jewish communities of the Balkan hinterland such as Monastir, Uskub, and Edirne that had been part of the textile manufacturing infrastructure around Salonika and that had not only provisioned it, but also benefited from the trade nexus based on it. Ethnic domination and specialization in one sector of the economy, while providing for the creation of economic networks that were advantageous, could lead to a serious weakening of the economic position of the whole group when the sector went into crisis and decline.[28] This is what happened to the Sephardim of the Balkans by the seventeenth century. Their position was not helped by Ottoman economic policies concerning the provisioning of internal markets and needs, which did not protect local industries, and were hostile to exports. The Ottomans were oblivious to evolving European mercantilist strategies where the state took a lead in encouraging the development of exports and foreign markets. Facing European mercantilist policies nurturing joint-stock companies such as the English Levant Company, an ethnically based Ottoman industry such as Jewish textile manufacturing could not survive.

The ethnic bases of much Ottoman economic activity eventually emerged as significant in the rise of guilds based on religio-ethnic affiliation. Guilds were important means of market regulation in the Ottoman Empire. They set prices, directed the distribution of raw materials, controlled production, and also acted as conduits for the social control of the urban masses by the government.[29]

Guilds based on ethnic affiliation existed from the beginning, as did guilds whose membership was mixed. Jews were present in both types of arrangements. In areas of production where Jews predominated, such as in the Salonika textile industry, Jewish guilds controlled dyeing and silk manufacture.[30] There were Jewish guilds in various textile occupations in Istanbul in the seventeenth century.[31] Some cartels functioned as guilds among certain Jewish merchants in Istanbul in the seventeenth century,[32] and among Jewish brokers in Izmir in the early eighteenth century.[33] However, on the whole, there were relatively few all-Jewish guilds in the earlier periods of Sephardi settlement in the Empire. Among the many guilds that existed in the city of Bursa in the seventeenth century, only three were all-Jewish.[34] As the economy of the Empire declined, ethnic economic conflict grew fiercer, and the number of ethnically based guilds increased.[35] Jewish guilds in various artisanal trades continued well into the modern period, with the ethnic division of labor and production lasting until the end of the Empire.[36]

It was a configuration of an ethnically based network of trade that catapulted some Sephardi Jewish merchants and traders into leadership positions in international commerce in the sixteenth century. Jews became particularly important in Ottoman trade with Italy, the Empire's prime commercial partner in Europe. Until the middle of the seventeenth century, Venice was the major European entrepôt of this trade, although other Italian cities also had a share. By the early sixteenth century, the Sephardim emerged as the linchpin of commerce between the two areas.

One of the major reasons for Sephardi preeminence in this domain was the international Jewish family and community networks that spanned the Christian and Muslim worlds. The existence of a single Jewish religious law that could be resorted to in the event of litigation facilitated the use of bills of exchange that oiled the wheels of commerce. Family and communal links made for security in transactions, facilitated the dissemination of accurate information about commodities and markets, and provided opportunities to exploit new developments.

Indeed, the migration process of the Sephardim in the aftermath of the expulsions from the Iberian peninsula and elsewhere created a Sephardi diaspora that by its very nature established far-flung commercial networks along the Mediterranean. Many Jews had stopped in Italy on their way to the Ottoman Empire, with some remaining there while others proceeded further East, settling along trade routes from the Dalmatian coast inland through Bosnia, Serbia, and Macedonia to Salonika and further to Edirne and Istanbul. The superimposition on this initial Sephardi dispersion of a new Marrano diaspora that emerged in the aftermath of the introduction of the Inquisition in Portugal after 1535–6 gave the decisive impetus for the rise of an Italian–Ottoman Sephardi trading axis. The Marranos were even more knowledgeable about developments in Europe, and upon their return to Judaism in Levantine cities such as Salonika and Istanbul could act as the ideal intermediaries between the worlds of Islam and Christendom. The very factors that fostered the rise of a Sephardi economic élite in Northwestern Europe in the seventeenth century, which was preeminent in trade with the Iberian peninsula and with Iberian colonies in the New World, also contributed to the making of a similar élite in the Mediterranean a century earlier.[37]

Commerce between Italy and the Ottomans had been in the hands of Ragusans, Armenians, and Greeks before 1492. Soon thereafter, this trade passed into the hands of the Sephardim. Jews imported Italian cloth and exported wool, cotton, and silk from the Balkans and from further East. The Abravanels of Salonika imported silk garments and exported textiles, while the Mendes family under Don Joseph and Doña Gracia Nasi imported European textiles and exported grains, spices, and other raw materials.[38] Their commercial activities went beyond the Mediterranean and they also engaged in trade with Poland, exporting wine and other commodities from Asia Minor.[39] Their economic power was such that they led a move in 1555 to boycott Jewish trade with the port of Ancona (which was under papal rule), where some ex-Marranos were burnt at the stake. However, the difficulties of trade with the alternative port of Pesaro led to the eventual failure of the boycott.[40] The commerce with Poland was continued by the wealthy trader Salomon Ibn Yaesh (Alvaro Mendes) later in the sixteenth century.[41]

Jews were also active in the commerce of the same commodities within the Balkans, and were significant in regional markets. Their importance in the trade of the Balkans, linking the various inland trade routes from the Dalmatian coast to Salonika in the East, through Sarajevo to Buda in the North, and through Sofia and Vidin to the Danube and further North, became a well recognized fact by the middle of the sixteenth century.[42] As a terminus point of this trade, the Dalmatian coast emerged as particularly significant. Already in 1520, there were to be found 528 Jewish households in the Ottoman Albanian city of Valona, an extraordinarily large Jewish population for the time.[43] Given the importance attached to Jewish economic activity, Ragusa (Dubrovnik) rescinded its 1515 expulsion of the Jews in 1538.[44] While Christian traders continued to be active and the Jews did not monopolize long-distance trade with Ottoman lands, the growing perception that they did so, fueled by the important role they played in this activity, affected policy *vis-à-vis* the Jews in Italy. In 1541 Venice issued a decree allowing the Ottoman Jewish merchants the right to settle for a limited period in the city, arguing that they controlled most of the trade between Venice and "upper and lower Romania" (the Ottoman Rumeli/Balkans).[45] This was a calculated move to relaunch trade which had been diverted to other Italian ports after the Turco-Venetian war of 1537–40.[46]

The same considerations, a mixture of myth and reality, lay behind the settlement charters granted to Jews by Venice in 1589 and by Livorno in 1593. Similar concerns were also in evidence in the Venetian senate's acceptance in 1590 of the Jewish merchant and financier Daniel Rodriguez's proposition to build a port in Split (Spalato) that would bypass Ragusa as the link to the land trade routes on the Dalmatian coast.[47]

Ottoman Jewish merchants, the *levantini*, benefited from the protection granted to them by the Ottoman government and from the privileges that they obtained as a result of the capitulation treaties signed by the Ottomans and the European powers. Often, a Sephardi Jew settled in Italy would go to the Ottoman Empire, and return after a short while as a full-fledged "Levantine," enjoying the various rights that this status entailed.[48] Indeed, the whole perception of economic achievement and Jewish preeminence in Ottoman trade acted as an important element in European policies, allowing for Jewish settlement in areas from which they had previously been barred. Ironically, the very Expulsion from Spain, which was one of the last expulsions from an increasingly *judenrein* Europe, eventually opened the path, through a circuitous route via the Ottoman Levant, to the resettlement and growing toleration of Jews in Western Europe.

The Impact of Changes in the World Economy

While Jewish involvement in the commerce between Italy and the Ottoman lands continued through the seventeenth century, the Sephardim were gradually displaced from their important position in it. The general decline in the fortunes of the Ottomans that began towards the end of the sixteenth century eventually affected the Jews. The Ottoman Empire's wealth had been predicated upon continuous expansion through war. By the end of the sixteenth century the expansion stopped as the Ottomans reached the limits of their power. Wars proved to be increasingly costly, and the need to meet the challenge posed by the European armies' use of firearms led to a restructuring of the Ottoman armies that had profound social consequences. The land-based *timar* system in which the holder of the land brought supplies and men to the war effort, was replaced by the ever-expanding infantry janissary corps which now came to include increasing numbers of Muslims recruited from the localities. Their upkeep added to the cost that increased taxation had to cover, which, in turn, was eroded by the janissaries' growing involvement in the local economy which siphoned off much-needed revenue and resources.

A severe price inflation, the result of the massive entry of American silver into local markets, threw the Ottoman financial system into disarray, with frequent devaluations of the currency eroding economic entrepreneurship. The Ottoman system of directing economic output to provision local markets, especially that of Istanbul, increasingly failed because of the insatiable demand for grain from Europe. Grain was smuggled or redirected to Europe from the Balkans, and especially from Asia Minor, bringing in yet more American silver, and further increasing inflationary pressures on the system. The shooting price of grain made the feeding of a growing local population more difficult. Loss of control by the center coupled with economic disaffection led to major uprisings at the end of the sixteenth and early seventeenth centuries, and the rise of banditry and piracy affected long-distance trade.[49]

Heavy tax exactions and monetary debasements, anarchy, and insecurity, all affected Jewish economic activity. A major realignment of the European economy also created new conditions that proved fateful. While economic activity around the Mediterranean remained important, the rise of the Atlantic economy and especially of Holland and England transformed old economic relationships. The English and Dutch Levant Companies, integrated into a global network of trade and commerce, eclipsed Venice's position in Mediterranean trade which went into a serious decline, especially after the costly Venetian–Ottoman wars over Crete which ended in 1669 with Venice's defeat.[50] Commerce passed increasingly through Dutch, English, and eventually French ships that came to Ottoman ports, bypassing the Balkan trade routes with Italy in which the Jews had occupied a special role. The decline of the Salonikan textile industry shook the economic position of the Jews as a whole in the Balkans. Greek, Armenian, and Slav Orthodox merchants managed to develop alternative trading networks that conquered new markets.[51] The Ottoman Jewish ethnic trading network with Italy was eventually supplanted by other more dynamic networks better integrated with the new economic configurations that had arisen by the seventeenth century.

While Marranos continued to arrive, especially to Izmir in the first half of the seventeenth century,[52] their numbers appear to have decreased overall, the group as a whole being attracted by better opportunities in Northwestern Europe. As a result, the intimate knowledge of economic opportunities brought by Marranos, and Marrano entrepreneurship as a whole, became much less significant in the economic life of the Jews of the Empire, leading to growing insularity. In the final analysis, the Ottoman Jewish trader, too entrenched in the old economic axis between Ottoman Rumeli (Turkey in Europe) and Italy, could neither rise to the challenges posed by new economic circumstances, nor reorient the Balkan Jewish ethnic economic network to face new realities. They would never again occupy the position of importance they had enjoyed in the Balkans in the sixteenth century.

However, the Jewish presence in Ottoman–European long-distance trade continued in the next two centuries, albeit in a diminished form. A new impetus came at the end of the seventeenth and the beginning of the eighteenth centuries with the arrival in the port cities of the Levant of Francos, Sephardim from the city of Livorno. The Jewish merchants of this city were particularly important in the trade with Tunis.[53] With new capitulations granted by the Ottomans to the French in 1673 which increased the privileges granted to French merchants in commerce with the Empire, many Livorno Jews sought the "protection" of French consuls to engage in commerce in the Levant. This soon emerged as a mutually beneficial relationship. While the Livornese benefited from their French "protégé" status, the French consuls benefited from the dues the latter paid to the consular coffers.[54] Increasing numbers of French merchants settled in the ports of the Levant, and the Francos were also to be found with them in cities such as Aleppo, Izmir, and Salonika by the early eighteenth century. French merchants and the Livornese were often economic rivals, a situation that prompted many complaints by the former.[55] Nevertheless, both the lucrative nature of the relationship between the Livornese and the French consuls, and their importance in certain key economic activities in the localities, did not alter the fundamental situation. The Francos often acted as middlemen between local Jews and the French, and especially in Salonika derived benefit from the fact that the Ottoman Jews still had the first right of purchase of raw wool, a commodity very much in demand in the West. While on occasion the Francos and the French entered into pacts, like the one in 1732 that stipulated that they would try to buy wool together,[56] local Jews managed to maintain their position, and the Francos reverted to the position of being the local Jews' first economic interlocutors.

The Livornese continued to be active in the Mediterranean cotton, wool, spice, and grain trade throughout the eighteenth century. They were especially significant in the first two thirds of the century in the Levant, Tunisia, and in Gibraltar which was the entrepôt of trade between Morocco and England. Their role in the commerce of the Levant decreased considerably towards the end of the eighteenth century,[57] with the overall decline of the importance of the trade between the Eastern Mediterranean and Europe also being noticeable in the activities of the English Levant Company.[58] But by then, colonies of Francos had taken root in cities such as Izmir, Istanbul, and Salonika where they were to play an important role in the internal life of the Jewish communities in the next century.

Jews continued to be present in several areas of the Ottoman economy throughout the seventeenth and eighteenth centuries. One important position that they seem to have occupied with great frequency together with other non-Muslims was that of middlemen between European traders and local markets, and between these merchants and Ottoman officialdom. Many played this role in the port city of Izmir, which rose to economic prominence in the early seventeenth century. Izmir became a boom town in this period due to increased European interest in the rich agricultural and raw material markets of Asia Minor. As the weakening Ottoman center lost its grip on the region which it had designated as a granary for the huge population of Istanbul, grain, fruits, cotton, and wool from Asia Minor were sold directly to European traders.[59] The English and the Dutch increasingly bypassed old trading centers in the region and focused their activities in Izmir. With the weakening of the position of Venice in the course of the seventeenth century, the English and the Dutch Levant Companies established a clear superiority in the international commerce of Asia Minor through Izmir.[60]

With the rise of the port, many Jews from the towns of Asia Minor, and especially from the declining center of Salonika, moved to Izmir and were soon active in many sectors of the city's economy. They were involved in a wide range of occupations such as artisanal and crafts trades and commerce, and were busy as brokers, factors, moneylenders, and wholesalers.[61] In the first half of the seventeenth century, they monopolized the collection of customs, acting as intermediaries between the Ottoman officials and the European traders.[62] By 1620, most customs officials in the port were Jewish.[63]

The great earthquake of 1688 killed 20,000 people in Izmir, destroying its economy.[64] The port was rebuilt 15 years later, and the Jews resumed their activities. In the early eighteenth century, a guild of Jewish brokers existed that acted as intermediaries with the foreign merchants and competed with the Greeks and Armenians, as well as with those Jews who remained outside the guild.[65] In the eighteenth century, the trade with Livorno, Holland, and England continued. Sixteen out of 22 firms doing business with Livorno in 1724, and 14 out of 19 exporters to Amsterdam in 1725 were Jewish.[66] Over 100 Jewish names are in evidence in British consular records between 1715 and 1726 as having paid fees for merchandise sent or bought through British ships.[67]

The Jews hence maintained some importance in their role as middlemen and traders, as is also apparent elsewhere in the Empire. According to the archives of the English Levant Company, 380 Jewish traders had business dealings with the British in Istanbul between 1646 and 1823.[68] Ottoman Jews were active in the Leipzig fairs throughout the second half of the eighteenth century, and their participation even increased in the early nineteenth century relative to Christian Balkan traders.[69] As late as 1812, 53 out of 100 merchants protected by the French consulate in Izmir were Ottoman Jews.[70]

However, there is no doubt that while still an integral part of the Ottoman economic mosaic,[71] the Sephardi role had declined in relative terms by the end of the eighteenth century. Fires, epidemics, religious crises such as Sabbateanism, economic instability, growing insecurity, increased arbitrary tax exactions from the authorities, and the general overall decline of the Ottoman Empire had taken their toll. Available statistics confirm the relative impoverishment of the communities. In Bursa, the percentage of the taxpaying Jewish population in the highest income bracket fell sharply from 48 to approximately 11 percent between 1598/99 and 1688/89.[72] The budget of the community of Istanbul for 1771/72 reveals an enormous debt, an insufficient tax base to cover both internal and state taxes, and great difficulties in meeting the government's tax exactions.[73]

The Greeks and Armenians were much more populous than the Jews, with a more diversified economic base. They were now better linked to new international economic configurations, especially in the Balkans, and had managed to eclipse the Jews in many domains. Most significantly, the Jews had not revamped their economic profile. By the nineteenth century, the Empire was increasingly integrated into a Western European dominated capitalist world economy. The economic leadership of Ottoman Jewry was, however, integrated into the old finance-oriented sectors of the declining Ottoman economy. They were provisioners, customs agents, and tax farmers, bankers and moneylenders, and were located overwhelmingly in the old financial nexus built around the Ottoman system of government. Families such as the Arié in Ottoman Bulgaria held extensive tax farming concessions, being responsible for the collection of the poll tax, customs dues, and the running of the salt mines in the region of Samakov through the eighteenth and early nineteenth centuries.[74] Jewish *sarrafs* still met the financial needs of the janissary corps throughout the eighteenth century,[75] with the Carmona, Aciman, and Gabay families amassing considerable fortunes from acting as its provisioners and moneylenders at the end of the century.[76] These families formed the lay leadership of the Sephardim of the Empire in the early nineteenth century, and their economic activities supported a whole network of subaltern Jewish agents and officials.

The abolition of the janissary corps in 1826 by the reforming sultan Mahmud II was a terrible blow for these families and for the Jewish economic élite and community as a whole. By the early nineteenth century the Sephardim of the Empire were economically ensconced in the Ottoman *ancien régime*, and they consequently suffered from its downfall. Bekhor Isaac Carmona, the principal *sarraf* of the janissaries, lost his life during the destruction of the janissary corps, his execution being a convenient way for the sultan to evade the assumption of the heavy debts owed to

Carmona.[77] The economic position of the other leading families was also seriously eroded. This episode was symptomatic of the final and now precipitous decline of the Eastern Sephardim. A reforming Westernizing state, rationalizing the administrations, reorganizing the finances, abolishing tax farming and tax collection concessions spelled the end of the economic livelihood of thousands of Jews. The Sephardim of the Empire now faced the major challenge of reorienting their economic activities to fit the era of Westernization and reform.

INTELLECTUAL LIFE

The sixteenth century saw a great outburst of intellectual activity among the Sephardim of the Ottoman Empire. Several developments converged to make this period the high point of Sephardi creativity after the Expulsion. Most of the exiles in the Ottoman Empire congregated in large numbers in relatively few centers, bringing together scholars who in the Iberian peninsula would have been scattered in many localities. Istanbul, Salonika, Edirne, and later Izmir emerged as the sites of a rich intellectual and cultural life, with Safed and Jerusalem in the Holy Land closely linked to these centers. The confrontation with the local Romaniot culture provided an additional stimulus. It did not prove easy to coexist with and eventually supplant the local Jewish rabbinical leadership, and numerous conflicts, especially in the area of *halakhah*, led to new developments and interpretations.[78]

Hebrew rabbinical culture

The relative prosperity that the economic élite among the Sephardim achieved in the sixteenth century provided a network of support for scholarly and cultural activity that nurtured intellectual achievement. Wealthy families amassed books and created large libraries open to scholars. Families such as the Beit Ha-Levi and the Ben Banvenest not only produced major intellectuals, but also oversaw major collections of past and present scholarship in their homes and elsewhere.[79] The Alatun family of Salonika created a special college, collected books, and supported its activities.[80] Wealthy philanthropists sponsored books, funded Torah academies, subsidized the work of scholars, and gave employment to many as tutors to their children.[81] Don Joseph Nasi and his aunt Doña Gracia supported writers, built academies of higher learning in Istanbul and in Tiberias, and financed publication projects.[82] The Hamon family likewise aided *yeshivot* and sages in Istanbul and Salonika.[83] The cultural ideals of the Jewish élite of the Iberian peninsula survived the transition to the Levant. Support for scholarship remained high in the list of priorities.

Many of the leading scholars of Spain brought their libraries with them.[84] Manuscripts and books circulated widely in the Sephardi centers. Printing presses were a considerable impetus. They had already revolutionized the world of books in Spain and elsewhere in the West and had major consequences for the diffusion of knowledge within the Jewish and non-Jewish spheres. The first Hebrew press was established in Istanbul in 1493 (?) by the brothers Samuel and David Nahmias, publishing the famous medieval code of Jacob ben Asher (1270?–1340), *Arba Turim* ("The Four Pillars"), in 1494. This was in fact the very first printing press in the Ottoman Empire as a whole and was followed by presses in Salonika in 1510, Edirne in 1554, and Izmir in 1646. The Ottoman Levant emerged as a major center for Jewish publishing, printing many works composed by Jews outside the Empire. The famous Soncino printing houses of Istanbul and Salonika, having relocated from Italy, were particularly noteworthy in this respect. Nevertheless, the bulk of the publishing was of local Jewish works, with hundreds of books, all on religious topics, being printed in the sixteenth and seventeenth centuries.[85]

The concentration of scholars in a few cities, the circulation of ideas made possible by the publishing of books and by the presence of libraries, and the support of a network of philanthropists of intellectual activity all operated in a context where education remained the highest priority. Considerable importance was assigned to the instruction of the young. In the traditional Jewish society that prevailed among the Sephardim of the Ottoman Empire, education consisted of the reproduction across the generations of the eternal verities, and through this reproduction aimed to perpetuate Jewish thought and culture that underpinned the Jewish people. For the masses, this meant learning to read the Hebrew alphabet and the prayer book, and beginning to decipher some of the religious works of the sages. The intellectual élite, aided by the economic one with which it often overlapped, did not shy away from the task of educating the general public in institutions such as the great *Talmud Torah* of Salonika. This establishment was one of the largest of its kind, dispensing education from the elementary to the most advanced levels, and was responsible for the instruction of hundreds of youth each year, often the poor and the orphans. It attracted students from throughout the Ottoman Levant, and also even from Ashkenazi centers in Eastern Europe.[86]

Nevertheless, it is quite clear that for the overwhelming majority of the public, instruction could not have gone very far, and did not proceed beyond a certain familiarity with the Jewish prayer book and ritual that sprung from the very nature of religious praxis itself. The female half of the population received next to no instruction, except among certain wealthy families where private tutoring sometimes took place. Except for a certain middle and upper middle-class élite, one cannot assume widespread literacy for the great majority of the Sephardim in the Levant. Furthermore, the people spoke and understood Judeo-Spanish, while Sephardi rabbinical culture remained overwhelmingly Hebraic. While imparting elements of this culture took place through the medium of Judeo–Spanish explanation, the bulk of élite culture, like in most traditional societies, remained a closed book for the masses.[87]

Education in this period, having achieved this minimalist task of the group's religious reproduction, had the economic and cultural critical mass at its disposal to aim to advance and transmit much higher learning. It appears that the *Talmudei Torah*, the Torah academies, and private tutoring by the learned sages, all created an audience among the intellectual and economic élite to receive the works of the rabbinical masters. The Torah academies of Salonika, Edirne, Istanbul, Safed, and Jerusalem provided the institutional setting in which sages could discuss and debate the wide range of issues deeply embedded in the various layers of rabbinical culture as it had been transmitted through a long chain of tradition, and add their interpretation, commentary, and exegesis to the rich corpus that they had inherited as their birthright. Of course, much of past scholarship was cast and recast, interpreted and reinterpreted in the light of the burning intellectual and cultural issues of the day, albeit under an overarching umbrella that stressed continuity with and reference to the past, with the accepted "chain of tradition" that provided the only source of legitimacy and value.

One of the most important scholarly domains which saw a remarkable efflorescence was religious law, *halakhah*. The process of resettlement in a new area, the creation of brand new communities and relations with other Jewish groups, all provided the impetus for works of religious law which by tackling these questions, provided guidelines for social and communal life. Responsa literature also flourished in this context, offering answers to specific questions. Furthermore, the need to consolidate the transplanted Spanish heritage, preserving the traditions of the past by adapting them to new settings, put the spotlight on works of compilation, codification, and clarification.

Among the first generation of *halakhists* of the sixteenth century, Jacob ben David Ibn Yahya (1475–1542), Joseph Taitazak (1487/8?–1545?), David Ibn Abi Zimra (1479–1573), Jacob Berav (1475–1546), Levi Ben Habib (1483–1545), and many others made major contributions to rabbinical responsa literature. Their works, whether in manuscript or printed forms, reached a large audience.[88] One particularly burning question was the reintegration of Marranos returning to the Jewish fold. A host of difficult issues accompanied this return, from the recognition of their Jewishness to their marital status. Rabbis such as Jacob Ibn Habib (1440/50?–1515/16?) showed great suppleness, interpreting the law to facilitate the successful absorption of the Marranos.[89]

Samuel de Medina of Salonika (1506–89), who emerged as the greatest *halakhist* among the first generation born in the Ottoman Levant, was the student of some of the leading sages of his time, such as Levi Ben Habib and Joseph Taitazak, and was largely responsible for the regulation of communal life in the city as well as for settling a host of questions that preoccupied the Sephardim of the Levant. His responsa were published in his own lifetime in two volumes in Salonika in 1585–7, with a new edition in three volumes appearing in 1594–8. His rulings were widely disseminated and respected throughout the Jewish world.[90]

The leading codifier of Jewish law whose influence has been decisive ever since was indisputably Joseph Caro (1488–1575). Arriving in the Ottoman Empire from Portugal after 1497, and living in various Balkan Jewish communities such as Nicopolis, Edirne, and Salonika, Caro settled in Safed and became a leader of the rabbinical scholars who congregated there. His magnum opus, *Beit Yosef* ("The House of Joseph"), on which he labored for decades, was a codification of all Jewish law organized as a commentary on the *Arba Turim*, and was published in 1555. The digest of this work, the *Shulhan Arukh* ("The Set Table"), aimed for the widest possible usage by bringing together the laws and practices that regulated all aspects of Jewish existence. It was printed for the first time in Venice in 1564–5. This became arguably the most popular of all rabbinical works and has been in use ever since.[91] The Spanish tradition of codification and compilation saw its apotheosis in Caro's achievements.[92]

Many other aspects of the intellectual traditions of Jewish Iberia continued among the Sephardim of the Levant. Exegesis and homiletics based on the Bible and the Talmud were a favorite genre, practiced in the synagogues, *yeshivot*, and in print. In the prevailing intellectual trends of the time, almost all scholars had to demonstrate their mastery of the Torah, Talmud, and the commentaries by leading Jewish thinkers down the ages. In the sixteenth century, figures such as Meir Arama (1460?–*c*.1545), Joseph Taitazak, Salomon Le-Beit Ha-Levi (1532–1600), Moses Almosnino (*c*.1515–*c*.1580), and many others prepared numerous anthologies and collections of commentaries. The nonlegal, *aggadic* (homiletic) texts were incorporated into these discussions, with selections of these and *midrash* being published frequently in the main printing centers.[93] One important example was the compilation of *aggadot* from the Babylonian and Jerusalem Talmuds with the addition of classical commentaries which Jacob Ibn

Habib published as a book under the title of *Ein Yaakov* ("The Source of Jacob") in Salonika in 1516. This work enjoyed enormous acclaim in the Ashkenazi as well as the Sephardi communities.[94]

For most of the sixteenth century, philosophical and scientific questions were prominent in rabbinical literature and discussions. Spanish Jewry had been the main site of the great debates over medieval rationalism, and philosophical inquiry continued to be practiced by the Sephardi exiles.[95] Joseph Taitazak cited Thomas Aquinas in his commentary, *Porat Yosef* ("The Tree of Joseph," Venice, 1599), and was clearly influenced by medieval scholastic Aristotelianism.[96] Moses Barukh Almosnino was a particularly notable example of a leading scholar who was totally at home in both Jewish and non-Jewish sources. His manuscript *Penei Mosheh* ("The Face of Moses") combined Aristotelianism with Maimonides and the Talmud to popularize science.[97] The famous physician Amatus Lusitanus (1511–68) shows the great imprint medieval and Renaissance philosophy and science had on Marrano intellectuals who continued to be interested in these trends after their return to Judaism.[98] Again in continuity with Spain, some scholars continued to fear the corrosive nature of philosophical inquiry on faith, as seen by the attacks on philosophy by such a figure as Meir Ibn Gabbai (1480–1540?).[99] But it was only towards the end of the sixteenth century that philosophy declined among the intellectual élite of the Sephardim of the Levant.

While certain personalities were masters of one type of intellectual exercise and genre, and had clear preferences as to which genres were the most appropriate ones, it is impossible to typecast most of the Sephardi sages of this period as rigid adepts of disciplines. Later categories establishing oppositions between philosophy and/or rationalism on the one hand, and mysticism on the other, clearly do not apply.[100] Joseph Taitazak, while a leading *halakhist* and also engaged in philosophical study, was also one of the most important mystics of his generation. David Ben Judah Messer Leon (*c.*1470–*c.*1535) a leading Italian thinker who moved to Istanbul, and then to Salonika and Valona, combined medieval Thomism, Renaissance humanism, and the Kabbala.[101] Joseph Caro, the leading rational codifier of Jewish law, was at the same time engaged in deep mystical endeavor, communing extensively at night with his own *maggid* (angel or spirit) in an attempt to reach a better understanding of the divine and of the divine law.[102] For much of the sixteenth century, the Kabbala was one among many fixtures of the extensive repertoire of rabbinical learning. It had its place, together with homiletics, exegesis, philosophy, science, and many other methods of inquiry in the attempt to construct and uncover knowledge of God, humankind, and the world. Indeed, for many, this was a minor field, and does not appear to have had much influence on the leading rabbinical sages of Salonika, Istanbul, and Edirne. The Kabbala remained an esoteric study limited in importance to a very small élite during the sixteenth century, and both in creativity and printing does not seem to have been at the forefront of rabbinical activity until that century's final decades.[103]

The main exceptions to this were the cases of Jerusalem and Safed, where Kabbala did become a very significant, indeed often the primary, focus of attention. The Expulsion from Spain and the dispersal of the Spanish Kabbalists had a fructifying effect on the whole field, leading to extensive cross-fertilization of ideas and methods in Italy and the Levant. One of the direct results was the rise in prominence of the great work of Spanish Kabbala, the *Zohar*, which was printed for the first time in Italy in 1558.[104] Many different forms of Kabbala, from the visionary, philosophical, and ecstatic to the theurgic had coexisted throughout the Jewish world, and many came to be represented in the writings and practices of the Kabbalists who congregated in the Holy Land. Many were active in Jerusalem.[105] But it was in Safed that the sixteenth-century Kabbala reached its apogee. Joseph Caro, Shlomoh Ha-Levi Alkabez (1505–45), Moses Cordovero (1522–70), and others were deeply engaged in mystical endeavor in the town, and clearly benefited from the confluence of diverse schools of Jewish mysticism.[106] Isaac Luria Ashkenazi (1534–72) developed the famous Lurianic school which was further elaborated and popularized by his disciple Hayyim Vital (1542–1620), exercising a deep influence on Kabbalists among Sephardim and Ashkenazim in the following centuries.[107]

One extraordinary feature of the whole range of Jewish intellectual activity in the Ottoman Empire in this period is the fact that, with the exception of a few lone figures, there does not seem to have existed a great deal of intellectual engagement with the surrounding society. There appear to be no major discernible traces of Ottoman Muslim thought and literary activity among the Sephardim. The efflorescence of Jewish culture in the Ottoman Levant seems to have taken place in a situation determined and conditioned by the horizontal context of contemporary Jewish developments. This culture was marked above all by its vertical referentiality and intertextuality with the Jewish, and most notably Iberian Jewish, past. Only in the realm of music do Ottoman forms and genres seem to have been adapted into liturgical Jewish music,[108] in all likelihood because of the great continuity this seemed to demonstrate with the Muslim Spanish historical cultural repertory of the Sephardim in this domain. Outside this isolated influence, and without further research that might unearth hitherto unexplored areas of intellectual interchange, it is hard to point to a symbiosis between Ottoman and Jewish high culture. On the whole, the Jewish rabbinical sage, like most of his fellow Jews, did not learn Turkish, because in the ethnic/religious mosaic that made up the Ottoman Levant, he needed it for neither economic nor cultural survival. Some influences certainly traversed linguistic and cultural barriers. Nevertheless, these remained weak and intermittent. The Sephardic intellectual world of the Levant remained an essentially Jewish one, and came eventually to be increasingly isolated from external stimulus in the domain of high culture.

The sabbatean explosion

In this cultural universe, the Expulsion from Spain remained for many the original trauma that became constitutive of the very experience of the life in the Levant. For rabbinical sages, whether personally or in collective memory, the loss the Expulsion entailed remained vivid and real. Many families had been torn asunder, some members converting, others remaining behind against their will, and still others dying en route to new destinations or in the new lands of refuge. While the Ottoman Levant provided a safe haven, disease and pestilence continued to take their toll, and for many a scholar, the loss of children and spouses remained vivid and colored their world view.[109] Both exile and personal misfortune had to be interpreted, and the Jewish tradition had well established answers to catastrophe. The rabbis, from Joseph Yaavez (d.1507) and Moses Almosnino to Salomon Le-Beit Ha-Levi interpreted the Expulsion as a punishment for the sins of the children of Israel, and as God's means of returning them to the path of righteousness.[110] And interestingly, while these Sephardim now found themselves in the land of Islam, they remained preoccupied with Christendom, and with the suffering that it had inflicted on them. Christianity remained the principal tyrant, the main foe.[111]

It is perhaps here that one can find the vital link in the messianic expectations that apparently existed as a significant current throughout the sixteenth century. Messianism has emerged as a potent force at various periods in Jewish history, and a major event such as the Expulsion from Spain renewed messianic ardor among the exiles, as can be seen in the thought of figures such as Isaac Abravanel.[112] But to this was added the extraordinary spectacle of the rise of the Ottoman Empire, an empire of Islam defeating over and over the world of Christendom. The end of days appeared at hand, from Elijah Capsali (1450–1523) observing the struggle from close at hand on the isle of Crete[113] to Joseph Ha-Kohen (1496–1578) writing in Italy the history of the kings of France and the sultans of Turkey.[114] In this context of febrile expectation, figures such as David Reuveni and Salomon Molho could emerge and tap the undercurrent of messianism, trying to implement fantastic schemes of geopolitical realignment and converting the Pope.[115] Rabbi Jacob Berav (*c.*1474–1546) attempted to reactivate the ordination of rabbis in the Holy Land in expectation of the reestablishment of the Great Sanhedrin which would herald the messiah's arrival.[116]

Scholarly opinion remains divided as to the links between Kabbala and messianism. For some, new developments in Kabbala, especially the Lurianic variety, resulted from the internalization of the themes of exile and suffering that explained the events after the Expulsion and that continued to affect subsequent generations. The shock of the Expulsion, according to this interpretation espoused by Gershom Scholem, remade Jewish mysticism and messianism, leading to the final explosion of Sabbateanism which consumed the Jewish Middle Ages in a cataclysmic outburst.[117] A more recent view sees the evolution of new esoteric trends as internal to the Kabbala itself, thus downplaying the impact of the Expulsion.[118] Given the wealth of material and the multiple layers of interpretation, it is impossible to enter into this debate. Suffice it to say that the psychic and spiritual impact of the Expulsion, affecting Sephardim for many generations, was only one of many factors that went into the making of the potent brew of Jewish mysticism and messianism in the sixteenth and seventeenth centuries that was fed by a multiplicity of currents.

By the end of the sixteenth century, philosophical and theological study were increasingly eclipsed by a strong emphasis on *halakhah* and rabbinical literature.[119] The Kabbala grew to be a popular mode of inquiry diffused widely among the learned élite, the *Zohar* achieving a status that it had not previously enjoyed. It is difficult to make direct links between socioeconomic developments and intellectual trends. However, the economic crises engendered by inflation, the fall of the Salonika and Safed textile industries, uprisings and social unrest, all provide the backdrop to the withdrawal of Sephardi intellectual endeavor from some of the themes and genres with which it had been customarily engaged. In times of economic downturn, scholars suffered from the uncertainty of philanthropic backing, and had to cope with the erosion of the support network that had made much of their production possible. Increased class conflict within the Jewish communities also took its toll, threatening the social position of the intellectual élite by challenges both from within its own status group over scarce resources, and from outside.

The period of relative economic decline at the end of the sixteenth century added to the deep existential insecurities of an intellectual élite that had internalized the trauma of the Expulsion. The Chmielnicki massacres in Poland in 1648–9, when tens of thousands of Jews were killed and thousands of others became captives who had to be ransomed, also left their mark on the Sephardim of the Levant.[120] With refugees streaming into the

Empire, the horrors of the massacres were all too vivid to a group which had itself dealt with catastrophe and exile. European, Russian, and Muslim messianic activities in the seventeenth century also undoubtedly played a role in increasing messianism and eschatological expectations. All these factors contributed to making the Sephardim receptive to a movement of Jewish messianism which erupted with great force with the rise of Sabbetai Zevi.

Sabbetai Zevi was born in 1626 in Izmir, the son of a family from Greece that had been attracted by the port city's great prosperity. Indeed, Zevi's father became a rather wealthy broker by working for English merchants,[121] and it is quite clear that the ebullient cosmopolitan atmosphere of this boom town with Europeans, Greeks, Armenians, and Muslims actively trading with each other, facilitated the transfer of ideas, expectations, and dreams. Sabbetai Zevi received a traditional Jewish education under the leading rabbinical figures in the town, such as Joseph Eskapa (1570–1662),[122] and was exposed to the Kabbala as a youth. While very successful as a student, early on he manifested eccentric behavior, and appears to have had a somewhat manic-depressive personality, given to exalted moods followed by deep despair. The Chmielnicki massacres had a deep impact on him, and he might already have been indicating as early as this period that he was the messiah. However, given the rapid change in his moods, and his bizarre behavior, he was not taken seriously. He fell into disfavor with the Jewish authorities of Izmir, who forced him to leave the town in the early 1650s. He wandered for more than a decade in many of the Jewish communities of the Levant, making friends and contacts attracted by his charismatic personality.

The decisive events for his emergence as messiah took place in 1665 when Zevi, who was then living in Cairo, visited Nathan of Gaza. The latter declared him to be the messiah, and brought to the fore Zevi's messianic inclinations and ardor. Nathan of Gaza spread the news far and wide through missives to Jewish communities. Encouraged by him, Zevi made his way to Jerusalem where he became the object of popular enthusiasm, but was not accepted by most of the rabbinical leadership. He left the city and traveled to Izmir, where word of him had preceded his arrival. It is while he was there in September 1665 that messianic fervor began to grip not only the masses but also much of the rabbinical leadership of the city and of other Jewish communities in the Sephardi Diaspora. Zevi deposed Aaron Lapapa (1604–67), the Chief Rabbi of Izmir, and replaced him with Haim Benveniste (1603–73), a previous naysayer to his messianic pretensions who "converted." Zevi performed many rituals designed to show that he was the messiah, publicly transgressed Jewish law, abolished fasts, declared forbidden food acceptable, and heralded the beginning of a new messianic age when accepted verities lost their validity. Messianic fever reached its peak when he left for Istanbul at the very end of 1665, with rumors widespread about his intentions to depose the sultan. Increasingly embellished stories about his powers and miracles were disseminated throughout the Jewish world, with rabbis and laymen alike becoming his followers, stopping all normal business activity, and preparing for the restoration of the Jewish people in the Holy Land.

Some leaders of the Istanbul community, worried about the impact of Zevi's arrival, warned the Ottoman government, who arrested him on his way to the city. He was treated extraordinarily leniently by the Ottoman Grand Vizir, Ahmed Köprülü, who kept him in comfortable confinement first in Istanbul, and then in Gallipoli. The latter became a place of pilgrimage for his followers, and agitation about the messiah in Turkey continued to foment feverish expectations in the Ottoman Levant and elsewhere. As the agitation appeared to get out of hand, the authorities finally brough Zevi to Edirne in September 1666, and presented him with a choice between conversion to Islam or death. Zevi chose conversion. Nevertheless, while outwardly a Muslim, he continued many Jewish/messianic practices with his followers in the next decade. In the end, he was exiled to a remote outpost, Dulcino, in Albania, where he died in 1676.[123]

The disappointment in the Jewish world was enormous, especially among the Jews of the Sephardi heartland. Many rabbinical authorities came to their senses, renounced Zevi, and repented their past gullibility, and returned to normative Judaism with renewed zeal. For others, however, Zevi had altered the contours of their existence irrevocably, with reality itself having undergone an epistemic shift. It was impossible to accept the enormity of the whole event having come to nought. Denial set in, together with rationalizations about the messiah's conversion. Many remained Sabbateans, believing that there was an internal logic to what had happened, and that Zevi's messiahship would eventually actualize itself. Others were prepared to go much further. Already within the lifetime of Zevi, many families followed in his footsteps and converted to Islam. Others followed after his death, with hundreds of families in Salonika converting. However, while outwardly remaining Muslims, this group, known as the *Dönme* in Turkish ("those who turned"), became an esoteric sect, with its own belief system revolving around Zevi, and its own rituals.[124] The sect continued to exist in Salonika until the conquest of the city in 1912, and eventually left with the Greek–Turkish population exchange of 1924 for Turkey, where it appears to have survived, in remnants, down to our own day.

Interestingly, Sabbateanism among Sephardim and other Jews who did not convert to Islam continued for a very long period after the debacle of

1666. While many scholars and rabbis appear to have returned to normative Judaism, in fact many overtly and covertly continued Sabbatean activity, meeting with each other to discuss, collect, and disseminate information about the messiah. Sabbateans among Jews after Zevi's conversion manifested themselves in a whole spectrum of activity and belief, from groups of hard-core adepts, sympathizers, and fellow travelers, to the merely curious who indulged intermittently.[125] It has increasingly come to light that some of the leading rabbinical figures of the Ottoman Empire continued to be secret Sabbateans long after the movement appeared to have run its course. Figures such as Abraham Rovigo and Samuel Primo, the latter the rabbi of Edirne until 1708, are examples of Sabbateans who appear to have persevered in their beliefs and led a double life.[126] Their activities continued well into the eighteenth century, as evidenced in the publication in Izmir of a three-volume set of Sabbatean writings under the title of *Hemdat Yamim* ("The Most Beautiful of Days") in 1731.[127] Indeed, a figure such as Rabbi Moses Hagiz (*c.*1672–1751) of Jerusalem who traveled widely in the Levant and Europe, spent much of his life trying to stamp out Sabbateanism and impose rabbinical orthodoxy among the rabbinical élite.[128] In spite of these efforts, it is likely that echoes of Sabbateanism survived through the eighteenth century.

While messianism and mysticism do not necessarily follow from each other, they do seem to have converged among certain elements within the intellectual élite in the messianic explosion of 1665/66 and its aftermath. Messianism was always latent in Judaism, with the potential for activation under specific circumstances. The events of 1648–9, the slowly declining economic fortunes of the Sephardim, the great instability and chaos in the Ottoman Empire, and above all the continuing predicament of exile (*galut*), with all its attendant miseries, all provided a context for the appeal of a charismatic "messianic" personality among the Sephardi intellectual leadership. The spread of the Kabbala, Lurianic or otherwise, with its implicit potential for antinomianism, was added to the equation, providing a rationale not only for the rise of a messiah, but also, if necessary, for his conversion.

This is not to say, however, that for the thousands of Jews swept off their feet by Sabbetai Zevi, the Kabbala was instrumental in shaping their zeal. The *Zohar* and Kabbalistic doctrines had been increasingly popularized. Nevertheless, for the barely literate and often illiterate Sephardi masses, the appeal of the messiah lay in folk religion, in the systems of thought and practice that, through an admixture of normative belief, superstition, and magic, tried to make sense of an often dismal reality. In communities riven by class conflict, poverty, disease, pestilence, and fire that were undergoing an ineluctable decline, it is not hard to understand the appeal of a messiah promising a radically altered reality to the individual and the collectivity.

In spite of the continuing presence of submerged Sabbatean currents, intellectual life among the Sephardim slowly reverted to a certain level of normalcy after the last decades of the seventeenth century. However, the fear of renewed messianic outbursts, and the concern to control antinomian impulses, narrowed the horizons of intellectual endeavor. The new became increasingly suspect. The favorite mode of rabbinical intellectual activity remained the *halakhic* work which, however, shied away from the innovation and vision that had been its hallmark in the sixteenth century.

The Rise of Religious Judeo-Spanish Literature

While many sectors of rabbinical culture lost their vitality, new areas of intellectual creativity emerged. One major intellectual innovation after Sabbateanism was the rising importance of religious literature in Judeo-Spanish. From being a secondary and marginal phenomenon, it acquired a certain legitimacy in the eyes of the rabbinical élite, and exercised a profound impact on the cultural universe of the Sephardi masses.

Books in Judeo-Spanish – Spanish written in Hebrew script (almost always in the *Rashi* script) – made their appearance in the Levant soon after the arrival of the Sephardim. The habit of writing the vernacular with the Hebrew alphabet had long been a feature of premodern Jewish existence, and several Jewish languages such as Judeo-German (eventually Yiddish), Judeo-French, Judeo-Arabic, and Judeo-Persian emerged at different times. It is important to distinguish between the Judeo-Spanish of the Levant, and the Castilian Spanish, written in the Latin alphabet according to standard rules, of the Marrano communities in Italy and Europe. While the latter remained in touch with the developments of Spanish in the Iberian peninsula, and was for all intents and purposes identical with contemporary Spanish, the use of Hebrew script and the eventual decline in contacts with the West led to the evolution of Judeo-Spanish as a distinctive idiom. The language of the Eastern Sephardim kept many words and phrases that became archaic in Spain and also replaced many Spanish expressions with loan words from Hebrew, Turkish, Greek, and Italian. Nevertheless, in essence, the language remained Hispanic.[129]

The very first book to be published in Judeo-Spanish was the *Dinim de Shehita y Bedika*, a book on ritual slaughter and inspection of animals that appeared in Istanbul in 1510.[130] This "how to" book was obviously of great use to a population in motion. A major turning point was the translation of the Pentateuch in Istanbul in 1547 at the press of Eliezer Gershon Soncino, the same translation appearing in Latin characters in Ferrara in 1553.[131] While the former had the Sephardim of the Levant as its audience, the latter clearly appealed to Marranos returning to Judaism for whom a text in Latin script was more accessible.[132]

Indeed, for much of its history, Judeo-Spanish literature was to consist essentially of translations and adaptations from the Hebrew. In the early period, one original work on ethics, Moses Almosnino's *Regimiento de la Vida*, was published in Salonika in 1564. The same author's *Extremas y Grandezas de Constantinopla*, an account of the city of Istanbul, while written in Judeo-Spanish, appeared by an odd twist of fate in Latin script in Spanish in Madrid in 1567.[133] In contrast to these original creations, a major book of Jewish medieval ethics, Bahya Ibn Pakuda's *Duties of the Heart*, was translated from its Hebrew version into Judeo-Spanish by Zadik Ben Yosef Formon, and published in Istanbul under the title of *Obligasion de los Korasones* in 1550, while extracts of Joseph Caro's *Shulhan Arukh* appeared under the title of *Meza del Alma* in the same city in 1568.[134]

In spite of the publication of these works, books in Judeo-Spanish appear to have been printed only rarely until the eighteenth century. The most important reason was this literature's lack of value in the Sephardi rabbinical mindset. Hebrew held pride of place, and any scholar worthy of the name had to demonstrate his virtuosity in the sacred language. Judeo-Spanish remained the quotidian language of both the rabbinical élite and of the masses, and the former did not hesitate to pepper responsa with Judeo-Spanish words and expressions. But Judeo-Spanish did not impart worth or prestige. Apart from the occasional work, the major genre that remained acceptable in Judeo-Spanish was the translation of scriptures, the prayer books, and the Passover *Haggadah*.

Once the latter were in place by the end of the sixteenth century, they soon reached sacral quality themselves. Following exactly the Hebrew word order of the original, and forming a calque, the Judeo-Spanish of these books became a highly stylized idiom that remained immutable, and in a few generations was thoroughly archaic. It became difficult to understand for the masses whose own language had been in constant evolution.

The language of these works was very often identified on the title pages as Ladino, from *enladinar*, which denoted the act of putting into the Latin, i.e. Spanish language. Some scholars take the term Ladino to refer solely to this calque translating archaic language.[135] Nevertheless, in the eighteenth and nineteenth centuries, as free translations of rabbinical texts gained currency, and many new original religious and ethical works such as the *Meam Loez* ("From a Foreign People") were written by the élite in the language of the masses, authors very frequently denoted the idiom of these books as Ladino on the title pages, in spite of the fact that no calque from the Hebrew was involved.[136]

In fact, the language of the Eastern Sephardim was marked for centuries by what sociolinguists call "diglossia." The latter is defined as a situation where

in addition to the primary dialects of the language (which may include a standard or regional standards), there is a very divergent, highly codified (often grammatically more complex) superimposed variety, the vehicle of a large and respected body of written literature, either of an earlier period or in another speech community, which is learned largely by formal education and is used for most written and formal purposes, but is not used by any sector of the community for ordinary conversations.[137]

Like many other Jewish and non-Jewish linguistic contexts, in Judeo-Spanish there existed a literary language of high culture, used by the educated, rabbinical élite mainly but not exclusively to translate Hebrew religious texts, and a popular, spoken language of the masses. The high culture written language, often referred to as Ladino, followed the Hebrew syntax and word order of the translated texts only when the latter were, or had assumed, a sacred nature. The language of quotidian speech remained much more fluid, and evolved in a dialectical relationship with the surrounding cultures, with the literary language of the rabbinical elite, and with Hebrew. Hence, "diglossia" marked a situation where the literary, high culture, written language, and the popular spoken language represented different stages of a complicated spectrum in perpetual flux. And one level higher on the hierarchy of value and esteem, Hebrew reigned supreme. Sephardi high culture intellectual life, until the onset of modernity, was marked by a linguistic situation that exhibited Hebrew/Judeo-Spanish bilingualism as well as Ladino/Judeo-Spanish diglossia.

The crisis Sabbateanism engendered increased the rabbinical élite's vigilance against future outbreaks. Moralization of the masses appeared prudent. Furthermore, there was a serious decline in the religious knowledge and practice of the Sephardi masses. Most did not know Hebrew and were quite removed from any serious learning, and could thus easily be swayed by a new charismatic personality. It was in this atmosphere that the magnum opus of Judeo-Spanish literature, the *Meam Loez* by Rabbi Jacob ben Meir Hulli (1689–1732), appeared in 1730 in Istanbul. This vast compendium of rabbinical lore was organized around the traditional format of commentary on the Bible, beginning with the book of Genesis. The whole range of rabbinical literature, from the Mishna, Talmud, and *aggadic* material to philosophical ruminations and Kabbalistic interpretation were all presented to explicate the relevant biblical passages. And all was written in the simple and clear Judeo-Spanish of the Sephardi masses (referred to as Ladino on the title page).[138] Arguably the most interesting product of Judeo-Spanish literature, the work proved to be an instant success, and after initial hesitation, received the approbation of the rabbinical élite. Hulli died in the middle of his endeavors, in 1732, and the second volume appeared posthumously in Istanbul in 1733.[139]

An important precedent had been set. Rabbinical literature in Judeo-Spanish had begun to appear as a valid genre in its own right. The eighteenth and the first half of the nineteenth centuries saw the high point of this trend. In the eighteenth century, Abraham Asa, more than any other figure, was responsible for following in Houlli's footsteps. His most important work was a new, hugely successful translation of the Bible which was published between 1739 and 1744. This translation broke with the archaic style and put the Bible in the language of the masses. Abraham Asa translated many other works, such as sections of the *Shulhan Arukh* under the title of *Shulhan Hamelekh* ("The Table of the King," Istanbul, 1749), and Isaac Aboab's work of ethics, *Menorat Hamaor* ("The Candelabra," Istanbul, 1762), and wrote a compilation of *dinim* (rules) under the title of *Zorkhei ha-Zibur* ("The Needs of the Community," Istanbul, 1733).[140]

Books on ethics, a *musar* literature in Judeo-Spanish, became a favorite genre in this period, and appeared throughout the eighteenth and nineteenth centuries in translations from Hebrew or as original works. Abraham Ha-Kohen published his *Shevet Musar* ("The Staff of Ethics") in Istanbul in 1740. Figures such as Isaac Amaragi, Eliezer Papo, and Moses Emanuel Shalem continued this literature until the end of the nineteenth century.[141] In the eighteenth century religious poetry also finally began to be seen in print with the publication of *Coplas de Yosef Hazadik* ("The Couplets of Joseph the Just") of Abraham de Toledo (Istanbul, 1732), and of *Los Maasiyot del Sinior de Yaakov Avinu* ("The Acts of the Patriarch Jacob," Istanbul, 1748).[142] Poems celebrating the festival of *Purim* also were printed with great frequency after this period under the title of *Coplas de Purim*.

However, it was the *Meam Loez* that proved the most successful and enduring. Houlli's work was continued by others in the next century and a half. His interrupted commentary on Exodus was completed in two volumes by Isaac Magriso (Istanbul, 1733 and 1746), who then proceeded to extend the work to Leviticus (Istanbul, 1753) and Numbers (Istanbul, 1764). Isaac Arguete tackled part of Deuteronomy (Istanbul, 1773) without finishing the whole book. In the next century, the tradition of adding to the *Meam Loez* persisted. Rahamim Menahem Mitrani of Edirne produced commentaries on Joshua printed in 1851 (Salonika) and 1870 (Izmir), Raphael Hiya Pontremoli on Esther (Izmir, 1864), Raphael Isaac Meir Benveniste on Ruth (Salonika, 1882), Isaac Judah Aba on Isaiah (Salonika,

1892), Nissim Moses Abud on Ecclesiastes (Istanbul, 1898), and Haim Isaac Shaki on the Song of Songs (Istanbul, 1899).[143]

The continuation of the genre demonstrates its enduring appeal. The works of Hulli and Magriso remained the most popular of all. Indeed, their *Meam Loez* became the most widely read work among the Eastern Sephardim, and was found even in the poorest households, often as the sole book owned by the family. The *Meam Loez* set the contours of the popular religious universe of the Sephardim well into the modern period.

There is no doubt that the bulk of rabbinical literature, most of it *halakhic* works, continued in Hebrew. However, by the eighteenth century, books in Judeo-Spanish had attained sufficient legitimacy to be accepted as an integral part of the learned élite's repertory. Aiming for a wide, popular audience, the rise of religious Judeo-Spanish literature was a response to real and perceived needs to strengthen the faith and resolve of the masses who were coping with increased economic and social problems which were making considerable inroads into traditional instruction in the post-Sabbatean period. This literature was the counterpart in the Levant of the large Jewish literature in Castilian Spanish and Portuguese that was produced in Western Europe in the sixteenth and seventeenth centuries in order to reintegrate Marranos returning to Judaism. Just as books about religious practices, laws, ethics, and explication of the Bible and Jewish tradition were needed in the language of the Marranos in this period,[144] a similar literature (in content) appeared in Judeo-Spanish in the eighteenth and early nineteenth centuries in the Levant to renew and reinvigorate the Judaism of the masses. On the eve of radical changes that would buffet Sephardi communities in the modern period, a relatively stagnant rabbinical culture had managed to produce a reservoir of popular religious works in the language of the people. It was from this source that a secular Judeo-Spanish literature and culture would emerge, in the age of Westernization.

3

Eastern Sephardi Jewry in the Era of Westernization

CHANGING FRONTIERS

The Judeo-Spanish community which survived for over three centuries as a unit distinguished by its language, religion, and culture, was an integral part of the Ottoman ethnic–religious mosaic. Of course, the content and frontiers of Judeo-Spanish ethnicity shifted and evolved over time. Constant exchanges with the surrounding populations and cultures in dress, food, music, popular beliefs, and economic activity all left their imprint. Nevertheless, outside influences were in the long run Judeo-Hispanicized through the overdetermining mediums of the Judeo-Spanish language and rabbinical Judaism. Levantine Sephardi identity remained distinct and all-embracing.

The West's progressive domination of the Ottoman Levant from the end of the eighteenth century had a profound effect on this community. The triumphant incursion of Western power had a twofold effect. On the one hand, it led to the Westernizing reforms carried out by the Ottomans. On the other, it resulted in the creation of new states in zones where Turkish power had lost its foothold. The fundamental concepts of political, cultural, and economic life had to undergo radical change in response to the challenge of growing Western domination.

One of the most visible manifestations of the change was the progressive fragmentation of the Ottoman Levant and the emergence of new nation-states in the Balkans. The kingdom of Greece was recognized in 1830, although the great Sephardi center of Salonika continued to form part of the Ottoman Empire until 1912. The Treaty of Berlin (July 1878), following the Russo-Turkish war (1877–8), redrew the frontiers of the Balkans. The Empire lost many of its European provinces. The *de jure* independence of Serbia was formalized (it had been recognized *de facto* since 1830). Greater Bulgaria, born of the Treaty of San Stefano (March 1878), was divided into three: the North became autonomous, but remained under Ottoman suzerainty; the center, Eastern Rumelia, became a semi-autonomous province, and was only definitively attached to Bulgaria in 1885; the South was returned to direct Ottoman control. Bosnia-Herzegovina, containing the important Sephardi center of Sarajevo, was occupied by Austria-Hungary in 1878 and annexed in 1908. This process inevitably gathered momentum in the twentieth century. During the Balkan wars (1912–13), Salonika, "the mother city in Israel," was incorporated into Greece; other towns changed masters as victories dictated. Macedonia was divided among Bulgaria, Greece, and Serbia. The First World War dissolved the Empire and the Turkish Republic emerged in 1923. The Balkans saw the creation of the kingdom of the Serbs, Croats, and Slovenes, uniting the Sephardim of the old Ottoman lands with the Ashkenazim of the Habsburg lands, and becoming Yugoslavia in 1931. Palestine came under the British mandate.

The creation of these new nation-states did not definitively undermine Eastern Sephardi unity. Nevertheless, although the Sephardim preserved the same language, traditions, and culture with some variations, they were henceforth destined to adapt themselves to local circumstance and follow the evolution of the different states. The policies undertaken by these nation-states, the rights granted to their minorities, the degree to which the Jews identified with the ideology of their new masters, the nature of the regime and the directions it chose, were some of the factors which determined development of these communities. The geographical situation of the countries in which they were settled and their relationships with their neighbors also played a part. In spite of these developments, it was still possible to talk about a Judeo-Spanish *Kulturbereich* in the Levant until the Second World War.

Jewish traditional society in its self-representation saw the present as the perpetuation of the past.[1] Until the first half of the nineteenth century, the Sephardi communities of the Levant corresponded to this model. But this did not mean that they remained static and sheltered from change. On the contrary, like any other society, they were subject to evolution, with every generation making its distinctive contribution.[2]

However, change is not synonymous with what has come to be called "modernization." "Modernity" has come to be associated with a specific type of civilization which emerged fully in the Western Europe of the Enlightenment and Industrial Revolution, and, spreading throughout the world in various political, ideological, and economic forms, often came to be synonymous with Westernization.[3] However, the internal dynamic of non-Western societies should not be underestimated in the latter process, marked as it was by the dialectic between internal and external forces.[4] The reactions of these societies depended on their degree of *rapprochement* with the West, and on the relative strength they maintained *vis-à-vis* European powers.[5] The process of change could be marked by direct conquest, as in the case of Bosnia-Herzegovina by Austria-Hungary. It could involve the creation of a new nation-state such as Bulgaria, which borrowed from Europe some of its typical state-building practices. Or again, it could be influenced by an economic type of semicolonization such as prevailed in the Ottoman Empire. Many different avenues of change existed, depending on local circumstances. In the case of the Jews, for example, specific trends such as the *Haskalah* (the Jewish Enlightenment movement) and the *Wissenschaft des Judentums* ("Science of Judaism") of the second generation entered the Levant via Eastern Europe, as a result of contacts between intellectual élites which ensured the circulation of ideas in the Jewish world, and left their imprint on paths of Westernization.[6]

The latter was not a passive process. The role played by local élites was a very significant factor. Unable to rely on anything but their own resources, these élites often went halfway to meet their Western Jewish counterparts. In this case, Westernization emerged with its corollaries, Frenchification and, to a lesser extent, Germanization, depending on the comparative strength of Western Jewish activity in the area and the local communities. In a number of cases, the Westernizing policies of European Jewry played the role in the East that the nation-state had in the West, where it used authoritarian means in an attempt to integrate its Jews in the name of centralization and the struggle against particularisms.[7]

In the Eastern Sephardi world "Westernization" was therefore polyvalent. Several parallel movements developed. They emerged in diverse ways in the different communities depending on local history and on the conditions in which contacts with the West were established – even if, over and above this diversity, the communities shared the same culture and historical origins.[8] On another count, a distinction must also be made – even if it is not easy to do so – between the process of internal communal change and the influence exercised by the models of societies deemed more "advanced."[9]

STATE WESTERNIZATION: THE OTTOMAN EXAMPLE

The modern European state, especially the strong bureaucratized and centralizing French state, eventually came to provide an important model for old and new élites in the Levant. The desire to resist Western incursion into the area led to the adoption and adaptation of Western military and state-building practices to strengthen Ottoman power. This policy, which was at the heart of the reform process known as the *Tanzimat* (reorganization), also fitted well the Ottoman state's centralizing aims to subdue alternative centers of power.

The emergence of the modern state in Western and Central Europe had a profound impact on European Jewry. The dissolution of the legally sanctioned autonomous Jewish community, and its steady "nationalization," imposed or encouraged by the centralizing state, posed a major challenge and gave rise to new forms of Jewish communal and societal existence as well as to far-reaching modulations in European Jewish identity.[10]

How did the adaptation of Western state-building practices affect the Judeo-Spanish community? The answer varies according to the context, and distinctions have to be made between the areas remaining under Ottoman rule and others which progressively fell under the control of the new nation-states such as Greece, Serbia, and Bulgaria.

In the case of the Ottoman Empire, the reforms carried out were the product of measures of self-defense taken against an imperialist and aggressive Europe.[11] The Empire was in some ways pushed into a "modernization"/"Westernization" process which posed the problem inherent in this type of evolution: a conflict between East and West.[12] This characterized the Islamic world where state and religion were intertwined – a situation which placed the process in a conflictual setting from the start and raised the question of cultural identity. The process aroused opposition from the traditional strata of society and from elements within the state: "modernization" could be seen as a victory for the Infidel West, the age-old enemy, long regarded as inferior.

The military reforms carried out by Selim III (1789–1807) were extended to the administration and the state institutions after 1830, an evolution which culminated in the promulgation of the Constitution in 1876. Sultan Mahmud II (1808–39), drawing his inspiration from the model of Peter the Great, tried to institute a program of reforms after 1826, when the corps of janissaries was abolished. His successor introduced the second phase of reforms, the *Tanzimat*.

The Western powers wanted to equip the Empire with institutions capable of guaranteeing its integrity and their own economic interests. To this end, they forced the hands of the leaders in order to ensure the protection of Christian subjects. The Jews reaped the advantages of this policy although it was not designed for their benefit. The imperial rescript of Gülhane, promulgated on 3 November 1839, marked the starting point of the *Tanzimat*. It guaranteed security of life, honor, and property to all Ottoman subjects. It fixed a regular procedure for determining the basis, as well as the distribution, of taxation. It established a standard system for conscripting troops and the length of their service. It ensured a fair and public trial for persons accused of a crime and equality before the law in general for all subjects, irrespective of religion.[13] This last decision broke with Islamic tradition, which stressed the juridical and social inferiority of non-Muslims. It met with disapproval from traditionalist Muslims, who considered it contrary to the principles of religion and morality.[14]

A new decree, the Decree of Reform (*İslahat Fermanı*) *was promulgated on 18 February 1856.*[15] This decree was drawn up under pressure from the ambassadors of Great Britain, France, and Austria on the eve of the opening of the peace conference in Paris (1856) and confirmed the principles of the 1839 rescript. It once again guaranteed, but in more precise terms and in a more formal manner, the equality of all subjects of the Empire – which was confirmed yet again by the 1869 nationality law.[16] It also announced that admission to all public offices and to civil and military schools was open to everyone, irrespective of religion, as well as the creation of mixed courts. In addition, it abolished the payment of the poll tax by non-Muslims and opened military service to everybody – from which, however, exemption could be obtained on payment of a tax (*bedel-i askeri*). In fact, enrollment of non-Muslims in the army did not come about until 1909, following the Young Turk revolution (1908).

These reforms contained many contradictions. They flowed from the Empire's dependent position *vis-à-vis* the European powers, and therefore took place in a situation in which limited margin for maneuver was left to the Ottoman leaders. A closer look at the measures concerning non-Muslims shows that although on the one hand the *dhimma* became, for all intents and purposes, nonoperational, on the other, the quasi-autonomous mode of organization for non-Muslims not only continued to exist but was actually institutionalized between 1862 and 1865, the period during which the non-Muslim communities were granted organic statutes governing their administration. This institutionalization prevented integration, but also went hand in hand with the failure of the policy of Ottomanism proclaimed by the authorities attempting to establish common structures and to provide a point where the loyalty of all Ottoman citizens, irrespective of religion, language, or race, could converge.

Notwithstanding the autonomy which the rescript ensured to non-Muslim communities, the state intervened directly. It called on them to institute reforms, including the creation of mixed councils, composed of religious and "lay" elements, charged with administering temporal matters. These councils later played an important role in the new area of activity open to these religious groups, introducing a modern political perspective and gradually secularizing the communal sphere. The state also provided salaries to the leaders of these communities, thus strengthening its supervisory rights. The organic statutes defined the role of these leaders and made them Ottoman officials, as in the case of the Chief Rabbi of the Empire.

Reforms significantly eroded the legal autonomy of the Jewish community. After 1856, criminal, civil, and commercial cases had to be tried according to new codes introduced in the middle of the century. The French commercial and penal codes were adopted in 1850 and 1858 respectively and were to be valid for all subjects of the Empire, since they were not based on the principles of Muslim religious law. Non-Muslims still had the choice of continuing to appeal to their own courts in disputes relating to personal status, such as divorce and inheritance. On the other hand, the autonomy of the *millet* lost all semblance of reality in questions involving commercial, civil, or criminal law. The restructured community institutions were henceforth basically religious organizations and no longer enjoyed the relative legal autonomy which had been theirs in the centuries before the *Tanzimat*.[17] They incarnated and strengthened the foundations of ethnic difference on the ideological and symbolic plane, whereas their authority lost the real significance that it had enjoyed in earlier periods.

There were 150,000 Jews in the Empire between 1844 and 1856 (not including Jews of foreign nationality);[18] by the early twentieth century, their numbers had risen to more than 250,000, although the Empire had lost a large part of its European possessions.[19] Even if the *Tanzimat* measures had few concrete effects, they encouraged Westernized local élites to strike out in new directions with the collaboration of European Jewish élites who interpreted the reform in the light of their own experience of emancipation. As early as 1840, the blood libel at Damascus had drawn the eyes of Western Jewry – undergoing a process of radical social integration and acculturation – to its coreligionists in the East. The Crimean War (1853–6) strengthened this interest at a time when public discussions on the equality Europe was demanding for Christians in the Empire appeared not to include Jews. The Jewish leadership in the West mobilized to achieve equality for Ottoman Jews together with the Christians. Relations between

Eastern Sephardi Jewry and the West, which had weakened over the centuries, were thus revived and strengthened.

The reforming movement was checked when the 1876 Constitution, which might have transformed the Empire into a more democratic state, was cancelled a year after its proclamation. The Constitution recognized the equality of Jews before the law and a few Jews began to enter the state apparatus. Its abrogation marked the beginning of the absolutist reign of Abdulhamid II (1876–1909) which was not propitious to democratizing initiatives. On 23–24 July 1908 the Young Turks, opponents of the regime, came to power by a peaceful *coup d'état*. As they, too, wanted to transform the Empire into a modern, centralized state, they restored the abrogated Constitution. A wind of liberalism blew through the country. The Jews welcomed this change with enthusiasm. New opportunities emerged. Five Jewish deputies sat in the Ottoman parliament on the morrow of the Young Turk revolution and some gained important positions in the higher civil service. The Jews took advantage of the situation to attempt to restructure their community. Lay élites, extolling the virtues of reform, seized strategic positions. This was the period when the World Zionist Organization set up its local branch in Istanbul (1908), the first in the East. The context was one in which Jewish political groups were able to clash openly with one another, ushering in a period of change.[20]

The choices now offered by this new context, even if theoretical, were also a factor in new attitudes towards traditional authority. The opportunity to turn towards non-Jewish society was the result of this transition to a supposedly more open society.[21] This process affected only a minority, and in any case, did not remain on the agenda for long, as growing Turkish nationalism discouraged any inclination to integrate manifested by certain élite Jews.

Generally speaking, the number of non-Muslims, including Jews, holding relatively secondary positions in the Ottoman bureaucracy rose during the *Tanzimat*, and particularly after 1856. But this was far from being a significant phenomenon.[22] Only 99 of the 22,394 Jewish men living in Istanbul in 1885 were in state service.[23] Therefore, 0.44 percent of the Jewish male population was working for the state, as well as 0.38 percent of the Greeks, 0.58 percent of the Armenians, and 4.67 percent of the Catholics. The opportunity the Jews now had to enter state civil and military schools encouraged the formation of a small intellectual élite mixing in non-Jewish milieus. In 1847, 24 Jewish students attended the Imperial School of Medicine, founded in 1827 to train military doctors.[24] The first graduates in pharmacology, this time from the School of Civil Medicine, created in 1867, were Jews.[25] The names of other Jewish graduates appeared regularly in all lists of appointments between 1874 and

1902.[26] However, their numbers were small. Nevertheless, traditional Jewish authority could not be exerted on men who were pursuing such careers. Similar developments had taken place in Europe but on a larger scale. But the Ottoman Jews, even the most privileged, did not yet have the chance to fulfil themselves completely in the surrounding society, and the community for a long time remained their mainstay.

The Ottomanist reforms failed in the long run. Interference by Western powers, resistance by traditionalist Muslims as well as Christian nationalist élites in the Balkans, blunted any real progress. The state itself was remarkably slow in fields such as mass education, considered decisive in the forging of a united citizenry in Europe. A start was not made in opening secular Ottoman primary schools until 1869, and this too proceeded very slowly. Only 80 non-Muslims in the whole Empire attended these schools in 1895.[27] When, after 1908, the Young Turks made Turkicization their aim, it was already too late. The separate education systems of the different *millets* survived intact to the end of the Empire, despite various attempts to control them more closely. Few non-Muslim schools taught Turkish effectively and inculcated any deep loyalty to the Ottoman state.

In this continuing multi-ethnic and polyglot configuration, Turkicization did not emerge on the agenda for the Jews until the early twentieth century. Instead, the cultural arena was left open to the intervention of Western Jewry working closely with local élites.

WESTERNIZING STRATEGIES

The role of élites

The Damascus Affair of 1840 brought Western Jewry closer to Eastern Jews by forcing it to take action. The accusation of ritual murder that initiated the affair was one of a series of libels common in the Empire at that time. A Capuchin monk, Father Thomas, and his servant disappeared. They were never found. At the instigation of the French consul at Damascus, Ratti Menton, the crime was attributed to the Jews. A number of Jews were arrested, imprisoned, and tortured; some of them died as a result of mistreatment. Western public opinion took a close interest in the affair because of the political developments in the Near East, in which Europe was involved.[28] The press devoted numerous articles to the matter. Emancipated European Jewry could not fail to react to the resurgence of this type of libel, which it had thought belonged to the past. It was up to the emancipated Jews to defend the violated rights of their Eastern coreligionists who did not have the means to do so. The Rothschild family used its relationships to intervene with the various governments in the great cities of Europe.[29] The famous philanthropist, Sir Moses Montefiore, representing British Jews, the French communal leader, lawyer, and politician Adolphe Crémieux, and the orientalist scholar, Salomon Munk, representing French Jews, visited the viceroy of Egypt, Mohammed Ali, whose army was occupying Syria during the summer of 1840 and obtained the release of the Jewish prisoners. The delegates also extracted a decree from the sultan in Istanbul condemning accusations of ritual murder in general and prohibiting them in the Empire. The mobilization around this affair and the publicity given it point to a new type of political solidarity in the Jewish world, prepared to intervene when necessary, even in distant lands. This was institutionalized in 1860 by the creation of the Alliance Israélite Universelle (hereafter Alliance).

The Damascus Affair also gave a tremendous impetus to the expansion of the Jewish press. A total of 18 Jewish newspapers were published between 1835 and 1840; between 1841 and 1846, their number rose to 53, with 13 in five European countries. Some of the papers, such as the *Archives israélites* (1840) in France, *The Voice of Jacob* and *The Jewish Chronicle* (1841) in England, actually made their appearance in the heat of the Damascus Affair. This press played an important role in relaying news inside the Jewish world, bringing different communities into contact with one another and acting as a conduit for the circulation of ideas. It created a Jewish public opinion. It would later not only spread the major movements of ideas such as the *Haskalah*, the *Wissenschaft des Judentums*, Jewish nationalism, and Zionism, but also bring the leadership and cultural élites of different countries closer together.

These newspapers, helped by the Damascus Affair, accelerated the *rapprochement* between Jewish West and East. The first article on the Jews of the Levant had already been published in the paper *Allgemeine Zeitung des Judentums* in 1840, just before the affair.[30] Shortly afterwards, the newly launched *Archives israélites* published it in translation. The following year, letters from the Istanbul correspondent of the paper *Allgemeine Zeitung des Judentums* appeared in a summarized, translated form in *Archives israélites*.[31] Eastern Jewry was described in somber tones. Ignorance, superstition, intolerance, the undue influence wielded by rabbis, early marriage, the absence of any education worthy of the name, the nonexistence of craftsmen, and the lack of knowledge of foreign languages were many of the charges made against Eastern Jewry. These descriptions were couched in the language of exoticism. They denounced a way of life regarded as backward which in fact sent back a negative image to Western Jewry, by reminding it of its own past. Since the Jews of the West had "regenerated" themselves, there was no reason why the same results should not be attained in the East by using the proven methods of the past. These derived from the process of change and acculturation that Western Jewry itself had been undergoing. The Eastern Jew had to be given "the feeling of the dignity of man," and to that end, schools had to be opened or young local Jews sent to study in Europe. It was also emphasized that the local Jews were without influence and deprived of protection. In 1842, Algerian Jewry was subjected to the same criticism in the pages of a "Rapport sur l'état moral et politique des Israélites de l'Algérie et des moyens de l'améliorer,"[32] written by two delegates the French Jewish leadership sent there. Interest in Judaism in the lands of Islam grew continuously. Other articles on the subject appeared in the press over the years. The connection between the Eastern Question, the subject of so much debate in Europe at the time, and the interest in this Jewry cannot be doubted.

At the same time, the Damascus Affair contributed to the development of the press in the East, by creating a dynamic which drew its source from the *rapprochement* with the West. The role the Judeo-Spanish press played in the introduction of modernizing ideas is extremely significant. The first attempts go back to 1842, when the short-lived periodical *La Buena Esperansa* ("The Good Hope") was founded in Izmir. In 1845 came *La Puerta del Oriente* ("The Gate of the East"), a Judeo-Spanish periodical in Hebrew characters, again in Izmir, which lasted only a year.

The Jewish leaders in Europe, interpreting the local Ottoman reforms in the light of their own experience, assumed the right to intervene directly in the communities in order to adapt them to the new context. The next step was to set up local branches of various European Jewish institutions such as the Alliance. Much later, in the same vein, the *Hilfsverein der Deutschen Juden*, a German Jewish organization founded in 1901 for the improvement of the social and political conditions of the Jews of Eastern Europe and the Levant, developed a small network of schools in the Ottoman Empire, competing with the Alliance network. The World Zionist Organization was to follow the same path. Some of these political groups participated directly or indirectly in the French or German "civilizing missions" of contemporary European imperialism.

This interventionism could not have come about without the aid of local élites, favorably disposed to change and ready to associate themselves with the efforts of European Jews. Most of these were Francos who already benefited from the capitulations, privileges granted by the Ottoman sovereigns to subjects of European states, authorizing them to trade freely and to enjoy the advantages of fiscal exemption, as well as providing protection by European consuls. Some of them were already in contact with Western élites through their commercial activities, primarily in banking, but they also needed support from outside the Empire in order to strengthen their economic position and their political status in the Eastern communities. The Jewish West could be instrumental for this purpose. These Francos worked closely with the local Jewish bourgeoisie who shared the same interests. The latter imitated the Francos, and gave their children a similar European education. However, neither the foreign nor Ottoman local Jewish élites had either the means or the infrastructures necessary to ensure the education or the "productivization" of populations doomed to precarious conditions of life. Most Jews in the East did not have a skilled trade, and lacked the training which could have made them competitive in a changing market increasingly under the sway of European capitalism.[33] Greeks and Armenians had long since overtaken the Sephardim. The small Jewish élite needed a restructured economic base to make headway in sectors held by other ethnic groups in a local marketplace where a division of labor by ethnic group often prevailed.[34] As the state was not in a position to act decisively, the Jewish élites needed external support to begin the process of reforming the community. They pursued the same goals as Western Jewry with respect to the "regeneration" of Sephardi Jewry. This common aim made *rapprochement* easier.

When Sir Moses Montefiore visited Istanbul in 1840, on the morrow of the proclamation of the imperial rescript of Gülhane, he put pressure on the Chief Rabbinate to publish a declaration inviting all the schools in the Empire to introduce the teaching of Turkish into their curriculum. Direct collaboration between the two élites was established from 1854 when Albert Cohn, the emissary of the Rothschilds, set up a committee in Istanbul to found a school. Cohn had gone to the Ottoman capital to make sure that the sultan would include Jews in the rescript stipulating equality between Muslims and Christians.[35] The same year, the first Jewish school to include the teaching of foreign languages alongside Hebrew and Judeo-Spanish in its curriculum opened in Istanbul. Other schools were founded in Jerusalem and Izmir. Another French Jew, Alphonse de Rothschild from the Paris Central Consistory, who was present at the proclamation of the Reform Decree in 1856, persuaded the Chief Rabbi to send a circular to all the communities in the Empire outlining the reforms to be undertaken.[36] Dated March 7, 1856, the circular gave a predominant place to the Francos in community administration and educational work.[37] This intervention to the advantage of the Francos was a perfect illustration of the alliance between local élites and the Western Jewish leadership, an alliance which was to become institutionalized by the work of the Alliance Israélite Universelle a few years later.

The plans of these economic élites, composed of bankers, financiers, and rich merchants, converged with the aims of a few local intellectuals connected with the *Haskalah*, although the number of the latter must not be exaggerated. It is difficult to distinguish the external from the internal factors in the emergence of the *maskilim* (supporters of the Jewish Enlightenment), who played a crucial role in creating new types of schools in their respective communities. They included men such as Yuda Nehama (1825–99) from Salonika, called the "Turkish Mendelssohn,"[38] or Joseph Halevy (1827–1917) of Ashkenazi origin, active in Edirne, who subsequently became a famous orientalist in Paris, and intellectuals like the Salonikan journalist Saadi Bezalel Halevy (1820–1903). In the second half of the nineteenth century they were joined by other *maskilim*, such as Barukh ben Yizhak Mitrani (1847–1919), Abraham Danon (1857–1925), who supported the Alliance projects, and Elie Isaac Navon (1857–1952), a poet and journalist. During the editorship of Nahum Sokolow (1859–1936), the future Zionist leader, Navon published various articles in the Warsaw Hebrew paper *Hazefirah* ("The Dawn," 1862–1931), close to *Haskalah* circles.[39] He worked for the rebirth of the Hebrew language and associated himself with the schemes of Eliezer Ben Yehuda (1858–1922), one of the founders of modern Hebrew.[40]

Improved means of communication forged ties between intellectuals in diverse lands and contributed to the emergence of similar values.[41] This was also to be true in the Judeo–Spanish context. The correspondence between the *maskil* Yuda Nehama and other *maskilim* in Western and Eastern Europe was significant in this respect.[42] His contemporaries and their successors maintained these contacts and succeeded in spreading the major ideas of the Jewish world and in making foreign works accessible to the public by translating them into the vernacular.

The machinery for change already existed in embryo in the Jewish bourgeoisie which was open to the West. Franco notables such as the Salonikan financier Moïse Allatini, Salomon Fernandez (honorary Italian consul in the same city), and others founded the first schools, even before the establishment of Alliance institutions. The close collaboration between Moïse Allatini and the *maskil* Yuda Nehama in attempting to create a modern educational system in Salonika once again demonstrated some of the common interests shared by the two groups. Albert Cohn's journeys in 1854 and 1856 hastened the creation of modern educational establishments in various cities, but the Francos were not content merely to follow the impetus coming from the outside. They also tried to reform what already existed, starting with the traditional infrastructure.

These wealthy bankers not only encouraged *maskilic* creation but also made the necessary arrangements for the realization of their plans. The *Kupat Hesed Olam* society (Mutual Welfare Fund), which taxed Jewish merchants on their transactions in order to reform community institutions, was founded in Salonika in 1853 under the sponsorship of Moïse Allatini.[43] Some years later, this body brought a young rabbi from Strasbourg to reform the existing *Talmud Torah* and to give evening classes in foreign languages and arithmetic. This sort of initiative became very frequent. In 1880, Moses Jacob Ottolenghi (1840–1901) was summoned from Livorno to introduce Turkish, Italian, and arithmetic into the syllabus of the same *Talmud Torah*. This desire to ally tradition and modernity within the existing structures did not disappear. In 1908 Isaac Epstein (1862–1943) was appointed to head the same institution. This important teacher, founder of the method of teaching Hebrew in Hebrew, played a considerable role in the rebirth of the language and the advancement of the "national" cause in Salonika. The *Kupat Hesed Olam* society, which was dissolved in 1861, also subsidized the cost of a new school founded by the Francos and run by the same Strasbourg rabbi brought over to reform the Salonika *Talmud Torah*. This school, which taught French and Turkish, soon closed for lack of funds. Similar experiments took place elsewhere.

These attempts at opening up to the outside world caused a stir among the traditionalist rabbis and their supporters in the communities. The rabbis were not only afraid of losing their livelihood which relied heavily on teaching within the framework of the *meldars* (religious primary schools equivalent to the *heder* in the Ashkenazi world). They were also afraid of losing their ascendency in the wake of the Westernization and secularization which would accompany the development of a European type of education. Judging by the violent reactions in their ranks which these schemes provoked, it is clear that they grasped fully the meaning of the changes being instituted. The local Jewish establishment also mistrusted the growing influence enjoyed by the Francos. Given their status as foreigners, they were not bound to comply with community requirements and thus avoided its control. The collusion between Western Jewish leadership and the Francos was clearly evident in Alphonse de Rothschild's circular. The reforming aims it expressed undermined the prerogatives of the local ruling group.

Many of these factors were in full evidence in the initial conflicts between religious and lay factions.[44] The pretext for one of the most famous confrontations was the school opened by Cohn in Istanbul, which the banking family Camondo – called "the Rothschilds of the East" – and Francos themselves, took charge of in 1858. The struggle between the ultraconservative rabbinate and the reformers became public. The school and those associated with it were excommunicated. Eventually the semblance of a compromise emerged. In the interim, Jacob Avigdor, sympathetic to the reformers, was appointed Chief Rabbi of the Empire in 1860.[45] He immediately formed an assembly of lay administrators, headed by Abraham de Camondo, the conservatives' target. The conservative ranks, on the defensive since the 1858 incident, were not slow to react to this takeover of community affairs by the secular faction. The conflict resumed in 1862 with the conservatives calling for the dismissal of the reformist Chief Rabbi and excommunicating Camondo.[46] The masses became involved in the affair, whose dimensions grew. The same trends were also in evidence at the same time in the Greek and Armenian communities. Significantly, the two warring Jewish groups were called *loussavorial* (enlightened) and *khavarial* (obscurantist), names borrowed from the disputing parties in the Armenian community.[47] The state eventually intervened to settle the conflict in favor of the reformers.[48] Later, however, following the conservatives' complaint to the government, a decree by the Sublime Porte disqualified Jews of foreign nationality from leadership in community affairs. In 1862, the Francos founded a separate "Italian" community with its own synagogue and administration.[49] They had come to the conclusion that it was impossible or at least premature to reform from inside a community still in the grip of the traditionalist rabbinate.

It was again the Francos who turned to the Alliance and requested that it found schools in the large Jewish centers of the Empire. They were seconded by the *maskilim*. The regional committee of the Alliance, founded in Istanbul in 1863, was in fact composed of Francos and foreign Jews associated with the establishment of Cohn's school in 1854. The opposition which the Alliance encountered from the conservative camp locally, in Bulgaria for example, was again considerable.[50] In fact, the élites recruited from among the Francos aimed to seize power and with the aid of their Western counterparts embark upon Westernizing reform. The strengthening of this leadership encroached upon the traditionalist leaders. The latter fought to retain their positions but eventually were to retire from the fray in defeat. These same élites did not come into contact with the West solely through its Jewish representatives. During the period of the rise in Freemasonry in the Ottoman Empire, between 1850 and 1875 and in the years which followed, their members were already present among the founders and members of Masonic lodges in towns such as Istanbul and Salonika.[51] The Grand Orient of France and Italy lodge was active in the city alongside English, Greek, and German lodges. In Salonika, where the Sephardim were in the majority, Francos, bankers, and merchants were prominent in these anticlerical, liberal lodges which were influenced by positivism. The Jewish intellectual élite also became involved. The links these groups had with Freemasonry were both a symptom and a vehicle of change, eroding the circumscribed frontiers of the Jewish community and contributing to links between Muslims and non-Muslims, even if these relationships were not always harmonious and reflected the intercommunal conflicts endemic to the Ottoman world.

Within the Jewish community, the top echelons of Jewish society, essentially composed of Francos but also including a certain number of Ottoman Sephardim, were the main beneficiaries of the changes in the Ottoman economy during the nineteenth century. Western industrial powers, such as Britain, France, Austria-Hungary, and Germany came to dominate the economy of the Levant, flooding local markets with European manufactured products and becoming the main consumers of raw materials such as cereals, cotton, and tobacco. The Anglo-Ottoman trade agreement of 1838, which lowered the Empire's customs tariffs and removed restrictions on the free movement of goods within the Empire, was one of the first measures to open up this region to Western products. It was followed by similar treaties with other countries. The Ottoman state embarked upon reform, and needing new technical skills to reform its army, was increasingly dependent on European know-how and equipment, but at the same time, it proved incapable of putting its house in order and maximizing its revenues by introducing a rationalized and efficient fiscal system. Its weak position made it particularly vulnerable to European interference and exploitation. Increased expenditure at the time of the Crimean War, along with a foolhardy deficit policy and the floating of successive loans, culminated in the bankruptcy of the Empire in 1875. In the 1880s Western economic interests institutionalized the administration of the Ottoman public debt, controlling the revenues from certain key sectors of the economy. The Empire had virtually become a semi-colony.[52]

The volume of trade increased in leaps and bounds, particularly when steamships came into regular use after the Crimean War. Between the 1870s and the end of the century, railways connected major centers with the hinterland and with Europe, facilitating and considerably increasing the transport of goods. Many modest craft workshops, guilds, and small trades could not hold out against competition from the cheap mass imports and collapsed, while others succeeded in adapting and thriving. In the commercial and financial sectors, the traditional middlemen, particularly Greeks and Armenians, and to a small extent Jews, took advantage of the new economic climate and managed to strengthen their key position between local and international markets.

Some influential figures still succeeded in amassing considerable fortunes in the traditionally Jewish areas, such as finance. Abraham de Camondo managed to rise from the classic status of *sarraf* to become a modern banker. He played an important role in financing the Ottoman effort during the Crimean War and maintained close relations with European banks. The

Camondos held an important place in the financial life of the capital until the 1890s.[53]

Nevertheless, it was relatively rare to find personalities of this stature in the mid-nineteenth century. For the majority of the Sephardim in the Empire, the situation was very difficult. Descriptions by travelers and journalists, and later by the Alliance teachers, paint a gloomy picture of the economic situation of the Jewish masses throughout this period.[54] Most lacked any real professional training and lived in poverty. A small group of notables held power in strongly polarized communities, which were sometimes torn by serious class conflicts, as was the case in Izmir on several occasions during the nineteenth century.[55]

The increased economic activity which accompanied European domination of the Ottoman market, in conjunction with the growing knowledge of French and of European ways, principally through the Alliance schools, came to improve the lot of certain sections of the Jewish population in large towns by the first decade of the twentieth century. It is hard to find reliable statistical data to support this, but all evidence indicates a certain upward mobility.[56] The ranks of the Jewish middle class, now increasingly Francophone, expanded to include not only merchants and small businessmen, but also white-collar workers such as bookkeepers in Jewish and European firms, bank employees and administrators. The liberal professions, doctors, pharmacists, and lawyers, were also beginning to appear, even if only on a very modest scale.[57] New trades appeared among craftsmen. However, there could be no radical transformation of this milieu as long as it remained exposed to the crises provoked by the wave of low-priced European finished products which flooded the local market, and as long as the ethnic division of labor continued to impede the acquisition of new skills.[58]

Not until the First World War did Jewish women leave the domestic world to enter the tertiary sector – and then in very limited numbers. The mass mobilization of the male population at that time encouraged this entry. Although a few Jewish women had begun to work outside the home as secretaries, switchboard operators, and shop girls in large towns such as Istanbul in the first decade of the twentieth century,[59] the great majority of the active female workforce consisted of poor young girls, mainly employed by the *Régie des tabacs* processing tobacco and manufacturing cigarettes.[60] Others still worked in the home as maids, dressmakers, and embroideresses. In Muslim sectors of the Sephardi culture area, under the influence of an environment which long continued to disapprove of women going out to work, the Jewish woman remained confined to her home.

Generally speaking, even though some advance can be noted in the economic position of the Jewish communities during the first decade of the twentieth century, it was not spectacular, and the Jews continued to lag behind the Greeks and Armenians until the end of the Empire. These two communities had diversified economic foundations; they included a broad peasant base alongside a large artisanal class, and possessed dynamic business leaders who were well placed to take advantage of the new opportunities. Jews were not dominant in the economy anywhere except in Salonika.

The port of this city went through a rapid economic and social evolution in the second half of the nineteenth century. This boom town tied with Beirut to become the third port of the Ottoman Empire and the volume of goods passing through it rose from one to two million tons between 1880 and 1912.[61] At the turn of the century, Salonika was connected by rail to Bosnia and Serbia and from there to Vienna, as well as to Istanbul. Until the 1870s, the city still exported raw wool and cotton from its hinterland, but it subsequently began to develop industrial infrastructures, with small factories supplying Macedonia and Ottoman markets with flannel, knitted goods, and wool and cotton products. Nevertheless, the export of cotton, hides, silkworms, and wool continued to represent an important part of its economic activity.[62] Turkey in Europe was transformed into an important tobacco-producing area – production rose 250 percent between 1892 and 1909.[63] The main tobacco-growing center was in northern Greece, near Cavalla, but Salonika was the hub of the tobacco trade, as well as an important center for tobacco processing and cigarette manufacture.

The growth of economic activity in the city, the establishment there of hundreds of European firms doing business in the Levant, and its rail and steamship connections with the major European centers of communication, all helped to improve the situation of the Jewish community. The old Franco élite, composed of families such as the Allatinis, Fernandez, Modianos, Morpurgos, Saias, and Torrès, rose to new heights. The Allatinis gained particular renown in international trade and banking. With the Modianos, they had hitherto operated in the cereal trade and in flour production, building a modern flour mill in 1857. They extended their activities to the tobacco trade, built a modern brickyard, and opened the Bank of Salonika in association with foreign partners.[64] The Jewish firm of Capandji, Jehiel and Bensussan set up a cloth factory in 1911, and Modiano and Fernandez created the famous Olympos distillery.[65] Of the large businesses in the town at this period, 38 were Jewish, most of them specializing in the import–export trade.[66] There were hundreds of smaller Jewish enterprises in every sector of the Salonikan economy and thousands of Jewish white-collar workers employed in Jewish and European firms.

The expansion in Salonikan industry resulted in the formation of the only important proletariat in the Sephardi world. It was mainly concentrated in the tobacco industry, though it was also to be found in other areas.

It numbered approximately 10,000 persons at the beginning of the twentieth century. The new class of factory workers coexisted alongside the old type of craftsmen and groups such as the Jewish porters and fishermen who were present in very large numbers in the town.[67]

Notwithstanding the overall improvement in the economic situation of the Jewish community in Salonika, there were still many Jews who were poor. Poverty was endemic to Sephardi life in the Levant in the contemporary era. In 1911, some 6,000 Jewish families in Salonika out of an estimated total of 13,000 families received some form of assistance from community benevolent societies.[68] Nevertheless, by the end of Ottoman rule, a substantial middle class had emerged. All our sources tend to show that the Jews (61,439 persons out of a total population of 157,889 souls according to the first Greek census in 1913)[69] clearly dominated economic life in Salonika.

The other Judeo-Spanish communities in the Levant certainly did not experience the same economic progress. Local circumstances were different. There were many more Greeks and Armenians in towns such as Istanbul and Izmir and they occupied many of the key positions in the economy of these centers. In Istanbul in 1885, for example, Jews represented 5.59 percent of the active population, and 5.24 percent of the population that worked in trade, craft, and industry.[70] Greeks and Armenians, on the other hand, formed 22.52 percent and 20.58 percent respectively of the active population, and 25.41 percent and 26.99 percent of the population working in trade, craft, and industry.[71] Muslims for their part were underrepresented, forming 49.4 percent of the active population but only 38.32 percent of the population working in trade, craft, and industry.[72]

In 1900, the position held by Jews in relation to other non-Muslims had scarcely changed. That year, Jews represented 17 percent of the total non-Muslim population of the town but only 13 percent of the population engaged in trade, 6 percent of the liberal professions, and 3 percent of industrial trades.[73]

Even if no community was destined to attain heights comparable to Salonika, there is hardly any doubt that the opening up to the West and the growing involvement in European interests contributed to an improvement of the Jews' economic position in the Empire in general. The acquisition by a large part of the community of a European language, French in particular, the lingua franca of trade in the Levant, contributed to the rise of an Ottoman Jewish bourgeoisie – hitherto relatively underdeveloped – within the mainly non-Muslim trading circles, who acted as intermediaries between the local market and the outside world. This accomplishment was linked directly to the work of the Alliance Israélite Universelle, assisted by the class of local notables and Francos.

The Alliance Israélite Universelle

The main task of providing the masses in Sephardi lands with a Western education fell to the Alliance, even if other European missionary and secular schools had a share in the process. Founded by French Jews in Paris in 1860, it represented Western Jewry's urge to reform its coreligionists in the East. It was famed for its defense of the rights of Jews throughout the world. But its real work was in education.

The Alliance's intellectual origins lie in the wider European Jewish movement of *Haskalah*. The latter argued for a better integration of Jews through the reforming of Jewish society and culture in conformity with modern European civilization. For the century preceding the foundation of the Alliance, the themes that were the hallmark of the *Haskalah*, such as the critique of traditional rabbinical Judaism, and the call for modern education and a transformation of Jewish social structure through the spread of manual trades, had all been widely discussed. For the Alliance, this social emancipation had to proceed in tandem with legal emancipation. Deeply marked by the French–Jewish path to modernity, the Alliance became a central conduit for the diffusion of these ideas in the Sephardi world. According to its ideology of emancipation, Jewish solidarity called for the remaking of "backward" Jewries in the image of modern Franco-Jewry. Hence, its massive educational endeavor to establish French–Jewish schools throughout the Middle East and North Africa.

The educational work of the Alliance began in Tetuan, in Morocco, in 1862, and culminated in the opening of primary, and then secondary, schools for Jewish boys and girls throughout North Africa and the Middle East. In 1913, it encompassed a network of 183 institutions attended by 43,700 pupils, covering an area which stretched from Morocco in the West to Iran in the East. Generations of Sephardim received their education in Alliance institutions, which provided them with an essentially French education with the addition of Jewish subjects such as Jewish history, religious instruction, and Hebrew. The Alliance thus played an important role in the Westernizing process of Sephardi Jewry.[74]

The first school founded on Ottoman soil, in the heart of a Judeo-Spanish culture area, was in Volos, Greece, in 1865. It was followed by similar establishments in Edirne, in Turkey, in 1867, and Shumla (Shumen), in Bulgaria, in 1870. Alliance schools for boys and girls were founded in Istanbul, Izmir, and Salonika in the 1870s. In 1911, 9,441 pupils attended such institutions inside the frontiers of present-day Turkey.[75] In Salonika, some 10,000 persons had passed through Alliance schools from the time they were created until the First World War.[76] In 1912, every Judeo-Spanish community of around 1,000 souls possessed at least one Alliance school.

These schools were slowly accepted by the local communities, often after initial difficulties. They eventually became quite popular and all of them mustered substantial numbers of pupils. As has already been noted, the Sephardi populations of the region were under pressure from local forces who, favorably disposed to such activities, often even invited the Alliance to found schools in a given location well before it would have dreamed of doing so. Active support came from local notables who were as aware as the Francos and *maskilim* of the need for Jews to acquire new skills in order to withstand Greek and Armenian competition. The deep-seated poverty of the communities softened the resistance of the more traditional sectors. Many of these schools gradually integrated into the life of the community, often receiving small subsidies from its constituent bodies.

For the first time in the history of Sephardi Jewry, girls also attended school in large numbers.[77] In the local context this was a true revolution. Traditionally, Sephardi girls were kept away from any formal education. The process of Westernization had everything to gain from the education which young Judeo-Spanish girls received in the Alliance schools and which they, in their turn, passed on to the next generation.

The Alliance's institutions grew at an accelerating pace by the turn of the century. Large centers such as Istanbul, Izmir, Salonika, and Sofia came to have several Alliance establishments, with a few dispensing a full secondary education. With the addition of vocational courses such as apprenticeship programs and bookkeeping classes, as well as the creation of youth clubs, alumni associations, libraries, and mutual-aid groups, a whole network of institutions came to be clustered around the major schools. The language used in all these establishments was French, even though Hebrew was not ignored (it was taught primarily to enable the pupils to read and understand the Bible and the prayer book).

The Ottoman Empire remained the favorite arena for Alliance activities. In a weakened state, colonized economically by the European powers, there was no risk of the Alliance schools meeting major difficulties from the authorities. Although the Alliance was theoretically aiming at the masses, its pupils also came from the middle classes. The Alliance's schoolmasters and schoolmistresses were the emissaries of Westernization. What infiltrated the local populations was not so much its ideology of emancipation as the Western education and receptivity to the West that it promoted. By adopting French ways, the small middle class was the first to benefit from this schooling. It needed foreign languages to obtain work in a market which was increasingly dominated by Europe and where the new economic issues transcended local frameworks. By picking and choosing among the repertory of ideas and trends brought by the Alliance, the local populations came to establish a balance between the old and the new.[78] Local conditions led ineluctably to this development, since the imported Western model of Jewish emancipation did not fit into the local circumstances.

The work of the Alliance Israélite Universelle in the Sephardi and oriental Jewish communities depended almost exclusively on the activities of the schools' teachers and directors. While they had to supervise the daily functioning of the educational system, they were very much more than ordinary pedagogues. They represented the Alliance locally, provided it with almost daily information on events which might concern it, protected the Jewish community by intervening with the authorities on its behalf, and also endeavored to change the community by encouraging the process of Westernization in every form. It is worth noting in particular that this teaching body, working for the Westernization of local Jewish populations, was itself composed mainly of Jews from North Africa and the Middle East. They had been trained by the Alliance in Paris, at its *Ecole normale israélite orientale* (ENIO), and had then returned to spread their newly acquired culture with all the enthusiasm of neophytes. The Alliance teachers thus formed one of the first autochthonous Westernized intellectual elites among the Jews in Muslim lands. The majority of the 403 teachers who were trained in Paris between 1869 and 1925 on whom information is available, were born in the Ottoman Empire and particularly in the Judeo-Hispano-phone area comprising present-day Turkey, Greece, and Bulgaria. This Judeo-Spanish culture area alone provided almost 60 percent of the teaching body. The figure rises to 70 percent in the case of women teachers.[79] The teaching staff, many serving the Alliance for decades, formed the backbone of its educational network.[80] Many teachers, upon leaving the service, became notables, journalists, heads of communities, and politicians, forming a compact group of Westernized elements capable of working in close association with local *maskilim* and the ruling élites of the communities.[81]

During the first decade of the twentieth century, the Alliance exercised an enormous influence on the Judeo-Spanish centers. Of course, its schools did not embrace the whole school age population. In Bulgaria in 1901, they contained 3,890 pupils as compared with 1,938 in Jewish community schools (boys and girls combined).[82] In Istanbul in 1905, 30.21 percent of Jewish boys attended Alliance schools.[83] Figures show that 1,808 girls were registered at these Alliance institutions, against 1,420 boys, while 1,470 children (boys in fact) continued to receive their education in the *meldars*, with a further 570 in small private schools; 500 children of both sexes attended the Protestant school, and almost the same number French Catholic schools.[84] In Salonika in 1908, the Jewish community schools took in 1,849 pupils, the Alliance schools 2,132, Jewish private schools, where the standard was considered to be mediocre, 3,250 pupils, while foreign schools, Turkish and later Greek, had between them a total of 1,300 pupils.[85]

The traditional *Talmudei Torah* survived for a long time. Nevertheless, the Alliance's activities also had an impact there. After many abortive attempts, it eventually managed to merge these establishments with its own schools or to introduce substantial reforms; it taught French, for example, by means of appointing one of the society's teachers as headmaster of a *Talmud Torah*. As a result, the Alliance's influence was not limited to its schools, but came to affect and alter the rapidly declining traditional education system.[86]

This influence varied from region to region depending on the importance of the more traditional type of school and the opportunities available in other educational establishments. The Alliance schools reached a considerable number of children who attended them for longer or shorter periods in one district or another. On average, most attended for three years.[87] It is hard to imagine that the Alliance's ideology could make an impact in such a short space of time. Children from affluent and middle-class homes stayed at school longer, while the rest acquired no more than a smattering of reading and writing, and those who left school after a year were as ignorant as when they entered. Most of the future "progressive" community leaders, some of whom rallied to the Zionist cause at the beginning of the twentieth century, had been through Alliance schools at some point in their educational careers.

The Alliance was not content solely to educate the young, but also wanted to teach it new trade skills. It also created new areas for educational and post-educational socialization which accelerated the process of change. The network of associations it set up turned it into an alternative area for politicization, making the Alliance an important pressure group which took its position on the political chequer-board of the community alongside other groups, such as the *Hilfsverein der Deutschen Juden*, the World Zionist Organization and B'nai B'rith,[88] which founded lodges in the Ottoman capital from 1911.

By taking over some of the prerogatives of the modern nation-state, such as education, the Alliance was at the same time replacing anemic community institutions. Those responsible for them did not take kindly to this intrusion. The "Alliancists" (leaders connected to the Alliance), many of whom were recruited from among the Francos, organized themselves on the periphery of the community leadership. The Young Turk revolution in the Empire and the selection of the Alliance's man, Haim Nahum, to head Ottoman Jewry, moved these notables to the center of power together with their protégé after 1908.[89] These men differed from their predecessors in their openness to modern ideas and their desire to see them realized locally, but they were not fundamentally different. In their class interests and management methods they rapidly came to resemble the conservative lay cadres who had hitherto supported the rabbis. Unlike the situation at the time of the 1858–65 conflicts, when rabbis had been their main protagonists, this time they had to meet opposition from both rabbis and conservative laymen. However, some of these "progressive" notables had previously sat alongside the conservatives and as soon as they seized power they in turn became conservatives. They did not cherish any fundamentally innovative social plans; they had used Westernization and the Alliance as a springboard to gain power. It was not enough to want to reform the communities. The new leaders had also to be able to develop and maintain structures capable of absorbing these changes.[90] These prevaricating notables, occupying themselves with community affairs in their spare time, were in no position to implement the policy demanded by the new situation of relative democratization which the Ottoman Empire experienced after the 1908 revolution. Other political pressure groups, also from abroad, took advantage of this context to take up their positions in the communal arena.

The only truly legitimate political area for Ottoman Jews remained their community. This was limited and subject to oligarchical administration; it offered no great opportunity for access to power. Those who held power guarded it jealously, all the more so because possession of community power generally set the seal on the Jewish notable's social ascent. By its very structure, the oligarchical system could not permit political pluralism. However, the Young Turk revolution, by ending the absolutism of the previous regime, inaugurated the era of open politicization. The Jews did not fail to follow these changes and engage in politics themselves.[91]

These winds of change also affected the Alliance establishments. Already before the First World War, their bourgeois clientele had gradually started to look elsewhere. Other institutions, whether missionary establishments or secular schools, had begun to attract the upper middle and middle-class Jewish students who were interested in a more extensive secondary education which the Alliance, concerned about the plight of the poor, was relatively late in developing. Hence in 1912, while there were 3,700 students in AIU schools in Salonica, 1,100 were attending that of the French *Mission Laïque*.[92] The numbers for the Alliance schools in Salonika had fallen to about 1,300 by 1927.[93] In Istanbul, other French and German schools had begun to have a substantial number of Jewish students in the years before the First World War, and slowly but steadily, the increased opening of secular Turkish secondary education institutions began to offer new opportunities for Jews.[94] The B'nai B'rith Jewish Lycée, opened in

Istanbul in 1915, also offered a complete secondary education in French, and was successful in attracting students away from the Alliance.

Nevertheless, most mass education in the Judeo-Spanish communities continued to take place in Alliance schools or in Alliance run or influenced *Talmudei Torah* until the end of the First World War. The great exception to this rule was in Bulgaria. Here, the new nation-state context and the growing politicization in the Jewish public sphere contributed to ending the Alliance experiment. As will be explained below, political developments within communities led to the Zionists' domination of communal councils and of the schools in the first decade of the twentieth century. Hebrew and Bulgarian replaced French, and by the First World War, the Alliance had lost almost all of its institutions in the country.

Apart from contributing to the upward social mobility of significant numbers of Jews through education, the Alliance was instrumental in bringing about a major cultural reorientation of the Levant Sephardim. The generations of Jews who attended its schools came to admire France and French culture, and many became fully Francophone. Indeed, with the exception of the Maronites, the Sephardim were the only group in the Levant to adopt a foreign language as the language of instruction in their institutions of mass education. While Turks, Greeks, Armenians, and others often attended French schools or learnt French and other European languages through the process of Westernization that was sweeping the Levant in the second half of the nineteenth century, no groups other than the Maronites and the Sephardim came to have a mass education system in French.

The consequences of this development were manifold. French and French culture became referents for the Eastern Sephardim, especially for the middle and upper classes. Substantial numbers adopted the language as the medium of cultural and intellectual life. The Jewish community became even more polyglot with the massive incursion of the new language. Like Sephardi Jews in North Africa, the Jews of the Levant made French a major part of their cultural baggage in the twentieth century.

However, this was not necessarily a transparent, unmediated process. The Alliance did not simply dispense a new culture which was then adopted wholesale by the recipients. Like the larger phenomenon of Westernization itself, Gallicization represented a complex spectrum. A small minority took the matter to its logical conclusion and, also motivated by economic goals, began to emigrate to France from the first decade of the twentieth century onwards. However, this was not an option for the vast majority of the Eastern Sephardim who stayed put. The ideology of emancipation they imbibed in the Alliance schools proved to be largely irrelevant in a Levant where group distinctiveness remained paramount and the equality of citizenship problematic. The new education that opened them to the larger world in general and to the Jewish world in particular, especially through the acquisition of a European language, prepared the ground for a complex politicization process which for many resulted in a growing receptivity to Jewish nationalism.

In the final analysis, the acquisition of French proved to be the most direct and long-lasting result of the Alliance interlude in the history of Eastern Sephardi Jewry. However, in the local context of persistent ethnic identities, this did not lead to a weakening of Judeo-Spanish ethnicity and to "assimilation" to France. The very opposite happened. The boundaries of Judeo-Spanish ethnicity shifted, and appropriated, coopted, domesticated, and Judeo-Hispanicized French. The very fact of speaking French (in a distinctive local accent common to all Eastern Sephardim) became yet another marker of Sephardi distinctiveness. The slow growth of the educational infrastructure of the Ottoman Empire and its successor states, which was preceded by the establishment of the Alliance institutions among the Sephardi communities, impeded the effectiveness of any assimilatory drive from the state until well into the twentieth century. By then, the new cultural topography of the Eastern Sephardim had already been formed and was working to dissociate the communities culturally from their local moorings.

Cultural Westernization in the Judeo-Spanish heartland overdetermined a process of change that separated the Jewish communities from the culture that the rulers slowly imposed on their subjects. The polyglot Judeo-Spanish communities were singularly ill-prepared to meet the new nation-state that was to become the norm in the Balkans by the twentieth century. All the Alliance schools in Turkey, Greece, and Yugoslavia (in Macedonia) were to be "nationalized" in the 1920s and 1930s. Nevertheless, the half-century Alliance dominance in most Judeo-Spanish communities considerably complicated the response of the Eastern Sephardim to the irruption of the nation-state, which carved up irrevocably the old Judeo-Spanish center that had remained a single unit during four centuries of Ottoman rule.

THE SEPHARDIM CONFRONT THE NATION-STATE

With the massive shift of frontiers in the nineteenth century, Sephardim who had previously lived in the Ottoman Empire came under the rule of different states, but the majority of them still continued to be subjects of the Ottoman regime. Serbia, with the important Sephardi center of Belgrade, broke away from the Empire and from 1830 became an autonomous province under Ottoman suzerainty. It held between 2,000 and 3,000 Jews.[95] When Alexander Karageorgevitch (1842–58) came to power in 1842, anti-Jewish laws were promulgated. Laws passed in 1846 and 1861 prohibited Jews from owning land and trading in Serbian provinces. This was followed by expulsions from rural Serbia.[96] Even though Belgrade, where half the Jewish population of the country lived, was not directly touched by these measures, their effects were considerable.[97] The Serb Constitution of 1869 guaranteed the freedom and individual rights of all Serb citizens, but the Jews had not yet gained full civil rights even though they continued to be recruited into the army.[98]

The year 1878 proved to be the turning point for these Sephardi communities. Whereas the Treaty of Berlin granted the Balkan states new territories and new status, the Jews of these regions found champions among their Western coreligionists, in particular the Alliance Israélite Universelle, which sent delegates to Berlin to work for their emancipation.[99]

Articles 5, 20, 27, 34, 35, 43, and 44 of the Treaty of Berlin directly concerned Jews.[100] The European powers recognized the independence of Serbia and Rumania, on condition that the equality of all religions before the law was introduced into the legislation of these countries. The same principles later served as the basis for the constitutions of Bulgaria, Eastern Rumelia, and Montenegro.

There was no lack of resistance to these conditions. They were opposed bitterly in Eastern Rumelia. In Serbia, the Jews had to wait until 1888 for definitive recognition of their civil rights in the new Constitution guaranteeing complete equality to all inhabitants of the kingdom.[101] The Jews achieved complete civil equality after 1918. When the "Kingdom of the Serbs, Croats, and Slovenes" was created in the same year, Jews were regarded as a religious minority and were given the right to establish, manage, and control their own charitable, educational, and religious institutions, with the opportunity to use their own language and practice their religion freely.

When studying the configuration in the region which later became Yugoslavia, a distinction has to be drawn between the Sephardi and Ashkenazi populations. The Sephardim inhabited the poor regions in the South and East, Serbia, Bosnia-Herzegovina, Macedonia; the Ashkenazim lived in the North of the country, in Croatia and Vojvodina. The unification of the South Slav lands after the Great War brought the two communities into contact. The two elements were already living side by side in some large towns, without truly mingling. The Ashkenazi communities, particularly those in the North from the Hungarian or German spheres of influence, while containing important ultra-Orthodox pockets, had mostly undergone an emancipation and acculturation process similar to the model current in Western and Central Europe. The Sephardim, on the other hand, were not necessarily acculturating, with variations depending on the environment and on the area of settlement. Acculturation was interpreted differently according to generation and class affiliation. In centers with large concentrations of Sephardim, the East versus West, the modernization versus tradition conflict, crystallized around the Sephardi–Ashkenazi dichotomy, the Ashkenazim representing the outside world, the West, and the foreigner.

In the multi-ethnic, Christian, and Western-oriented South Slav lands, a relative degree of integration was achieved without loss of identity. If this phenomenon is compared with what occurred in the Ottoman Empire, the differences are obvious. To be good Yugoslavians did not prevent these Sephardim from claiming to be good Jews as well. In the Empire a person was defined first by religion, while here the Jew could claim national membership parallel with religious affiliation (like a Slovene who could claim both Slovene and Yugoslav identities), which was itself formally recognized. It was to this that the Zionists in Yugoslavia attached themselves when they demanded the recognition of the Jews as a national minority after the Great War. On another score, the absence of the Alliance from most of the community scene (except for Bitola [Monastir] and Skopje [Uskub] in Macedonia) removed the option of Frenchification, and this favored a smoother integration.

The Jewish community of Belgrade, the majority of whom were Sephardim, increased from 2,599 in 1890 to 4,844 in 1921, and then to 7,906 in 1931.[102] The growth in the Jewish population was part of the demographic growth of the whole city. On the eve of the Second World War, there were more than 10,000 Jews, comprising 8,500 Sephardim and 1,888 Ashkenazim. This increase was due to immigration to the capital by native inhabitants from other parts of the country, to the improvement in living conditions and the resultant security, and to the fall in the death rate linked to better hygiene.[103] The Sephardi birth rate was higher than the Ashkenazi but fell considerably between 1899 and 1939. Sarajevo, under Austro-Hungarian rule, also experienced significant demographic growth, the number of Sephardim rising from 2,618 to 4,985 between 1885 and 1910.[104]

From the second half of the nineteenth century, Serbo-Croat and German were introduced into the curriculum of Jewish schools, which allowed those who wished to continue their studies in state schools. It became increasingly common for Jewish children to attend the latter. The absence of Alliance schools in these regions made the transition easier. Towards the end of the century, the progressive secularization of education encouraged mobility towards new areas of activity, including the tertiary sector and the liberal professions. In Serbia, Jewish schools were not state-maintained but only subsidized. Jews had the right to establish kindergartens and primary schools.

With growing nationalism, and under pressure from the school and the political environment, secularization became real, and a relatively rapid linguistic acculturation ensued. Although Judeo-Spanish was predominant until the end of the nineteenth century, the trend was gradually reversed. Thus, 2.79 percent of Serbian Jews stated that they spoke Serbo-Croat in 1895, whereas the figure in 1931 was 48.99 percent. Conversely, the percentage of those who spoke Judeo-Spanish was 80.35 percent in 1895 against 29.86 percent in 1931.[105] In Belgrade, more than 50 percent of the Jewish population spoke Serbo-Croat in 1931.[106] As for Sarajevo – the city with the most multi-ethnic population – which had 6,397 Jews in 1910, including 4,985 Sephardim,[107] the proportion of Sephardim speaking Judeo-Spanish was still 51.13 percent in 1931, compared with 41.63 percent speaking Serbo-Croat.[108] The latter language was used in public life and in the administration of many Jewish institutions. Sarajevo also established a rabbinical seminary in 1928 reflecting its more traditional orientation.[109] Although Yugoslavia saw less antisemitism than Bulgaria, Jews neither entered the ranks of the bureaucracy nor played an important role in the country's political or cultural life.

Under the Austrians, a good proportion of the Sephardim in Sarajevo engaged in trade, specializing in the import and export of hardware, textiles, and colonial products. The Shaloms and Alkalays made their name in small-scale industries such as tanning, manufacturing matches, and flour mills.[110] However, the overwhelming majority of the Sephardi population of Sarajevo remained impoverished, and the situation did not change during the interwar period. Jews were responsible for a third of the town's economic activity, and more than half the merchants working in the textile trade were Jewish.[111] Nevertheless, however great the wealth the community amassed in this way, it seems to have remained concentrated in a few hands. In 1935, 1,700 out of a total of some 6,000 to 7,000 Sephardim were sunk in poverty and 1,116 had no income at all.[112] The Sephardim in Macedonia were no better off. The war had a devastating effect on the region. The Jewish population of the town of Bitola fell from 1,250 to 650 families in 1918, 400 of whom were extremely poor.[113] The situation was relatively better in Belgrade, where the Sephardi community as a whole had a more middle-class socioeconomic profile.[114]

The reorganization of community structures on the model of the communities of Central Europe, state intervention in their affairs and the subsidies it accorded their clergy and religious institutions, and the progressive predominance of secular groups in their administration, all in their way contributed to the transformation of Yugoslav Sephardi life.

These trends can also be observed in Bulgaria, another cradle of Sephardi Jewry. However, the influence of the Alliance locally as well as the extent of local antisemitism produced a different situation, marked by an expansion of Zionism unknown elsewhere in Sephardi lands.

In April 1879, the clause in the Treaty of Berlin concerning minorities in Bulgaria and Eastern Rumelia (Article 5) was incorporated in the Constitution of Turnovo.[115] The communities were again assured of a certain degree of autonomy. This was followed in 1880 by provisional regulations for the administration of religious communities through the synagogue.[116] Jewish life would be governed by democratically elected councils and subject to the authority of a Chief Rabbi paid by the state. The clergy was thus placed under the authority of its own spiritual leaders, but supervised by the state. The Jews themselves showed a wish to adapt their institutions to the new situation.[117] As state intervention became more active, the clergy's task was gradually limited solely to religious matters. In 1890, communal organization became centralized with the establishment of a French type of central consistory which, however, the state did not recognize.[118] Here too, the reorganization of the community structures encouraged the admission of greater numbers of laymen and offered these élites new avenues of power.

Jews formed approximately 0.90 percent of the total population of Bulgaria, 96 percent of them Judeo-Spanish speaking.[119] The majority lived in urban centers. Here, too, there was appreciable demographic growth, which was not related to a rise in the birth rate under the Bulgarian regime. On the contrary, the number of births fell considerably between 1891 and 1922, declining from 39.2 percent to 12.4 percent.[120] On the other hand, the death rate in the same period also decreased from 24.1 percent to 12.4 percent, and was below the rate for the general population.[121] The Jewish population of 20,503 in 1881 rose to 33,663 in 1900 and to 51,000 on the eve of the Second World War.

The part that education played in the process of change was central. The Alliance schools Gallicized certain classes of Jews, putting them into direct contact with the West. Bulgarization, on the other hand, took place in the primary school where the practice of teaching some subjects in Bulgarian was adopted, and then by attendance at Bulgarian secondary schools. After 1891 Jewish schools were officially recognized by the state, and pupils who left them were entitled to continue their studies at Bulgarian schools. The Jewish schools were maintained by the communities but subsidized by the state. These schools adapted themselves to the national curriculum and taught Bulgarian, while still continuing to teach Jewish subjects. In 1931, despite the considerable Bulgarization of the Jews and their relative integration into the country, the majority of children in towns like Sofia,

Philippopolis, and Ruse still attended Jewish schools, the remainder receiving their education from state and foreign schools.[122] Moreover, in 1926, 89.43 percent of the Jewish population stated that Judeo-Spanish was its mother tongue. On the other hand, in 1934 it appeared as the spoken language of 57.86 percent; in the same period, Bulgarian, which was the declared mother tongue of 7.62 percent in 1926, was claimed as the language spoken by 39.80 percent in 1934.[123] Even if Judeo-Spanish remained predominant in the family, this did not mean that those who claimed it as their mother tongue did not know Bulgarian. Statistics drawn from information on Jewish conscripts show that the percentage of those who were illiterate in Bulgarian fell from 8.70 percent to 1.52 percent between 1898 and 1910.[124] The percentage was higher for women in view of their lesser school attendance in the same period; the gap subsequently diminished.[125]

The spread of Bulgarian among the Jews was facilitated by the early disappearance of the Alliance schools, important instruments of Frenchification. Conversely, in Ottoman lands where their role was crucial, the state did not succeed in imposing its authority on non-Muslims, particularly in educational matters. In the absence of a national language comparable to the languages of the Balkan nation-states, no real Turkicization of the Jewish populations began until the eve of the Second World War. To some extent, the failure of the Alliance's attempt to teach Turkish in its schools contributed to this development.[126] On another score, the Alliance with the help of the Westernized élites also waged war on Judeo-Spanish. The question of its abandonment at a time when literature and journalism in that language were in full bloom was raised with frequency at the beginning of the twentieth century and the Judeo-Spanish press periodically echoed these discussions.

In Bulgaria, where the situation was substantially different, Jews still did not obtain high positions in the army or administration despite their knowledge of the language of the country. Nor did the precarious nature of salaries encourage them to enter these professions. Nevertheless, after the Great War and the subsequent economic crisis, Jews did make some attempts to enter the civil service, though apart from a few they did not succeed in making much headway. The situation was the same in the liberal professions. The Jews of Bulgaria did not particularly distinguish themselves in the political and cultural life of the country. The prevailing antisemitism was not unconnected with this state of affairs.

During the first decades after Bulgarian independence, most Jews were petty traders and craftsmen. They were to be found in the cotton and cereal trade and in a variety of small crafts. Their economic situation was very precarious.[127] There was no radical change in the profile of the community after the First World War. Jews were only important in a few limited sectors. Before the war, they controlled 90 percent of the country's exports of cereals, tobacco, fruit, and dairy produce – a proportion which fell to 60–70 percent in 1932.[128] They dealt, in particular, with Greece, Turkey, Italy, France, and England, and actively contributed to the country's commercial expansion. They controlled between 30 and 40 percent of imports of soap, oil, and colonial produce. In these areas, they competed with Greeks and Armenians.[129]

Nonetheless, despite this activity, the Jews never played a decisive role as far as the country as a whole was concerned. No large-scale Jewish merchants, financiers, or industrialists came to the fore. The majority of the community remained active in small-scale businesses. According to statistics for 1920, 54.8 percent of the active Jewish population of Bulgaria was engaged in trade, 35.2 percent were in small industry, crafts, and transport, and only 6.2 percent were in the liberal professions and the civil service (their place in this last category being limited to a few elected officials).[130] Of those working in the commercial sector, 63 percent were independent.[131] Statistics for 1926 show some movement into salaried jobs. In Sofia, Plovdiv (Philippopolis), and Ruse, where the bulk of the Jewish population was concentrated, the proportion of independent workers fell from 49.3 percent to 41.2 percent, while the proportion of wage earners rose from 30.5 percent to 36.1 percent.[132] The same year, Sofia recorded 1,952 Jewish traders and 84 industrialists alongside 2,090 small craftsmen, 1,133 employees in private enterprises, and 1,707 workers.[133]

The expansion of cooperative activities in the peasant and also in the business world, as well as the government's policy of using state agencies in the import–export trade, put the community in a difficult position. Many Jewish merchants lost their means of livelihood. The situation worsened after the great depression of 1929, and Jewish crafts were also seriously affected. The Jews reacted by developing their own cooperative movement with the help of the American Joint Distribution Committee. Loan banks (*kasas*) were created in Sofia in 1920, and other localities followed this example. The *Geulah* ("Redemption") cooperative bank of Sofia and other *kasas* in provincial centers were of considerable help in strengthening the Jews' economic position by providing loans and creating office jobs for educated Jews in their own establishments.[134]

However, white-collar workers remained few in number, as did members of the liberal professions. In 1940, only 146 of the 3,200 doctors and 77 of the 2,606 advocates were Jews.[135] The great majority of the Jews of Bulgaria were still concentrated in the trade and craft sectors, with few really large fortunes. Pauperization was rampant during the interwar period, particularly after 1929. In 1940, 17.4 percent of the Jewish population of Sofia needed support and was registered with the charitable association *Bikur Holim*.[136]

It was during the Balkan wars of 1912–13 that the most important and populous of all Judeo-Spanish Jewries, that of Salonika, came under Greek rule. Old Greece, formally independent since 1830, had had a few small Jewish communities, the most notable of which was Athens. However, it was with the annexation of Salonika and other smaller communities of the North that one can speak of the creation of modern "Greek" Jewry, and much of the group's history is that of the Jews of Salonika. According to the official Greek census of 1913, the city contained 157,889 inhabitants, including 61,439 Jews, 39,956 Greeks, 45,867 Turks, 6,263 Bulgarians, and 4,364 foreigners.[137]

The new rulers, whose entrance into the city was accompanied by antisemitic incidents,[138] were not welcomed by the Jews. Greeks had long been the Eastern Sephardim's economic rivals throughout the Middle East, and most of the blood libel incidents that had emerged with great regularity in the nineteenth century had been fomented among Greek Orthodox populations. Furthermore, the Jews of Salonika had benefited tremendously from the boom years of the second half of the nineteenth century, and were perfectly satisfied with the benign neglect of the Ottoman Empire.[139] Constituting more than half the population of the city in 1910,[140] and dominating its economic activities, their interests were well served by the preservation of the status quo.

Hence, both the fear of antisemitism and distrust of Greek rule, as well as economic calculations – keeping Salonika as an entrepôt of Balkan trade with a large hinterland – lay behind the attempts of the Salonika Jewish leadership to prevent the Greeks' formal annexation of the city. The French-educated upper bourgeoisie, the Zionist militants, as well as the Jewish socialist movement appealed throughout 1913 to the governments of the great powers, and to international organizations, as well as to the leading Jewish figures and societies in the West, to find a non-Greek future for Salonika. They presented a variety of scenarios. While the ideal remained Turkish rule, the internationalization of the city as a free port was another solution that would have served Jewish interests. Even Bulgarian rule, which would have provided a large hinterland and free trade links with the North was preferable to annexation by Greece.[141] However, international diplomatic realities, and the configuration of forces on the ground, precluded all these options, and Salonika remained in Greek hands.

A nonintegrated and suspicious Salonika Jewish community presented a serious problem for the fiercely nationalist Greek regime, and the years until the Second World War were punctuated with conflict and friction between the state and the Jews. In fact, in many ways, the worst fears of

Salonika Jewry came to pass. This was not only because of antisemitism, which was widespread among certain sectors of the surrounding population, but was also the result of the inherent logic of the modern nation-state which the Greeks adopted with a vengeance. An ethnically distinct group which dominated the most important port city of the country could not escape "nationalizing" policies that aimed to subvert its "minority" distinctiveness.

Initially, the state was prepared to be quite liberal and to assuage the Jews' doubts and fears. The religious liberty guaranteed by the Constitution was extended to New Greece. An act of 1914 recognized the right of the Jews to use Jewish law in marriages. With the laws of 1920 and 1922, the legal existence of individual Jewish communities was recognized by the state. They could be formed wherever there existed 20 Jewish families in a locality, were free to implement internal taxation for the support of communal institutions, and could elect communal assemblies through universal suffrage, which in turn could choose a Chief Rabbi for the community. The law of 1920 affirmed the right of the Jews to keep their commercial books in the languages of their choosing, to conduct business on Sundays and to observe the Sabbath, and to choose the language of instruction in communal schools so long as Greek was taught and was also used to teach history, geography, and the natural sciences.[142]

The enactment of these liberal laws coincided with the period of Greek irredentism, with the drive to annex new territories in Anatolia, when the government was concerned about international opinion about its treatment of non-Greeks and about the future of the Greeks of Asia Minor.[143] This legislation also came on the heels of the most important blow to the Salonika community before the Holocaust and might have been designed to smooth the Jews' hurt sensibilities. The fire that broke out in August 1917 consumed most of the Jewish quarter and left most of the community, 10,000 Jewish families (out of 15,000 affected by the fire), homeless. One hundred and twenty hectares of the historic town center were completely destroyed and 72,000 people found themselves on the street. Three quarters of the 4,101 property owners in the fire area were Jews. Although aid provided by the government and by the major world Jewish organizations helped to support the victims, nevertheless, the social fabric of Salonikan Jewry was irremediably broken. Schools, synagogues, and community centers were almost entirely reduced to ashes and the centuries-old infrastructure of the community destroyed overnight. The liberal government of Eleutherios Venizelos (1864–1936) launched a vast scheme for the modernization of the former Ottoman city. It decided to take over the disaster area, which meant that the Jews had to leave the heart of the town. The new plan was not without political motives. Under a law promulgated by the minister of transport, Alexander Papanastassiou, the government took over the zone and distributed bonds to the property owners at a value determined on the basis of the government's own assessments. In most cases, these bonds fell far short of the lost properties' true value, which seriously eroded the Jewish community's economic position.[144] By the same stroke, the town lost its specific Jewish character. The Jewish masses were relegated to the periphery. The government could then give the hitherto cosmopolitan Ottoman city a Hellenic hue. In this way, any concentration of Jews in the central, commercial, and harbor zones of the town would also be averted.[145] Investment by Greeks coming from outside Salonika, who bought land in the expropriated zones, was encouraged.

In the wake of this event, the Jewish population showed a continuous decline, with waves of emigration to Europe, the Americas, and Mandatory Palestine during the twenties and thirties. With the Greek debacle in Asia Minor in 1922 and the subsequent exchange of populations with Turkey, tens of thousands of Greek refugees were settled in Salonika as part of a deliberate policy to counterbalance the Jews' predominance. The 1928 census puts the number of refugees for the whole of Greece at 1,221,000, compared with a native population of 4,982,835. As for the Jews, the number of Sephardim was put at 63,000 and the figure for Greek Jews in Old Greece at 9,090, 1.02 percent and 0.15 percent respectively of the total population.[146] The mass of refugees, bitter, downwardly mobile, and abandoned to their fate, became fertile soil for the antisemitism which began to grow in the interwar period.

By 1923, the period of relative liberalism *vis-à-vis* the Jews ended. This was a result of the state's renewed "nationalizing" Hellenizing policies. But it was also a product of the cleavages and conflicts in the Greek body politic that ensnared the Jews into particular political alignments.

Ever since the elections of 1915, the Salonika Jews and the liberal Venizelist political movement and its allies found themselves at loggerheads. In the elections of 1915 and 1920, the Jews of Salonika voted overwhelmingly against Venizelos, being on the whole against the entry into the war and against irredentism. The middle and lower middle classes that supported Venizelos were the Jews' economic competitors. Liberalism in Greece, emerging in the form of Venizelism, went hand in hand with an assimilationist nationalism that aimed to Hellenize minorities. The opponents of Venizelism, associated with the monarchy and the old landed and bureaucratic élites, were just as nationalist, but were somewhat less intransigent *vis-à-vis* the minorities. Since the electoral weight of the Jews was significant in Salonika, their votes could and did block the Venizelist candidates in city elections. Minorities appeared to have a disproportionate impact in the political process of Macedonia where they were concentrated. In the elections of 1920, anti-Venizelists won 69 out of 74 seats in Macedonia, with the Venizelists winning only one seat in Salonika, which at the same time elected four Jewish anti-Venizelists to parliament.[147]

With the revolution of 1922 which brought Venizelists to power, a remedy for this "anomaly" was found in the creation of electoral colleges for the Muslims of Macedonia and Thrace which were extended to the Jews of Salonika in 1923. Jews could vote only for a set number of Jewish candidates which would represent them in the Greek parliament, and hence could not make their voices heard as electors in national politics.[148] While the official rationale for the new system pointed to clause 7 of the Treaty of Sèvres, which guaranteed minority representation in elections, the real reason was electoral considerations and Venizelos himself conceded this on many occasions.[149]

The Jews boycotted the first elections under the system in 1923 and continued to protest against the electoral college.[150] While no separate vote was used in the elections of 1926, Venizelos reimplemented the policy upon his return in the elections of 1928, 1929, 1931, and 1933. This electoral system was found unconstitutional by a higher court in 1933 under anti-Venizelists who had in the meantime come to power.[151]

The episode of the separate electoral college highlighted the contradictions of the new nation-state's relations with its minorities. While concerned to Hellenize all of the population, the most assimilationist of politicians could not and did not act as if they truly believed that these minorities could ever be "real" Greeks. Electoral politics aside, it is not hard to see the echoes of the old Ottoman paradigm of the *millet* just beneath the political surface in all the Ottoman successor states. In spite of the adoption of the West European forms of the modern nation-state, with citizens existing in an unmediated relationship with the center irrespective of religious and ethnic origins, the persistence of old notions about the primacy of the religio-ethnic group continued to corrode the political process and complicate relations with minorities.

A series of measures in the early 1920s began to whittle away some of the specific privileges granted to the Jews in the 1920 law organizing communal life that was affirmed in the Sèvres treaty. In 1923, the Jews lost the right to keep their accounting books in the language of their choosing.[152] In 1924, Sunday was made the compulsory day of rest for the whole population irrespective of religion.[153] This was a serious blow to the Jewish economy in Salonika where Jews had been accustomed to closing their businesses on Saturdays only. In spite of local and international protests, this law did not change, and many Jews, especially small shopkeepers who could not afford to stop working two days a week, were obliged to forego their religious scruples if they hoped to survive. In the same year, the exemption for Jews from military service in return for the payment of a certain sum was ended for those who had reached the age of 21.[154]

The state also began to demand more in the realm of education. A separate Jewish educational infrastructure continued to provide education for the majority of the school-age Jewish population. Of the 9–10,000 in Salonika who fell into this category in 1929, only 412 attended the state primary schools, while a mere 67 were in state institutions of secondary education. Jewish communal schools were attended by 3,500 students, while 1,243 were frequenting the Alliance establishments.[155] The rest were to be found in foreign secular or missionary institutions. The state paid a regular subsidy to the community to support these schools in return for which the community accepted the teaching of the Greek language and the instruction in Greek of history, geography, and the natural sciences. However, in spite of the increased hours of exposure to Greek, most of the schools still used French as the language of instruction.

In 1930, all Greek citizens were forbidden to attend foreign elementary schools, which dealt a major blow to the 2,000 Jewish students attending the foreign establishments. This law did not affect the Alliance schools, as they operated under the fiction that they were communal bodies.[156] However, the Alliance institutions could not escape from the measures that banned the teaching of foreign languages in all schools until the fifth grade. A series of protracted negotiations with the government only yielded a short delay in the implementation of this policy.[157] By 1935, the Alliance had to obey the new rules, and its institutions were effectively transformed into communal schools following the Greek-imposed curriculum as with all other establishments.[158]

The economic position of the Jewish community of Salonika deteriorated considerably during the interwar period. Several factors contributed to this: the disruption caused by the 1917 fire; the new economic profile of the city within a nation-state; the authorities' negative attitude towards the role played by Jews; and, lastly, the great depression. The situation deteriorated even more with postwar inflation and the crisis in the tobacco industry.[159] Many of the Jewish firms engaged in the sugar, rice, and coffee trade closed their doors and transferred their activities overseas.[160] Poverty remained a serious problem. However, in the thirties Jews again took a relatively active share in the economic life of the town. Representing a sixth of its total population, they were responsible for a fifth of its economic activity. They were still very much in evidence in the paper and textile industries, in pharmaceuticals, glass, ironmongery, tanning, and the timber trade. Two Jewish banks, the Amar Bank and the Union Bank, were considered among the best in Greece.[161] On the eve of the Second World War, there were

2,300 Jewish businesses in Salonika out of a total of 9,800.[162] In addition, certain Jewish textile firms, such as Britannia and Alhadef, and the Levy spinning mills, were among the most important in the country.[163]

A serious wave of antisemitism continued to worry the community through most of the 1930s (see below). On the eve of the Second World War, Greek Jewry, much weakened, with its economic power much diminished, still represented a sizeable urban minority that was, on the whole, unintegrated. The encounter with the nation-state had not proven to be a very pleasant one, in marked contrast to (especially) the half century of Ottoman rule when the community had flourished in the cosmopolitan, multi-ethnic, and multireligious Levant only marginally affected by modern state-building practices. Jewish creativity and political activity, in Greece as elsewhere in the Balkans and the Middle East, turned inward, operating on the communal and intra-Jewish level. The separate Jewish ethnic identity remained primordial and had only just begun to engage with the new "national" identity being imposed from above.

The situation which prevailed in neighboring Turkey was very similar, even though the nationalist policy of the government there was one of the most intransigent of any that were set in motion in the successor states of the Empire.

The birth of the Republic of Turkey in 1923 from the ashes of the Ottoman Empire after a decade of crises and struggles radically changed the map of non-Muslim life. The Armenian community was decimated, the Greeks, except for the Istanbul community, were transferred to Greece, and Greece returned the majority of its Turks to Turkey. The sizeable non-Muslim middle class of the prewar era was greatly reduced in number.

The Jews, numbering 81,872 according to the first republican census of 1927,[164] were mostly concentrated in the towns of Istanbul, Izmir, and Edirne. Emerging from the traumatic experience of the collapse of an empire, the Turks were strongly xenophobic during the interwar period. All non-Muslim minorities were suspect, and suffered the consequences. This was particularly apparent in economic matters. The victorious nationalist Turkish state was determined to encourage the formation of a "naitonal," that is to say, Muslim Turkish, middle class, and its economic policy used every means to this end.

The peace treaty of Lausanne, signed by Turkey and the powers of the Entente in 1923, guaranteed the rights of non-Muslims. They were to be free to use their own languages, even before the courts, could continue to administer their schools and charitable institutions, and also determine questions of personal and family status according to their own religious laws.[165] However, the non-Muslims themselves waived this protection in 1925–6, following the abolition of the caliphate and of the Muslim religious courts in 1924, and the announcement of the creation of a new juridical system on the model of the Swiss, Italian, and German codes. There is every reason to suppose that pressure was applied to make them take this course, and that this renunciation was not voluntary. The official announcements by the non-Muslim communities explained that, since the state legal system would no longer be based on the principles of Muslim law but would conform to those of Western secular codes, non-Muslims no longer had any reason to apply their own laws in matters of personal or family status. However, this decision was secured in a context of closed commissions, composed of non-Muslims appointed by the state, and placed under the presidency of a Muslim Turkish official. It was then presented as a *fait accompli* to the non-Muslim community bodies who had no choice but to accept.[166]

By the end of these developments, the last remnants of the old privileges attached to the *millet* system had disappeared. The new secular juridical system made no legal distinction between Muslims and non-Muslims. To complete the process, Islam ceased to be the state religion in 1928. Religious organizations and communal life became entirely voluntary. Indeed, the state showed some reluctance even to formalize Jewish communal infrastructures, despite several attempts by the community which wanted to formulate new statutes for its administration. The death of Chief Rabbi Haim Bejerano in 1931 was followed by a long period in which no successor was appointed. The vacancy was only filled in 1953 when Rafael Saban took office,[167] even though he, and his successor, David Asseo, were appointed on a provisional and *ad hoc* basis,[168] by decrees which carefully avoided regularizing the position of the Chief Rabbinate and of the communal bodies.

The republican state also initiated a Turkicization policy. This process had already started under the Young Turk regime. In 1915 new regulations relating to the operation of private schools made it compulsory to teach the Turkish language and also required that history and geography be taught in Turkish by Turks (that is to say, only by Muslim Turks).[169] The republican state reiterated these measures in 1923.[170] In 1924, Alliance schools were forbidden to maintain the slightest connection with a "foreign organization" and they now became community schools. Later the same year, official syllabuses were imposed on all Jewish establishments, and the place reserved for French in the curriculum was severely curtailed. All the Jewish elementary schools were eventually forced to opt for Turkish as the language of instruction. In 1931, all Turkish citizens were also forbidden to attend foreign primary schools.[171] By then, the process of Turkicization of the educational system had made great strides. The use of Judeo-Spanish was also viewed unfavorably and a number of organizations were founded to encourage Jews to speak Turkish. A veritable campaign of harassment against those who spoke "foreign" languages in public was launched in the 1930s, a campaign supported and encouraged by the ultra-assimilationist Jewish jurist and publicist Munis Tekinalp (alias Moïse Cohen).[172] The slogan "Citizen, speak Turkish!" was indefatigably repeated in the press and in public places. Jews were severely criticized for persisting with Judeo-Spanish. A recurrent theme in these polemics consisted of reminding the Jews that they ranked as "guests" and that it was therefore incumbent on them to demonstrate their gratitude to the Turks by Turkifying themselves as rapidly as possible.

The ubiquitous secularism of the Republic accelerated secularization of Turkish Jewry which had already been well under way since the introduction of European-style education half a century earlier. The prohibition on all religious instruction in schools dealt a serious blow to the teaching of Hebrew and made questionable the maintenance of a separate Jewish educational system. In 1929, Istanbul had ten Jewish schools attended by 2,510 pupils, not including the 500 pupils enrolled at the Jewish Lycée.[173] But the number of children attending this type of establishment steadily declined, and after the Second World War, only a limited number of Jewish schools remained. Most Jews attended state primary institutions (which was obligatory by law). Many then chose to continue their studies in secondary schools teaching in foreign languages, though subjects such as geography and history in these establishments had to be taught in Turkish by Turks. In the 1950s, Jewish religious education had disappeared from the institutionalized educational system and only just managed to survive outside the curriculum on a voluntary basis. Religious and community institutions wasted away and essentially lost their grip on the community. For the first time, the new republican generation, now educated in Turkish schools, was gradually beginning to become completely Turkophone.

However, the community's integration was patchy at best. Several events showed the existence of discrimination. In 1923–4, all non-Muslim state officials were dismissed from their posts.[174] Until 1945 Jewish conscripts could not reach officer rank. Legal equality of rights did not guarantee *de facto* equality in the social and public spheres.[175]

The majority of Jews remained concentrated in trade, although the important role the élite played as middlemen between local and world markets declined as a Turkish "national" bourgeoisie slowly emerged. In 1935, 24 percent of Jews worked in trade, 20.5 percent in industry and crafts, and only 4.4 percent in the administration and service sector.[176] The category "no known occupation" accounted for 45.9 percent, reflecting the importance of the makeshift activities which required no training that Jews continued to pursue. This group, with the rest of the poor, later formed the bulk of the massive wave of emigration to Israel after the Second World War, leaving behind a community with a more middle- and upper-class profile.

The Jews' social integration was limited by the state's exclusivist nationalism. From this point of view, as in the case of most of the Sephardi communities elsewhere, the process of change did not bring a significant integration into the surrounding society. The Jews remained apart, anxious to keep a low profile. They internalized the label of "guests" given to them during the first two decades of the Republic.

A few general conclusions emerge from this overview of the relationships of the Judeo-Spanish communities with the new nation-states which succeeded the Ottoman Empire. The Judeo-Spanish *Kulturbereich* in the Orient, which had formed a unit, began to break up in the nineteenth century and was completely shattered in the twentieth, when the communities came under the authority of diverse states and regimes. The transition from the multi-ethnic and multireligious context of the Empire to the nation-states which succeeded proved to be problematic.

In non-Turkish states, these populations were perceived as having been staunch upholders of the old Ottoman regime, and antisemitic actions and incidents worsened the relationships between Jews and their new masters. In Bulgaria, the war of independence of 1878 saw the harassment of Jews by Russian and Bulgarian soldiers, the burning of several Jewish quarters in the towns, and the flight en masse of various communities to Istanbul. When they returned in 1879 they had to make a completely fresh start.[177] The entry of Greek troops into Salonika was also accompanied by antisemitic incidents. Although these disturbances rapidly subsided, thousands of Salonikan Jews nonetheless emigrated to Turkey and the West immediately after Greece's annexation of the city.

In all the new states, while the Jews were granted legal equality, a formalized Jewish community, reminiscent of the Ottoman *millet*, came to pose a problem for the rulers. In Bulgaria, the synagogue remained the only legally sanctioned Jewish communal unit, in spite of attempts in 1900 and 1920 to have a centralized communal structure recognized by the state.[178] A nationwide Jewish body did not come into being in Greece, and likewise the Chief Rabbinate was only recognized *de facto* by the Turkish authorities. Only Yugoslavia saw a statewide Jewish communal federation emerge in 1929 which did not, however, function successfully because of friction between ultra-Orthodox communities and other groups.[179]

The most visible signs of the "nationalization" policies of these new states were in education. The Alliance schools were gradually closed and in effect "nationalized" with the rest of the community institutions. Nevertheless, despite action taken to spread the use of languages supported by the state, change only took place slowly. Judeo-Spanish remained the mother tongue of a considerable proportion, even a majority, of Sephardi populations until the Second World War. The policies of cultural nationalization were, in fact, fairly slow to yield results.

Although a certain degree of acculturation had made some inroads by the eve of the Second World War, it cannot be said that the Judeo-Spanish community – apart from a small number of individuals – had assimilated or even integrated in any country. The new states, ruling over extraordinarily complex multi-ethnic and multireligious populations came to represent the interests of élites associated usually with one of the dominant groups. Nationalist governance closed access to those defined as "outsiders." The nationalist discourse on "majority rule" crystallized, indeed brought into being, groups defined as "minorities." This was inherent in the very structure of the nationalist world view. The nation as an "imagined community"[180] had to have shifting boundaries that generated sites of conflict and antagonism by excluding groups outside and including groups inside the imagined reality.[181] For the very discourse on the nation, adopted in the abstract and applied to mold an intransigent reality, had embedded within it the binary opposition of majority/minority, a "majority" incarnating the "nation," and a "minority" with its distinctiveness to receive expression only in private, and destined eventually to disappear within the majority. Hence, the state of being of the "minority" group was by definition a provisional, transitory one. The "minority/other" was to be tolerated only insofar as it proved able to accommodate the demands of the fictitious majority represented by the state which it was expected to join by attenuating its distinctiveness.

It was inevitable that the Jews, the quintessential "other" of all discursive frameworks since the very inception of the notion of the "West" itself, found themselves transformed into one such "minority" wherever they were situated in the post-Ottoman Levant which imported and adapted the Western nationalist discourse. The Judeo-Spanish community had to face the fact that the old Ottoman mosaic of which it had been a constituent element had ended and accept a new status, that of "minority" under various political units.

However, the new nation-states did not necessarily import the liberal elements of the nationalist ideology prevalent in Western Europe at the time of its emergence in the early nineteenth century, but rather stressed the more authoritarian parts of the modern state and nation-building strategies. The nation-state in the Levant blocked access to the minorities, and hence to the Jews. In the face of this development, it is not surprising that, for the Sephardim of the Balkans, in direct continuation with Ottoman times, a separate Jewish identity remained in the foreground.

THE INTERNAL DYNAMIC

The manifold processes of Westernization generated internal change in more than one direction according to the local context, sometimes going beyond what was entailed by the premises of Western "modernity."[182]

Haskalah and the science of Judaism

The *Haskalah* movement, with literature and the press as its main vectors of diffusion, situated itself in a continuum with the traditional past. Unlike imported Western institutions, it did not meet strong opposition in the Judeo-Spanish context. Introduced from Eastern Europe through the intermediary of intellectuals, it was neither imposed nor institutionalized and, above all, affected small numbers of people. The Sephardi *maskilim* came from the traditionalist milieu, like the initiators of the movement in Western Europe and the majority of their counterparts in Eastern Europe. Religious circles in the Sephardi world did not present the same highly ideological trends as in the Ashkenazi world, such as those upheld by *hasidim*,[183] *mitnagdim*,[184] and the orthodox who did battle with the *Haskalah*.[185] For all that the social credo of the Sephardi *maskilim* was modern education and "productivization," they did not radicalize as did some of their counterparts in Europe. One of the earliest, Yuda Nehama, wrote in both Hebrew and Judeo-Spanish, producing biographies, poetry, and history. He corresponded in Hebrew with other *maskilim* in Europe and even created a newspaper in Judeo-Spanish, *El Lunar* ("Moonlight," 1865–6), which aimed to educate the people. Barukh Mitrani, like Nehama, fought for modern methods of education, founded a school for this purpose in Edirne, *Akedat Yizhak* ("The Binding of Isaac"), and devoted many years of his life to teaching. He wrote books on education in Hebrew and a grammar of spoken Judeo-Spanish, and also contributed to Hebrew periodicals such as *Hamagid* ("The Preacher," 1856–1903) and *Havazelet* ("The Lily," 1863–1914). In particular, he founded newspapers, such as *Karmi* ("My Vine," 1881–2) and *Karmi Sheli* ("My Own Vine," 1890–1) in Hebrew and Judeo-Spanish, arguing for colonization in Palestine and national rebirth. Historian, storyteller, and poet, neither his career nor his aspirations were very different from those of certain *maskilim* in Eastern Europe of the same period. Many of them appealed to people to return to "true" Judaism and tradition, and eventually advocated a type of Jewish nationalism. In Sephardi lands, the *Haskalah* did not develop assimilationist currents, as did some of its counterparts in Eastern Europe, and did not call for Ottomanization. This would seem to point to its adaptation to local realities.

One of the best representatives of the *Wissenschaft des Judentums* of the second generation in the Sephardi world was the *maskil* from Edirne, Abraham Danon. A student of Joseph Halevy, who imported the *Haskalah* into Edirne, Danon devoted himself to academic and literary work. Like the Salonikan Nehama, he composed and published a number of works in Hebrew. While working at the *Bet Din* (rabbinical court), he contributed to the opening of the Alliance school in Edirne. In 1879, he founded the society *Hevrat Shoharei Tushiah* ("Society for the Friends of the Intellect") or *Dorshei Hahaskalah* ("Friends of Culture") with young men filled with the desire to acquire knowledge and to bring the Jews out of their moral and material poverty.[186] In this association, a determined effort was made to discuss Hebrew and Judeo-Spanish newspapers and to encourage the study of Jewish history and literature in the light of research by the greatest scholars.[187] The society sought to bring to Ottoman Jewry the European *Wissenschaft* movement.[188] There was even the suggestion of creating a journal which would encourage works on the history of Ottoman Jewry utilizing the latest research. These champions of modernity were aware that the traditional heritage could be lost in this *rapprochement* with the West. Awareness of the possible breach with the past was in itself a symptom of the "modernity" for which Danon was the self-appointed spokesman. In 1888 the first issue of *Yosef Daat* ("The Increase of Knowledge") or *El Progreso* ("Progress") appeared, published both in Hebrew and in Judeo-Spanish. Suspended by the government, the journal only survived from March to December 1888. Danon wanted to establish harmony between traditional and Western knowledge. He called for study of the texts of Maimonides and secular languages, while still emphasizing the importance of the rebirth of the Hebrew language and the protection of the Judeo-Spanish mother tongue. A scholar of international repute and founder of a rabbinic seminary in Edirne in 1897 which moved to Istanbul in 1899, he shared several of the characteristics of the *Wissenschaft* of the second generation.

Other *maskilic* societies were born in the Empire. Working within the larger context of Westernization, they became sites for strengthening Jewish identity. These societies aimed to study the Hebrew language and to promote its appreciation by the public, to educate the masses through the medium of Hebrew, and to clarify and strengthen religious faith by the study of the Jewish disciplines. This was a program which, while linked to tradition, at the same time used methods inspired by the most recent developments in Western Judaism.

The society *Dorshei Leshon Zion* ("Friends of the Language of Zion"), founded in Istanbul in 1890 with Abraham Frumkin as secretary, opened a Hebrew school and library in 1892.[189] This school was the fruit of collaboration between Ashkenazim and Sephardim. It aimed to fill a vacuum in education. Whereas Jewish children in the other schools were becoming strangers to Judaism in the absence of adequate Hebrew teaching, this new establishment proposed to train men who would remain true to their people and their God. It rejected the type of education offered at the Alliance schools. Teaching was in Hebrew and children were accepted at six to eight years of age so that they gradually became accustomed to the language and would, in the course of time, be able to use it in their contacts with each other outside school. It aimed to create four classes. The first class would teach exclusively Hebrew. In subsequent classes, the children would be taught Turkish as well as Hebrew, so that they would then be able to enter state secondary schools if they so wished. It can be seen from this that the school did not propose to prevent the Jews' acculturation; on the contrary, the aim was to establish harmony between Hebrew culture and the culture of the land. The library was to serve to create a link with the Jews of the city. Appeals went out for teachers and experts in the Hebrew language for advice, and requests were also made for Hebrew works and Jewish books in other languages. The society defined its stance as "Judeo-national." The moderate position it adopted permitted Jewish dignitaries, connected with the state apparatus, to become members. A few months after its foundation, the school claimed 150 pupils, including 30 Ashkenazim, most of whom did not pay fees. The founders hoped to resuscitate the Hebrew language. "Regeneration" through the ancestral language had replaced the "regeneration" that the emancipating forces of the West had so much wanted. The Sephardi *Haskalah* established the link between emancipation and national renaissance.

There were other societies of the same type in other areas. The *Dorshei Leshon Ever* society ("Friends of the Hebrew Language") for the teaching of the Hebrew language and literature, in accordance with the program of the *Haskalah*, was created in Izmir in the same year.[190] The *Sfat Emet* society ("Language of Truth") was founded in Salonika in 1891.[191] The society aimed to contribute to the rebirth of Hebrew – "language of truth" – through teaching, reading, comprehension, oral practice, and writing, all in the most correct and grammatical way. Subscriptions were to cover the society's expenses: rent, purchase of books and journals, and also, in case of need, salaries for teachers. Membership carried the obligation to attend this educational establishment in accordance with a timetable determined by the board of directors. The curriculum consisted of the study of the Bible, Hebrew grammar, and the books and journals of the *Haskalah*. Three months after the society was founded, members were forbidden to speak any language except Hebrew.

The *Kadimah* society ("Forward" or "Eastwards," that is to say, towards Palestine), created in Salonika in 1899, showed the most visible proof of the links between the Sephardi *Haskalah* and Jewish nationalism.[192] Its founders were *talmidei hakhamim* (scholars in the traditional sense) who had been educated in *yeshivot* (schools of higher religious education) and studied French and secular subjects. They aimed to study the Hebrew language, spread appreciation of it among the public, educate the masses through it, and illuminate and strengthen "true" religious faith by deeper study of Jewish subjects. In addition to the *talmidei hakhamim*, the society's membership included teachers engaged in traditional Jewish education, journalists, educated elements, and merchants. It organized various activities: book lending, evening grammar classes, teaching Jewish history and other Jewish subjects, as well as lectures and discussions. It also helped to establish a library containing books in Hebrew and European languages. It was not long before it came to be regarded as a clandestine Zionist association. After the Young Turk revolution and the beginning of the Zionist revival in Salonika, *Kadimah* resumed its activities under the name of *Bibliotheque israélite* and it eventually joined the Zionist Federation of Greece when it was founded in 1918.

These societies and *maskilim* softened the shock of the new, at the same time as they shared its message. In a sense, they established a bridge between "modernity" and Jewish nationalism in the Sephardi culture area. Even though they did not have a significant impact on the masses, they helped to train a new generation of intellectuals who, in their way, became the vectors of this transition. Influenced by the *Haskalah* and the *Wissenschaft des Judentums* and inspired by the romanticism of a paradise lost, a whole string of historians of Sephardi Jewry appeared who did their utmost to write the history of their community. These historians, champions of modernity and guardians of a past which was no more, included Salomon Rozanes (1862–1938)[193] from Bulgaria, Abraham Galante (1873–1961)[194] from Turkey, Joseph Néhama (1880–1971), headmaster of an Alliance school in Salonika, and Michael Molho (1891–1964), also from Salonika. Other people began to collect various aspects of Sephardi folklore. The mass newspapers continued the process.

Literary creativity

In the mid-nineteenth century, even before changes began to appear on the ground, Eastern Sephardi Jewry was, of its own accord, looking for means to replenish its resources in the West, particularly through the intermediary of its intellectuals. The literary and journalistic production of that period demonstrates also that the influence that East European Jewry exerted on this process must not be neglected. However the receptivity to the West relegated creative work in Hebrew to second place; this was limited to scholarly and religious circles, although the nineteenth century produced a vast rabbinic literature. Judeo-Spanish was the principal medium of Westernization among the masses.

Translation of works on Jewish subjects from Hebrew and other foreign languages into Judeo-Spanish began from the first decade of the nineteenth century and subsequently increased among *maskilim*.[195] Then came historical works. In fact, the infatuation with history, not only Jewish but also world history, was evidence of a degree of secularization and also of a wish to know one's own history, which might be lost. Some of the classics of Jewish historiography, few though they were, were also translated into Judeo-Spanish, such as *Shevet Yehudah* ("The Sceptre of Judah") by Salomon Ibn Verga (second half of the fifteenth century, first half of the sixteenth), or *Emek Habakhah* ("The Vale of Tears") by Joseph Ha-Kohen (1496–1578).[196] The newspapers also played an important role in the diffusion of history. For example, Alexander Ben Ghiat began to publish the famous historian Heinrich Graetz (1817–91) in Judeo-Spanish translation in his paper *El Meseret* ("The Joy"), in 1897, the year of the paper's foundation in Izmir.[197] He himself contributed articles on history. Historical romances abounded. This interest in history was an integral part of the cultural profile of a Sephardi Jewry in a new era and showed its growing openness to the outside world. After the 1880s, there was an outburst of publications, biographies of famous Jews such as Moses Montefiore, the Rothschilds, and Adolphe Crémieux, anthologies of poetry, plays, ethical works, educational books on various subjects, books on Ottoman law, sermons, and prayer books with poems in Judeo-Spanish.[198] This mixture of translations and original works in the vernacular, borrowing as much from traditional as from secular literature, reflected Sephardi Jewry's complex evolution at the time.[199] The Protestant mission in Istanbul also contributed to the new Judeo-Spanish culture both with the newspaper *El Manador* ("The Source," 1855–8), and by publishing Jewish and Christian religious works in Judeo-Spanish.[200]

The beginning of the twentieth century saw a wave of translations of French, Italian, Russian, and Hebrew novels, which continued until the thirties.[201] This literature embraced the best foreign works of the day, appearing in abridged adaptations, and in installments in newspapers. *Manon Lescaut* by Abbé Prévost was reduced to 82 pages, *Paul et Virginie* by Bernardin de Saint-Pierre to 23 pages, *La Dame aux Camélias* by Alexandre Dumas to 64 pages, *Les Mystères de Paris* by Eugène Sue appeared in a version of 187 pages from 1876. Journalists such as Alexander Ben Ghiat and Elia Carmona published dozens of these works. The leading translators became known to a wide public. These serials were then sold in bound form to an adoring public. There were also penny novellas aimed particularly at women. Even though the Alliance was fighting to introduce "good" literature in the original language, the masses opted for the translated, diluted and abridged versions in Judeo-Spanish. Nevertheless, Western models made their way by these means, primarily reaching the female population, which, in turn, brought them into the family. Translations of the great authors of Hebrew literature of the day into Judeo-Spanish and of the works of Yiddish literature produced by such men as Shalom Aleichem (1859–1916), Isaac Leib Perez (1852–1915) and Sholem Asch (1880–1957) established a link with the rest of the Jewish world.

Drama did not lag behind. Molière and Shakespeare were translated from the beginning of the century. Theater began to make headway in the Sephardi centers. Original plays came to be written outside the usual biblical themes.[202] Zionist societies also helped to develop this art form by making it a popular leisure activity. Two theater groups operated in Salonika from 1910, one socialist and then communist, the other Zionist, with a varied repertoire of plays, most of which remains unpublished.[203]

This profusion of translations in some ways stifled local creation. The end of the nineteenth century and the beginning of the twentieth century were not notable for the production of great original works. The writer-journalists who wrote novels in Judeo-Spanish could not compete with the novelists whose works they often translated. Judeo-Spanish popular literature was heavily influenced by European, particularly French, literature. Nevertheless, there was a certain flowering of poetry in Judeo-Spanish. Local poets such as Shlomoh Shalem, Alberto Taragano, Moïse Cazès, and others published in the Jewish press.[204] An important representative of popular literature was the Salonikan Jacob Jona. He wrote songs in Judeo-Spanish about individuals, events, disasters.[205] Everyone in Salonika knew this colorful man, whose profession was town crier (*combidador*) and who also devoted himself to safeguarding love-songs, proverbs, anecdotes, and short stories in Judeo-Spanish by collecting them.

More emphasis was placed on didactic works. The expansion taking place in modern teaching made it essential to publish books which introduced into the home the latest developments in science in popularized Judeo-Spanish form. Side by side with the extraordinary boom in French in Ottoman and Bulgarian towns, the publication of spelling books for learning Judeo-Spanish proliferated, while Hebrew continued to decline. Istanbul, Izmir, Salonika, and Jerusalem, with the famous printing house of Israel Sherezli, himself a translator, became great publishing centers for Judeo-Spanish at the end of the nineteenth and the beginning of the twentieth centuries.

The role of newspapers in disseminating the current intellectual trends and at the same time in continuing traditional culture, at least in its popular version in Judeo-Spanish, is indisputable. The great expansion of the press occurred in 1870–80. That was the period which saw the birth of stable, remarkably long-lived newspapers. There had emerged already in the 1860s a proliferation of newspapers in Judeo-Spanish in Vienna which contained a considerable Sephardi community. In the Ottoman Empire too, there was a profusion of newspapers in the Judeo-Spanish language and a couple in Turkish in Hebrew characters (four between 1867 and 1889), but only a small number of publications in French, despite the success that language enjoyed with the élite at the time.[206] After the Young Turk revolution and the subsequent liberalization of the press, encouraging the growth of these new means of communication in the whole of the country, the number of newspapers in the Jewish centers also increased. The number of Jewish newspapers, covering all communities, reached 389.[207] Every trend was represented and reflected the politicization of the communities. Zionist newspapers, subsidized by the World Zionist Organization, mainly in Judeo-Spanish but also in French and Hebrew, strengthened their hold after the revolution and became important means of propaganda. They worked to develop national consciousness and to disseminate the broad themes of the movement among the people. They also helped to spread Hebrew novels in serialized form, activist literature and news about the development of the movement in the Jewish world, thereby strengthening Jewish "unity" and identity. The Kemalist republic brought the boom in this press to an end, replacing it by newspapers which were careful not to displease the authorities, despite a slight burst of energy at the time of the foundation of the state of Israel. It was after the 1908 revolution too that a considerable number of popular humorous newspapers were born.

Salonika, which had become Greek in 1912, continued the tradition of journalism in Judeo-Spanish, reflecting a variety of trends in opinion and style, ranging from the political to the humorous. With the Hellenization imposed in the thirties, newspapers in the Greek language were added to those already existing in Judeo-Spanish, but the latter dominated journalistic activity.

Journalists such as Saadi Bezalel Halevy and his son, Sam Levy, Yehezkiel Gabay, Isaac Gabay, Aharon de Yosef Hazan, David Fresco, David Florentin, David Elnekave, Rafael Uziel, and others, each defended a particular ideology. Their influence was considerable. They made themselves spokesmen for the currents of ideas flowing across the Jewish world without, however, renouncing either their local ties or their historical and cultural heritage. For example, David Fresco, enthusiastic champion of the work of the Alliance, wrote and translated various works into Judeo-Spanish: *The Jews and Science; The Divine Resemblance* (on the concordance of the Jewish religion with science and progress); *A Victim of Ignorance* (a booklet against superstitions); *Love of Zion* by Abraham Mapu (1808–67), the famous novelist of the East European *Haskalah*; *The Marranos of Spain* by Ludwig Philippson; *Les Mystères de Paris* by Eugène Sue; *Jerusalem* by Moses Mendelssohn. This eclecticism was a sign of the times and gave voice to the range of options faced by world Jewry.

From the 1880s the press in Bulgaria also experienced a considerable boom. Between 1880 and 1932, there were more than 50 newspapers in Judeo-Spanish, seven in Hebrew, and over 70 in Bulgarian.[208] More than 50 percent of the newspapers were Zionist and those that called themselves independent followed a Zionist line. Unlike the Empire, where papers in the language of the country were in the minority, in Bulgaria, where the Jews were increasingly familiar with Bulgarian, there was a balance between it and the traditional Jewish languages.

In Yugoslavia, where the Jews had lived longest outside the Ottoman sphere, newspapers in Judeo-Spanish were few in number.[209] The last newspaper to appear in that language, *La Alborada* ("The Dawn"), ceased publication in 1901. It published articles primarily on Jews in the world, the Bible, the Jewish festivals, folklore, and essays on the history of the Jews of Bosnia. This educational emphasis reflected the awareness of a world in the process of disappearing and an attempt to safeguard it in the traditional language of daily life. After the Great War, newspapers appeared in Serbo-Croat and followed a more Zionist trend, despite the large number of non-Zionist Jews. Palestine also followed the movement with newspapers in Judeo-Spanish directed at the Sephardi communities.

In the nineteenth century, while the Jewish West began to intervene in the affairs of Eastern Sephardi Jewry which it regarded as exotic and backward, and while Western ideas, values, and languages were finding their way into the Levant, this world was experiencing a cultural "golden age," especially in Judeo-Spanish. A remarkable efflorescence occurred in Judeo-Spanish within the context of the spread of European languages, particularly French, and the decline of Hebrew in the traditional arena. The intellectuals were very frequently able to write in both a Western language and Judeo-Spanish, as was the case in Eastern Europe with Yiddish at the same time, where the introduction of Russian or German did not prevent, and even encouraged, the development of creative literary work in Yiddish. Even if the literature produced in Judeo-Spanish did not fall within the canons generally valued in the Jewish world, it was still evidence of the unprecedented explosion that took place in popular literature in the vernacular. Hundreds of books and newspapers appeared, often in difficult financial conditions. Judeo-Spanish became studded with new words borrowed from the West. French headed the list. Gallicization affected both vocabulary and syntax. Judeo-Spanish adapted itself to the new situation. It was Judeo-Spanish, indissociable from the culture of this *Kulturbereich*, which became synonymous with self-defense against a progressively encroaching Westernization – while at the same time transforming itself into an instrument of the same process. The abundant literary production of this period has been ignored for a long time. Being neither in Hebrew nor in a known or esteemed Western language, it has had no way of reaching posterity. But it was very much the quintessential expression of a culture area which was now creating and translating on a massive scale in its own language, just before it disintegrated in the turbulence of the twentieth century.

The thirties sounded the death knell of this "golden age." The Judeo-Hispanophone audience began to diminish with the imposed acquisition of both local and Western languages. Salonika still remained relatively active in Judeo-Spanish literary production, since it contained a very considerable Jewish community. In Turkey, the reform of the script adopted by the new regime, replacing the Arabic Ottoman characters with Latin ones, put local Jews in a dilemma. Should they, too, replace the Hebrew *Rashi* script – until then the main medium of writing in Judeo-Spanish – with Latin characters? This replacement gradually took place. The change was not propitious to literary production in Judeo-Spanish. As in the other nation-states, the challenge of acculturation now appeared with great urgency, and this ineluctably involved the abandonment of the distinctive mother tongue. The waves of emigration during the twenties and thirties also destabilized these communities, often robbing them of their most vocal elements. Even though the language long remained rooted in the daily lives of these Sephardim, it no longer showed the dynamism needed to promote literature, even translation, or a stable press. The Holocaust finally destroyed the wellsprings of the language. Only vestiges of that period continue to exist, a few newspapers scattered here and there which struggle to prevent the Judeo-Spanish language from dying out. The Judeo-Spanish community transplanted in Israel has come up against the same obstacles. In a nationalist state, the languages and cultures of ethnic groups belong to folklore rather than to a state-imposed reality which demands the acquisition of the national language. A culture area cannot be reproduced elsewhere, even if individuals continue for a time to hand down their linguistic and cultural heritage.

The emergence of the new states and the changes undergone by these Jewish communities did not, on the whole, converge. The process of transformation of European Jewry received a central impetus from the state and developed in its local framework. Elsewhere, the process took multiple and distinctive paths. In Judeo-Spanish communities, the Ottoman heritage and local realities saw to it that the group continued to be perceived as a distinct minority in spite of imported models. This perception undeniably tied the Jews to their condition. They could not claim to assimilate; when they tried, they failed. However, within the boundaries of the Sephardi lands themselves, circumstances created a highly variegated picture. Where there were nation-states, these states barely had the time needed to assimilate their Jews when the latter, in touch with contemporary Jewish developments elsewhere, were themselves already envisaging new perspectives in the Jewish world, such as nationalism and Zionism in particular.

Assimilationist movements confronted the same obstacles. Assimilation/acculturation when it occurred only concerned certain regions and this belatedly. In the Ottoman Empire, the Alliance wanted the Jews to integrate into the surrounding society. In a paradox which is at the very foundations of this sort of Westernization, by teaching them French and inculcating Western values, it itself checked their integration into the local society. In fact, the Alliance, despite itself, nurtured Jewish particularism.

There was no single model or single process of change. The responses to the latter were equally manifold. Westernization was appropriated locally by those involved. A source of conflict, it was not able to supplant tradition completely; on the contrary, it was adapted to the new context, and could only affect the masses by allying itself with them. It was often utilized by élites anxious to take over the leadership of the communities. Another important phenomenon, Jewish nationalism, associated with the impact of the West but showing a specific local dynamism, emerged as a vocal symptom of nonintegration and itself contributed to the politicization of the Sephardi communities.

4

Paths of Politicization

The forerunners of Zionism and the Zionist movement in the Sephardi culture area cannot be separated from the Westernization process, particularly in the second half of the nineteenth century. Jewish nationalism appeared at an earlier or more advanced stage of the process of Westernization, depending on the local patterns in the culture area. Whether symptom or outcome, it was one facet of Westernization.

The rise of Zionism in the Balkans and the Ottoman Empire, after the foundation of the World Zionist Organization in 1897, took place on ground already prepared by individuals and movements which had nurtured earlier nationalist plans. The subsequent development of Zionism was determined by the specific situation in each of the countries concerned. Of particular importance here was the nature of the regime and the options open to it, its relations with neighboring countries, its policy in respect of the Jews, the degree of communication between these Jews and the non-Jewish environment and the rest of the Jewish world, and the geographical locale. For this reason, one must talk of a variety of Zionisms in the East, rather than of one unique model.

These nationalisms took different routes, depending on whether they emerged in Ottoman lands – which included Palestine until 1917 – or outside them. From this point of view, Bulgaria is a significant example. If one denotes by "pre-Zionism" the range of Zionist thought and political activity before its organization as a political movement with the first Zionist Congress in 1897, then Bulgaria can be considered to have been the single most important center of pre-Zionism in the Sephardi world. Bulgaria was able to become the cradle of pre-Zionism, and Herzlian Zionism and its diverse trends, because it was no longer Ottoman after 1878. That was the time when pre-Zionism began to take shape, reaching a crucial turningpoint in 1895. In the great Ottoman centers such as Salonika and Istanbul, on the other hand, there was no such upsurge in this period. Any movement which aimed to colonize Palestine or foresaw its eventual independence was likely to question Ottoman sovereignty and was consequently regarded as suspect by the Ottomans and by the Jewish establishment, as it risked compromising the Ottoman Jewish community. For all that, various strata of Ottoman Jewish society did not accept their leaders' policy in this matter. Depending on the circumstances and specific interests of these groups and despite opposition from the governing groups, Zionism, in the form of a sort of composite of Jewish nationalisms, gained ground until the advent of the Turkish Republic (1923), which drove it underground.[1]

The Ottoman presence in Palestine was a determining factor in the development of pre-Zionisms in the Sephardi culture area. It was even more crucial for Herzlian Zionism after 1897, the year of the first Zionist Congress in Basel. Even the World Zionist Organization adapted its policy on Palestine at the Hamburg congress in 1909 and then at the Basel congress in 1911, at least as far as appearances were concerned, and for a short period adopted the principle of the political integrity of the Ottoman Empire. Broadly speaking, within the Eastern Sephardi communities, a distinction can be made between the various pre-Zionisms and Zionisms, with or without specific reference to Palestine, depending on whether these movements did or did not develop under the Ottoman regime.

THE PRE-ZIONIST ACTORS

The last years of the first half of the nineteenth century saw the appearance in both the Sephardi and Ashkenazi worlds of men who were not only champions of the Jewish national idea but also called for action to achieve it. Parallel with the Ashkenazim Zvi Hirsch Kalisher (1795–1874) and Eliyahu Guttmacher (1795–1874), the Sephardi side was represented by the less well known Judah Bibas (1780–1852) and his more famous successor, Judah Alkalay (1798–1878), a contemporary of the important figures in nascent Jewish nationalism.[2] Even if the audience for the pre-Zionists remained limited, the ideas conveyed fitted into both a Jewish and non-Jewish context open to their diffusion.

Pre-Zionism in the Sephardi *Kulturbereich* also showed a wide degree of diversity. Although Barukh ben Yizhak Mitrani from Edirne was close to the pre-Zionist model set by Alkalay, other types of figures and doctrines also appeared on the scene, which expanded the hitherto accepted range of the movement. The visionary Reuven Isaac Perahia, a little-known figure in pre-Zionism,[3] the Serb H. G. Nahmias,[4] and Marco Barukh (1872–99), a militant activist,[5] directed their efforts towards finding concrete means of achieving the national ideal. This marked them off from their more passive predecessors. The establishment of colonization societies derived from this trend. These modes of more direct action developed in Bulgaria, whereas in the surrounding countries under the Ottoman ragime the aspiration for national rebirth was confined to *maskilic* societies which gradually became seedbeds of nationalism. In fact, the methods used in Ottoman lands were clearly distinct from those employed in the adjacent country.

Bulgarian beginnings

The pogroms of 1881–2 in Russia raised the burning question of the absence of a land for the Jewish "nation," the victim of constant persecution. The *Hibat Zion* movement ("Love of Zion"), born of this traumatic situation, recommended the reestablishment and rehabilitation of the Jewish nation in its historic homeland to populations who were most receptive to ideas of this sort. This new turn had considerable influence on Bulgarian Jewry which welcomed these ideas. Antisemitism, certainly present in the region, was not the only factor in this development.

A crucial role in the awakening of Jewish national consciousness in Bulgaria was played by Bulgarian nationalism from its earliest days, with its battles against the Ottomans, and finally with its victory in the advent of a nation-state and total independence. This new nation-state was born of a break with Ottoman rule. Local Jews unquestionably projected this example onto Palestine, and identified with the course of Bulgarian nationalism.[6] The tribulations of Armenian nationalism inside the frontiers of the Ottoman Empire, from the end of the nineteenth century, on the other hand, were hardly an encouragement to overt Jewish nationalism within its borders. It did not develop until the World Zionist Organization opened the first Zionist agency in Istanbul in 1908, on the morrow of the Young Turk revolution (1908) – and then always with support from overseas. Nor did the relative absence of organized antisemitism encourage the expansion of such a movement.

Once Ottoman subjects, now citizens of Bulgaria, the Jews had not had time to integrate before they came into contact with Jewish nationalism. Given the prevailing antisemitism, the illusion of assimilation rapidly dissipated. On the other hand, the adoption of the Bulgarian national curriculum in Jewish schools alongside the teaching of Jewish subjects, and attendance at Bulgarian secondary schools, enabled young Jews not only to learn the Bulgarian language but also to become familiar with its national literature. Neither passive identification with Bulgarian nationalism nor gradual Bulgarization diminished the Jewish population's nationalist aspirations. Although the élite, which was Westernized and connected with the Alliance, showed its opposition to nationalism, no organized hostility was expressed either by rabbinic circles or by the Chief Rabbis, who were generally recruited from the Ashkenazi world and were already familiar with this new credo. In fact, rabbinic circles actually helped to propagate the ideas of the *Hibat Zion* and were active in the colonization societies. In the Ottoman Empire, on the other hand, both traditionalist and "progressive" Chief Rabbis opposed Jewish nationalism. Apart from their own opinions on the subject, the formal position they held within the frontiers of the Empire left them little room for freedom of action or expression. The proof of loyalty was opposition to the Jewish national movement. On the other hand, traditional rabbinical circles were more receptive to the emotional appeal of the Jewish national plan, and from the outset did not reject it. There was even a degree of collusion with the Zionists in certain circumstances.[7]

The Bulgarians, for their part, had no great sympathy for their former masters, and could not but encourage any movement in opposition to the Empire, including Zionism. An additional factor was the proximity of the country to the capitals of Central Europe, Vienna in particular.[8] There is no doubt about the influence of these cities on Bulgarian Jewry. Thus, the repercussions of the national movement which arose in Jewish intellectual circles in these centers supplemented the effects of ideologies which had emerged in Eastern Europe.[9] Nor were the Alliance schools divorced from the local introduction of these new ideas which were developing in the Western world. A number of Alliance graduates became Zionist supporters for a variety of reasons. Whereas the Alliance's work in the Empire continued unhampered, in Bulgaria most of the Alliance's schools were closed from the beginning of the twentieth century as a result of Zionist pressure. An important bastion of anti-Zionism and a sizeable obstacle to Bulgarization thereby disappeared. These schools became community schools and successfully introduced a national Jewish education which in turn strengthened the foundations of Zionism.

Bulgarization and identification with Bulgarian nationalism, some acculturation and the predominance of Jewish education, and Jewish nationalism: these were the dialectics at the heart of the development of both pre-Zionism and Zionism in Bulgaria.

The modern personalities of Bulgarian pre-Zionism, in particular Marco Barukh, came to the fore on the ground which the settlement societies had prepared. Barukh was very different from most pre-Zionists, who are often simplistically placed in the "messianic" category. He was clearly closer to the future leaders of political Zionism and should more accurately be regarded as a pre-Herzlian Zionist. Barukh established societies which he called Carmel. He started a French-language Zionist newspaper in Plovdiv (Philippopolis), the *Carmel*, which appeared between September 1895 and January 1896 and only published six issues.[10] Above all, he was able to create a real Zionist dynamic and gather people around him who would later lead the movement locally.

In Bulgaria, news about the *Hibat Zion* movement and the Palestine colonization societies was spread by Hebrew newspapers coming from Eastern Europe. Colonization and other mutualist-inspired societies appeared in different Bulgarian towns in 1880–90.[11] Their statutes resemble those of the societies set up in Eastern Europe by the *Hovevei Zion* ("Lovers of Zion"). The declared aims were to propagate the virtues of manual work, to spread the idea of settlement in Palestine among members of the society, to purchase land and to settle some families on that land. The idea of "regenerating" the Jews through working the land was at the very foundation of these projects. They enjoyed the support of religious circles, which propagated their ideas in places of worship.[12] There were a few actual attempts at settlement in Palestine, but the only one that really succeeded was at Hartuv near Jerusalem.[13] This was the first nationalist Sephardi settlement in Palestine.

At the same time as the leading personalities were coming to prominence and the colonization societies were enjoying support, associations with a variety of aims were also emerging and playing their part in strengthening national consciousness among the local populations. The establishment of this sort of association was undoubtedly influenced by the East European version of the *Haskalah*. Local newspapers also played their part in disseminating Zionist projects. They included *El Amigo del Puevlo* ("The People's Friend," 1888–1902), one of the first Judeo-Spanish papers in Bulgaria; *Evreyski Glas* ("The Jewish Voice"), published in Bulgarian with a Judeo-Spanish supplement between July 1896 and January 1897; and *La Boz de Israel* ("The Voice of Israel").[14] All these papers, in addition to those which arrived from other countries and were discussed regularly, made local populations fully aware of the vicissitudes of the nationalist and Zionist Palestinophile plans throughout the Jewish world and in Bulgaria, thereby linking local Jews to the rest of Jewry.

In lands under Ottoman rule, pre-Zionism did not show as much diversity as in Bulgaria. The *Haskalah* played an important role. Even though most *maskilim* were striving for a modern type of education and collaborating with the élites who were determined to Westernize local society, they were opposed to "assimilation." It was in a dialectic between receptivity to the West and continuing the traditional cultural heritage with a vestigial internalization of the separate *"dhimmi"* status that Ottoman Jewish national consciousness was forged, particularly among the masses who were most susceptible to the emotional appeal of the Jewish national project.

ZIONISTS WITHOUT ZIONISM UNDER THE OTTOMANS

The Palestine question

Zionism experienced a certain degree of dynamism in the Empire in the aftermath of the Young Turk revolution (1908). Whereas before the revolution it was confined to *maskilic* societies, working discreetly to propagate Hebrew language and culture, it emerged from underground a few months after the revolution with the establishment of a Zionist office in Istanbul. This operated under the cover of a banking group, the Anglo-Levantine Banking Company, and was run by Victor Jacobson (1869–1935), a representative of "practical" Russian Zionism. This form of Zionism favored concrete achievements and fought for emigration to Palestine with a view to changing relative political strength on the ground. Most of the Zionist leaders temporarily posted to the Empire were proponents of this orientation. But once in the Empire, they rarely agitated in favor of emigration to Palestine. Even during the period between the revolution and the end of the First World War, when the movement made intermittent progress, the question of Palestine was rarely raised. So long as the country remained Ottoman, it was better not to highlight this sensitive question and thus prevent a break in negotiations with the Ottoman authorities.

Zionists had several expectations from the new regime in the Ottoman Empire. Following the pogroms in Russia and the subsequent waves of immigration into Palestine, the Ottomans had introduced restrictions on Jewish immigration (1882), and limited land purchase by Jews (1892).[15] Their opposition to Jewish immigration was not new. They were afraid that Jews from Russia, who retained their Russian nationality, would strengthen the local influence of the Russians, their long-standing enemies, and destroy the fragile equilibrium in the region. In addition, the Empire was facing worsening national problems at the end of the nineteenth century; there was no need to add yet another. Massive Jewish immigration was likely to subvert the pan-Islamic policy of the sultan Abdulhamid II that aimed to introduce political and social cohesion to a collapsing Empire.

Moreover, these restrictions were subsequently strengthened under pressure from the Arab populations. But, as we know, they did not yield the expected results, since the Jewish population of the Holy Land tripled between 1882 and 1908. This made a solution of the Palestine question an urgent matter on another count. Theodor Herzl, founder of political Zionism, failed in his negotiations with the sultan, despite visiting the Empire five times between 1896 and 1902. The Zionists wanted to take advantage of the new post-1908 situation. They cherished hopes of progress on the Palestine question under a more liberal regime.[16]

At first, they strove to have the restrictions lifted. Their optimism was short-lived. The new regime did not change policy on the Palestine question. It only differed from its predecessor on one point: it now offered the persecuted Jews of Eastern Europe new regions for settlement, such as Mesopotamia, on condition that they avoided mass concentration in any single area. No tangible results came from the adjustment of Zionist policy to favor Palestine remaining under Ottoman suzerainty. Direct negotiations were equally unproductive, as was the propaganda on behalf of the cause obtained by subsidizing newspapers, including the Turkish nationalist paper, *Le Jeune Turc* from 1909.

In Palestine, the commandant of the 4th Ottoman Army, Cemal Pasha, who had become unchallenged master of the region, was indefatigable in his anti-Zionist maneuvers in 1915–16, followed by the anti-Jewish persecutions of 1917. The inhabitants of Jaffa, Jews and non-Jews alike, were driven to the north. The Jewish population, however, was particularly hard hit. After the Balfour Declaration (November 2, 1917) and the British occupation of Jerusalem on December 9, 1917, the Ottomans chose to make some concessions. But it was too late. The armistice of Mudros on October 30, 1918 ended the Ottomans' centuries-long hegemony in Palestine.

Seeing this Ottoman hostility to Zionism, the governing Jewish élite very early on tried various means to check the movement's rise, in order to protect communities. They were afraid that the movement would spread in the Empire. The majority of the economic élite was legally dependent on foreign consulates under the terms of the capitulations and could at any time be accused of betraying the Empire's interests. This élite had backed the Alliance in order to restructure the Ottoman Jewish community and equip it to meet the new situation. It had also found in the Alliance a source of support: since its offices were situated overseas, it could intervene in case of difficulties, even if this did not form part of the Alliance's original plan. Ideologically speaking, it felt closer to the Alliance than to the Zionist plan, which it regarded as a utopia, a view it shared with leading Jewish circles in France of the same period. Its credo was the Westernization of the masses, with the corollary of "productivization." For all that, it did not really believe in the eventual integration of the Jews in Ottoman society.

Even though the *dhimma* ceased, for all intents and purposes, in 1856, non-Muslims were still not transformed into full citizens, and vestiges of the previous status persisted long after. The desire for integration was absent both among the Ottoman leaders and the non-Muslim groups, who had learned to adapt to the relative autonomy that the system granted. The organization into religious groups – the very foundation of the *dhimma* – as well as the surrounding society's perception that non-Muslims were members of these groups, combined with their failure to integrate, all helped to endow them with a certain type of religious unity, even if, as in the case of the Jews, it was increasingly expressed neither by assiduous synagogue attendance nor sustained religious practice. This unity went further: the Jew perceived him or herself first and foremost as a Jew; this self-perception coincided with the perception that others had of the Jew and thus strengthened Jewish identity.

The communal arena

Although the Zionists' claims met with no success with the governing circles of the Empire, their actual institutional presence did breathe a certain national dynamism into the community, thus preparing its ultimate receptivity. Even though fear of repercussions had precluded nationalist agitation as, for example, in Bulgaria, the setting was not absolutely unfavorable to the movement's expansion under experienced Zionist leaders from abroad. In order to promote the Palestine question, these leaders aimed to build strength so as to counterbalance Ottoman power when the time was ripe. Above all, they aimed to win over the élite, which had access to the government and was connected with the Alliance. This was a strategic error which inevitably slowed their activities and resulted in political conflicts inside the community, without directly serving the leaders' avowed goals. It was in order to win the support of these élites that they turned towards the masses, in the belief that once the latter were enrolled in the movement, the former would give way.

The Zionist leaders sent to work in the Empire did not hope to create an organized Zionist movement. They pursued pragmatic aims, convinced that the future of Zionism would not be determined in Sephardi lands. This attitude persisted. The Sephardim had been second class subjects in the lands of Islam; were they not also second class Jews in the eyes of the key Zionist workers, the future leaders of the future state of the Jews? They wanted to conquer the ruling institutions of Ottoman Jewry in order to give their policy a new look as much inside the community as in the confrontation with Ottoman power. The notables, who had a stranglehold on these institutions, and the Chief Rabbi of the Empire, appointed to this position since the revolution, were both "Alliancist." This new issue by itself would already politicize community life. By setting up as an opposition party, the Zionists were declaring war. They employed various means to achieve their aims. The principal methods were propaganda in the press, activism on the ground, the development of an associational life, populism, infiltration of community institutions, and alliances with groups hostile to the Chief Rabbi and the oligarchy that surrounded him.

By taking over local Jewish newspapers or creating others, the Zionists set up a veritable press complex, an unquestionable mainstay of the movement.[17] This press was directed at the different strata of Jewish society, and the language chosen, French, Hebrew, or Judeo-Spanish, varied according to the population they wished to reach. Gifted leaders were working on the spot, such as Vladimir Jabotinsky (1880–1940), future founder of the Revisionist movement, Richard Lichtheim (1885–1963), and Arthur Ruppin (1876–1943), and they strengthened the movement by their diverse journalistic and militant activities. They relied on the middle class which wanted to gain community power, hitherto held by notables from bourgeois backgrounds. This relatively Westernized middle class now possessed a certain amount of economic power which enabled it to bear the cost of running the community, and was waiting to be entrusted with communal responsibilities – the consecration of social ascent for the Ottoman Jew. Political power could only be exercised within the community, for want of any other arena. These new aspirations found their outlet in those societies where the militants served their political apprenticeship before seizing power.

The Zionists were better informed on community life than the Alliance, because they had actually established themselves locally. They turned to the masses at their traditional meeting place: they became active in the synagogues and attempted to enroll the congregants in their ranks. Their ultimate aim was to gain power. The watchwords were nationalism and democratization of the community's political machinery. To those ends, the Zionists did not hesitate to ally with the enemies of the Alliance, including the *Hilfsverein der deutschen Juden*, B'nai B'rith, and the traditionalist religious faction. This last group had not looked kindly upon the Alliance's establishment of a European type of school network, since they thought it to be incompatible with traditional education.[18] The Zionists also took advantage of interethnic conflicts between Sephardim and Ashkenazim in the Ottoman capital, those odd-men-out of the community institutions. The Zionist leaders assigned to Istanbul were of Ashkenazi origin; they formed a "Germanic" block combining most of the Alliance's opponents. Local leaders also emerged, taking advantage of Zionism to move into key positions in the community arena. The Zionists shared power intermittently with the supporters of the Alliance associated with a Chief Rabbi connected with the society, but they did not succeed in democratizing the institutions they controlled and pursued the same policy as their opponents, since the system did not make it possible to do otherwise. In this way, the Zionists helped to destabilize still further the community's delicate equilibrium.

The conflicts between local Alliancists and Zionists were not about ideology but about power, along with personal conflicts and attacks on the Chief Rabbi, which made them all the more unproductive. In their zeal, local Zionists overstepped the aims of the Zionist leaders abroad. The World Zionist Organization had to intervene to stop this development.[19] The eventual result was a clear-cut division between Zionist and non-Zionist leaders, who were all trying to influence the Jewish population – each group striving to align this population against its opponents.[20]

This rowdy antagonism broke with the Jews' traditional discretion–carefully avoiding any conduct capable of attracting the rulers' attention. The uproar in the community in the aftermath of the Young Turk revolution was augmented by the barrage of calumnies and insults which each party released in its newspapers. These papers caused a considerable stir even if they did not have large circulations. Most of them had not joined the Zionist ranks through ideological conviction. Journalists, who wrote, edited, and owned their periodicals, very often came down on the side which was able to pay to keep their paper alive. It is true that some acted out of conviction, such as *El Avenir* ("The Future") of Salonika, owned by David Florentin, an active militant Zionist, who eventually emigrated to Palestine. Some, such as *Le Journal de Salonique* ("The Journal of Salonika") and *La Epoca* ("The Epoch"), belonging to the descendants of Bezalel Halevy, one of the first well-known Salonikan journalists, did not always make their choices clear and were at one time subsidized by the World Zionist Organization.[21] *L'Aurore* ("The Dawn"), which appeared in French, was one of the first Jewish papers to be subsidized by the Zionists with a view to reaching the educated classes of Jewish society, the mainstay of the Alliance. The Zionists sometimes agreed to pay Alliancist papers in order to neutralize them, fully aware that it would not be easy to make them change their political line. This was the case with *El Tiempo* ("The Times"), established in the community since the second half of the nineteenth century and owned by a keen supporter of the Alliance and of Westernization. Other papers, such as *El Judio* ("The Jew") and *La Boz* ("The Voice") in Istanbul, and *La Tribuna Libera* ("The

Free Tribune") and *El Puevlo* ("The People") in Salonika, directly subsidized or supported by the Zionists, declared war on the enemy camp's press. These papers played a considerable role in destroying the community's equilibrium. What is more, some of their founders had themselves been through Alliance schools and were thus very knowledgeable about the opposing views they aimed to undermine. The only paper to preserve a certain degree of decorum was the Hebrew-language *Hamevaser* ("The Spokesman"), founded in 1910 by the Zionist leaders posted to the country.[22]

This activity was not unconnected with the spread of the movement's key ideas, which were also passed on by new associations. The latter created new areas of socialization, politicization, and leisure activities under the nationalist banner.[23] They not only attracted people who wanted to serve their political apprenticeship in peripheral structures – those excluded from power – but also drew the masses who were seeking new outlets for their aspirations.

For a long time, the network of societies born of the Westernization era had existed under the auspices of the Alliance and of the privileged strata of Jewish society. The uneducated masses, not molded by Alliance schools which they rarely attended or which they only attended for short periods, came together in the mass arenas that the Zionists established. Through lectures, excursions, Hebrew lessons, gymnastic classes, and film screenings, the latter attracted impoverished youth who long remained loyal to Zionism, even after the advent of the Republic, when the movement went underground. Even if the Zionist leaders in the country saw themselves overtaken by the local political dynamic, they were able to adapt their strategy not only to the Ottoman situation but also to local issues and to the different social strata. This explains their public success, in contrast to the Alliance. Despite its schools, the organization had neither the logistics of a party, nor the ability to engage in *realpolitik* to enable it to fight Zionism effectively, even though the supreme head of Ottoman Jewry, the Chief Rabbi Haim Nahum, was a member.

Zionism not only introduced a certain national and political consciousness. Above all, it appeared to be a cure for the lethargy of a once flourishing community, now taken over by foreign Jewish philanthropic societies engaged in a relentless struggle to secure local predominance, and associated with imported identities. Zionism also came from abroad, but it was able to summon this community to assume its responsibilities and take itself in hand. The struggle between the Zionists and their opponents set up a real dynamic which, albeit conflictual, promoted the propagation of Zionism. This in some ways furthered the process of Westernization of those Jews who were in transition without cutting them off completely from their traditions. It led them to discover one of the extensions of Westernization that was also a Jewish identity. As ethnic distinctiveness had not been eroded, the task was relatively easy, at least as far as the masses were concerned. In this transitional phase, Zionism, for many, therefore held a position somewhere between tradition and modernity, a stance which served its aims, even if it did not enable it to win over the economic leadership. Eventually the intellectual élites, the majority of journalists, a couple of Alliance teachers, and above all a considerable number of Alliance graduates sided with the Zionists. Not everyone who supported Zionism did so for the same reasons, which accounts for the movement's complexity in the country and partly explains the different directions it gradually took. It is also true that Zionism took advantage of the dissatisfaction prevailing among the different strata of Jewish society.

A favorable conjuncture

The end of the First World War was marked by the rise of the local Zionists at the expense of the World Zionist Organization in London which had decided to withdraw from the scene. The Empire was dismembered and Ottoman power at Istanbul was tottering, with occupying forces in the city itself. All this dealt a death blow to the lingering hesitations of local Jews over Zionism. As they were no longer afraid of the Ottoman authorities, they allowed their expectations free reign. In November 1918, a few days after the Allies occupied the capital, the Jewish National Council, a sort of national coalition of the various factions in the community, held a meeting. In fact, this council took the place of the constituent bodies of the community. Its program also revealed its adaptation to the new situation.[24] To begin with, it ratified the principle of the transfer from religious to lay communal organization. It gave official sanction to the opening up of Ottoman Jewry to overseas Jewry, and to some extent prepared the ground for its representation at the future peace conference. Ottoman Jewry was envisaged as an independent interlocutor alongside Western Jewry, thus asserting its independence. It took its stand on the principle of national rights stipulated in President Wilson's Fourteen Points. It was surprising to find such boldness on the part of Ottoman Jewry. Even more astonishing was the call to form a common front with the other minorities in the Empire, that is to say, the Greeks and Armenians. In addition, the authors of the autonomy plan demanded proportional representation of Jews in state institutions and public office. The Jews thus violated the limits of their old status as *dhimmi*. When the Chief Rabbi returned from a mission to Europe on behalf of the Ottoman leaders, he took steps to weaken this council. He succeeded, with the help of notables who were alarmed by this display of strength, and who now made haste to reestablish "order."[25] However, fortune favored the local Zionists. In any case the official recognition of Zionism (the Balfour Declaration) secured the support of populations who had hitherto flirted with the movement. The British, concerned with the mandate in Palestine, had an interest in cooperating with local Zionists, in particular with those who might influence the choice of mandatory power.

It was also in 1919 that the Zionist Federation of the East was set up in Istanbul, and the local Zionist movement became official. The functions of this federation, through its different bodies, included collecting money for various Zionist funds, as well as dealing with emigration to Palestine. It held regular congresses. The presence in the country of a representative of the World Zionist Organization did not, however, prevent this organization from becoming a tool of a few ambitious local activists, who pursued narrowly self-interested goals. This could only widen the gulf between the central leadership in London and its local branch.[26]

After the October revolution, Istanbul became a transit point for Jews fleeing the Russian and Ukrainian pogroms. The newcomers had already had contact with Zionist ideology and they therefore helped to consolidate the local movement. With institutionalization, Zionism lost its contestatory character which had hitherto enabled it to attract the discontented. Most Zionists in the capital appeared to be under the Federation's thumb. Nevertheless, it was in this same period of intense nationalist activity that membership of the various societies fell. This decline did not prevent a proliferation of small societies most of which disappeared soon after they emerged, but which nonetheless gave testimony to the movement's dynamism. The movement reaped the benefits of intensive prewar propaganda. In the twenties, the Federation had a membership of between 4,000 and 5,000.[27] This is a substantial figure considering that the Jewish population of Istanbul amounted to 70,000.[28] The Federation incorporated 18 societies in the capital and ten in the provinces.[29]

Alongside these organized Zionists, there grew up a movement of sympathizers without affiliation, organization, or ideological structure. This represented a genuine landslide due to the circumstances and to the hopes Zionism aroused among the masses. The discontented, the desperate, the misfits, appear to have sought salvation outside of institutions. In addition, there were a variety of Zionist trends which did not identify with the Federation: the labor branch, *Hitahdut* ("Union"), founded in 1920, for example, and the *Makabi* gymnastic society. Both these organizations were youth-oriented and continued to exist on the community scene in various guises during the period when Zionism went underground.

This period was punctuated by demonstrations, blatant propaganda, fiery articles in the Federation's official organ, *La Nation*, and reports of congresses. The great difference with the prewar period lay in the fact that all this was done openly. The same ebullience also prevailed in Salonika at the time of its annexation by the Greeks. Freed from Ottoman rule, the Jews were no longer afraid to demonstrate a nationalist orientation. The weakening of Ottoman power in the occupied Empire encouraged this outburst. As in Salonika, uncertainty as to what the future might hold also promoted the movement.

The war between the Zionists and the community organizations resumed with renewed vigor. The Zionists reinforced their class and demagogic discourse with proposals for an egalitarian society in a Jewish country. This attracted not only the proletarianized Russian Jews, but also certain fringe groupings. The war had impoverished families of modest means and enriched mainly the upper-middle classes. Strangely enough, in this case, Zionism acted as a buffer in the face of economic problems, deflecting the crisis which might have threatened or even overturned community structures. It facilitated the reduction of serious social tensions by channeling them towards a nationalism capable of meeting the requirements of the time. It is equally true that the absence in the capital of a workers' federation like that in Salonika, and the small degree of proletarianization among local Jews were not unconnected with the advance of this brand of Zionism.

The local Zionists succeeded in obtaining the Chief Rabbi's dismissal, who they regarded as their primary enemy, in winning decisively the elections which were held between 1919 and 1920, and also in seizing the leadership of community organizations, until the eve of the Republic. The World Zionist Organization was still absent from the local scene.

Is it accurate to use the term Zionist to describe this movement, which became active after 1908 and subsequently experienced periods of great popularity? When the tactics of the World Zionist Organization are considered, it is apparent that, as an organized movement, it used Ottoman Jewry and utilized the community arena and its networks for its own ends. Conversely, certain groups and individuals made use of the movement locally for their own advancement. For most people however, Zionism represented Jewish nationalism and hope for the poor masses, for most of the *Luftmenschen* who had not been able to benefit from Westernization and, in particular, for the youth born into these classes, who expected to reproduce the family model with no great opportunity for social mobility. Zionism thus oscillated between a sort of nationalism, capable of restoring dignity to people who had nothing to lose in an increasingly isolated and hierarchical Jewish society, and an autochthonous social and cultural Jewish nationalism, barely distinguishable from the former. These were the groups which emigrated en masse to Israel after its establishment, without having been entirely molded by official Zionist ideology.

Official Zionism was overtaken by local Zionism, and local Zionism by a spontaneous movement, independent of organizations. Istanbul was not an isolated example; it was a model only because it contained the seat of the Chief Rabbinate, and precisely because of this, the conflicts there appeared to have been particularly harsh.

Clandestinity

Even without the Zionist movement, would there not have been Zionists in Turkey, as Meir Dizengoff (1861–1937), Zionist leader and future mayor of Tel-Aviv, claimed as early as 1919?[30] Comparison of the situations in Turkey and Bulgaria clearly shows the differences. In Bulgaria, there was an organized movement, a number of ideological trends with clear affiliations to the world and local headquarters, a substantial ideological discourse, participation in Zionist congresses, the organization of local congresses, and the usual fundraising. This continued up to the eve of the Second World War. Even Salonika and the Sephardi communities of Greece differed from Turkey. After the advent of the exclusivist Kemalist Republic, Turkish Jewry officially broke its ties with the organizational framework of the movement, but this did not stop Zionism continuing underground, including the maintenance of a Palestine Office in Istanbul from 1920. This office also operated clandestinely and was concerned mainly with emigration to Palestine, especially of Russian Jews in transit, and only very incidentally with local Jews.[31] The office comprised representatives of the different Zionist factions and was subordinate to the Zionist executive in London. The office helped 4,200 Russian immigrants between June 1920 and June 1921. They consisted in the main of Ukrainian immigrants who arrived at Istanbul after crossing Bessarabia and Rumania and, once there, waited for an emigration permit for Palestine.[32] The Palestine Office also passed through various phases, including closure. When Russian Jews were barred entry to Kemalist Turkey, the office turned its attention to the Sephardi population.[33] The inadequate number of certificates for Sephardi emigration to Palestine inevitably lessened the impact of the national project on this Jewry, who lived in fear of the authorities who considered Zionism a betrayal of the state.[34]

Zionism in republican Turkey was clandestine. It was difficult to carry on the activities involved in enrollment, propaganda, indoctrination, and education under such conditions. An effective Zionism could not develop where Zionist leaders took relatively little interest in local Jews.[35]

Istanbul still remained important, since it was also the point from which the Palestinian Jewish colony initiated the rescue of persecuted Jews from

Central and Eastern Europe and effected their transfer to Palestine. A number of Zionist leaders, some of them future rulers of the state of Israel, stayed in Istanbul for this purpose. By a decree published in 1941 after much negotiation, the Turkish government granted transit to persecuted Jews through its territory once they had secured their Palestinian visa (see below).[36] At the time of the Second World War, Turkey's attitude to Jews both inside and outside the country passed through a number of phases which were, to say the least, contradictory. Nevertheless, more than 37,000 Jews were sent on their way to Palestine between 1934 and 1944.[37] Various Zionist institutions organized this underground immigration which violated the British restrictions. Istanbul was transformed for a time into a focal point of Zionist activity, responsible for collecting information for rescue operations and the dispatch of parachute commandos.[38] It was there that delegates of the Jewish Agency for Palestine forged links with the different diplomatic corps. When the Turkish authorities closed the Palestine Office in 1935, this agency took over and established links with other rescue centers.

In the last years of the war, when operations directed towards the occupied countries were delayed, this agency turned its attention to local Jewry.[39] Generally speaking, the impression emerges that the official bodies of Zionism ceased to take a systematic interest in local Jewry after the Balfour Declaration. Despite everything, this agency kept the Zionist flame burning in the country, even if its principal aims did not directly concern Turkish Jewry, either at the time when it was set up or during the war.[40] Until the end of the thirties, the Jewish Agency was the only Zionist institution in the country. In fact, it was the only one to provide information on Palestine. The period which preceded the advent of the Kemalist Republic was rich in Zionist activity; but the period which followed was characterized by enforced silence. Exclusivist nationalism, such as Kemalism, was not inclined to accept another nationalism, certainly not one which emanated from former *dhimmis*.

Clandestinity offered few opportunities for pioneer and other training preparatory to emigration. This can, therefore, be described as a Zionism without ideological preparation. The years which preceded Kemalism were not long enough to imbue the population with the ideological message of Zionism. It is also legitimate to ask whether Turkish Jews were not simply resistant to any political ideology. After all, the Zionists failed, as the Alliance before them had failed. For the Jewry of the Turkish Republic, as for the Jews during the last years of the Ottoman Empire, it appears to be true to say that they were Zionists without Zionism.

The majority of emissaries sent regularly from Palestine to train local youth knew neither Judeo-Spanish, nor Turkish, nor even French, which did not make communication easy. The leadership in Palestine had no coherent strategy in respect of this Jewry and acted in fits and starts. Disputes frequently broke out between the emissaries from Palestine and the local leaders, on the same lines as those which emerged during the Ottoman period, but this time at a lesser pitch because of the clandestinity which made it imperative that the clash not percolate through to the outside world. It was in this atmosphere of tension that Zionist work, now reduced to a minimum, was carried out. When the Turkish government shut down the Palestine Office in 1935, the only "official" link between Turkish Jewry and Palestine was cut.[41]

Despite clandestinity, a *Neemanei Zion* society ("The Faithful of Zion"), consisting of school-age youth, was formed in Istanbul in 1938.[42] Its object was to introduce Zionism to all strata of the Jewish population. It thus aimed to raise the level of Zionist knowledge, to develop both Zionist culture and numbers, spread Zionist literature, hold meetings and, above all, make propaganda for Jewish Palestine. At roughly the same period, there was also a small revisionist youth movement; however, this failed through lack of leadership. A year later, because of events in Europe, the Jewish Agency and an illegal immigration branch (*Mosad Lealiah Bet*), began operations in Istanbul for the rescue of Jews in Nazi-occupied countries.[43]

Even though Turkey remained neutral, the war period was rich in Zionist activities. Local Jews were frightened by the repercussions of the conflict, with its accompanying rise of antisemitism. The *Neemanei Zion* society was controlled by the Jewish Agency representative in Istanbul. It is also true that the achievements of the representatives of the Jewish colony of Palestine in rescuing Jews from Eastern Europe encouraged Zionist work locally. Its membership was not large, but the local Palestinian Zionist society was active, unstintingly dispensing Hebrew language teaching, collecting the Zionist tithe (*shekel*), raising money for various funds, publishing reports. From the end of 1942, it opened branches in towns with large concentrations of Jews, such as Izmir, Edirne, and Bursa, where educational meetings, sports events, and excursions were organized. The number of members in the provinces was still low. Emigration to Palestine accelerated despite the difficulty of obtaining certificates. Other Jewish institutions refused to help and there was some fear that they might denounce the Zionists to the government.[44] Meetings were held in private houses which restricted the number of potential recruits. Families were afraid to let their children participate in this type of activity; few young girls were able to attend meetings of this sort, as local customs, as well as the fear of abduction, barred them from going out in the street alone, even in large centers.

During the war, a nucleus inside *Neemanei Zion* formed a pioneer group sympathizing with *Hehaluz* ("The Pioneer"), a socialist movement, founded in Odessa in 1905.[45] Their 1926 "profession of faith" placed an emphasis on individual growth, acquiring the Hebrew language and culture, attachment to the *Histadrut*, the trade union, and participation in every venture undertaken by the workers for Palestine in the Diaspora. This first nucleus had branches in various provincial towns. It was mainly composed of young people from working class backgrounds, which caused problems since the founders of the society were educated youths from more privileged strata.[46] The ultimate aim of this society was emigration to Palestine. Several groups of pioneers left during the war. In 1944, there was a schism. The pioneer nucleus became *Hehaluz Turkiah* ("The Pioneer of Turkey"), organized by emissaries from Palestine; it was, in effect, a movement directed from abroad. The *Neemanei Zion* society shut down; part of its membership joined the pioneer movement; the other formed what became the "Zionist Organization" (*Hahistadrut Hazionit*).[47]

The conflict between these two Zionist groups, within an isolated Jewry abandoned by the leading Zionist bodies, inevitably grew worse. The class struggle had repercussions inside the movement, but this was no more than an extension of the situation during the Ottoman period. In addition, there were the usual intrigues and conflicts between the Palestinian emissaries and the local Zionists, a common scenario in the region. Amidst all this, there were also sports clubs, such as *Makabi*, a youth association founded in Istanbul in 1895,[48] societies for spreading the Hebrew language (*Hasafah*: "The Language"), and youth groups supporting local Zionist work.

The achievements of the pioneer movement were not negligible. In Turkey, where there was neither a Jewish proletariat, nor a socialist movement, as in Salonika or Bulgaria, the Zionist movement served as a substitute for socialism. The end of the First World War increased this tendency and, in clandestinity, when Turkish Jewry had no direct access to socialism because the movement was banned, the Zionist group with socialist sympathies emerged as predominant, bringing together the poorer elements. In the provinces, particularly in Izmir, this tendency took root. The emissaries from Palestine showered praise on the more traditional, more militant provincial youth, particularly the young people of Izmir. After the war, some of them were to be found living on the kibbutzim of Givat Brenner and Givat Hayyim in Palestine.[49] Activists from Neemanei Zion, on the other hand, founded kibbutz Hagoshrim in Galilee.

The majority of Turkish Jewry did not belong to Zionist groupings. In 1946, only 1 percent of the Jewish population of Istanbul was enrolled in their ranks.[50] The shortage of educators from Palestine contributed to this lack of organization. In the postwar period, Zionism was again viewed unfavorably in Turkey. Hostility to the foundation of the state of Israel appeared among the country's governing bodies, and the press echoed their sentiments.[51] The Zionist leaders had always striven to cultivate good relations with Turkey. That was why its policy on the Palestine question was followed very closely locally. In the Ottoman period, it was in order to negotiate; in the Kemalist period, when Palestine was no longer Ottoman, it was from fear lest Turkey side with the Arabs. This anxiety continued into the contemporary period since Turkey was the only country in the Middle East, apart from Egypt, to maintain formal relations with Israel.

Internally, Turkey followed a rigid line of categorical opposition to Zionism, while at the same time being more or less cognizant of Zionist activities, and the Jews suffered from some antisemitism, but obviously not on a level comparable to Europe. The ban on Zionism was not due to any specific opposition to the movement, but was one aspect of a nationalist policy forbidding any independent or associational activity with a foreign affiliation.[52] This ambiguity was at the very heart of Turkish policy on the Jews. Even today, local Jews, who are very attached to Israel, do not engage overtly in an activity capable of being even remotely related to Zionism.

With the foundation of the state of Israel, underground Zionist activities became even more dangerous. Arrests took place regularly. In Istanbul, adult Hebrew classes were given by Berlitz in order to be above suspicion. In the fifties, the community leaders and the Chief Rabbinate opposed any Zionist or pro-Israel meeting for fear of compromising the community.[53] The newly rich, hit by the tax on wealth during the war (see below), avoided all outward display of affluence and were afraid of involvement in any type of Zionist activity which might endanger the fortunes they had made after 1943.[54] Zionism continued to operate underground inside youth clubs, revisionist Zionist groups, or religious societies, observing the greatest possible caution. If this can be barely called Zionism in the strict sense, it is still true that a number of local Jews, despite the appearance of Turkicization, regarded Israel as the principal escape route in case of danger.

ZIONISM IN GREECE

In Salonika, the core of the Sephardi cultural area in the Balkans, Zionism under the Ottoman regime did not follow a very different course from neighboring cities such as Istanbul or Izmir. The transition from unobtrusive Jewish nationalism to more visible militant Zionism was not made until the time of the Young Turk revolution which, to some extent, made associational life possible. A few societies appeared and the Zionist press expanded. Here, too, it was a Zionism without Palestine, at least without direct reference to the question.

A certain degree of vitality came from Salonika's proximity to Bulgaria, stronghold of Sephardi Zionism in the Balkans, as well as from the interest some Zionist leaders showed in a town where Jews formed a majority, and the presence at the head of the community of a Chief Rabbi, Jacob Meir, who was sympathetic to Zionism. In fact, this vitality was such that Salonika was able to send five delegates to the Ninth Zionist Congress held in Hamburg in 1909 in the aftermath of the revolution.[55] As the number of delegates sent depended on the number of *shekels* sold, it is legitimate to suppose that not only did Zionist militancy exist but also that some sectors of the population showed concrete support for the movement. When the liberalism which marked the early days of the revolution lost its edge, caution regained the upper hand, all the more so as the powers within the community took a stand against Zionism for the same reasons as in the Ottoman capital. Here, too, they clustered around the Alliance and a group called the *Club des Intimes*, while Zionism gained ground within the religious groups. The schools of the *Hilfsverein der deutschen Juden*, the rivals of the Alliance schools, as well as the town's great *Talmud Torah*, then run by the eminent pedagogue from Palestine, Isaac Epstein, fought against the French camp. Only two delegates from Salonika attended the Tenth Zionist Congress in Basel two years later (1911) and none at all from the Ottoman capital, because of fear of arousing the central authority's animosity.

On the other hand, Zionism took root in the south of the country, belonging to the kingdom of Greece, earlier than in the lands under Ottoman rule, parallel with the development of the movement in the rest of the Jewish world, and it did so openly. In Corfu, the first Zionist orientated paper appeared between 1899 and 1901; in Larissa, the first Zionist society dated from 1902 and in Corfu from 1906; the socialist Zionist society *Poalei Zion* ("Workers of Zion") was set up in Volos in 1910.[56]

The Balkan wars (1912–13), which signalled Salonika's break with the Ottoman regime, brought a considerable expansion of Zionism. From 1912 the Jews, who had lived with the Ottomans for four centuries, had to come to terms with the Greeks. The advent of the Greeks was accompanied by antisemitic incidents. The authorities tried to win the confidence of the Jewish population, an ethnic–religious group which was almost in the majority. For Salonika Jews, the change of regime was traumatic. It was aggravated by the instability the town experienced as a result of plans for internationalization. The Greek army entered Salonika on 10 November 1912; it was followed by the Bulgarian army. Rivalry between the conquerors aggravated the situation.

The context proved favorable to the Zionist movement, which seemed like a refuge at that particular juncture. The only thing the Jew could really be certain of was that he or she was Jewish. It was also at this time that there was mention of forming an autonomous state in the city, a sort of free port where the Jewish element would predominate, and this did not fail to arouse strong feelings. The community was torn asunder by a bitter battle between Jewish socialists and Zionists. There emerged unprecedented Zionist activity. The new occupants of the city could not but support Zionists at this stage. In fact, the Greeks were favorably disposed to anything which ran counter to the Ottomans. This attitude was not solely the result of Greek hatred for their former masters; it was also justified by the very existence of the Greek nation-state, born in 1830 from the struggle against the Ottomans. There was still the aspiration to recover the provinces outside the frontiers of the Greek kingdom which were still inhabited by Greeks. In this way, the idea of national liberation became synonymous with restoration of the Byzantine Empire. This irredentist policy became more pronounced when the conservatives came to power in 1843. To begin with, anything that contributed to the dismemberment of the Empire was viewed with satisfaction. Greek nationalism and Jewish nationalism in some ways appeared to converge. Zionism also claimed return to the ancestral land in order to found a state. Similar considerations explain Bulgarian support for Zionism. In Salonika, the fact that the Greeks wanted gradually to break Jewish supremacy in the town acted in Zionism's favor. In fact, the Greeks hoped that in the long term local Jews' support for Zionism would lead to their departure for Palestine.[57]

The fire in August 1917 was a turningpoint for the Jewish community of Salonika. The spatial reorganization of the city could not fail to have repercussions on the economy, hitherto dominated by the Jewish population. The latter fought back vigorously but even so did not succeed in making its voice heard. Jewish ghettos of a sort were then formed on the periphery of the town, a way of life that the Jews had not experienced under the Ottoman regime. They became bastions of the Jewish Left and also targets for antisemites. Like the other national minorities in northern Greece, the Jews voted against Venizelos in 1915 and 1920, expressing opposition to Greek domination and sovereignty.[58] It is only possible to understand Zionism in Salonika after 1912 in the framework of this refusal by a good part of the Jewish population to shed its distinctive identity and thereby lose its privileged position in the town. In the interwar period the Sephardim of Greece, 86 percent of whom lived in Salonika, still regarded themselves as a distinctive ethnic–religious group.

In this Greek nation-state into which they were now incorporated, the Sephardim, in a sort of prolongation of their status in Ottoman society, continued to perceive themselves as distinct from the majority of the population, which was Greek and Christian, and displayed their particularist attachment. Their political behavior, on the other hand, was totally different from their customary conduct during the four centuries under the Turkish regime. As they had no support from any foreign state, they could engage in disputes with both the Greek majority and the Greek state more openly than any other national minority.[59] This political attitude broke the custom of silence and submission which they had long adopted. Their Zionism was also public. Even if the reasons for a vocal and active Zionism lay in the geopolitics of the region and in the national struggles between the Christian minorities and the Ottoman leaders, it is no less true that this Zionism was sanctioned even after Palestine ceased to be Ottoman. The same can be said of the socialism and communism which developed in the same states, movements in which Jews participated to a greater or lesser extent depending on the country. On the other hand, in the Turkish nation-state, risen from the ashes of the Ottoman Empire, these movements had to come to terms with clandestinity for a very long time, as did Zionism. Were these nation-states more democratic and therefore closer to their Western models? It must be noted, however, that under the dictatorial regime of Ioannis Metaxas (1936–41), Zionist activity in Greece came to an end after 1936.[60] In fact, it is impossible to say that these states were more tolerant, particularly bearing in mind that antisemitism in the Christian nation-states was more virulent than in the lands of Islam. What is involved here is the whole history of the cohabitation of Jews and Christians on the one hand, and Jews and Muslims on the other, which did not have the same trajectory or the same religio-juridical foundations. All things considered, the Jew was not truly integrated in these states, whether in Christian countries or in the lands of Islam. And this was so, on the one hand, because of the weakness of these states which did not succeed in achieving their assimilatory plans and, on the other, because of passive or active resistance by the Jews who continued to perceive themselves as active *dhimmis* in the Christian Balkan states, taking advantage of the introduction of relative democracy, or as passive *dhimmis*, as in modern Turkey.

On the model of political behavior in general, Zionism and its practice in these regions remained linked to this perception and evolved in accordance with the local situation. Inside the community, Jewish social groups took up political positions in line with their own interests. Thus, the Jewish working classes in the suburbs of Salonika opted for socialism and communism, and voted accordingly. The Westernized bourgeoisie formed a small group of moderates, appealing for integration, harmonious relations with the Greek state, and supported Venizelos. The Zionists, who were gradually building a majority in the community bodies, and rallying the opponents of Greek hegemony in the town, lined up against Venizelos.[61]

If the period before 1912 is compared with the following years, it can be seen that the Alliancists, who had been in the majority in the community bodies, gradually lost their position to the Zionists. Were the Zionist ranks made up solely of the middle classes? A number of Alliancists slid over to the Zionist side for ideological and pragmatic reasons. The leader of the religious Zionists and then of the Revisionists, Abraham Recanati, had been an Alliance pupil himself. The élite of Jewish society figured among the supporters of certain Zionist initiatives; in 1921, for example, a Salonika–Palestine investment company, aiming to develop commercial relations between Salonika and the new Jewish center in Palestine, was set up with a membership of 300.[62] This company bought land in the center and vicinity of Tel-Aviv (one such area became the "Florentin" district named after the Zionist militant, David Florentin). It also transferred ships belonging to Jews to the ports of Haifa and Tel-Aviv. Bank Discount, the large Israeli private bank, was also founded by members of this company.

It was very much in the Jews' interest that Salonika should not lose its Jewish coloring. Its Hellenization meant the end of the Jews' state within the state and everything that this implied in economics. A close look at the composition of the Zionist leadership shows that although it remained heterogeneous, its militants came from the middle and upper classes, those Frenchified circles which had looked towards the West until the recent past. Moreover, the Zionist vote was primarily conservative and therefore anti-Venizelist.

The Jewish population regarded the Zionists as good Jews, ready to support every good cause and to fight for the community's interests.[63] They helped Jewish refugees during the Balkan wars and the Great War, came to the aid of Jews who were attacked, of victims of the 1917 fire, and formed loan funds for small shopkeepers. Members of the revisionist Jewish youth organization, *Betar* (initials of *Brit Yosef Trumpeldor*, "Joseph Trumpeldor Alliance") fought side by side with Greek partisans during the Second World War.[64] The real function of Zionism in Salonika was its resistance to Greek hegemony. It therefore set out to be a national "minority" party in the new centralizing nation-state. From the beginning of the Greek occupation of the town, the Zionists, through their leader David Florentin, actively supported the internationalization of the town as a means of safeguarding the Jews' preeminence. The Congress of the Jews of Greece, which the Zionists organized in 1919 to prepare for the Peace Conference in Paris, passed the following resolutions: equality for Jews wherever they were; their right to self-determination in countries containing national minorities; the establishment of a Jewish homeland in Palestine under

British mandate; and the representation of the Jewish people at the League of Nations.[65] Similar proposals had already been formulated in 1917 in the program prepared for a congress scheduled to take place that year but postponed because of the fire.[66] At the time of the struggle for the abolition of Sunday as a compulsory rest day, the Zionist religious movement *Mizrahi* proposed that the Jews be recognized as a national minority in Greece.[67] This was contrary to the state's interest and aroused the resentment of the Greek leaders. The authorities' negative reaction and the hardening of their attitude encouraged Zionist expansion. In some ways, this vicious circle benefited the Jewish national movement.

In 1919, the General Federation of Zionists in Greece was founded, while the authorities began to rebuild the city. In its organizational activities, and in its official newspaper in Judeo-Spanish, *Esperansa* ("Hope," which had existed since 1915), later replaced by the *Renesensia Djudia* ("Jewish Renaissance"), *Tribune juive* ("Jewish Tribune"), a short-lived publication in French, and a Greek-language periodical, *Israel*, intended for the Jews of the old Greece, the Federation reflected a desire for regrouping, despite the dissent within its ranks which emerged later as other Zionist trends developed in the country. In 1922, it embraced 35 Zionist societies, including seven in Salonika, or 1,000 male and female members.[68] With the rise of antisemitism at the end of the twenties, membership rose to 2,500, including 1,400 in Salonika.[69]

In 1919 a branch of the conservative and orthodox *Mizrahi* Zionist faction was established in the city. Its credo was Palestine for the Jewish people under the guidance of the Torah. This society gradually came to encompass some 15 associations of various age groups, social classes, and both sexes. Throughout its existence, it published several periodicals in Judeo-Spanish, French, and Hebrew, such as *Hashahar* ("The Dawn"), *El Djidio* ("The Jew"), *La Nation, Israel*, and *Tikvatenu* ("Our Hope").[70] The movement joined the Zionist Federation, but subsequently turned into a federation itself, regularly sending delegates to Zionist congresses until the Second World War. This Zionist group supported a national–religious point of view, at the same time as it fulfilled functions of the traditional associations. This was also true of all those Zionist organizations which combined political activity in the modern sense without discarding the elements they had inherited from the premodern Jewish past. This is still partly the case in the Jewish world of the Diaspora today. The Zionist societies excelled in this role because of their self-representational ideological situation between tradition and modernity.

The *Mizrahi* movement, in its turn, embraced dozens of societies with names denoting their religious character. It carried on charitable activities, such as founding an orphanage, a medical assistance scheme, and a cooperative for the sale of kosher meat at competitive prices to the needy. At the same time, because of its religious but politicized ideology, it waged a fierce battle for the abolition of the compulsory Sunday rest day. This was a political battle, justified, on one hand, by the perception that *Mizrahi* sympathizers had of Zionism and, on the other, by the ideology of this type of Jewish organization, which was also religious. If Jewish shopkeepers closed on Sundays, they could no longer observe the Sabbath on Saturday. This was therefore contrary to one of the most important Jewish commandments. In collaboration with the rabbinate, the *Mizrahi* movement went so far as to set up a Sabbath observance society. It is from this perspective that the enrollment of a certain part of the population in the association's ranks must be understood in spite of the fact that it did not draw large numbers and that the general Zionists attracted more members.[71]

The audience of this religious trend must not be assessed purely by the size of its membership, and the same is true of the others. The movement also participated in the political life of the city. For example, its leader, Abraham Recanati, was elected to the municipal council where he acted as deputy mayor between 1929 and 1931. Thus, Salonika was the only area in the Judeo-Spanish culture area of the East where the national–religious trend acquired any real political representation. Elsewhere, it was almost nonexistent, for the simple reason that, despite their strong Jewish identity, the Sephardim of the region were not noted, at least in the contemporary period, for intense religiosity.[72]

It was also within the *Mizrahi* organization that the core of Salonika Revisionist Zionism was formed. At the beginning of the twenties, disagreements emerged between supporters of the *Mizrahi* movement and the General Zionists. The latter opted for selective emigration to Palestine, preferring people with a trade which would be useful in the new country, together with agricultural pioneers and a certain number of privileged persons. The Mandatory government in Palestine also carried out a selection policy. *Mizrahi*, on the other hand, advocated mass emigration. The General Zionists tried to stem the supporters of the religious movement's advance into the governing bodies. The World Zionist Organization was going through a crisis in this period. All these factors favored the creation of the Revisionist movement in Salonika which emerged in 1924.[73] Abraham Recanati, head of the *Mizrahi*, was one of its founders and its president. He had already published articles by Vladimir Jabotinsky, spiritual father of the Revisionist movement, in the French-language paper *Pro-Israël*, founded in 1917, which subsequently became a pillar of this new tendency. This paper had also intervened with the Greek and British authorities in 1918 with a view to enrolling 300 volunteers in the Jewish

Legion founded by Jabotinsky, which later fought on the Middle-Eastern front. The end of the war prevented the plan from becoming a reality.

Isaac Cohen was Salonica's representative at the first Revisionist assembly organized in Paris in April 1925. He and Abraham Recanati were subsequently elected members of the central committee of the world Revisionist movement. At the Fourteenth World Zionist Congress, held in Vienna in 1925, at the initiative of Abraham Recanati, two Sephardi delegates, one from Palestine, the other from Bulgaria, together with Jabotinsky, formed the Revisionist faction, which enabled Jabotinsky to set out his program and proclaim his independence. The following year, Jabotinsky's visit to Salonika relaunched the local movement and widened the gulf with the General Zionists. The *Bnei Mizrahi*, or religious youth, joined *Betar*, or Revisionist youth, and formed the largest youth organization: *Bnei Mizrahi–Brit Trumpeldor* ("Sons of Mizrahi–Trumpeldor Alliance"). The religious movement and the Revisionists merged – a development unique to Salonikan Jewry. A Right bloc was thus formed and faced a Left bloc, made up of socialists who opposed Zionism. Even though a *Hashomer Hazair* group ("The Young Guard"), a Zionist pioneer youth group with Marxist leanings, was founded in the same period, socialist Zionism failed in Salonika. Both the situation at the time and the composition of the local Zionist audience recruited from the conservative middle class, account for the formation of this radical Right bloc within Salonikan Jewry. In addition, the existence of a strong socialist movement in Salonika, directly linked to the Jewish working class in the city, was a crucial factor. The religious demands of *Mizrahi* within this joint operation gave rise to disputes, bringing to an end collaboration between the two movements in 1933. The departure of Recanati for Palestine, after the wave of antisemitism in 1931, helped to weaken these movements. Until the advent of Metaxas in 1936, the Revisionists continued their activities, with their own societies and newspaper, *La Boz Sionista* ("The Zionist voice").

In Salonika, the antisemitism of the thirties was combined with anticommunism. Jews were associated with communism in the eyes of their opponents. The rise of antisemitic movements strengthened the Zionist Right, even though Jews continued to be described as communists. The pogrom in the Jewish district of Campbell in Salonika, in 1931, provoked by groups with fascist tendencies, took place in the same tense atmosphere. It caused waves of emigration and, in its turn, gave a boost to right-wing Zionism, even though its leaders had already left the city for Palestine. This hardening in non-Jewish attitudes contributed to the Zionist supremacy in community institutions.

Zionism in Salonika therefore went through several phases. Until the Greek occupation a low-key Zionism prevailed; subsequently, it emerged in full bloom. The Balfour Declaration in 1917 opened up new perspectives, all the more so as the Zionists were supported locally by the Greek authorities. After the Greek occupation, Zionism operated as a Diaspora nationalism, more concerned with local problems than with emigration. The overlap between Zionism and national policies in the country was linked to the historical past of the city and the circumstances of its Jewish inhabitants. What emerged was a type of Zionism peculiar to a city which had been overwhelmingly Jewish in the past and which was faced with loss of this specific feature, a key element in the way of life and social and political aspirations of a large part of its Jewish population. This self-assured nationalism developed overtly since Zionists were regularly elected to parliamentary and senatorial bodies. This was, in addition, a bourgeois brand of Zionism. It was only after the pogrom in Campbell that active left and right-wing Zionism, oriented towards emigration to Palestine, was to be found side by side with Diaspora nationalism. Antisemitism channeled it in this direction and encouraged the various trends to regroup to implement their plans.[74] Zionism advocating emigration to Palestine was not predominant, but circumstances certainly encouraged it.

In 1929 the Salonika community possessed 14 periodicals including seven dailies, three in French and four in Judeo-Spanish, most of them having between one and two thousand readers, primarily in Salonika.[75] *L'Independant*, founded 43 years earlier, was sympathetic to Zionism. *Le Progrès*, once Zionist, had opted for what the Zionists described as assimilation but was actually only timid integration. *Le Flambeau* ("The Torch") had been created by the Zionists. *El Puevlo* ("The People"), with a large circulation, was strongly Zionist, *Avanti* ("Forward"), was communist, *El Tiempo, La Renesensia Djudia*, and *Israel* were Zionist, and *L'Echo de Salonique* pleaded for an assimilation of sorts.

Ten years later the mood was for integration; even the Zionists called for it.[76] Jewish schools were empty; Jewish youth associations no longer attracted many members. As in neighboring Turkey, Zionism now existed without Zionist culture and with no real leadership. Metaxas's dictatorship had wreaked havoc. The Zionist Federation was almost nonexistent, the struggles between the different trends a thing of the past. The poor hoped to emigrate to Palestine. Only four newspapers favorably disposed to Zionism and emigration to Palestine survived in Salonika. This represented the rout of Zionism, linked to the closing of the public sphere under the authoritarian rule of Metaxas.

On the eve of the Second World War, Zionism had been reduced to silence.[77] The war itself decimated the Jewish population of Greece. An attempt was made to reorganize Zionism in the postwar period and relaunch a publication to revive the movement.[78] Salonika had become a

Jewish desert. In July 1945, 200 Jews were left in the town. There was everywhere an urgent need to create ideological and spiritual leadership.[79] After the foundation of the state of Israel, Greek Jewry was only a shadow of its former self. There was no longer a Zionist organization.[80] There were ten Zionists in Salonika; in Athens, a Zionist youth association had a hundred members. Those who had left for Palestine before the war, after the Campbell pogrom, had escaped death in the Holocaust and were able to bear witness to the glorious period of Zionism in the "mother city in Israel," Salonika. Although Zionism made an impact and seized control of the community bodies, it acted primarily as a Jewish Diaspora nationalism, as it did in most Central and Western European countries.

SEPHARDISM

In the multi-ethnic region that became Yugoslavia, Zionism was introduced into the context of a Jewry which was already composite in consisting of Ashkenazim and Sephardim. According to the official census of 1931, 13 years after Yugoslavia was created, the country contained 68,405 Jews, 57 percent of whom were Ashkenazim, 38.25 percent Sephardim, and 4.72 percent who defined themselves as Orthodox.[81] The past history of the two groups, their existence under different regimes, depending on their geographic location, and consequently their degree of integration into the surrounding area, all influenced the community. Zionism erupted in the midst of this diversity, and for the same reasons obtained varying results. In regions such as Croatia, where there were large concentrations of Ashkenazim, Zionism emerged amidst a Westernized Jewry in the process of integration, as it did in Europe. It encouraged a return to origins among those who were moving away from Judaism or passing through an identity crisis. It also offered an alternative to the Jew faced with the impossibility of becoming an "authentic" Croat.[82]

The occupation of Bosnia-Herzegovina by Austria-Hungary from 1878 and its permanent annexation in 1908 brought Central European Jews into a country which was primarily inhabited by Sephardim. As the local Jews had lived under Ottoman rule for four centuries, neither their perceptions of themselves nor of the surrounding society were the same as the Central Europeans'. In a Sephardi milieu, which was still close to tradition, Zionism did not operate in the same way as in Croatia and Vojvodina, where the Jews took their stance in a radically different environment.

The creation of the Kingdom of the Serbs, Croats, and Slovenes after the Great War brought two groups with different cultures into contact, the

Ashkenazim from the Habsburg lands and the Sephardim from Ottoman countries. The politico-social environment in which these populations lived and their relationship to their Jewish identity influenced their behavior with regard to Zionism. There were, on the one hand, the Ashkenazim, comprising two-thirds of Yugoslav Jewry, living in the most urbanized and Westernized areas in the North. On the other hand, the Sephardim were settled in the poorer zones in the South and East of the country.[83]

Being a Zionist in Belgrade in the interwar period did not prevent the Jew from considering him or herself a Serb patriot, whereas in Zagreb it meant that he or she was not a Croat of the Israelite faith.[84] In any case, the geographical position of this region played an important role in the spread of the Jewish nationalist movement.[85] The area came into contact with Vienna, where the first Zionist executive had been set up, with the other countries of Central and Eastern Europe, which were active in Zionist affairs, and with nearby Bulgaria, a Sephardi stronghold of Zionism. Inter-ethnic conflicts within local Jewry also had repercussions on the development of Zionism. The populations involved reacted in different ways and their conceptions of Zionism were not always identical. The Zionist leadership very soon fell into the hands of Ashkenazim, even though a number of societies had both Sephardi and Ashkenazi members from the beginning of the twentieth century. These societies were set up by the intellectual élite who had studied in Vienna. Exiled Serbs supported Jewish nationalism which was akin to their own aspirations. Before the First World War, Zionism primarily attracted young people; the societies *Bnei Zion* ("Sons of Zion") in Sarajevo, *Gideon* in Belgrade, and *Theodor Herzl* in Osijek were created in this milieu.[86] Zionism expanded without meeting any fierce opposition from the authorities, especially as various ethnic groups had fought either against the Habsburg occupation or against the Ottomans in order to regain their independence. In fact, the region, where different religions came into contact, was the cradle of contending exclusivist nationalisms, each with its own history and, as we know only too well, has remained so to this day.

Zagreb, the capital of Croatia, became a great Zionist center in both its financial contribution and the size of its membership. In the mid-twenties, more than 50 societies in Yugoslavia belonged to the Zionist Federation, most formed after the Great War. Forty-eight societies with 1,600 members in 45 centers were associated with the Federation of Jewish Youth Societies, and Zionists were beginning to constitute a majority on most community bodies.[87] They had no representatives, however, in parliament. The Federation of Jewish Youth Societies operated as a youth wing of the Zionist Federation. At the end of the interwar period, it had a membership of 3,500 and, with its press and its various activities, formed an important network. At this time, the Zionist Federation incorporated 126 societies, representing different Zionist trends, ranging from the Union of General Zionists to the Marxist Zionist Youth, and played an important federative role.[88] The Zionists came to have supreme control over all the communities in the thirties. Nevertheless, Zionism never became a mass movement. The well-to-do were active in charitable societies and did not opt for active Zionism. As for the underprivileged Sephardi classes in Sarajevo, they did not join the Zionist ranks directly, even though they constituted the active mainstays of the movement. It was the Sephardi and Ashkenazi middle classes who formed the bulk of the membership. As has been seen, these groups had turned towards the Alliance wherever it operated; in its absence, they gravitated towards Zionism.[89] The Zionist Federation itself was the product of this class, which formed the Federation's backbone. The Zionist leadership, on the other hand, was concentrated in the hands of members of the liberal professions.

Zionism offered a ray of hope to the Sephardi Jewish population living in very great poverty in Macedonia, and some Jews left Bitola (Monastir) for Palestine in the twenties.[90] At that time, Yugoslavia was the 21st largest contributor to the Jewish National Fund.[91] Here, too, the Zionism which predominated was not, on the whole, directed towards emigration to Palestine. Once again, it resembled the Zionism of Western Europe, where it was thought that a Jewish national home was necessary for those in distress. The generation born before the twentieth century was attracted to General Zionism. The cohort born at the beginning of the century did not join forces with Serb or Croat nationalism, but also opted for Zionism, in tandem with communism. It was the children of the middle class who chose a left-wing socialist Zionism (*Hashomer Hazair*) at a time when socialism and communism were expanding in the country and Jews could not participate fully in them. The reverse was true of Salonika, where the Jewish socialist movement was inseparable from the Jewish group, which had founded it and formed its base, until it was absorbed into the Greek communist party. This left-wing Zionism, which took root within a relatively integrating Jewry, was predominant in Yugoslavia in the inter war period, whereas religious Zionism and Revisionism expanded in Salonika. It was very successful among student youth from Sephardi as well as Ashkenazi middle-class backgrounds, who preferred a more radical Zionism to their parents' moderate variety.[92]

Sarajevo, a Sephardi center which had a weak Zionist organization but where an important Sephardist movement was created, was also transformed into an active center for this trend in the thirties. Other youth groups close to socialism, such as *Kadimah* ("Forward") and *Thelet Lavan* ("Blue and White") appeared at this time. There existed other groupings in the country, such as *Akibah* or the *Young Girls of WIZO*, as well as societies affiliated to the Zionist Federation of Yugoslavia. *Hapoel Hazair* ("Young Worker") and *Ahdut Haavodah* ("The Workers' Union") also emerged, advocating the establishment of a socialist society in Palestine. *Zidov* ("The Jew"), the Federation's official organ, was still appearing on the eve of the war. Written in Serbo-Croat and published in Zagreb, it had a long life, covering the whole interwar period. *Jevrejski Glas* ("The Jewish Voice"), a Zionist paper with a Sephardi orientation, appeared in Sarajevo.[93]

After 1933, there was also a Revisionist organization which aimed to attract Sephardim, with its militarist youth offshoot, *Betar*. Even though Revisionism was active, it did not make great strides. The context was not conducive to this type of movement. This was a period which can be described as a "golden age" of Zionism. In 1939, this Jewry, consisting of 70,000 people, a third of them Sephardim, sent six delegates to the Twenty-first Zionist Congress – resounding proof of the scale of the Zionist activity by a population which made a large contribution towards financing the movement as a whole.[94]

The *Hashomer* movement went on to form the seedbed for the *kibbutzim* in Palestine. It was primarily directed towards pioneering emigration. Thus, Yugoslavia had 20 centers preparing people for pioneering emigration in these years, training candidates both from its own movement and from rival groups.[95] These branches, situated in rural and urban centers, such as the agricultural center of Golenic, were used by refugees from Germany on the eve of the Second World War, as Yugoslavia was a transit point between Nazi Europe and Palestine.[96]

Zionist propaganda and the schemes of the World Zionist Organization, as well as the efforts of its leaders, were concentrated on the acculturated Jews of Croatia and Vojvodina. This attitude did not only concern the region but was for long a constant factor within the Zionist Organization. The history of Zionism among the Sephardim of the future Yugoslavia and the birth of the "Sephardist" movement were both the symptom of, and the reaction to, the "Ashkenazi" character of local Zionism.

Sephardism, which appeared at the end of the nineteenth century among the Sephardi Jews of Bosnia, in the emancipatory context of Central Europe, was a specific response to the West. The Sephardist movement was born exactly where Westernization seemed to find the best conditions for its development. Whereas this process implied the abandonment of particularism, this movement, confronted with the Ashkenazi environment and with centralizing Zionism, put forward its "Sephardi" character as a "refuge-value" and as a means of preserving Jewish identity in the face of possible assimilation.

In 1898, Sephardi students, studying in Vienna and exposed to Western ideologies, formed the *Sosyedad Akademika de Djudios Espanyoles: Esperanza* ("The Academic Society of Spanish Jews: Hope").[97] Its founding members included Vita Hayon from Sarajevo, who later became the spiritual leader of the movement. Aiming to protect their linguistic and historic heritage, they sought organizational and cultural means to rouse the Sephardim from their lethargy and make them contribute to the progress of Jewry as a whole. A large number of Sephardi intellectuals were active in this society. The next generation, which studied in Zagreb, a town with a preponderantly Ashkenazi community, founded its own *Esperanza* society in the interwar period. In the end, this culturalist trend changed into an ideological movement. The Sephardim hoped to develop a Diaspora-type Zionism that would flourish in both the Diaspora and Palestine.

This movement developed among the Sephardi Jewry of Bosnia who had continued to retain a strong Jewish identity in surroundings which were multi-ethnic, and which had been passed from Ottoman to Habsburg rule. The environment permitted such self-assertion. The Habsburgs' arrival was accompanied by the arrival of the Ashkenazim. In reaction to this Westernised Jewry, the Bosnian Jews, whose religiosity was beginning to flag, took refuge in their Sephardi identity.

Under the Ottoman regime, Judaism had been the Bosnian Jews' distinctive characteristic, and they both perceived themselves and were perceived by the surrounding society, in relation to it. Now, confronted with another brand of Jewry, their Sephardi identity became a specific marker. In this region which had long been Ottoman, the Sephardim had continued to maintain their language, lifestyle, and customs within the framework of the autonomy they had been granted on Islamic soil. Their Sephardi distinctiveness, present in their daily lives, was inseparable from their Jewishness. Those young students who came into contact with the West, rediscovered their Sephardi identity away from home, at a time when there was a danger that this Sephardi uniqueness would disappear under the steamroller of nationalisms which were increasingly intolerant of particularisms. Helped by the nostalgia of exile, they recreated the lost paradise through this affirmation. This was a luxury available only to individuals who had enjoyed the privilege both of discovering the West and of assessing the dangers of possible assimilation. When Zionism became increasingly the prerogative of the Ashkenazim, the Sephardim in Sarajevo, and to a certain extent the less traditional Sephardim in Belgrade, like other ethnic groups, identified with a specifically Sephardi nationalism without emigrationist aims. In fact, Yugoslavian multinationalism had replaced Ottoman multiconfessionalism. Instead of seeing themselves, and being seen, as Jews, these Jews first and foremost perceived themselves, and demanded to be perceived, as Sephardim.

The Sephardist movement was nationalist, but rejected the Zionists' unitary ideology leading to the establishment of a national home in Palestine. They considered themselves no less Zionist than the Ashkenazim, but claimed that the latter did not understand their interests and needs. Sephardi nationalism did not favor work in Palestine at the expense of the Diaspora. The Ashkenazi leadership, dominant in Zagreb, did not look kindly on the Sephardist attitude to Zionism and their choice of a Diaspora-type nationalism. Relations between Sephardim and Ashkenazim underwent a serious deterioration in Sarajevo in 1924 over the Zionist issue, provoking what was later known as the Sarajevo dispute, lasting until 1928.

While all this was going on within Yugoslavian Jewry, Sephardi nationalist notables at the Thirteenth Zionist Congress at Carlsbad in August 1923, decided to hold a meeting to discuss the changes and expansion of Zionist propaganda among Sephardim, as well as their participation in the rebuilding of Palestine.[98] The list of individuals present at this meeting represented the regions where the majority of descendants of the expellees from the Iberian peninsula lived, with the exception of North Africa. It appears that 20 delegates in all attended, coming from Bulgaria, Jerusalem (a city with a heavy concentration of Sephardim), Salonika, Italy, Yugoslavia, and France, which had become a major center of Sephardi immigration since the beginning of the twentieth century. Participants called for the organization of a Sephardi committee in the Diaspora which would work for the Zionist movement. They adopted an eight-point program aimed at forming a Sephardi lobby, which would work both in the Diaspora and in Palestine for the benefit of Sephardim, and would become their accredited mouthpiece. The Carlsbad meeting then called for a general conference of representatives of the Eastern communities to be held in Jerusalem. The Zionist leadership in Bulgaria immediately rejected this proposal on grounds of the unity of the Jewish people in respect of the Jewish national question and argued that the diversity of the Sephardi world would make such a policy null and void.[99]

The Zionist executive in Jerusalem, on the other hand, showed sympathy for this movement which it thought could stimulate Sephardi activities towards the rebuilding of Palestine.[100] For example, Menahem Ussishkin (1863–1941), one of the heads of the Zionist executive, thought that regrouping the Sephardim would restore their self-confidence and encourage the rise of Zionist ideology in their ranks. He also rejected the argument of the Bulgarian Zionists about diversity – and linguistic diversity in particular – of the Sephardim. In fact, Ussishkin recognized that there were greater differences between Sephardim and Ashkenazim than among the Sephardim themselves.

The future conference intended to spread the Sephardi Zionist field to North Africa, Mesopotamia, and Syria. Was it an ethnic reflex action that caused the Sephardim of Bulgaria, proud of their Sephardi character, to declare that they had nothing in common with their coreligionists in Arab-speaking regions? The office preparing the way for the new Universal Confederation of Sephardi Jews sent a questionnaire to all the Sephardi communities in order to monitor their respective situations and their participation in the Zionist cause.[101] Yugoslav Jews played an important role in the creation of this Confederation in 1925, on the occasion of the second world conference of Sephardim organized in Vienna.[102] Its headquarters, which were originally to have been in Jerusalem, were established in Paris. The Sephardim of Belgrade established their own branch, the Organization of Sephardi Jews of Belgrade, which concerned itself not only with cultural questions in the Diaspora, but also worked for the improvement of the status of Sephardim in Palestine. Strangely enough, Sarajevo, the Sephardi town *par excellence*, did not have its own branch. Belgrade, on the other hand, became an important center for the Sephardist movement. As for the Confederation, it did not yield the anticipated results and remained of no great moment either in the eyes of the Zionists or of the Jewish world in general.

Towards the end of the twenties, there was an attempt to organize Sephardi youth, which did not support Sephardism, the domain of their parents. This youth turned towards the Zionist Left, looking to the pioneering ideal to resolve its crisis of identity. After the German occupation, the Belgrade *Hashomer* movement was to join Tito's partisans.[103] Young Sephardim who were outside the Zionist circle enrolled in Sephardi clubs and sports associations. A number of those who belonged to the Zionist Left joined the communist youth or the communist party.[104] This section of the population therefore shook off the yoke of their parents' identity and chose radical paths.

The Sephardist movement was in fact directed primarily at Sephardi intellectuals; the masses remained outside its ideology. It cannot be said that the Sephardist movement made any real contribution towards improving the condition of Sephardim in the Diaspora or Palestine. Nevertheless, it placed the Sephardi problem on the public agenda and reminded the Zionist movement that it was a prime concern. Marriages between Ashkenazim and Sephardim, youth organizations and the activities of *B'nai B'rith* gradually drew the two groups closer together.

The Holocaust destroyed a good part of Yugoslavian Jewry. In the new postwar situation, Jewish youth joined the ranks of the communists, opposing the spread of Zionism.[105]

In the multinational context of Yugoslavia and of a multi-ethnic Jewry, the Sephardim were thus able to assert their Jewishness and their Jewish nationalism in an ethnic and Diaspora manner, and in this way, express the self-consciousness which was emerging within the Eastern Sephardi world. The Sephardis' Jewish nationalism did not choose just a single route. Several factors affected the form it assumed. Austro-Hungarian rule, the multinational state of Yugoslavia created after the First World War, the transition from religious identity to national and ethnic identity, all made an important contribution to the development of a nationalism which was both multifaceted and specific in this region.

TRIUMPHANT ZIONISM IN BULGARIA

In its own way, the case of Bulgaria also illustrates Zionism's diversity in the Balkans. The movement's different trends were represented here in a pattern which bore only scant resemblance to the situation in Salonika, Turkey, or Yugoslavia, where the predominance of Ashkenazim in Zionism altered perspectives considerably. At the elections which took place at the time of the Seventeenth Zionist Congress in Bulgaria in 1928, the General Zionists obtained 45.7 percent of the votes, the socialist wing, *Poalei Zion*, close to 30 percent, and the Revisionists 25.4 percent.[106] These ratios were maintained until the *coup d'état* in 1934, which brought democracy in the country to an end. The socialist Zionists then withdrew, to avoid reprisals from the new government, and disappeared entirely in 1939, with the rise of fascism. The progress of local Zionism therefore remained closely linked to the country's political development – which also explains Zionism's variations between Jewish communities in the Sephardi culture area.

From the first decades of the twentieth century, Zionism in Bulgaria operated as a proactive movement and not as a party of opposition to the Alliancist notables. The struggle against the Alliance Israélite Universelle certainly marked the early years of the movement, as it did in the Ottoman Empire. But by the beginning of the century, the Zionists had already ousted the Alliance's schools from the communal scene, and thus gained a larger margin for maneuver. The strength that the movement acquired locally also arose from its own history, the way it was integrated into the community landscape, its freedom of action and the support it received in the country, as well as its popularity with the different strata of Jewish society. Thus, in 1922, out of a total Jewish population of 50,000, 6,827 paid the *shekel*, all of them adults, as only adults were liable to this charge.[107] This is a considerable number, even if it does not reflect the movement's actual strength, as not all *shekel* buyers were necessarily affiliated to local Zionist organizations. On the eve of the Second World War, 10,000 people were affiliated to the Bulgarian Zionist Federation, embracing some 30 societies, even though it was not officially recognized by the Bulgarian authorities.[108] This represented 25 percent of the Jewish population which, according to the World Zionist Organization, numbered 42,000 souls. All these figures are significant, particularly when they are compared with the situation prevailing elsewhere in the Eastern Sephardi culture area, where Zionism could not reach such heights, even when it dominated community bodies. Here again, Yugoslavia remains an exception, because of the heterogeneity of its Jewish population; the statistics always show overall totals which conceal the proportion of Sephardim involved.

In 1923 the Zionists polled 90 percent of the votes in elections for synagogue councils and schoolboards and thus began to dominate the community scene.[109] The Zionist Federation, which had been planned as far back as 1898 and which survived until 1942, became a full-fledged community institution at this time. In fact, the conquest of community power had been planned since the early years of the twentieth century. The Zionists had not only to fight the Alliancist notables, but also the socialists, communists, and the religious head of the community, the Chief Rabbi Marcus Ehrenpreiss.[110] Bulgaria bears some resemblance to Salonika in this respect. With the departure of the Alliance, the Zionists gradually succeeded in giving the Jewish schools a national character and spreading the study of Hebrew, alongside teaching in Bulgarian, thus contributing to the revival of the Jewish national language.[111] On the one hand, the notables had to be persuaded to accept Hebrew as a language of instruction parallel with Bulgarian; on the other, the socialists had to be convinced that Judeo-Spanish could not fulfill that function.[112] The conflicts between the various community partners at that time crystallized around the question of the language of instruction.

Once at the head of the community institutions, the Zionists succeeded in creating a true Jewish nationalist life. The resounding result of this was the massive departure for Israel of Bulgarian Jews from every social class after the establishment of the state. All things considered, it was in Bulgaria that the Zionist Federation was unquestionably transformed into a community leadership and remained so until the eve of the war. It did not, of course, have a completely free hand, since it had to confront the various Zionist movements, which were tearing each other apart, and also, sporadically, the socialists and communists, as well as the groups of notables opposed to the Zionist plan, who were now enrolled in the lodges of *B'nai B'rith*.[113] However, as there were not very many Jewish socialists and communists, their freedom of action within these parties was also restricted.[114]

The Zionists' hegemony in the community lasted until 1942, when all Zionist and political organizations were dissolved.[115] The Zionist Federation had already suspended its activities the previous year.[116] Zionist activity did not regain its vitality until September 1944. The *coup d'état* on 9 September that year ended the authoritarian regime, during which the Jews had suffered spoliations and virulent antisemitism.[117] A single federation was founded, without Revisionist representation, because of the communists' hostility to this right-wing Zionist movement, but including the various moderate and left-wing groups.[118] The Jews rallied around Zionism in the confrontation with communism; the Zionist Federation had more than 19,000 members at this time.[119] The visit by David Ben Gurion (1886–1973) to Bulgaria in 1944 gave Zionism a boost. From the end of December 1947, the Bulgarian government authorized emigration to Palestine. This was the subject of fierce disputes between Jewish communists and Zionists who both wanted to monopolize this activity. Eventually, the organization of emigration was entrusted to the Central Consistory, which was in communist hands. The end for the Zionist Federation came at the beginning of May 1949: the majority of the community had emigrated to Israel and local Zionism had lost its raison d'être. A remarkable feature of the postwar Federation was the dominance of socialist tendencies. *Poalei Zion*, founded in Philippopoli in 1910, with its paper *Probuda* ("Awakening"), was the largest movement in 1944–8, with a membership of 7,000.[120] There again, the situation in the country exerted a significant influence on the complexion of the Zionist Federation.

The fact that Zionism was transformed into a community leadership over a period of some 20 years makes Bulgaria unique in the Sephardi culture area. In one fell swoop, Bulgarian Zionism took its place at the center of the community's political structures and not on the margins, as was the case elsewhere in the region. While it is true that the movement did from time to time reach the political center in several communities in the Balkans, nowhere did it attain hegemony as in Bulgaria.

The upheavals, which the Zionist Federation itself experienced in the course of its long existence, throw light on the tensions which pervaded the Zionist movement as a whole. In the first years of the twentieth century, the discussion of the Uganda project caused the territorialists to leave the Federation. The Balfour Declaration then created a dynamic leading to a considerable increase in local membership. Revisionist Zionism began to emerge from 1924 and, from 1927 to 1940, its official organ was the

Bulgarian-language newspaper *Rassviet* ("Dawn").[121] Youth was organized into the Democratic Zionist Activist Group, under the leadership of Benjamin Arditi, a future Revisionist leader. Another group belonging to the same faction was created inside the socialist movement, *Hashomer Hazair*. In the thirties, *Poalei Zion* and the Revisionists left the Zionist Federation.[122] On the other hand, the religious Zionist movement, *Mizrahi*, which was timidly set up in 1935, never really made a breakthrough in Bulgaria, unlike Salonika where, as we know, it was very influential.[123] In addition, there were sports clubs, youth associations, Zionist women under the banner of WIZO, and various socialist trends. There were also a variety of fundraising bodies, including the Jewish National Fund, contributions to which the Zionists imposed on all the Jews of the community, from the twenties until 1935.

Regular participation by Bulgarian delegates can be noted at the time of the Second World Zionist Congress up until 1946.[124] The Bulgarian Zionists also held their own congresses, 25 in 50 years, the last in October 1937.[125] They went so far as to reject the Sephardist option which might have competed with Westernization and Zionism in this culture area. Not only the shape of the community, which contained few Ashkenazim, but also the orthodoxy of local Zionism affected this decision, unique in the Sephardi *Kulturbereich* of the East at this period. Journalistic activity within the community also indicates considerable Zionist vitality. The majority of the 228 papers published in the country between 1897 and 1948 were Zionist.[126] There were Zionist periodicals in Judeo-Spanish, Bulgarian, and Hebrew, including the official organ of the Zionist Federation, *Hashofar* ("The Ram's Horn"), which appeared between 1901 and 1941 in Bulgarian, and was replaced between 1944 and 1948 by *Tsionistika Tribuna* ("Zionist Tribune"). Among those which survived for relatively long periods were *El Dia* ("The Day," 1897–1914), *Jvrejski Glas* ("The Jewish Voice," 1922–6), *Jvrejski Tribuna* ("The Jewish Tribune," 1926–9), *El Djidio* ("The Jew," 1927–9), and *Hatikvah* ("The Hope," 1928–32).[127] Bulgaria was thus not only the motherland of pre-Herzlian Zionism in the Sephardi world but also the motherland of institutionalized Zionism. It was in addition the home of a community governed in its diversity according to the Jewish nationalist ideology, and ultimately destined to disappear as a result of emigration to Palestine, which cannot, of course, be dissociated from the postwar situation. This story is relatively unknown in Jewish historiography, and merits further study.

The responses to Zionism were therefore as varied as the responses to imported Westernization. Zionism also came from outside the Sephardi world, but it was nonetheless better able to blend into the framework of local Jewish and non-Jewish realities. The multiplicity of responses did not prevent either the Zionisms or the Jewish nationalisms from forming the most vital Jewish public arena in the Sephardi culture area. This was the domain where the Sephardi underwent genuine politicization, transcending the frontiers of his or her community, particularly within non-Jewish bodies, as was the case with the Zionist-inclined Jewish deputies and senators in Salonika. Zionism was also at the heart of the political debates concerning Jews at the time when Salonika was Hellenized. The ranks of the socialist-oriented Zionist movements were swollen by people who did not have the opportunity of enlisting outside their community in the service of those new nineteenth and twentieth-century ideologies with which they identified. Yugoslavia is a case in point, or Bulgaria, where Jews were still not able to play a full part in non-Jewish socialist and communist movements (unlike Salonika, where the Jewish role in the socialist movement was enormous). Nationalism and Zionism were major means of socialization and politicization, for both women and men. Women moved from the bourgeois type of societies founded by the Alliance to areas of active socialization where, at least in questions which concerned them, they could attempt to shape the destiny of their people.

Thus, through Zionist societies and activities, these Sephardi girls and women crossed the threshold of their homes for the first time, at a juncture moreover, when they did not have access to the world of labor. However, it was one thing for Zionism to be a movement going out to meet women; it was something else for women to succeed in actively investing their energies in the cause. Like other nationalisms, Jewish nationalism too was a male movement, putting a high value on virility. Bulgaria, for example, where Zionism was so powerful, demonstrates this amply. Zionist women there were organized outside the Zionist Federation and in fact could not belong to it individually until 1936.[128] If Jewish nationalism and Zionism were indeed one of the facets of a modernization that did not break totally with tradition, for women they extended the Westernization begun at school by socialization and a relative politicization.

SOCIALIST OPTIONS

Even if Jewish nationalism and Zionism were major Jewish political and social options in the Judeo-Spanish communities in the twentieth century, they were of course not the only ones. The formation of the Workers' Socialist Federation of Salonika, the only Jewish socialist trade union in the Sephardi world, was also part of the wave of change. Founded in May–June 1909 by a group of Sephardim, with a few Bulgarians and a few Macedonians, it was the expression of the grassroots.[129] Its leading light, Abraham

Benaroya, a native of Salonika who had learned about socialism in Bulgaria, was involved in a series of socialist-oriented ventures.[130]

The Second International recognized the Federation the year it was established. Its membership included various non-Jewish elements, but the majority, recruited from among workers in the Tobacco Monopoly and various sectors of nascent industry – typographers, craftsmen, clerks, and dockers – were Jews. This organization involved some 7,000 to 8,000 people and played a leading role in Salonikan life[131] through its papers, *Jurnal del Lavorador* ("The Worker's Paper," 1909–10), *Solidaridad Ovradera* ("Worker Solidarity," 1911–12), *Avanti* ("Forward," 1911–34), which had a print run of more than 5,000 in 1912, its pamphlets, and its tremendous impact on the laboring masses. Jewish circles were thus introduced to socialism and its vicissitudes in the Western world via Judeo-Spanish, in constant use in activist literature, even though newspapers appeared in several languages, which were also used in verbal propaganda. Eleven of the 12 pamphlets published by the Federation were in Judeo-Spanish.[132] For the masses, socialism represented a new opening onto the world beyond the community and also onto the non-Jewish West. The polemics between the socialists and the Zionists were memorable. Although there were contacts with David Ben Gurion, Yizhak Ben Zvi, and other leaders of the socialist Zionist organization *Poalei Zion*, these had no lasting results.

Moreover, the mere fact that the Federation existed, and the place the Jews held in it, prevented socialist Zionist movements from developing in Salonika, whereas this was possible in Volos in Old Greece, for example. The Federation also siphoned off the Zionists' usual working class support. Actively adopted, and not imposed from above, this ideological trend is evidence of the growing politicization of the Sephardi world, which at the beginning of the twentieth century remained a privilege of the notables and was primarily limited to the organs of the community. But it is also proof of the search for an international solution to the worker question beyond ethnic–religious divisions. This process represented a new stage in the emancipation of the Salonikan Jews from their community, in a political situation which was favorable to this type of venture, such as after the Young Turk revolution. Directed in principle towards the whole Salonikan proletariat, its mainly Jewish officials strongly influenced the Federation's policy. Nevertheless, neither the Jews who belonged to the movement nor its leaders were alienated from their Jewishness, and in that respect, this mode of Westernization did not lead to assimilation. That option was not yet on the agenda in the region, even for socialists fighting for a universal cause. At the same time, because recruitment was taking place among the laboring masses who were still largely attached to the traditional Jewish way of life, because the framework remained Jewish as a result of its mainly

Jewish composition, and because socialist education took place in the Judeo-Spanish vernacular, membership of the Federation in no way necessitated a break with the Jewish world, even if it ensured contact with modern ideas and the non-Jewish world. Moreover, its leader, Abraham Benaroya, had long championed the formation of a Jewish sector inside the movement.[133] When the Greeks established their own socialist club, few non-Jews stayed in the Federation.[134] In 1918, it finally merged with the young Greek workers' party, losing its specifically Jewish character. In 1924, the founder of the movement was barred by the communist party, which henceforth controlled the movement.[135] The Federation had survived the transition from the Ottoman to the Greek era, but could not withstand the Hellenization of the town. Socialism was no longer Jewish, but it remained a choice for those who aimed to support it in appropriate conditions, most frequently outside any specifically Jewish context, as in Bulgaria or Yugoslavia.

There were Jewish sections inside the Bulgarian socialist party from the beginning of the century. Established in large towns, their membership consisted of typographers and intellectuals.[136] For a short time, they published a paper, *El Ovrador Djudio* ("The Jewish Worker"), which declared that Jewish socialism could not be Zionist, since Zionism was contrary to internationalism, and that the solution of the Jewish question lay in the struggle against capitalism. This paper was replaced by *El Puevlo* ("The People") and then by *Evreyski Rabotnik* ("The Jewish Worker") in Bulgarian, which appeared intermittently between 1909 and 1932. In the twenties, the number of Jewish sections in the country rose to 13. The socialists were active in Jewish institutions and participated in the great debates of the day on Jewish schools and their language of instruction. These socialists rebelled against Hebrew and declared that Judeo-Spanish was the mother tongue of Bulgarian Jews. After the Great War, they demanded the introduction of Bulgarian as the language of instruction alongside the teaching of Judeo-Spanish and of Hebrew for prayer. Here again, socialism not only remained close to the traditional Jewish world, but also in a way demanded, by its educational claims, that it be protected. The socialists did not play a very important role in the communities; they competed with the Zionists, who attracted their customary audience.

As for the strict Marxists, their place in the community was insignificant until the October revolution, even though they did publish a newspaper between 1912 and 1923. They waged war against the notables, the Jewish socialists, and the Zionists, and urged the Jewish proletariat and the poor to prepare for the class struggle. With the 1923 *coup d'état*, they went underground until the middle of 1944, but published a few newspapers. The underground Bulgarian communist party revived when the German armies invaded the Soviet Union in the middle of 1941. Young Jews, some Zionists among them, joined the communists and subsequently took to the countryside with the partisans, a move for which a number of them later paid with their lives. With the advent of the communists in September 1944, the Jewish communists forcibly seized all the community councils and dominated Jewish public life.[137] Nevertheless, they did not succeed in making mass inroads among the Jewish population who had overwhelmingly enrolled in the Zionist ranks. Moreover, few Jews succeeded in occupying important positions in the communist party and their influence remained minor.

The massive emigration in 1948–9 cancelled any Zionist predominance; in fact, there was virtually no longer a Jewish community, apart from a tiny number of Jews who remained in Bulgaria. A number of Jewish communists also set out for Israel. All in all, except in the immediate postwar period, the communists remained on the periphery of community life, their entry into the mainstream blocked by Zionist strength at a local level.

It is not possible to measure the proportion of Jews in the membership of the Yugoslav communist party, since after the party went underground in 1921, affiliation became secret and members' religion remained unknown.[138] In the thirties, educated young Jews, who had belonged to the Marxist *Hashomer* movement, enrolled in the communist movement. But overall, the party did not include large numbers of Jews. Nor did Jewish communists play an important role in the Jewish life of the country. Here, too, they competed with the vital socialist and Marxist Zionist groups.

It can thus be seen that politicization did not remain limited to the community alone, since Jews also had opportunities for action, if only in a limited way, within municipal, parliamentary, or senatorial bodies. Nevertheless, the community scene, with its proliferation of opinion groups, continued to offer the widest choice and it was here, too, that Jews could best invest their energies. Zionism was not the only option, and for a long period it had to meet the challenge of opposing ideologies. How is it possible to compare the impact of Zionism with the impact of the Workers' Federation in Salonika when Zionism brought 30,000 Jews out onto the streets on the anniversary of the Balfour Declaration,[139] and a signal from the Federation managed to summon, 7,000 to 8,000? What do these figures really mean? In any case, both played an important role in the politicization or, more accurately, the political socialization, of the Salonikan Jews. Can their long-term success be assessed on the basis of the figures for emigration to Palestine, and then to Israel? The Holocaust which decimated local populations in the greater part of the Sephardi culture area, also does not permit conclusions, except in the case of Bulgaria and Turkey, where massive emigration took place. In any case, Zionism and its allies appeared as the only political movements at a local level to suggest, in their words, a Jewish answer to the Jewish question, and as such they were crucial for the future of Sephardim, who did not hope for integration in the Western meaning of the word. Socialism and communism, too, offered alternate solutions. However, in the industrialization that Salonika was experiencing, a number of Jews who joined the Workers' Socialist Federation of Salonika surely did so to defend class, rather than ethnic, interests. Did the solutions socialism and communism offered, answer the needs of the Jews in these countries? The future would demonstrate the contrary. In conclusion, it is clear that the Sephardi culture area did not remain isolated from developments that affected the Jewish and non-Jewish worlds, and was fully engaged with the social, political, and ideological currents of the modern period.

5

The End of the Judeo-Spanish Balkans: The Holocaust and Migrations

ANTISEMITISM

The mid-twentieth-century Nazi cataclysm that annihilated much of European Jewish life also destroyed the great Judeo-Spanish centers, and dealt a death blow to the Judeo-Spanish language. Most of the Judeo-Spanish Diaspora was obliterated or displaced during the Second World War and the years that followed it. The centuries-old Judeo-Spanish presence in the Balkans disappeared forever.

The Ottoman Levant had not seen much antisemitism, certainly not when compared to the Christian West. The Jews, like other non-Muslims, did not enjoy juridical and social equality with the Muslims, and had been subject to occasional harassment by the authorities at various levels, especially in times of instability and weak central power. Nevertheless, there was no theologically based ideological antisemitism in Muslim lands until the modern period.[1]

In fact, the Jewish communities of the Middle East and of the Balkans generally had to face anti-Jewish acts from their non-Muslim neighbors, rather than from Muslims. This was usually manifested by accusations of ritual murder that began to crop up with great regularity after the Damascus blood libel of 1840. It seems that almost every spring one Jewish community or another was accused of kidnapping and murdering a Christian for ritual purposes.[2] The accusations were followed by riots in the Jewish quarters until the Turkish authorities intervened to quell the disturbances and act as the Jews' protectors. Nevertheless, the myth of this medieval libel, once revived, proved remarkably tenacious both in Eastern Europe and among the various Christian groups in the Balkans and the Middle East. In Izmir, ritual murder disturbances took place in 1872, followed by those in Istanbul in 1873.[3] There was another major incident in Izmir in 1891.[4] Candia had its own case in 1873,[5] and Corfu in 1891–3.[6] Between 1887 and 1898, many locales in Bulgaria saw similar accusations and riots against the Jews, the most notorious incident taking place in 1891 in the town of Vratsa, 60 km north of Sofia.[7]

The accusations were fed by resentments from many sources. Once the myth had become established in the popular imagination, it was difficult to dislodge from poorly educated populations deeply imbued with a popular Christianity disseminated by relatively ignorant clergy. The socioeconomic changes that accompanied the European domination of the marketplace, the economic rivalry between non-Muslims in a Levant where the traditional ethnic division of labor was being corroded by new economic circumstances, the search for scapegoats, urban–rural clashes, all played a role in the second half of the nineteenth century to keep the problem alive.

Nevertheless, in spite of the persistence of the blood libel charge, it cannot be said that it constituted a major threat to Jewish existence. Incidents flared up and subsided periodically. By the early twentieth century they were less frequent, and eventually became a lurid literary trope, a fixture in the antisemitic gutter press and pamphlet literature that made sporadic appearances in Bulgaria and Greece.[8]

Several factors contributed to keep antisemitism weak in this area. With the exception of a few cities such as Salonika, the Jews constituted a relatively small proportion of the overall population, and were not greatly visible. More significantly, they were one among many "minorities" and ethnic groups that inhabited the region, and were the only group without the irredentist or separatist aspirations that threatened the states in which they found themselves. On the whole, they were not the main concern of their rulers. During the Ottoman period, the Turks had to preoccupy themselves with Greek, Armenian, and Slav aspirations for independence. The Bulgarian state feared and resented its Turkish Muslim population, and was obsessed with the "Macedonian" problem after the First World War. Greece, too, was worried about its Muslim Turks, but also kept an eye on the Bulgarian, Vlach, and Albanian populations in the country, all of whom could be seen as working with foreign states. Republican Turkey resented all non-Muslims, but was more preoccupied by the Greeks and Armenians. While the Jews became one of the inevitable targets of the "nationalizing" policies of these states, they were not necessarily perceived as constituting the primary threat. Indeed, their very nonintegration and lack of political participation muted their significance in the eyes of the political classes among their compatriots.

Salonika was the obvious exception; here one finds considerable antisemitic popular agitation after the Greek conquest of the city in 1912. The Jews were a highly visible, distinctive group that constituted more than half the population and dominated the economic life of the country's great port city. As discussed above, the Greek state put into place a series of measures during the interwar period designed to Hellenize this population and to erode its economic and political power. The frictions and conflicts that this engendered fueled popular antisemitism, especially among the refugee population that had arrived from Asia Minor after the population exchange with Turkey in the early 1920s. The Jewish boycott of the elections in 1923 to protest against the electoral college to which they had been relegated was followed by the creation of the antisemitic organization Gregorios VII, and shrill press polemics in the Venizelist newspaper *Makedonia*.[9] This continued over the Sunday closing controversy in 1924–5.[10]

The deteriorating economic situation in the late 1920s, which exacerbated the resentments of the Asia Minor refugees, found a voice in the fascist-type organization, the *Ethnike Enosis Hellas* (Union of the Greek Nation) founded in 1927. In 1931, the organization had 7,000 members, 3,000 of whom were in Salonika, drawn mostly from the Asia Minor refugee population.[11] Members of this group as well as others were involved in the sole pogrom in Salonika in the interwar period. In 1931, the newspapers of the city, especially *Makedonia*, gave great prominence to an alleged story whereby a Bulgarian Jewish delegate at the *Makabi* (Zionist) congress in Sofia was said to have remarked that Bulgaria should annex the whole of Macedonia, including Salonika. The mob, composed of about 2,000 people mostly of refugee origin and of army reservists, broke into the poor Campbell quarter where 300 Jewish families had been living since the fire of 1917, and burnt their dwellings.[12] The instigators of the pogrom were all acquitted in 1932.[13]

The antisemitic campaign in the Venizelist press continued in the following years, especially over the issue of the abolition of the electoral college. Metaxas' authoritarian measures after his seizure of power in 1936 stopped all popular political agitation, including antisemitism.[14] Nevertheless, on the eve of the Second World War, Salonika Jewry still faced considerable friction with a segment of the city's non-Jewish population.

In neighboring Turkey, anti-Jewish sentiment as an ideology was not particularly acute. The Jews, together with other non-Muslims, were subject to the Turkicization policies of the state, but they were not singled out as Jews, and an antisemitic popular movement did not develop. However, the Jews suffered from the general suspicion with which all non-Muslim groups were treated, and were subjected to considerable harassment. Jews in public service as well as in companies having extensive dealings with the government systematically lost their jobs.[15] Jewish conscripts, together with other non-Muslims, did not serve in regular army units but in special battalions which performed hard labor building roads and bridges.[16] There were frequent boycott movements against Jewish businesses.[17] The Jews were heavily criticized in the press and in daily life for continuing to speak languages other than Turkish throughout the late 1920s and the 1930s.[18] While some prominent Jewish leaders such as Munis Tekinalp (Moïse Cohen) and Marcel Franco were prominent in organizations created to urge the adoption of Turkish as the Jews' language, such as "The Association for Turkish Culture" founded in 1933, most of the press polemics that this engendered had antisemitic overtones.[19] This was in ample evidence during the Elsa Niego affair of 1927 when a Jewish girl was murdered by a Muslim. In the sensationalist reporting of the event, the press accused the Jews of organizing an ostentatious public funeral which gave rise to anti-Jewish agitation. In the end, the state authorities had to intervene to end a potentially explosive situation.[20]

A law on residence was promulgated in 1934[21] which forbade those whose mother tongue was not Turkish from forming a compact group, a new village or quarter, an association of workers and artisans, and for the latter, to transmit any type of work or profession to members of their ethnic group in order to create a monopoly. It also aimed to take measures against those who had not assimilated into Turkish culture and continued to speak a language other than Turkish. And finally, it limited to 10 percent the number of foreigners in any given locality.

Some journalists such as Cevat Rifat Atilhan were clearly influenced by Nazi ideas (and received money from Germany). Atilhan, who penned scores of pamphlets against the Jews, began to publish the infamous antisemitic newspaper *Milli İnkilâp* (National Revolution) in 1934 after a visit to Nazi Germany, and engaged in vitriolic attacks on the Jews of Turkey.[22] The press emerged as an important factor in the fomenting anti-Jewish feeling which led to the one episode in this period which saw overt anti-Jewish action.

Pogroms broke out in 1934 in Eastern Thrace in the towns of Çanakkale (Dardanelles), Kırklareli, and Edirne. On June 24, 1934, crowds attacked the Jewish quarter in Çanakkale, destroyed several Jewish homes, and looted Jewish property. Similar incidents followed in the town of Kırklareli on July 3, 1934. The news from these towns, along with agitation by mobs in Edirne involving some physical attacks on Jews, and threats against the community as a whole, led to panic among Edirne Jewry. In spite of the fact that the government intervened to stop the attacks, and made declarations to protect the Jews and to calm public opinion, large segments of the Jewish population of these towns were either forced to leave or fled in fear of their lives.[23] Thousands of Jews emigrated from Thrace to Istanbul.

The Thrace events remain murky. While generalized xenophobia, a particularly anti-"minorities" governor of the region, and the general economic decline of this border region all played a role, it is also clear that the end result fitted the overall policy of Ankara to diminish the presence of non-Muslims in frontier areas, especially in this sensitive territory contiguous with Bulgaria and Greece.

As the Nazi German reports themselves indicated,[24] in spite of the Thrace pogroms, antisemitism in Turkey was not an ideology and functioned mainly as part of the overall antiminority xenophobia which was the hallmark of public opinion in the Republic's first two decades.

In Bulgaria and the areas of Yugoslavia where the Sephardim lived, antisemitism was not very significant in the interwar years. The Macedonian question, irredentist aspirations, and agitation over the area of Macedonia now under Serbian control, continued to destabilize Bulgarian politics, going so far as to contribute to the overthrow of the Stambolisky government in 1923, and widespread terrorist action by Macedonian militants.[25] This ferment also affected the Jews. In 1924, 170 Jewish notables in Sofia were approached by the Macedonian militants, and "taxed" about 20 million levas (3.25 million French francs) accompanied by dire threats as to what might happen if payments were not made. Many among the notables complied out of fear, until the government finally stepped in to stop the demands.[26] However, there is no evidence to suggest that the Macedonian militants saw in the Jews anything more than a ready source of cash. The Macedonian issue was not, on the whole, associated with antisemitism.

Some movements of fascist character came into being in the 1930s. The Union of Bulgarian National Legions which aped the Nazis was founded in 1933. Other groups such as *Branik*, which copied the Hitler Youth movement, and the Guardians of the Advancement of the Bulgarian National Spirit (*Ratnitsi*) followed suit. These organizations, influenced by developments in Italy and Germany, developed an antisemitic agenda in the late 1930s, spread antisemitic literature, occasionally harassed Jews, and broke windows of Jewish shops. However, their excesses were not tolerated by the government who prosecuted the troublemakers. On the whole, the fascist groups remained on the fringe and did not acquire a mass base.[27] They are significant only because of the association with them of personalities such as Petur Gabrovski and Aleksandur Belev (1900–44) who would later rise to prominence during the war years and have a direct impact on anti-Jewish policies.

Yugoslavia also did not see organized antisemitism in the interwar years. There were isolated episodes of anti-Jewish incidents, mostly in Croatia and in Vojvodina. The Croatian Peasant Party was largely unfriendly to Jews and occasionally used outright antisemitic language in its propaganda.[28] With the spread of Nazi ideas and tactics in the 1930s, antisemitic literature also began to make headway and certain newspapers in Serbia and Croatia became the vectors of its dissemination. By 1936, the *Protocols of the Elders of Zion* had been published in Serbo-Croat.[29] "Foreign" Jews, whether Jewish refugees from Hitlerism or relative newcomers from old Habsburg lands, were easy targets of antisemitism. With the growing *rapprochement* with Germany at the end of the 1930s, Nazi policies became more appealing to groups in power. In 1940, the government of Cvetkovich-Machek (1879–1964) passed legislation banning the Jews from wholesale food occupations, and also established a *numerus clausus* in high schools and universities.[30]

The Sephardi communities concentrated primarily in Macedonia, Bosnia, and Serbia encountered considerably less popular antisemitism than their Ashkenazi counterparts. The one episode of a boycott of Jewish business organized by the Yugoslav Muslim Organization in Bosnia in 1925 was in response to the Jewish vote for an opposing political party, and did not succeed.[31] Antisemites considered the Sephardim as somewhat more autochthonous and "native" than the previously German-oriented pro-Habsburg Ashkenazim of the areas in the West and North that had been under Austro-Hungarian rule.

The survey of developments in the various states that ruled over the Judeo-Spanish communities in Southeastern Europe in the interwar years leads to the conclusion that antisemitism was not a significant problem in the region. While there was some anti-Jewish sentiment that found expression in legislative measures and in popular agitation, nowhere did this sentiment find an organized mass base or reach an intensity that could threaten Jewish life. The situation was infinitely better than the one that obtained in Central and Eastern Europe in the same period.

The destruction of the Sephardi heartland was to be the result of external developments that came as an avalanche during the Second World War. The fate of the Sephardim of the Balkans during this period depended on the fortunes of war, geography, and the type of rulers under whom they found themselves.

GERMAN-OCCUPIED AREAS – SERBIA AND NORTHERN GREECE

The regions that fell under the direct rule of the Germans bore the full brunt of the Nazis' extermination policy as it evolved during the war years.

Of the Sephardim of the Balkans, those of Serbia, Greek Macedonia including Salonika, and Greek Eastern Thrace fell into this hapless category.

The Kingdom of the Serbs, Croats, and Slovenes fell to the Germans in April 1941. Dalmatia and half of Slovenia were annexed by Italy, the other half becoming part of the German Reich. A new state, Croatia, was created by the Axis and ruled over most of Bosnia-Herzegovina. Bulgaria annexed Macedonia, and Serbia proper fell under the rule of the German military administration that governed with the help of a puppet regime.

Most of the Sephardi population of Serbia was concentrated in Belgrade where it formed 80–90 percent of the total Jewish population of 11,000 who lived there before the Germans' arrival.[32] The new rulers took anti-Jewish action very soon after their conquest, limiting the Jews' role in the economy, confiscating their property and bank accounts, making compulsory the wearing of badges, and severely limiting their movement. The puppet Serbian regime collaborated in this action. All male Jews between the ages of 16 and 60 were drafted into forced labor battalions. With the Serbian communist-inspired uprising in the summer of 1941 after the German attack on the Soviet Union, the Germans began to engage in savage retaliations. In October 1941, the military leaders formalized their policy. Attacks against Germans were to be answered by the killing of 100 Serbian hostages for each German killed, and the death of 50 for each German wounded, and the killing of "all Jews."[33] All the male Jews in labor battalions, and others interned in camps, faced imminent death. As a result of this policy, most of them were executed in various camps in Serbia by the end of 1941. The *Wehrmacht* took a leading role in these atrocities, aided by the Security and Order Police of the SS.[34]

The Final Solution proceeded with remarkable rapidity in Serbia. Already in October 1941 it was decided to concentrate all the remaining Jews, mostly women and children, in one camp at Sajmiste, a fairground in the town of Zemun (Semlin), just across the Sava River from Belgrade. By March there were 6,280 Jews in the camp and others brought there in the next few months swelled the number to an estimated 7,500.[35] With the final decision for mass murder of European Jewry receiving its logistical framework at the Wannsee conference in January 1942, their fate was sealed. It was part of the tragic distinctiveness of the Holocaust in Serbia that, like in the occupied areas of the Soviet Union after the mass shootings by the *Einsatzgruppen*, the task was handled locally by a gas van that was dispatched to Sajmiste in the spring of 1942. On each trip, up to 100 women and children were loaded into the van for "resettlement," gassed while traveling through central Belgrade en route to the outskirts of the city, and then buried in mass graves. The population of the camp at Zemun was liquidated in this way between March and May 1942.[36] Serbia became *Judenrein* very early in the Final Solution's unfolding.

After having successfully defended itself against attack by the Italians, Greece fell to the Germans in April 1941. The King and many of the leaders fled, and a puppet regime obedient to the Axis powers was established. The general who signed the armistice, Georgios Tsolakoglu (1887–1947), became Prime Minister, and was eventually succeeded by Konstantinos Logothetopoulos and Ioannis Rallis. Greece was divided into several zones. Northern Thrace, with the exception of the Eastern border zone with Turkey, was given by the Germans to Bulgaria as a reward for having become an ally and for allowing the passage of German troops through its territory. The border zone and Greek Macedonia fell under German military rule, the Eastern Aegean Military Administration Division, and the Italians ruled the South, Athens, and the Epirus.[37]

The bulk of the Jewish population in the German-controlled areas was in Salonika, where there were some 56,000 Jews in 1940.[38] It was here that the Nazi policies as they applied to the Jews of Greece were developed and implemented. The German entry to the city on April 9, 1941 was accompanied by the usual restrictive measures. The two French-language Jewish newspapers, *L'Indépendant* and *Le Progrès* and the Judeo-Spanish newspaper, *El Mesagero*, were closed.[39] The latter was the last Judeo-Spanish newspaper in the world to publish in the traditional *Rashi* script, other Judeo-Spanish newspapers elsewhere having adopted Latin characters. A new pro-Nazi Greek newspaper, *Nea-Evropi*, appeared and engaged in antisemitic polemics from the beginning.

The members of the communal council were all arrested, to be released later. The archives of the community as well as libraries were ransacked and crucial historical documents, manuscripts, and books were confiscated by the *Einsatzstab* Rosenberg and taken to Frankfurt to the Nazi *Institut für Judenforschung* to be lost forever later during the war. Saby Saltiel, previously a rather ineffectual leader, was appointed to the presidency of the community, and acted as the main liaison between the German military administration, the SS, and the Jews of Salonika.[40]

A lull in the anti-Jewish measures followed the initial restrictive legislation. The greatest problem for the Jews of Salonika as well as for the rest of the population in this period was the scarcity of food in the severe winter of 1941–2. Many died of starvation and disease. Arbitrary arrests and some executions of Jews took place sporadically. In the meantime, crucial decisions concerning the fate of European Jewry had been taken in Germany and put into practice in Eastern and Central Europe. It was only a matter of time before the Jews of Salonika would become the victims of the extermination process.

On July 11, 1942, all Jewish men between the ages of 18 to 45 were called by a communiqué appearing in the pro-German newpaper *Apoyevmatini* to assemble at the city's central square, Liberty Square. Around 9,000 men gathered, and were subjected to harassment, beating, and insults, and were made to perform humiliating exercises. Two days later 2,000 were sent to labor battalions in various neighboring regions where they had to work for the German army in quarries, constructing roads and general hard labor. Because of the severe conditions under which they labored 250 died. The community created a committee to alleviate the conditions under which the labor conscripts worked, and attempted to ransom its youth, entering into extensive negotiations with the *Kriegsverwaltungsrat* Dr Max Merten, the military administrator for civilian affairs. The latter asked the Jews of Salonika to raise 3,500 million drahmas. In the end, the sum was lowered to 2,500 million drahmas. The community agreed to transfer the centuries-old Jewish cemetery to the municipality which had coveted it throughout the interwar years. The cemetery was promptly destroyed and the University of Salonica was eventually built on its grounds. The community had signed an agreement to raise the money by December 1942. In ways reminiscent of premodern taxation of Jews, all the leading personalities of the community, and those of Athens, were assessed according to their wealth, and eventually, 1,650 million drahmas were raised.[41] The Germans continued to harass the Jews, expropriating and plundering the property and business of the leading Jewish personalities.[42]

In the meantime, the Chief Rabbi of Salonica, Dr Zvi Koretz, who had been imprisoned by the Germans in Vienna, was released and brought back to head the Jewish council, the *Judenrat*, in December 1942, replacing the weak and incompetent Saltiel. Koretz remains a controversial figure, with some accusing him of collaboration with the Nazis. He was certainly predisposed to do the Germans' bidding in order not to alienate them and not to bring further misfortune upon the community, and became, like some of the *Judenrat* leaders in Eastern Europe, a cog in the machinery of destruction, facilitating rather than hindering the Nazis' task. Many of the Nazi measures were implemented with great severity by some Jews such as Salomon Uziel, Albert Hasson, and Jacques Albala, who in effect became collaborators.[43]

It was in January 1943 that the relevant departments of the German Foreign Ministry and the division under Eichmann in the Reich Security Main Office of the SS began to chart the logistics for deporting the Jews of Greece. Dieter Wisliceny and Alois Brunner, Eichmann's collaborators, arrived in Salonika during early February and began to coordinate plans with Merten. In the same month, the Nuremberg Laws were put into operation. Wearing of a yellow badge became compulsory for all those above the age of five, and Jewish homes and businesses were to be marked. With the aid of Koretz, a definitive list of all Jews was drawn up. Two ghettos in areas of Jewish concentration were established and the whole of the city's Jewish population was resettled by February 25. Most were settled in the Baron de Hirsch district close to the railway station. This area had been built in the early twentieth century by charitable donations of the famed Jewish philanthropist Baron de Hirsch to help refugees fleeing the Kishinev pogroms. Congregating the Jews in compact areas was a crucial prelude to deportation.[44]

On March 6 the Jews were forbidden to leave the ghettos. Their fortunes were confiscated and transferred to accounts under German control. The first train carrying Jews departed the city on March 15 and arrived at Auschwitz-Birkenau on March 20. Of the 2,800 on board, 2,191 were gassed upon arrival, and 417 men and 192 women were taken to the labor camps.[45]

One hundred and fifty Salonika lawyers protested the deportations, appealing first to the Greek Governor of Macedonia and then to the Greek government in Athens, to intervene and divert the transports to other parts of Greek territory. Athenian intellectuals and religious leaders, including Archbishop Damaskinos, also intervened, trying to save the Jews.[46] These appeals were met by the collaborationist regime's dragging its feet and feeble intercessions with the Germans which yielded no results. Nevertheless, the Greek government did protest the deportations.[47]

In the meantime, Koretz tried to buy time. When Eichmann agreed to release 3,000 Jews from the deportations for forced labor with the *Todt* organization outside the city, Koretz proposed that 15,000 be drafted for this purpose, an offer which was refused. Next, Koretz managed to see the puppet Greek Prime Minister Ioannis Rallis through the good offices of Archbishop Genadios of Salonika, asking him to intervene to stop the deportations. The tepid intercession of Rallis did not yield any results, except for the dismissal of Koretz by the Germans, and his imprisonment.[48]

Apart from some Jews who managed to escape and join the Greek resistance,[49] the only ones who eluded the grasp of the Germans, at least for the time being, were those few hundred who were foreign nationals, mostly of Spanish and Italian nationality. The question of what to do with foreign Jews in the German-occupied lands was present from the beginning of the war. There were extensive discussions between Eichmann's bureau and the German Foreign Ministry as to whether they were to be included in the Final Solution. By 1943, a decision was taken to include the citizens of conquered countries, as well as those of allies such as Bulgaria and Rumania, while those of other countries were to be "repatriated."[50]

In Greece, this concerned mostly Jews who were Spanish and Italian citizens, the largest groups among the Jews of foreign nationality.

Since the time of the Ottoman capitulations, and especially in the nineteenth century, many non-Muslims in the Empire, including the Jews, had taken up the citizenship of European countries which had used the policy to extend their sphere of influence in the region. Spain especially had made it easier for Sephardim to claim Spanish nationality in the 1920s, and many had availed themselves of the offer.[51] There were 511 Jews holding Spanish citizenship in the records in Salonika in 1943.[52]

However, "repatriation" to Spain was no easy task. Even though these Jews had the same legal status, and hence the right of entry to Spain, as any other Spanish citizen, the Spanish government balked at accepting them, and engaged in protracted negotiations with the Germans. However, the Spanish consul in Athens, Sebastian Romero Radigales, energetically protected this group. Largely due to his efforts and contacts with the Italians in the South, 150 Spanish Jews managed to escape to the Italian zone. In the meantime, the Spanish Foreign Ministry finally agreed to take the Spanish citizens of Salonika, but only after guarantees from international Jewish organizations that these Jews would transit through Spain to Morocco and elsewhere, and that they would arrive in Spain only after an equal number of refugees had left the country for other destinations. In the end, 367 Sephardim of Spanish nationality were deported by the Germans to Bergen-Belsen in August 1943 where they waited for the conditions to be met. They were treated relatively correctly, and entered Spain in February 1944.[53]

The Italian consulate in Salonika was very helpful to the Italian nationals, and also granted citizenship documents to any person who could show any link to Italian citizens. The consular staff, including the consul Guelfo Zamboni and Captain Lucillo Merci, the military liaison officer, protected these Jews and their property, and did their best to limit the impact of the Nazi legislation on its protégés. Largely through their efforts, around 750 Jews managed to move to the Italian zone in the South.[54]

The deportations from Salonika proceeded apace. Most of the transports took place between March and May 1943. The last one left in August, carrying the remnants of the *Todt* laborers to Auschwitz, while in the same month members of the *Judenrat* and the collaborators, 74 in all, were deported to Bergen-Belsen. All in all, 19 transports totaling 48,533 Jews left the city. About 77 percent, 37,386, were gassed upon arrival at Birkenau, and most of the rest perished in the next months at the labor camps in Auschwitz.[55]

The Jews of the border zone were mostly left alone until the moment of deportations. On May 8, 970 Jews of Didhimotikhon (Demotica), 32 of Souflion (Sofulu), and 160 of Orestias were taken to Salonika where they joined the transport that departed for Auschwitz on May 9.[56] By the end of August 1943, Salonika had become *Judenrein*. More than 450 years of Sephardi life in the city had come to an end. The "mother city in Israel," the Jerusalem of the Balkans, was no more.

ITALIAN-OCCUPIED AREAS – SOUTHERN GREECE

While they were allies of the Germans, and had themselves passed extensive antisemitic legislation in 1938, the Italians' behavior towards the Jews in areas that fell under their control was dramatically different from that of their Axis partner. In no instance did the Italians agree to deport the Jews under their control, and indeed did all in their power to nullify German demands for this action. A combination of humanitarianism, distrust of their allies, independent action among the military, a long tradition of obfuscation of orders through inaction, and an eye for world public opinion all combined to bring about an extraordinary set of circumstances whereby the Germans' principal ally came to block, at least temporarily, the Final Solution.[57]

The Italian zone on the Dalmatian coast along the Adriatic provided a safe haven for thousands of Jews fleeing the Germans and the Croatian fascist regime. Approximately 5,000 Jews, many of them Sephardim from Croat and German-occupied Yugoslavia, fled to this region, and lived under Italian protection. While some were captured by the Germans when Italy fell in September 1943, most survived thanks to being located in areas the partisans controlled.[58]

From 1941 to 1943, the Jews of Athens and other areas of Italian-controlled Greece lived in relative tranquility. The Italian Police Commander and administrator for Southern Greece, General Carlo Geloso, and his successor, General Vechiarelli, protected the Jews. Even though the German SS was active in Athens, the Italians were in charge and held in check most of the Germans' antisemitic actions.[59] The Italian zone became a refuge for Jews fleeing the German-occupied regions, and the Jewish population of Athens swelled to almost 10,000 by 1943.[60]

Athens was the site of the collaborationist Greek regime and of the Greek fascist organization (Patriotic National Socialist Organization, ESPO) under the leadership of Dr Speros Sterodimos, whose youth groups engaged in sporadic attacks on the Jews and ransacked the central synagogue. When the Greek resistance blew up the headquarters of the fascist organization and killed Sterodimos, the Germans took nine Jewish notables as hostages. They were released under pressure from the Italian military administration.[61]

The Chief Rabbi, Eliahu Barzilai, had been appointed the communal president by the Gestapo according to the Nazi policy of selecting a few

Jewish interlocutors who would act as intermediaries with the community, and supervise the implementation of orders. However, Barzilai was an entirely different kind of personality from Zvi Koretz, his counterpart in Salonika. He was constantly on guard, and believed in obfuscating German orders as much as possible. At his bidding, the Jewish communal council dissolved itself and created a secret committee to deal with the situation. Hence, Athens, unlike Salonika, did not have an open chain of command within the Jewish community whose very existence helped the process of spoliation and deportation.

Conditions deteriorated rapidly with the fall of Italy in September 1943. The Germans lost no time in taking control of the Italian zone, and all the antisemitic legislation that had been in place in the North was introduced in the South. Dieter Wisliceny came to Athens and established a *Judenrat*. Rabbi Barzilai was ordered to hand over a list of all the Jews from the communal records. In response, Barzilai burned the relevant documentation, and fled the city. While many other Jews escaped the city at this time, harsh living conditions in the countryside, and difficulties of transportation to safe havens outside Greece, made this a successful option for relatively few.[62]

The Germans ordered the Jews to register in October. Initially, few responded. In time, however, more obeyed the German directive, having been lulled into a relative sense of security by the SS's lack of further action.

In March 1944, the machinery of destruction became operational once again, the Germans having resolved to deport the remaining Jews of Greece. Dieter Wisliceny coordinated the deportations with the SS General Jürgen Stroop. In March 1944, the Germans arrested 800 Jews in Athens.[63] The Jews of the various towns of the Greek mainland such as Ioannina, Arta, Preveza, Volos, Larissa, and Trikala were seized between March and April. In some localities, such as Volos, many Jews managed to escape with the aid of the Greek population and the secular and religious leaders.[64] Those who fell into the hands of the Germans were initially sequestered in the notorious Haidar camp in Athens. Jews transported from there to Auschwitz in April 1944 numbered 5,200.[65] Around 1,800 Jews from the island of Corfu and 1,700 from the island of Rhodes were deported in June and July 1944.[66] By the end of the summer of 1944, between 60,000 to 68,000 Greek Jews had been transported to Auschwitz.[67]

While accurate figures are difficult to ascertain, the broad outlines of Greek Jewry's destruction during the Holocaust are clear. There did exist an active Greek resistance movement, and Greek collaboration with the Germans remained weak throughout. Nevertheless, according to the statistics compiled by the Central Board of the Jewish Communities of

Greece immediately after the war, almost 87 percent of the prewar Greek Jewish population of 75,357 died during the Holocaust, one of the highest percentages of loss suffered by any Jewish community.[68] The disaster in Salonika was one of the worst. Of a prewar population of 56,000 Jews to which were added 4,000 Jews from the surrounding towns, about 46,000 perished.[69] A small remnant survived in hiding, and a smaller remnant still survived the death camps. The immediate postwar Jewish population numbered only around 1,950 in Salonika, and about 5,000 in Athens, with smaller communities of a few hundred souls each to be found in provincial towns.[70]

"INDEPENDENT CROATIA" – SARAJEVO

Croatia came into being as an independent state for the first time in April 1941. The Germans and Italians created this satellite state to rule over large numbers of non-Croats, most notably Serbs and Bosnians. The largest numbers of Jews were to be found in the cities of Zagreb and Sarajevo. Most of the Sephardim were located in the parts of Bosnia annexed by the new state, most notably in Sarajevo where 8,000 to 9,000 Sephardim and 1,000 Ashkenazim lived.[71]

Croatia saw some of the worst atrocities in the Second World War. The fascist Ustasha regime under the leadership of Ante Pavelich massacred hundreds of thousands of Serbs in random and planned violence. The regime put Nazi antisemitic legislation in place to please its German masters, introducing the compulsory yellow badge in 1941 and expropriating Jewish property. The Germans' arrival in Sarajevo was accompanied by a Croatian pogrom which destroyed the Sephardi synagogue. Many Jews were arbitrarily arrested and executed. Between September and November 1941, the Croations deported most of the Jews of Sarajevo to local camps. Most of the men were taken to the infamous Jasenovac camp and murdered. Tens of thousands of Serbs were killed in this camp as well. The women were taken to the camp at Djakovo, and were transferred to Jasenovac in January of 1942, where most of them were killed. At German bidding, many of the remaining Jews in Croatia were taken from Croatian camps in August 1942 and handed over to the Germans who deported them. Further deportations took place in May 1943.[72] The Croatian Jews who survived, including 2,400 from Sarajevo, managed to do so by fleeing to the Italian–contolled region in Dalmatia where they received protection and help, and many were transferred to islands like Rab which had been annexed by Italy.

The area under the rule of Yugoslavia had the sad distinction of including zones such as Croatia and Serbia where most of the Jews were murdered locally.[73] The severe interethnic animosities in the region, while not directed against the Jews in the prewar period, gave rise to an explosive situation of massacre and murder with the destabilization introduced by the Axis conquest. Under the shadow of the German-inspired Final Solution, local hatreds, in their terrible denouement, consumed the Jews as well.

BULGARIA AND BULGARIAN-OCCUPIED AREAS

The fate of the Jews of Bulgaria diverged sharply from those of neighboring countries. It was one of the paradoxes of the Holocaust's unfolding in Europe that the Jews of a state that became a formal ally of Nazi Germany were not deported and were saved from death. Many theories have been put forth to explain this twist of fate. While some have argued about the philosemitism of the Bulgarian people, and the resoluteness of the King not to hand them over, others have stressed the role of the communist resistance. The picture is very complex, and indeed full of contingencies that could have led to a different outcome at any moment.

One of the most important factors that affected the situation was the nature of the political system during the war years. In spite of the fact that King Boris III (1918–43) ruled as a dictator after the coup of 1935, this was a relatively benign form of authoritarian rule when compared to other regimes of the time. In spite of the *dirigisme* of the center, parliament was not disbanded, political parties were allowed to continue and indeed take part in the political process, and the public expression of political dissent was, within limits, relatively free. Hence, when the crucial moments came, the Jews and their friends had avenues of communication and intercession that they used to avert disaster.

The Jews were a small part of the Bulgarian population, numbering 48,398 according to the official census of 1934.[74] The close to 50,000 Jews in 1940 made up under 1 percent of the total population. The Jews were most visible in the capital Sofia where half of the community lived. Composed of small businessmen, merchants, and artisans, the Sephardim of Bulgaria had not faced any significant threat to their existence until the Second World War.

Many factors contributed to the convergence of interests between Bulgaria and Nazi Germany. Bulgaria had also emerged vanquished after the First World War. It had lost the region of Southern Dobrudja in the North to Rumania and had been obliged to pay heavy reparations. Its irredentist dreams of incorporating Macedonia and reaching the Aegean in the South had been thwarted, and it had remained bitter and resentful throughout the interwar period. With growing trade relations between Germany and the

Balkans in the 1930s, most of Bulgaria's economy was tied to Germany. With the outbreak of the war, Bulgaria leaned heavily towards the Germans. The pro-German politician Bogdan Filov (1883–1945) was appointed Prime Minister,[75] and Bulgaria became Germany's formal ally in March 1941, allowing the passage of German troops for the invasion of Yugoslavia and Greece in April of the same year. It was rewarded by the Germans with Southern Dobrudja, most of Thrace, Macedonia, and a small part of Eastern Serbia.

The appointment of Petur Gabrovski, who had been associated with the fascist *Ratnitsi* as Interior Minister, made clear the country's new direction. One of the few antisemitic ideologues of Bulgaria, Aleksandur Belev, also entered the Interior Ministry, and was in charge of judicial affairs, the section that eventually developed the new state's Jewish policies.[76]

German interest in the development of anti-Jewish legislation converged with the new government's desires, and Belev spent the summer of 1940 in Germany studying the issue. In October 1940, the government published the project of "The Law for the Protection of the Nation." The proposed legislation was based on the Nuremberg Laws, defined who was a Jew, banned international Jewish organizations, excluded the Jews from public office, established quotas in universities, and put severe restrictions on Jewish economic activity.[77]

However, the law did not pass without opposition. Joseph Gueron, the President of the Jewish Consistory, and other leading Jews, lobbied against the legislation, and managed to rally certain sections of public opinion. Twenty-one leading writers, the Holy Synod of the Bulgarian Orthodox Church and leading religious personalities, the Medical and the Bar Associations, all protested. However, other groups such as the Merchants' Association (with many Jews among its membership), the pharmacists, and army groups all expressed support for the law. In the end, the government's intention of using the legislation to curry favor with the Germans prevailed, and the law was passed in February 1941.[78] Petty restrictions and economic spoliation followed in the wake of the law, and the economic and social position of the Jews began to be weakened. Many Jews were drafted for forced labor under harsh conditions.[79]

The antisemitic legislation was extended to the annexed territories where Jews had not been allowed to become Bulgarian citizens. Indeed, the Bulgarians behaved with great ferocity not only against the Jews but against all the non-Bulgarian groups of these regions, engaging in murder, looting, and rape. Thracian and Macedonian Jews were put into the most dangerous and vulnerable legal status for any Jew during the Second World War, statelessness.[80]

Nevertheless, the public debate that accompanied the law in Old Bulgaria, the existence of independent political forces, and the lack of German troops in the country, all provided for a context in which the Final Solution met with some serious impediments along the way.

Following the clear formulation of German policy at the Wannsee conference in January 1942, the demand for deportation of Bulgarian Jewry, like all other Jews, came with increasing insistence onto the German agenda. Belev was fully aware of German intentions, and began to prepare the groundwork for the transports.[81] In the summer of 1942, the government passed a law that authorized it to take action *vis-à-vis* the Jews with whatever measures it saw fit, submitting its decisions to the parliament for approval only afterwards, thus effectively sidestepping debate. This was followed in August by the establishment of a Commissariat for Jewish Questions under Belev's directorship. The Commissariat worked to confiscate the Jews' property, and to prepare for their "emigration" by gathering information about their exact location. All Jews were made to wear a yellow badge, and Jewish homes and businesses were to be clearly marked. Furthermore, a representative of the Commissariat was appointed at each Jewish consistory to oversee its activities and maintain tight control.[82]

Some of these laws were broken repeatedly by exemptions the authorities granted, and the manufacture of the badges to be worn by Jews was notoriously slow. Many Jewish cooperative banks managed to salvage their holdings by merging with some other cooperative establishments affiliated with the Social Democrats.[83] However, for the majority of Bulgarian Jews, the laws inaugurated a period of extreme hardship and danger.

Quite a few Jews were active in antigovernment activities. It is estimated that 400 partisans out of 10,000 were Jews, four times their percentage of the population. Many were associated with the communist resistance after the German invasion of the Soviet Union. The first partisan action against the pro-German regime was committed by a Jew, Leon Tadzher, who blew up a military depot in Ruse in October 1941. Violeta Iakova killed General Hristo Lukov in 1943, and others were involved in sabotage and clandestine activities throughout the war years.[84]

By the fall of 1942, the Germans, through their minister in Sofia, Adolf Beckerle, began to put considerable pressure on the Bulgarian government to begin deportations. An associate of Eichmann, SS *Sturmführer* Theodor Dannecker, arrived in Sofia, and on February 1943 signed an agreement with Belev by which 20,000 Jews were initially to be deported to the East.[85] While the original text had included the words "from Thrace and Macedonia," these were removed from the final draft. The government approved the agreement in early March.

Clearly, the Bulgarians took the same path as many other European countries under the German sphere of influence, including Vichy France, i.e. satisfying German demands by agreeing to part with "foreign Jews" first. This was much less problematic than deporting Jews who were actually citizens. The Jews of Thrace and Macedonia annexed by the Bulgarians were considered stateless, and hence were dispensable. As decisions of this gravity were never taken in Bulgaria without the consent of the King, Boris III must have approved the agreement.

However, Jews of the new territories numbered about 12,000. The remaining 8,000 stipulated by the agreement were evidently to come from Bulgaria proper. Here was the Rubicon to be crossed.

Belev had prepared the necessary means of transportation by February. In March 4, 1943, the Jews of Thrace were arrested by the Bulgarian police and placed in warehouses and makeshift camps for a couple of days. There were many cases in which the police and other officials looted their property. They were taken to camps in Gorna Dzhumaya and Dupnitsa in Southwestern Bulgaria. The 4,058 Jews who were deported from Thracian towns such as Serres, Komotini (Gumulcine), Kavala, Alexandropolis (Dedeağaç), and Xanthi stayed in these camps for two weeks. On March 18 and 19, two trains took them, together with 158 Jews that were brought from the town of Pirot in the area annexed from Serbia, to the city of Lom on the Danube in Northwest Bulgaria where they were to be handed over to the Germans. On March 20–21, they were put on four barges and taken along the Danube to Vienna.[86] The fate of these Jews remains shrouded in mystery. While some accounts indicate that the ships arrived in Vienna and the deportees were then taken to Treblinka by rail where they were all killed, others suggest that most of them were drowned in the Danube. There were no survivors from these Thracian deportations.

On March 11, 1943, Bulgarian police arrested the Jews of Macedonia. There were 3,493 Jews in Skopje (Uskub), 3,342 in Bitola (Monastir), and 546 in Shtip, making a total of 7,381.[87] A few managed to escape or evade arrest and it appears that over 7,300 were taken to makeshift camps at tobacco warehouses in Skopje to await deportation. Their houses were pillaged and their remaining property was taken from them in the camps. A total of 165, including 67 pharmacists and physicians needed by the Bulgarian state as well as foreign nationals, were released. The rest were deported on transports on March 22, March 25, and March 29 to Treblinka where almost all were gassed upon arrival.[88]

Belev had also prepared for deportations from Bulgaria proper to reach the desired number of 20,000 that the agreement with the Germans stipulated. In February, the Commissariat prepared a list of 8,400 Jews, among them prominent Jews from Sofia and Plovdiv, and the rest from other cities in the southwest of the country.[89] However, before the deportations could be effected on the designated date of March 9, word got out, and through a most remarkable intervention by many leaders of public opinion, the *Aktion* was stopped.

Belev's secretary, Liliana Panitsa, regularly supplied information to her friends among Sofia's Jews, and warned Buko Levi, the vice-president of the Consistory, of the impending event.[90] At the same time, a Jew from the town of Kiustendil in the Southwest, whose community was slated for deportation, was warned by a Bulgarian acquaintance from the Ministry of the Interior, and also by the Kiustendil district governor.[91] The Jews of the city had become aware of physical preparations for the deportations, and were gripped by panic. Many tried to bribe leading officials. Some Bulgarians assisted the Jews. A delegation of five Bulgarians from Kiustendil left for Sofia to plead the Jews' case.[92]

In the meantime, Iako Barukh, the Jewish Agency's representative in Bulgaria, was apprised of the facts by his brother, who was based at Kiustendil. Together with other intercessors, Barukh appealed to the highest officials in the government, to no avail. However, Dimitur Peshev, a classmate of Baruh and vice-president of the parliament, agreed to help, and raised the issue in the chamber, arguing for the illegality of deporting Bulgarian Jewish citizens. In the meantime, Petur Gabrovski had also been contacted by the delegation from Kiustendil, and finally agreed to postpone the deportation.[93]

Peshev continued to agitate in favor of the Jews, and obtained the support of 42 deputies who signed a protest manifesto. While this raised the ire of the government's supporters who unseated him, the protest's point had been made.[94] The chorus of opposition, which included personalities of the first rank, rendered future action increasingly problematic. Boris III dragged his feet during a visit to Berlin when he was urged to continue the deportations. He and others in the government were also under pressure from the Allies and the Red Cross not to proceed.[95]

While Belev resigned after the debacle of March 1942, he soon took up his post again and with the support of Gabrovski began to devise new plans. The Ministry of the Interior prepared two plans, one for deportation to Poland and another for deportation of the Jews of Sofia to the provinces. Boris III approved the second plan in May 1943. In spite of public protests by the Jews who demonstrated in front of the central synagogue, and the explicit support given to them by opposition parties and the Holy Synod under the Metropolitan Stefan in the previous months (and who now intervened again),[96] the deportations to provincial towns did take place. Between May 26 and June 7, 19,153 Jews of Sofia were taken to 20 provincial centers were they were made to live under cramped conditions in the homes of local Jews. A total of 7,000 Jews were in forced labor batallions during this period.[97]

Nevertheless, this action also presaged the end of the threat of deportations. Both the changing fortunes of war, and the depth of opposition from leading quarters, convinced even the Germans that further pressure was useless. Boris III died in August 1943. His role remains controversial. While he was not the savior of the Jews as has been claimed, he was nevertheless prepared to resist German pressure for pragmatic internal and foreign policy reasons. On the other hand, it is quite clear that the deportations from the annexed territories took place with his full consent. His death changed the political scene. Gabrovski lost his position of Interior Minister. Leading international Jewish personalities such as Chaim Weizmann (1874–1952) and Stephen Wise (1874–1949) worked together on rescue plans to transport Bulgarian Jews to Palestine. The United States War Refugee Board also intervened. These actions, together with the pressure in favor of Jews from the Allies and looming German defeat, convinced the Bulgarian government to amend its anti-Jewish policies and act in a more benign manner. The anti-Jewish legislation was repealed in August. Finally, on September 9, 1944, the Soviets entered Bulgaria.[98]

While some property was returned to the Jews, the economic damage was great, and most of the community, never particularly wealthy, was seriously impoverished by the measures taken during the years of persecution. Nevertheless, unlike most of their coreligionists in other lands, Bulgarian Jewry survived the Holocaust.

The Bulgarian attitude towards the Jews in this period was complex. There was little radical, racist antisemitism except among a few ideologues such as Belev. On the other hand, there were many opportunists who were all too ready to profit from the occasion by robbing the Jews. Others believed in the rule of the law and in humanitarian action, and rebelled against outright persecution. A relatively open political process allowed opinion to be heard and influence policy.

This was not enough to save the Jews of Thrace and Macedonia. Like other countries in the German sphere of influence, most notably Vichy France, Bulgaria was all too ready to do the Germans' bidding and deport "foreign" Jews. Under legal smokescreens, the indifference to the fate of the group designated as outsiders led to active complicity with the Germans. Other allies of Germany like Rumania also refused to deport indigenous Jews, but behaved with even greater ferocity towards the "foreign" Jews of newly occupied lands, massacring them in the hundreds of thousands. Bulgaria was likewise complicit in the murder of the Jews of Thrace and Macedonia, but saved its own Jews through a mixture of both humanitarian and hard-nosed pragmatic considerations. And last but not least, Bulgaria, unlike Greece or Yugoslavia, was not overrun by the German army, and could maintain relative autonomy which made these considerations effective.

NEUTRAL TURKEY

Turkey did not enter the Second World War, and as a result the Jews of Turkey did not face the same dangers as their brethren elsewhere. Nevertheless, the war years were an extraordinarily difficult time, and the community did not emerge unscathed.

In the 1930s, Turkey developed a selective policy of admitting well-qualified Jewish refugees from Central Europe. Three hundred distinguished doctors, scientists, artists, and intellectuals were given asylum, and many came to occupy positions in universities.[99] However, there was no plan to accept the Jewish masses fleeing the Nazis, and with the onset of the war, the possibility of admitting foreign Jewish refugees disappeared. The granting of resident or tourist visas to Jews persecuted in their home countries was forbidden by a law passed on January 30, 1941. Exceptions could be made only for a few qualified individuals whose skills might be needed in Turkey. However, transit visas for those who had a visa from their final destination and could show tickets for transportation were allowed.[100] While authorities maintained strict controls on the number of visas, this law enabled 13,240 Jews to use Turkey as an avenue of transit to Palestine throughout the war years with an additional 3,234 emigrating from Turkey proper.[101]

The law was observed to the letter, without exception, even in extreme situations, as the Struma incident demonstrated. In December 1941, 769 Jews from Rumania set sail on a rickety old boat for Palestine. None had entry visas to the country. The ship arrived in Istanbul on December 15 with engine failure. The vessel and its inhabitants were sequestered by the Turkish authorities while negotiations took place with the British. After ten weeks of fruitless haggling between the Zionist leadership and the British, the Turks lost patience, and towed the boat out to the Black Sea on February 23, 1942, in spite of the fact that it had no food, fuel, or water. On the same day, the ship was sunk by an explosion. It is conjectured that a Soviet submarine mistakenly torpedoed the boat. Only one person survived.[102]

Both the British and the Turks maintained a hard legalistic attitude during the incident. The British were afraid of unregulated migration to Palestine, and the Turks did not want to become the recipients of thousands of refugees who might get stranded in the country en route to other destinations. Furthermore, Turkey had been embarrassed by the sinking in December 1940 of another ship, the *Salvador*. This boat carrying 350 people was traveling from Bulgaria to Palestine, and sank during a storm in the Sea of Marmara, with the majority on board drowning.[103] While Turkey was not responsible for this disaster, it had been blamed by Bulgaria for having allowed the ship to redepart from Istanbul in an unseaworthy condition. Turkey wanted to stop sea adventures on its waters en route to Palestine, and did not want to appear weak on the refugee issue. As Prime Minister Refik Saydam put it immediately after the Struma incident, Turkey could not "become a settlement ground for people not desired elsewhere."[104]

Of course, Turkish Jewish citizens living in countries occupied by the Axis powers were free to return as long as they had valid documentation, and many did so. The problem arose with those who had let their documentation expire. A law of 1935 had passed stringent regulations which stipulated that those Turkish or ex-Ottoman citizens who had not traveled back to the country between 1924 and 1927, and those who had not renewed their passports, were no longer recognized as Turkish nationals.[105] Since very few Muslim Turks were settled abroad, this law was designed to deprive as many non-Muslims as possible of Turkish citizenship. As a result, already by 1939, 200 Turkish Jewish families living in Germany had been rendered stateless, and were in a dire situation.[106] It is estimated that there were at least 10,000 Jews of Turkish origin in Vichy France alone who lost their citizenship because of this law.[107] Very often, the situation of these Jews depended on the goodwill of local Turkish consuls who had to make decisions as to whether to claim them as Turkish citizens in order to save them from deportation. The consul at Rhodes, Selahettin Ülkümen, interpreted the regulations in the most elastic sense possible and saved 43 Jews whom he declared were Turkish nationals.[108] Some Jews who still held valid Turkish citizenship in France, and even some who were no longer citizens, were helped by Turkish consuls.[109]

There is some evidence to suggest that in 1942, upon the urging of Haim Barlas, the director of the Jewish Agency office in Istanbul, and Laurence Steinhardt, the American Ambassador to Turkey, the Turkish government intervened with the Vichy government to stop the deportations of its "irregular citizens." Other sources, by contrast, doubt Turkey's interest in their welfare. This episode remains unclear, and requires further research.[110] Unfortunately, a great number of these Jews, together with some who were Turkish citizens or whose citizenship was in the process of being verified by the consular authorities, were indeed deported from France and perished in the death camps.[111]

As Germany appeared to be winning the war in 1941–2, pro-German elements began to increase propaganda in favor of the Axis.[112] There was already a small core of Nazi sympathizers around Şükrü Kaya, the former Minister of the Interior and Secretary General of the ruling Republican People's Party. Many Turks who had been trained in German universities in the 1930s were also sympathetic to the German cause.[113] Turkey was already heavily involved with Germany economically, with 50 percent of its foreign trade in 1939 conducted with that country.[114] The German–Turkish nonaggression treaty of 18 June, 1941 also pointed to a *rapprochement* just prior to the German attack on the Soviet Union.[115]

The ground was increasingly favorable to overt antisemitism, with the newspapers *Cumhuriyet*, *Akşam*, *Vakit*, *Ülkü*, and the humoristic paper *Akbaba* taking a leading role, extending the old xenophobic discourse against non-Muslim minorities to focus increasingly on the Jews, relying heavily on stereotypically racist caricatures. While the government occasionally intervened to control excessive language, it often tolerated inflammatory statements.[116]

The government itself developed increasingly discriminatory policies towards non-Muslims in the exceptional circumstances of the war years. With the outbreak of the War, 20 classes of reserves between the ages of 18–45 were mobilized. The Jews together with other non-Muslims were not given arms, were separated from other conscripts, and were sent to labor camps where they engaged in hard labor such as road building under very harsh conditions.[117]

The reporting of the Struma incident by the official Anatolia news agency was severely criticized in a debate at the National Assembly on April 20, 1942 as being unpatriotic. As a result, 26 Jews who worked at the agency, from editors to secretaries, were summarily dismissed in early May.[118] Harassment of Jews also took place occasionally, such as the case of six Jewish youths being prosecuted in 1942 for Zionist activities.[119]

But it was in the economic realm that these policies hit hardest. The government passed the National Protection Law on 18 January, 1940 which gave it total freedom to closely regulate and direct economic activity throughout the land, and take exceptional measures because of the prevailing international situation.[120] The aim of the law was to enable the government to mobilize resources to put the country on a war footing so that it would be ready for any eventuality.

In spite of this law, and the control that it exercised over the economy, the war period saw inflation, smuggling, and shortages. Many engaged in profiteering and made fortunes out of smuggling, while the majority of the people struggled economically. The frictions that arose as a result of this situation led to great resentments which were increasingly directed towards the traditional scapegoats of republican Turkey, the non-Muslim minorities. Any non-Muslim caught in illegal activity that many Muslim Turks were also engaged in was singled out and became the pretext for fierce press polemics in which antiminority sentiment was vented.[121]

In this atmosphere, the government of Prime Minister Şükrü Saraçoğlu saw fit to pass on November 16, 1942 an extraordinary piece of legislation, the Capital Tax (*Varlık Vergisi*). The putative purpose was to tax the new wealth that was being made because of the war conditions. In reality, however, this law was designed to destroy the economic position of non-Muslims.

Proposals for an extraordinary tax had already appeared in the press in May 1942.[122] In September 1942, the government began to gather information for the tax and divided the population into four groups, resident aliens, non-Muslims, Muslims, and *Dönmes*.[123] Each group was to be taxed at a different rate. What is striking is the inclusion of the *Dönmes*, the descendents of the Sabbatean converts to Islam in the seventeenth century, who were by then well-integrated into Turkish society, with many occupying leading public positions. Islamist and racist circles had always attacked and resented this group, and their inclusion showed the levels which xenophobia could reach in exceptional circumstances.

The application of the tax was discriminatory from the start. Commissions composed of public officials and Muslim Turkish businessmen came into being in all the cities, and taxes were assessed based on previous tax records, and on the recommendations of the commission's businessmen. Wildly inaccurate estimates of fortunes were made, very often with the express purpose of ruining a competitor or a non-Muslim entrepreneur. No appeal was possible, and the taxes had to be paid in cash 15 days after the assessment.[124]

It is estimated that on average, per capita, Muslims were taxed 5 percent of their annual income, Greeks 156 percent, Jews 179 percent, and Armenians 232 percent.[125] For many non-Muslims, the tax involved sums several times the value of their total fortune. The tax on resident foreign citizens was assessed according to the rates applied to Muslims, with the exception of Jews who were citizens of Axis countries and their allies and were no longer under the protection of their consulates. These Jews were assessed at the same rates as the indigenous non-Muslims.[126] All foreign embassies, including those from the Axis, protested the tax, helped their nationals to pay it, engaged in extensive negotiations with the government, and in the end succeeded in stopping the payments altogether.[127]

Turkish citizens had no recourse but to pay, but many faced absurd sums which could not be met even with the sale of all possessions. Nevertheless, many did sell their businesses and all that they owned, and still fell short.

The law stipulated compulsory labor for those who did not pay the tax in time, and this measure began to be put into practice in January 1943. However, only non-Muslims were subjected to forced labor. They were deported to the work camp of Aşkale in Eastern Anatolia where they were employed in snow clearance and road building. A total of 2,057 were slated for deportation, although some managed to come up with the required cash at the last minute. Finally, 1,400 were deported.[128] Conditions in Aşkale were harsh, but not terrible when compared with other work camps in Europe at the same time. Twenty-one of the deportees died of disease and natural causes in the camp. Most were eventually transferred to Sivrihisar in Western Central Anatolia in September 1943, and released a few months later as the tax began to be wound up. Reports indicate that at least half of the inmates of the camp were Jews.[129]

The retreat of German forces in 1944 and the altered international situation which made it imperative to pay attention to public opinion in Allied countries made the tax a liability, and it was repealed in March 1944. In the end, 74.11 percent of the total assessments of 465,384,820 Turkish liras was paid. Of this, 53 percent was paid by non-Muslims, 36.5 percent by Muslims, and 10.5 percent by foreign nationals. Non-Muslims paid 70 percent of the assessments in Istanbul where they were concentrated.[130]

The tax in many respects was the culmination of the aims of Kemalist Turkey to create a "national" Turkish-Muslim bourgeosie by ending the supposed non-Muslim domination of the economy. The non-Muslims of the war period reaped a bitter harvest of long-standing resentments.

The Capital Tax was not directed against Jews but all non-Muslims. Antisemitism, though present now more than at any other time in Turkish history, was subsumed under generalized xenophobia. In a comparative perspective, this episode appears as relatively minor compared to the horrors visited upon the Jews elsewhere in Europe. Even in Bulgaria, which did not hand over its own Jews, the economic antisemitic measures alone were immeasurably harsher. However, from the standpoint of Turkish Jewry, the Capital Tax came at a time of great anxiety due to the events beyond Turkish borders. The first decades of the Republic had not been a period of great harmony between Jews and Turks, and heated press polemics and discrimination on many fronts did not help matters. Measures such as the Capital Tax legislation and its implementation, with its overtones of economic spoliation, forced labor, and deportations raised the specter of the horrors taking place in Europe well known to Turkish Jews by 1943. The psychosis that all this created led to widespread insecurity, panic, and nightmarish flights of fancy fueled by rumor. For example, a new bakery constructed in Balat, one of the old Jewish quarters of Istanbul, was widely reported to be a crematorium designed to liquidate the Jews.[131]

The Jews no longer trusted the Turks. The Capital Tax was largely instrumental in creating this psychosis which severed many Jews' links with Turkey, and prepared the way for the widespread emigration that took place after the war.

In the old Sephardi heartland in Southeastern Europe and around the Aegean littoral, the historic communities of Salonika, Belgrade, Sarajevo, and the hundreds of smaller Jewish centers in Greece, Serbia, Bosnia-Herzegovina, Macedonia, and Thrace disappeared during the Second World War. The extent of the destruction was greatest in those areas that fell under direct German control. The Jews of Bulgaria lived in a country that was allied to Germany but that did not have German troops on its soil. Primarily because of this factor, but due also to the vagaries of internal politics and the changing fortunes of the war, they were spared the fate of their fellow Jews in the Balkans. Nevertheless, they faced severe antisemitic legislation, economic spoliation, and displacement, and emerged traumatized and pauperized from the war. Neutral Turkey also saw the worst antisemitic excesses in its history during these years. The discriminatory acts and legislation during this period impoverished the community, leaving it disoriented, mistrustful, and cowed.

For many Sephardim of the region who survived the experiences of the war years, the old moorings in these lands had disappeared. The destruction of Salonika, the jewel of Judeo-Spanish life and creativity, and the last remaining large Judeo-Spanish center that had preserved its distinctiveness and had continued to influence the whole Judeo-Spanish Diaspora, heralded the end of the old world. For many of the survivors and the communities that had not undergone the horrors of the Holocaust but had nonetheless faced harsh antisemitism at home, emigration appeared as the logical next step.

A LAST EXILE?

The Sephardim who chose to leave the Ottoman Empire in the nineteenth century for other countries in the Near East or North Africa were motivated primarily by new economic opportunities. Few went to Europe in this period except to study. The dismemberment of the Empire, the creation of new nation-states on its lands, the resulting political instability, and the precariousness of the conditions in which they lived also drove these Jews to seek sanctuary in other lands. The process of Westernization opened up new horizons. The Young Turk revolution and the subsequent introduction of compulsory military service for non-Muslims provided the impetus for a considerable wave of emigration: 8,000 Salonikan tobacco workers left for New York.[132] Hundreds of young people went to France, Italy, Spain, Morocco, and the United States.

The same movement can be seen in Macedonia between 1907 and 1927, when the Jewish population of the town of Bitola (Monastir) fell from 6,000 to 3,000 inhabitants.[133] The phenomenon also occurred in large towns, such as Istanbul, Izmir, and other Eastern Sephardi centers. From 1900, Sephardim from Rhodes settled in New York, then in the South of the United States. They were also to be found in Seattle, in the Pacific Northwest, where they lived alongside Jews who came from what today is Turkey.

A certain number went to Latin America, while others chose to emigrate to Africa. Sephardi communities were formed in Belgian Congo, Rhodesia, and later in South Africa. It was the Ottoman territories which saw the waves of departure; the Jewish populations of Bulgaria and Yugoslavia generally remained more stable. There were also regional migratory movements,[134] particularly from Bulgaria to Turkey, primarily for economic reasons. The Balkan wars were an additional factor in this regard.

In Salonika, under the Greek regime, every anti-Jewish measure provoked a wave of emigration. With the advent of the Republic in Turkey, and the host of petty annoyances for non-Muslims which resulted from the nationalist measures, many Jews sought to leave the country. Curiously, it appears that it was those without sufficient capital to reach Palestine who left for other places – contrary to the later pattern when the state of Israel received mainly the poor and middle classes, the rest preferring to stay where they were or subsequently opting for the United States or Europe.[135] France, Spain, Belgium, Italy, Cuba, Mexico, and Argentina became the favorite destinations.

In 1939, it was estimated that 20,000–25,000[136] Eastern Sephardim lived in Paris, clustered at first in the ninth and eleventh *arrondissements*, then, as a result of social mobility, dispersed over various quarters of the city. In the eleventh *arrondissement*, their numbers rose to some 1,700 in 1926, 2,200 in 1931, and 2,600 in 1936.[137] It is estimated that 10,000 Jews of Turkish origin were in Paris under German occupation.[138] Cities such as Marseilles and Lyons also had Judeo-Spanish communities. According to data provided by Joseph Néhama, in the twentieth century 25,000 Greek Jews went to France; 15,000 to 20,000 to the United States and Canada; 4,000 to Turkey; 10,000 to Latin America, particularly Argentina and Mexico.[139] These figures appear to be exaggerated, and are used here only to point to the overall trends of the migration movement. They also give some idea of the importance that these departures assumed in the imagination of a contemporary witness.

Between 1899 and 1924, the number of Ottoman Jewish immigrants in the United States rose to 20,027, the majority coming from Thrace and the

Aegean regions.[140] The figure of 20,000 is also put forward for the number of "Levantine" Jews in the United States in 1913.[141] Most of those who went were men, who later brought over their families. As inaccurate as the figures for departures are, a considerable decline can be observed in the Jewish population of some large centers. One source suggests that the number of Jews in Salonika, for example, fell from 65,000 in 1928 to 45,000 in 1940.[142]

During the republican period in Turkey, emigration to Palestine, then Israel, offered a means of escape from local problems. Of course, a certain number of religious Jews had always chosen the Holy Land as their final destination; however, this phenomenon was on the whole episodic.[143] The same phenomenon had already been noted also among the Jews in Spain.[144]

In 1909, when the large waves of emigration began, the Zionists had not yet obtained a sufficient foothold in the Ottoman Empire to channel emigrants towards Palestine. Subsequently, Palestine and Israel were transformed into genuine havens of refuge, while many intending to emigrate there chose other destinations because of the small number of entry certificates available under the British mandate.[145]

Towards the end of the twenties, many Turkish Jews felt that their future in the new nation-state was no longer secure. Every crack in the fragile status quo provoked departures. This was the case in 1934 at the time of the anti-Jewish pogroms in Thrace, and again in 1942 when the Capital Tax was imposed.[146] Although the Zionist movement was illegal and few certificates were available, some 4,000 Turkish Jews left for Palestine between 1943 and 1944; less than a third settled in the various rural settlements there.[147] In fact, local Jews did not only have to contend with the petty harassments of the Turkish government. They also suffered from negligence on the part of the Jewish Agency.[148] This was regularly denounced by the Union of Immigrants from Turkey in Palestine. Notwithstanding these problems, 5 percent of the 80,000 Turkish Jews left in less than a year. This was in a context of general mobilization during the war, despite Turkey's neutrality, when most adult Jewish males were enrolled in the army and were consequently unable to leave. Those who wanted to leave were not the wealthy affected by the Capital Tax – who, in any case, were sent to labor camps in cases of nonpayment – but actually the young. This emigration took place clandestinely via the Syro-Palestinian frontier.[149] By the end of 1943, 3,000 applications for emigration had been registered, mostly from workers aged between 18 and 22.[150] A year later, 5,000 requests for emigration had been received from adults.[151] Most of those leaving had no Zionist education. The clandestine nature of this movement required a certain element of risk for participants, and many migrants might well have been dissuaded from coming forward for fear of getting into trouble with the authorities.

As a result of the vicissitudes of the war and its repercussions on the Jews, a massive wave of emigration to Israel took place when the frontiers were opened in 1949. More than 30,000 people were involved in this movement, mostly from the poorer strata of society and from the lower-middle class, with youth particularly prominent. Poverty had increased during the war period and also afterwards. There are frequent allusions in accounts of Turkish Jewry to the many children who were working from the age of nine or ten.[152] In the postwar period, Turkey had a small Jewish middle class with a very small fringe of wealthy individuals. The rest of the Jews were very poor. Young people worked in conditions reminiscent of the early days of industrialization in Europe, with very low wages. They sought salvation in the Zionist dream. A section of this youth formed the audience of the Zionist societies.

At the end of 1948, the Turkish government banned emigration to Israel.[153] Thenceforth, it took place in difficult conditions. Young people of an age to do military service deserted. Helped by representatives of the illegal immigration organization, financed by the American Joint Distribution Committee, groups of youth were shipped to Palestine, under a variety of covers and with considerable risk.[154] Some were arrested as deserters and imprisoned. These clandestine departures primarily involved people who did not have exit visas, particularly youth of conscription age. Others left via Italy. A number of people who had left their provincial towns, others their work, with the firm resolve to leave, were put in a difficult position by the closing of the frontiers. Their opening in 1949 unleashed a new wave of mass departures; the provinces, particularly the provincial towns, lost tens of thousands of Jews in a brief period.[155]

Turkey was the only country in the Eastern Sephardi culture area where this phenomenon of mass departure can be observed without the factors of push which normally provoke such emigration.[156] Nor can it be said that the Jews evinced a great traditional religious fervor, capable of feeding the migratory movement. Observers noted that Jews in Turkey lived their lives in a strange mixture of religiosity and areligiosity, with knowledge neither of Jewish history nor of the Talmud and traditional religious literature.[157] *Shabbat* was practically unobserved. In postwar Jewish schools, there was little religious instruction or attempt to make the pupils aware of their Jewishness; the learning of Hebrew was also optional. While the profile of the average provincial Jew differed slightly from this one, it did not affect substantially the overall trend of religious indifference. Because of factors which have already been mentioned, the ground had also not been sufficiently prepared for a strong, self-conscious Zionism which might have provided the impetus to leave.

The Jews were Jews in Turkey because they were perceived as such; that was enough to perpetuate and reinforce their Jewish identity. Since the establishment of the state of Israel, waves of emigration have taken place regularly whenever the political situation suggests any sort of danger, however remote. The majority of those who left when the state was established clearly did so to improve their socioeconomic situation. This primarily applied to the poor who left Turkey in large numbers; young people also left because they had little hope of participating in public life. As for the Zionists, impelled by idealism, they primarily consisted of pioneering youth who helped create agricultural settlements (*kibbutzim* or *moshavim*). Above all, people emigrated because they were Jewish and hence set apart, and because there was a strong chance that this would remain so in the foreseeable future in a postwar Turkey in which the Republican People's Party had shown little sympathy for the Jews. For a long time, the Jews of Turkey maintained unhappy memories of this party and tended not to vote for it.

Between the Second World War and the mid-fifties, 40 percent of Turkish Jewy left for Israel; most of the 10 percent who subsequently went back to Turkey did not remain there.[158] As a result, the Jewish population of Turkey decreased from 76,965 in 1945 to 45,995 in 1955.[159] Today, there are barely 20,000 Jews left in the country. Nonetheless, Turkey still contains the largest number of Sephardim from the old Judeo-Spanish culture area.

For the first generation in Israel, the Turkish background became part of a distinctive ethnic identity. This was the inevitable result of emigration without Zionism, of an untutored Zionism without indoctrination, or simply the effect of the inability to integrate completely the legacy of 500 years of *dhimmi* status.

In Salonika the pogrom in the Jewish district of Campbell in 1931 provoked a large wave of emigration not only to Europe but also to Palestine. A few thousand Jews left illegally as tourists. Very few possessed Palestine immigration certificates.[160] Those who did adopted children to enable them to share the privilege; young bachelors contracted fraudulent marriages so that one valid certificate could be used for two.[161] Those from the lower-middle class – shopkeepers, craftsmen, fishermen, boatmen, and clerks – settled mainly in Tel-Aviv, though a certain number went to Haifa.[162] In Salonika Jews had long followed trades related to the sea. In 1936, Salonika dockers played an important role in opening the port of Tel-Aviv.[163] Salonikans also set up shipping companies, thus contributing to the development of sea communications in Palestine; the sailors, dockers, fishermen, shipping agents, and various other workers likewise played their part in the economic development of the country. In 1937, Salonikans created the collective farm *Zur Mosheh* (Rock of Moses) named after the Zionist leader and deputy, Mosheh Kouffinas, a native of Volos. This wave of emigration, which lasted from 1932 to 1938, can be considered the most important, even in comparison with the movement which followed the establishment of the state of Israel. The Zionist movement in Salonika went into decline with the departure of its most active leaders.[164] Between 1939, when the White Paper restricted immigration into Palestine, and 1945, some illegal immigration took place, as it did from Yugoslavia and Bulgaria, but this did not involve large numbers.[165]

After the war, local Zionists tried to obtain certificates to send orphans to Palestine, together with some 200 to 300 families who wanted to emigrate.[166] An authentic desire to emigrate is apparent in this period.[167] In 1948–9, some 1,500 Jews from Greece chose Israel as their destination;[168] others went elsewhere. For example, it is estimated that 1,200 went to the United States, and 500 to Latin America and Europe.[169]

The establishment of the state of Israel had a decisive influence on the migration movements from the Sephardi culture area of the Balkans. The Jews of Salonika perished in the Holocaust so it is impossible to know how they would have acted after the war. The same is true of Yugoslavia, where emigration to Palestine remained very limited until 1941 because of the White Paper. It must also be added that, despite the intense nationalist activity which characterized the interwar period in Yugoslavia, Zionism grew stronger within communal politics, with only a minority pioneering movement turned towards Palestine. Emigration was not seen as an actual option; this was also the case in the rest of Western Europe. In the twenties and thirties, despite the establishment of a Palestine Office to help individuals and groups who wanted to emigrate, an attempt by the Zionist Federation of Yugoslavia to set up an agricultural settlement in Palestine ended in failure, and few people left. It is calculated that 15,000 Jews, Ashkenazim and Sephardim combined, survived in Yugoslavia at the end of the war.[170] Many emigrated to Italy, Switzerland, and the United States. Sarajevo, the main Sephardi community, was decimated. In 1946, only 1,413 Jews lived there, while in Belgrade their numbers stood at 2,236. Between 1948 and 1952, 7,578 Jews left for Israel; very few returned.[171] It is difficult to divide this number into Ashkenazim and Sephardim. Six to seven thousand remain in the area covered by ex-Yugoslavia and are to be found in the large centers. Most of them feel that Israel is very important, even though total assimilation seems to hover over their future.

The case of Bulgaria and its massive emigration, largely ignored by Zionist historiography, remains exceptional, both in the Sephardi culture area and in the Jewish world as a whole. Despite an intense Zionism inseparable from community life, emigration to Palestine between 1919 and 1939 did not take place on a particularly large scale. As no major event forced this population to leave the country, and as Zionism was institutionalized, Jewish life came to merge with Zionism. Between 1939 and 1945, some 3,000 Jews left the country clandestinely.[172] As conditions were relatively better for them than for the rest of the Sephardi culture area, the Jews of Bulgaria proper and Turkey did not experience very heavy losses during the war. This explains why these two countries could send the largest number of emigrants to the young state of Israel. The Bulgarian Jews emerged from the war plundered and demoralized. From September 1944 the country was ruled by the government of the communist-dominated Fatherland Front. The economy was in ruins and the majority of the population had no work. Furthermore, antisemitism did not totally cease. The Jews did not feel safe and demanded to leave.[173] By September 1945, the Palestine Office received 12,000 emigration requests: at least some of the applicants were heads of families, which would considerably increase the real number of applicants.[174] Illegal emigration got under way, involving around 1,000 people. The massive demand for emigration on the part of the local Jewish populations put the communal leadership in a dilemma. If this emigration took place, it would jeopardize the future of community life through a lack of Jews.[175] In the end, this leadership also opted for mass emigration. Between 1948 and 1949, 35,000 Bulgarian Jews reached the young state of Israel. This is very close to the figure for the Jews of Turkey who chose the same destination; the difference is that in this case it represented the majority of the Jewish population.[176] The Bulgarian immigrants settled in urban centers, though a certain number chose agricultural settlements, such as Beit Hanan or Kfar Shitin. No more than 5,000 to 7,000 Jews remained in Bulgaria.[177]

A close examination of the relationships between the Zionist establishment in Palestine and Eastern Sephardi Jewry reveals a real indifference on the part of the former, particularly when it came to the emigration of these populations to Palestine. Local Sephardi Zionist leaders regularly complained about the low number of immigration certificates granted to them and about the lack of enthusiasm showed for promoting emigration. The same sort of indifference was seen upon arrival in Palestine and then in Israel after the establishment of the state, leading to complaints by the Sephardi immigrants' associations as well as to disputes. The Jews from North Africa would experience a similar situation.

Among the various streams of Zionism, Revisionism, supported from its beginnings by the Sephardi leaders of Greece, Bulgaria, and Palestine, showed a much greater awareness of the Sephardim; statements by the leader of the movement, Vladimir Jabotinsky, make this clear. But on the whole the language and the geographical and cultural affiliations of the founders of official Zionism did not make them receptive to Sephardi Jewry, about which they knew very little.

The populations of the Sephardi culture area of the Balkans integrated relatively well into the new state of Israel, particularly those who had come from the predominantly Christian nation-states. A look at the popular perception of these Sephardim within the Israeli population shows a position midway between Jews from Central and Eastern Europe and Jews from North Africa.[178] The Jews of Yugoslavia, who are regarded as Ashkenazim, given the composite nature of their original community, hold first place in prestige ratings, followed by Bulgaria, Greece and, at the bottom, Turkey. The low prestige of Jews from Turkey is due to a large extent to the fact that they are natives of a Muslim country in a state where the élites are recruited from Jewish populations who had come from what they saw was the more "civilized" West.

Israel today houses the largest number of Sephardim descended from the exiles from Spain; those in France and other European countries were decimated by the Holocaust. Only a small number remain in the Balkans, while the Americas contain a few small communities. Generally speaking, the bulk of the survivors from the destroyed Sephardi culture area of the Balkans are to be found in Israel. It remains to be seen whether a distinct Judeo-Spanish "ethnic–cultural" entity in this vastly different geographical and cultural context can remain viable.

Conclusion

This book has followed the trajectory of a Jewish group from its expulsion from Spain at the end of the Middle Ages to its settlement in the Levant, where a new *Sepharad* was constructed. The *Sepharad* of the East came to an end in the Holocaust and in the migrations that followed. Our aim was not to narrate a saga but to write the *history* of these transplanted Judeo-Spanish communities. It is sometimes said that happy people have no history. But these communities, whose fate has not been so happy, have not, until now, had their history told.

To write the history of the Sephardi Jews of the Balkans is a challenge. One has first to confront neglect and blind spots in the historiography. One has to face and transcend a host of myths, not in order to rediscover the "truth" (since peoples never have one single truth) but in order to crystallize a certain "reality" with the hope that the Sephardi culture area of the Balkans will attain its rightful place in the general history of the Jews and in history *tout court*.

The historiography of the Sephardim is so rife with myths that it is tempting to wonder whether they emerged to provide palliatives to the gloomy "lachrymose" episodes in Jewish history. These myths have various origins but end in throwing a halo of shadows around the Sephardim. First, there is the foundation myth that the Jews had a sort of right to the Iberian land. This myth, created by the Jews themselves, dated the presence of Jews in the area from the destruction of the first Temple. Its equivalent is found elsewhere and at other periods in the history of the Jews. This myth was reinforced by the resentment of those who were expelled from their adopted land.

Then there is the myth which puts the number of expellees at the astronomical figure of 400,000, whereas recent estimates, erring on the other side, do not exceed 50,000. The exaggeration inevitably reflects the scale of this event in the Jewish imagination. This question is still a subject of lively discussion.

And what is to be said of that famous myth of the Spanish "Golden Age," which certainly pleases everyone? It is there to show that Jews were able to integrate and live harmoniously with their environment, either under Arab rule or at the beginning of the *Reconquista*. For a long time, the Judeo-Iberian creativity of those two periods, highly esteemed in the Jewish world, overshadowed the creations of the post-Expulsion period. Nothing could equal the richness of a cultural creativity which formed a glorious page in the history of the Jews as a whole.

These "golden ages" succeed in making one forget the rest, to the point of transforming the Peninsula into a mythical place where the three monotheistic religions developed in harmony. Where there was in fact fluctuating and circumstantial coexistence, there is instead talk of a "symbiosis," another myth. This mythical symbiosis provides the twentieth century, riven with incessant wars and conflicts, with the material with which to nourish fantasies of peace. It is not a matter of chance that this was so often mentioned on the occasion of the five hundredth anniversary of the Expulsion of the Jews from Spain in 1992. How strange to recall this symbiosis with a fanfare of trumpets, while commemorating the Expulsion which testifies to the contrary!

If all this is not false, neither is it entirely true. Spain was a land of asylum and a land of fanaticism, of coexistence and persecutions, of war and peace, of intellectual and economic expansion and the Inquisition. Judeo-Iberian creativity is put on a pedestal, perhaps at the expense of other culture areas, where Jewish achievement is concealed to an always ungrateful posterity. Then comes the Jewish Enlightenment (*Haskalah*), which in its turn wove a myth around this culture, seen as harmonious, balanced, both Jewish and open to the outside world, providing the champions of emancipation and integration with a ready-made model.[1]

The post-Expulsion period also had to yield to a status hierarchy. Victory in that case fell to the Sephardim settled in Western Europe, however few they were. The Sephardim of the Balkans, on the other hand, were only found worthy of attention when it came to recalling a few incontrovertibly significant figures, such as the halakhist Joseph Caro, Joseph Nasi, banker and Duke of Naxos, or his legendary aunt Doña Gracia Nasi (who catches the interest of Western imagination periodically, probably because very little is actually known about her). Similarly, the Balkan Sephardim figure in the historiography in connection with great intellectual movements, such

as Kabbala, or with fascinating deviant movements, such as Sabbateanism –
and intermittently with the Marrano saga as a terminus point for those
fleeing persecution. And it is not by chance that when it comes to
commemorations, these are the personalities and movements which regularly occupy the forefront of the stage. All the interest seems only to reside
in this image that others – Jews and non-Jews alike – possess of the
Judeo-Spanish communities, who are on the whole ignored. Their supposed "greatness" and their "great men" have succeeded in making one
forget them. Can one write the history of gods?

To return to the specific life of the Sephardi *Kulturbereich* itself, one
again is confronted by a history woven of myths, pasted onto it from
outside to suit the ideological conventions and *a priori* arguments of the
authors. Moreover, these myths have been adopted by the last descendants
of the expellees themselves, in a sort of centuries-long internalizing. There
is first of all the new Ottoman foundation myth, the exceptional welcome
given to the Jews. Five hundred years later, the last numerically sizeable
Sephardi bastion outside Israel, present-day Turkish Jewry, the last remnant of the Ottoman Empire, is appropriating this myth and prolonging it
by bringing it up to date. Anxious to enter the European Community, with
the semivoluntary collaboration of local Jews, Turkey is proclaiming its
long tradition of tolerance towards Jews in an attempt to reduce somewhat
the ill-effects of its treatment of some minorities in its recent history.
Elsewhere in the Balkans today, there are no such issues requiring the
collaboration of Jews or the creation of a reconciliatory myth. This explains
why the Jews of Turkey have emerged at the forefront of commemorative
"festivities." Nor is it pure coincidence that a certain number of books
devoted to the Jews of the Ottoman Empire published in 1992 systematically leave whole sectors of the Sephardi culture area in the shadows.

The myths follow one another, all of them different. There is the myth
of the economic success of the expellees, the myth of their integration, the
myth that a Chief Rabbi always existed, the myth of autonomy, and lastly
the myth of peaceful existence, including the period of the Second World
War, in Turkey at least. The contemporary period and the West have
fabricated their own myths: the Marranos as architects of modern capitalism, and the attachment of the Sephardim to Spain and to their Hispanicity
in the twentieth century, trumped up by Spanish ideologists for political
reasons. In this category too is the myth of the decline of the Sephardim,
an ideological interpretation by a Western Jewry, confident of its own
triumph, which interpreted a long-standing crisis by its own criteria (and
by comparison with the equally mythical Spanish "Golden Age") in order
to pose as savior, indifferent to the local context and the real needs of the
populations concerned. On the basis of this myth and coming from the

outside, the Jewish West embarked on concrete action aimed at Westernizing the Sephardim. In the process, it contributed decisively to a very complex process of change which resulted in a fundamental reorientation of Sephardi Jewry in the modern period. More recently, other Westerners, Sephardi and non-Sephardi, in a sort of desperate attempt to appropriate a heritage, are engaging in intellectual speculations (largely cut off from the realities of history), in interminable discussions about the name of the Sephardi language for example. Should it be called Ladino, Judeo-Spanish, or *djudezmo*? This great debate has not yet reached a conclusion.[2]

The Sephardim of the Balkan cultural realm also created their own myths. The mythification of the Spain they had lost when they arrived in the Empire; then, with the beginning of Westernization, the mythification of a Europe from which they in fact borrowed the signifiers and languages rather than the values. Once the *Kulturbereich* was transplanted in Israel, some of its components, the Jews of Turkey for example, mythified in their turn the country they had left.

Would the history of this group have become a myth in any case? Or did the fact that this history disappeared from view in the East actually encourage the birth of long-lasting myths? All this contributed to their status as "invisible" Jews, wherever they are, even in Israel.

The problem is already apparent in the name given the group. All Jews born in Muslim countries are now called Sephardim, in a sort of simplistic dichotomy which divides the Jewish world into Sephardim on one hand, and Ashkenazim on the other (a term reserved for Jews originating from Europe). And yet, the differences within each of these "units" are just as great as between the two groups themselves. *Sefarad*, in the sense of Spain, already appears in ancient Jewish texts. The term "Sephardim," in its proper application, designates Jews originating from the Iberian peninsula. And yet not all those who today are called Sephardim originated there. In fact, the Jews of North Africa, or for example of Mesopotamia and Iran, have their own identity, with a long and rich history. This confusion is not a contemporary phenomenon. Very early on, Sephardim from the Iberian peninsula adopted the practice of affixing next to their signatures the terms *sefaradi tahor* ("pure Sephardi") as if to protect themselves from possible counterfeiters, in a brand of ethnic chauvinism, projecting a sort of aristocratic image of themselves within the Jewish world.

The local culture of the Sephardim of the Balkans was dismissed by the very people from the West who came to extricate them from their crisis by imposing Western models on them. While this aim was praiseworthy, the measures taken were more ambiguous. Confronted with a mythified Western model, the less traditionalist classes came to the point of wishing to shed a lowly esteemed identity. A repudiated people cannot lay claim to its history. Every effort was made to replace Judeo-Spanish by French in the Balkans, where perhaps the more urgent need was to learn the language of the country. Their culture was despised, the better to be ignored. Nor did the Zionists who followed have a very high opinion of the vernacular language or culture of their public. They reacted in the same way as they did to Yiddish in the Ashkenazi world. In the course of Westernization, certain local intellectuals grasped the loss and began to write a history, *histories*, to salvage what could be saved. Others were to assume the task when the Sephardi culture area was drained of Jews and partially transplanted to Israel, where a new risk of loss of specificity threatened. In the Balkans, amateur historians wrote sagas which opened the way to more thorough, scholarly research. These pioneers wanted to record their history with the tools available to them. While still following the specific evolution of each of its components, it was not yet possible to envisage an overall history of the culture area. This period also saw an unprecedented expansion in literature in Judeo-Spanish, Sephardist movements, and folkloric-type ventures, in a sort of reaction to Westernization.

Neglect also haunts the tragic fate of the Sephardim who died after being deported to death camps. We need only to point to the fate of the immigrant Sephardim, whose mass arrest by French police started in the eleventh *arrondissement* in Paris in August 1941, not mentioned in most history books.[3] As for the fate of Sephardim who stayed in the Balkans, they remain until this day on the margins of the history of the Holocaust.

The Eastern Sephardim continued to retain many features of an overall cultural and linguistic unity which had marked them in Ottoman times even after the break-up of the Ottoman Empire. However, the Sephardi *Kulturbereich* did not emerge unscathed from this transition from a pluralist society to monolithic ones, from a geographical zone without frontiers to that of nation-states. The fate of the different communities which formed the Sephardi Balkans varied in relation to the new national context into which they were now inserted. The Ottoman model of ethnic organization had favored the preservation of a specific cultural heritage. It had made it possible to strengthen an almost autonomous Judeo-Spanish identity, without a direct or mythified link with the Iberian peninsula, which had become a distant memory. Although familiarity with the language of the country was acquired somewhat more quickly in nation-states such as Yugoslavia and Bulgaria, Judeo-Spanish persisted. Some 85 percent of Jews in Turkey in 1927 still claimed Judeo-Spanish as their mother tongue.[4] Equivalent percentages were recorded in 1945. It must be noted that this language was not taught in Jewish schools but was simply transmitted in daily life. It was in the sixties that Turkish really became the mother tongue of Turkish Jews, although Judeo-Spanish did not disappear. The continuity of the culture and of the Judeo-Spanish language throughout the Balkans in no way meant closure to outside influences. Even Judeo-Spanish was studded with words borrowed from local languages. Daily life, music, dress, culture, cookery were influenced to varying degrees by external additions though it cannot be said that there was a genuine integration – a concept which is alien in the Ottoman context – and even less a symbiosis with the surrounding cultures. In the states created on former Ottoman lands, the Jews continued to be perceived in a *dhimmi* category borrowed from Ottoman times, and above all, they perceived themselves as such.

The group was thus distinguished by the enduring quality of its specifically Balkan Judeo-Spanish identity, an identity with regional variations, becoming in the modern period multicultural and multilingual, receptive not only to the local environment but also to the French, Austrian, or German West. Despite this permeability to outside influences, which was initially voluntary but later imposed from above, leading to national or Western acculturation, the Judeo-Spanish identity managed to adapt and to survive in various forms, with greater or lesser strength depending on the region and social class until the Second World War.

What is the position of Judeo-Spanish communities today? Some 100,000 reached Israel between 1919 and 1949. Does this mean that the Sephardi culture area has been recreated in a new geographical center? It is hard to say yes. Even emigration statistics make a distinction between Jews from Turkey, on the one hand, placed under the heading of Asia, and Jews from Greece, Bulgaria, and Yugoslavia, on the other, who appear under the heading of Europe. In the minds of the authorities, these Sephardim therefore belong to different states instead of a single culture area. Israeli society has also adopted this image and perceives its Sephardim by countries of origin, classifying them according to a hierarchy of prestige. Some Sephardim are therefore more highly esteemed than others, with those who came from so-called European countries forming the upper crust.[5] In Israel, they are now Turkish, Bulgarian, Yugoslav, or Greek (Salonikan) Jews, with their own specific characteristics, their own districts with large concentrations of people from the same place, their associational life. In the last resort, the identity of their country of origin takes precedence when faced with the unifying mold of a modern nation-state such as Israel. The culture area could only exist in a multi-ethnic context, where the Jewishness of these populations was inseparable from their Sephardi affiliation, the two making for the unity of a group which attempted to withstand the era of nation-states in the Balkans. It did so in a sort of tradition of a common image, shared by the Jews themselves and the new masters of the country, for whom Jew was synonymous with

Sephardi, with few exceptions, such as Yugoslavia, where Sephardim and Ashkenazim existed side by side.

In Israel, the Judeo-Spanish language is spoken by the first generation and understood by the second, Israeli-born generation. There is a material culture which continues to be handed down through the small details of daily life. It is, however, not possible to talk about a Judeo-Spanish identity, common to all and asserted as such. Only the older generation clings to a common fund of language and culture which is on the path to extinction.

This book has endeavored to study a Jewish group which has all but disappeared as a distinctive unit and a culture area which has been lost. It mostly asks questions, through shadows, myths, sometimes commonplaces. It provides some answers, while waiting for others to bring further clarification, and to ask new questions.

Notes

1 COMMUNITY AND SOCIETY

1   For a general history of the Ottoman Empire, see Stanford J. Shaw and Ezel
    K. Shaw, *History of the Ottoman Empire and Modern Turkey* (2 vols,
    Cambridge University Press, Cambridge, 1976–7). For a recent publication
    in French, cf. Robert Mantran, ed., *Histoire de l'Empire ottoman* (Fayard,
    Paris, 1989). On the early period of the Empire: Halil İnalcık, *The Ottoman
    Empire: The Classical Age, 1300–1600*, tr. from Turkish by N. Itzkowitz and
    C. Imber (Weidenfeld & Nicolson, London, 1973).

2   From the large literature on this subject, see Antoine Fattal, *Le Statut légal
    des non-musulmans en pays d'islam* (Imprimerie catholique, Beirut, 1958); Bat
    Ye'or, *The Dhimmi: Jews and Christians under Islam*, tr. from French by
    David Maisel, Paul Fenton, and David Littman (Fairleigh Dickinson
    University Press, London and Toronto, 1985); Bernard Lewis, *The Jews of
    Islam* (Princeton University Press, Princeton, 1984), pp. 17–85; Esther
    Benbassa, "Comment être non-musulman en terre d'islam," *L'Histoire*, 134
    (June 1990), pp. 86–91.

3   Which included the Sabaeans and Zoroastrians.

4   See two articles by Simon Marcus, "Contribution to the History of the Jews
    of Adrianople," *Sinai* 29 (7–8), 1951, pp. 10–11 (in Hebrew); and "The
    History of the Rabbis of the Gueron Family of Adrianople," *Sinai* 25 (7–8),
    1947, p. 48 (in Hebrew); Isaac Moscona, *On Some Historic Moments of*

Judaism in Bulgaria and in Balkan Lands (unpublished ms., Sofia, 1980; in Judeo-Spanish); Mark Alan Epstein, *The Ottoman Jewish Communities and their Role in the Fifteenth and Sixteenth Centuries* (Klaus Schwarz, Fribourg, 1980), p. 20.

5   Quotation in Lewis, *Jews of Islam*, pp. 135–6. We know nothing about the actual impact of this missive on the migration plans of the Jewish communities of Europe. It is nonetheless a reflection of the state of mind of a number of exiles arriving in the Ottoman Empire.

6   Moscona, *On Some Historic Moments.*

7   Epstein, *The Ottoman Jewish Communities*, pp. 20–2; Yavuz Ercan "The Juridical, Internal and Economic Situation of Non-Muslims in Turkey in the Fifteenth and Sixteenth Centuries," *Belleten*, 48, 188 (Sept. 1983), pp. 1,129–30 (in Turkish).

8   Moscona, *On Some Historic Moments.*

9   The most recent general study of Byzantine Jewry is Steven Bowman, *The Jews of Byzantium, 1204–1453* (University of Alabama Press, Tuscaloosa, 1985). For a depiction of the Romaniot intellectual milieu, which passed from Byzantine to Ottoman domination, see Jean-Christophe Attias, *Le Commentaire biblique: Mordekhai Komtino ou l'herméneutique du dialogue* (Cerf, Paris, 1991).

10   On the Karaites of the region, see Abraham Danon, "Documents Relating to the History of the Karaites in European Turkey," *Jewish Quarterly Review*, 17, 2 (Oct. 1926), pp. 165–322; and "The Karaites in European Turkey," ibid., 15, 3 (Jan. 1925), pp. 285–360.

11   Ömer Barkan, "Quelques remarques sur la constitution sociale et démographique des villes balkaniques au cours des XVe et XVIe siècles," in *Istanbul à la jonction des cultures balkaniques, méditerranéennes, slaves et orientales, aux XVIe–XIXe siècles* (AIESEE, Bucharest, 1977), p. 287.

12   There is a large literature on this subject. The most detailed study of the *sürgün* as applied to Jews is Joseph Hacker, "The *Sürgün* System and Jewish Society in the Ottoman Empire during the Fifteenth to Seventeenth Centuries," in Aron Rodrigue, ed., *Ottoman and Turkish Jewry: Community and Leadership* (Indiana University Turkish Studies Series, Bloomington, 1992), pp. 1–65.

13 See Halil İnalcık, "Jews in the Ottoman Economy and Finance," in C. E. Bosworth, Charles Issawi, Roger Savory, and A. L. Udovitch, eds, *Essays in Honor of Bernard Lewis: The Islamic World* (Darwin Press, Princeton, 1989), pp. 513–14.

14 See Hacker, "The *Sürgün* System," pp. 27–33.

15 Lewis, *Jews of Islam*, p. 122; İnalcık, "Jews in the Ottoman Economy," p. 514.

16 Epstein, *The Ottoman Jewish Communities*, pp. 105–12.

17 Ibid., p. 118.

18 İnalcık, "Jews in the Ottoman Economy," p. 526.

19 Elijah Capsali, *Seder Eliyahu Zuta* ("The Little Order of Elijah"), ed. Meir Benayahu, Shlomoh Simonsohn, Aryeh Shmuelevitz (Ben Zvi Institute, Jerusalem, 1975–7), vol. 2, p. 218 (in Hebrew). The English translation of this quotation can be found in Jacob Barnai, "On the History of the Jews in the Ottoman Empire," in Esther Juhasz, ed., *Sephardi Jews in the Ottoman Empire: Aspects of Material Culture* (Israel Museum, Jerusalem, 1990), p. 19.

20 Quoted from Immanuel Aboab, *Nomologia o discursos legales* (Amsterdam, 1629), in *Encyclopaedia Judaica* (Keter, Jerusalem, 1972), vol. 16, col. 1,533.

21 For an example of this state of mind, see Joseph Hacker, "The Despair of Redemption and the Messianic Expectation in the Writings of Rabbi Sholomo of the House of Halevi of Salonika," *Tarbiz*, 39, 2 (1970), pp. 195–213 (in Hebrew).

22 Joseph Hacker, "The Ottoman Policy towards the Jews and Jewish Attitudes towards, the Ottomans during the Fifteenth Century," in Benjamin Braude and Bernard Lewis, eds, *Christians and Jews in the Ottoman Empire: The Functioning of a Plural Society* (Holmes & Meier, New York, 1982), vol. 1, p. 124.

23 Ibid., p. 121; Epstein, *The Ottoman Jewish Communities*, pp. 29–33.

24 Quoted by Abraham Danon, "La Communauté juive de Salonique au XVIe siècle," *Revue des études juives*, 40 (1900), p. 207.

25 Ibid.

26 On this subject, consult Jacob Barnai, "The Portuguese Marranos in Izmir in the Seventeenth Century," in Menahem Stern, ed., *The Nation and its History* (*Proceedings of the Eighth International Colloquium of Jewish Studies*), Zalman Shazar, Jerusalem, 1983), pp. 289–98 (in Hebrew); Zvi Ankori, ed., *From Lisbon to Salonika and Constantinople: Annual Lectures on the Jews of Greece* (University of Tel-Aviv, Tel-Aviv, 1988) (in Hebrew). On the Iberian background, see the latest account in Jane Gerber, *The Jews of Spain: A History of the Sephardic Experience* (Free Press, New York, 1992).

27 *Religious composition of the main towns in the Ottoman Empire between 1520 and 1530*

Towns	Households			Total households
	Muslims	Christian	Jewish	
Istanbul	9,517	5,162	1,647	16,326
Bursa	665	69	11	76,351
Edirne	3,338	522	201	4,061
Ankara	2,399	277	28	2,704
Athens	11	2,286	–	2,297
Tokat	818	701	–	1,519
Konya	1,092	22	–	1,114
Sivas	261	750	–	1,011
Sarajevo	1,024	–	–	1,024
Monastir	640	171	34	845
Uskub	630	200	12	842
Sofia	471	238	–	709
Salonika	1,229	989	2,645	4,863
Siroz	671	357	65	1,093
Trikala	301	343	181	825
Larissa	693	75	–	768
Nicopolis	468	775	–	1,343

Source: Lewis, Jews of Islam, p. 118.

28 On this subject, see Avigdor Levy, *The Sephardim in the Ottoman Empire* (Darwin Press, Princeton, 1992), pp. 7–11.

29 On this, see Heath Lowry, "Portrait of a City: The Population and Topography of Ottoman Selânik (Thessaloniki) in the year 1478," *Diptykha*, 2 (1980–1), pp. 254–92. See also İnalcık, "Jews in the Ottoman Economy," p. 514.

30 İnalcık, "Jews in the Ottoman Economy," p. 514.

31 Lewis, *Jews of Islam*, p. 123.

32 Stanford Shaw and Ezel Kural Shaw, *The Jews of the Ottoman Empire and the Turkish Republic* (New York University Press, New York, 1991), pp. 38–9.

33 Harriet Pass Freidenreich, *The Jews of Yugoslavia: A Quest for Community* (The Jewish Publication Society of America, Philadelphia, 1979), p. 26; Zvi Loker, "Les Séfarades parmi les slaves du sud," in Henry Méchoulan, ed., *Les Juifs d'Espagne: Histoire d'une diaspora, 1492–1992* (Liana Levi, Paris, 1992), p. 272.

34 Freidenreich, *Jews of Yugoslavia*, p. 12; Yakir Eventov, *History of the Jews of Yugoslavia* (Union of Yugoslav Immigrants in Israel, Tel-Aviv, 1971), vol. 1, p. 186 (in Hebrew).

35 Loker, "Les Séfarades parmi les slaves," pp. 268–70; Eventov, *Jews of Yugoslavia*, vol. 1, pp. 73–114. On the same subject, in Serbo-Croat, see Jorjo Tadić, *The Jews in Dubrovnik up to the Mid-Seventeenth Century* (La Benevolencia, Sarajevo, 1937); and Duško Kečkemet, *Jews in the History of Split* (n.p., Split, 1972).

36 Amnon Cohen and Bernard Lewis, eds, *Population and Revenue in the Towns of Palestine in the Sixteenth Century* (Princeton University Press, Princeton, 1978), pp. 128, 94.

37 Ibid., p. 161; Levy, *Sephardim in the Ottoman Empire*, p. 12; Joseph Hacker, "The Natives of Spain in the Ottoman Empire in the Sixteenth Century – Community and Society," in Haim Beinart, ed., *The Sephardi Heritage*, (Magnes Press, Jerusalem, 1992), p. 462 (in Hebrew).

38 On this town, see two articles in Hebrew by Jacob Barnai: "The Origins of the Jewish Community of Izmir in the Ottoman Period," *Peamim*, 12 (1982),

pp. 47–58; and "Rabbi Joseph Eskapa and the Izmir Rabbinate," *Sefunot*, 18, 3 (1985), pp. 53–81. On relations between the Jews in the town and the English Levant Company, see Eliezer Bashan, "Contacts between Jews in Smyrna and the Levant Company of London in the Seventeenth and Eighteenth Centuries," *Transactions of the Jewish Historical Society of England*, 29 (1988), pp. 53–73.

39   İnalcık, "Jews in the Ottoman Economy," p. 514.

40   Haim Gerber, *The Jews of the Ottoman Empire in the Sixteenth and Seventeenth Centuries: Economy and Society* (Zalman Shazar, Jerusalem, 1982), p. 48 (in Hebrew).

41   For this last figure, see Shaw and Shaw, *Jews of the Ottoman Empire*, p. 40.

42   Barkan, "Quelques remarques sur la constitution sociale et démographique," p. 281.

43   Hacker, "The *Sürgün* System," p. 35.

44   Ibid., p. 5.

45   Uriel Heyd, "The Jewish Communities of Istanbul in the Seventeenth Century," *Oriens*, 6, 2 (1953), p. 300 (in Hebrew).

46   Joseph Hacker, "Superbe et désespoir: l'existence sociale et spirituelle des Juifs ibériques dans l'Empire ottoman," *Revue historique*, 578 (April–June 1991), pp. 280–3.

47   Ibid., pp. 270–80.

48   For a study of the Romaniot community of Ioannina, see Rae Dalven, *The Jews of Ioannina* (Cadmus Press, Philadelphia, 1990).

49   Levy, *Sephardim in the Ottoman Empire*, p. 60.

50   Leah Bornstein-Makovetsky, "Structure, Organisation and Spiritual Life of the Sephardi Communities in the Ottoman Empire from the Sixteenth to Eighteenth Centuries," in R. D. Barnett and W. M. Schwab, eds., *The Sephardi Heritage: The Western Sephardim* (Gibraltar Books, Grendon, Northants, 1989), vol. 2, p. 318.

51 On this subject, see Joseph Hacker, "The Chief Rabbinate in the Ottoman Empire in the Fifteenth–Sixteenth Centuries," *Zion*, 49, 3 (1984), pp. 225–63 (in Hebrew).

52 See Mark A. Epstein, "The Leadership of the Ottoman Jews in the Fifteenth and Sixteenth Centuries," in Braude and Lewis, eds, *Christians and Jews in the Ottoman Empire*, vol. 1, pp. 101–15.

53 Heyd, "Jewish Communities of Istanbul," p. 308.

54 Hacker, "Superbe et désespoir", pp. 285–9.

55 Jacob Barnai, "Les Juifs de Palestine à l'époque ottomane," in Méchoulan, *Les Juifs d'Espagne*, p. 440; Abraham David, "The Immigration of the Expellees from Spain to Palestine and their Influence on the Native Inhabitants," in Beinart, *The Sephardi Heritage*, p. 458 (in Hebrew).

56 Levy, *Sephardim in the Ottoman Empire*, p. 64.

57 Jacob Barnai, "Sephardi Jewry after the Expulsion: The Sephardim in North Africa," in Beinart, *Sephardi Heritage*, p. 429 (in Hebrew).

58 Haim Zafrani, "Les communautés juives d'origine ibérique au Maroc depuis 1492 jusqu'à nos jours," in Méchoulan, *Les Juifs d'Espagne*, p. 524.

59 See *inter alia* Yaron Tsur, "France and the Jews of Tunisia: The Policy of the French Authorities towards the Jews and the Activities of the Jewish Elites during the Period of Transition from an Independent Muslim State to the Colonial Régime, 1873–1888" (unpublished doctoral thesis, The Hebrew University, Jerusalem, 1988; in Hebrew), pp. 10–13; André Chouraqui, *Histoire des Juifs en Afrique du Nord* (Hachette, Paris, 1985), pp. 193–4.

60 Heyd, "Jewish Communities of Istanbul," pp. 299–309; Haim Gerber, "The Jews in Adrianople in the Sixteenth to Seventeenth Centuries," *Sefunot*, 3, 18 (1985), pp. 46–8 (in Hebrew).

61 Hacker, "Natives of Spain in the Ottoman Empire," p. 463.

62 Bornstein-Makovetsky, "Structure, Organisation and Spiritual Life," pp. 317–18.

63   Barnai, "Rabbi Joseph Eskapa," p. 81; Jacob Barnai, "The Jews of the Ottoman Empire in the Seventeenth to Eighteenth Centuries," in Beinart, *Sephardi Heritage*, p. 496 (in Hebrew).

64   On the role of the guilds as an administrative link between the ruling class and the populations, see Gabriel Baer, "The Administrative, Economic and Social Functions of Turkish Guilds," *International Journal of Middle East Studies*, 1, 1 (Jan. 1970), pp. 28–50.

65   Jacob Barnai, "On the History of the Jewish Community of Istanbul in the Eighteenth Century," *Miqqedem Umiyyam*, 1 (1981), p. 62 (in Hebrew).

66   Epstein, "Leadership of the Ottoman Jews," p. 101.

67   On this subject, see Benjamin Braude, "Foundation Myths of the *Millet* System," in Braude and Lewis, eds, *Christians and Jews in the Ottoman Empire*, vol. 1, pp. 69–88.

68   Joseph Néhama, *Histoire des Israélites de Salonique* (Durlacher/Molho, Paris/Salonika, 1935–78), vol. 2, p. 17.

69   Leah Bornstein-Makovetsky, "Jewish Lay Leadership and Ottoman Authorities during the Sixteenth and Seventeenth Centuries," in Rodrigue, ed., *Ottoman and Turkish Jewry*, pp. 96, 110.

70   Joseph Hacker, "The Limits of Jewish Autonomy: Jewish Autonomy in the Ottoman Empire in the Sixteenth to Eighteenth Centuries," in Shmuel Almog, Israel Bartal, Michael Graetz *et al.*, eds, *Transition and Change in Modern Jewish History: Essays Presented in Honour of Shmuel Ettinger* (Zalman Shazar, Jerusalem, 1987), p. 385 (in Hebrew). See also Amnon Cohen, *Jewish Life under Islam: Jerusalem in the Sixteenth Century* (Harvard University Press, Cambridge, Mass., 1984).

71   Hacker, "The Limits of Jewish Autonomy," p. 385.

72   Michael Molho, *Contribution to the History of Salonica* (Akuaroni and Behar, Salonika, 5692/1932), pp. 17–18 (in Judeo-Spanish); Néhama, *Histoire des Israélites de Salonique*, vol. 2, p. 75.

73   Hacker, "Limits of Jewish Autonomy," pp. 381–4.

74   For an example, see Gilles Veinstein, "Une communauté ottomane: les Juifs d'Avlonya (Valona) dans la deuxième moitié du XVIe siècle," in Gaetano

Cozzi, ed., *Gli Ebrei e Venezia, secoli XIV–XVIII* (Edizioni Comunità, Milan, 1987), p. 812.

75 On this subject, see Esther Benbassa, *Haim Nahum: A Sephardic Chief Rabbi* (The University of Alabama Press, Tuscaloosa, 1995).

76 Danon, "La communauté juive de Salonique," p. 230; Néhama, *Histoire des Israélites de Salonique*, vol. 2, p. 75.

77 Hacker, "Natives of Spain in the Ottoman Empire," p. 467.

78 Danon, "La communauté juive de Salonique," p. 208; Néhama, *Histoire des Israélites de Salonique*, vol. 2, p. 46.

79 On the organization of the congregations, see Danon, "La communauté juive de Salonique," pp. 213–19; Leah Bornstein, "The Leadership of the Jewish Communities in the Middle East from the Fifteenth to the Eighteenth Centuries" (unpublished doctoral thesis, The Hebrew University, Jerusalem, 1978) (in Hebrew); Joseph Hacker, "The Jewish Society of Salonika in the Fifteenth and Sixteenth Centuries: A Chapter in the History of Jewish Society in the Ottoman Empire" (unpublished doctoral thesis, The Hebrew University of Jerusalem, 1978) (in Hebrew); Azriel Shohat, "Notes on the Communal Organisation of the Jews in the Ottoman Empire in the Sixteenth Century," *Miqqedem Umiyyam*, 1 (1981), pp. 133–7 (in Hebrew); Aryeh Shmuelevitz, *The Jews of the Ottoman Empire in the Late Fifteenth and the Sixteenth Centuries: Administrative, Economic, Legal and Social Relations as Reflected in the Responsa* (E. J. Brill, Leyden, 1984); Hacker, "Natives of Spain in the Ottoman Empire," pp. 467–77.

80 On the role of the rich in the communities, see Eliezer Bashan, "The Position of the Salonikan Rabbis in the Sixteenth to the Eighteenth Centuries in the Dispute Relating to the Influence of a Wealthy Minority on Public Life," *Mimizrah Umimaarav*, 2 (1980), pp. 27–52 (in Hebrew).

81 On this subject, see Bornstein-Makovetsky, "Jewish Lay Leadership," pp. 87–112.

82 For an example, see Minna Rozen, "The Activities of Influential Jews at the Sultan's Court in Istanbul in Support of the Jewish Settlement of Jerusalem in the Seventeenth Century," *Michael*, 43 (1982), pp. 394–430 (in Hebrew).

83 Meir Benayahu, "Facts about the Jews of Spain in the First Century of their Settlement in Turkey," *Sinai*, 14, 3–4 (1951), p. 183 (in Hebrew).

84 On the Jewish courts, see Leah Bornstein, "The Structure of Law-Courts in the Sixteenth and Seventeenth Centuries in the Communities of the Ottoman Empire, as Portrayed in Rabbinical Literature" (unpublished paper presented at the International Conference on Jewish Communities in Muslim Lands, Ben Zvi Institute, Jerusalem, n.d. [197?])

85 Hacker, "Natives of Spain in the Ottoman Empire," p. 471.

86 On the congregations in this town, see Jacob Barnai, "The Congregations in Izmir in the Seventeenth Century," *Peamim*, 48 (1991), pp. 66–84 (in Hebrew).

87 Jacob Barnai, "Ottoman Jewry in the Seventeenth to Eighteenth Centuries," in Beinart, *Sephardi Heritage*, p. 495 (in Hebrew).

88 Ibid., p. 496; Jacob Barnai, "The Status of the Chief Rabbinate in Jerusalem in the Ottoman Period," *Cathedra*, 13 (1980), pp. 47–69 (in Hebrew).

89 Abraham Shaul Amarillo, "Benevolent Societies," *Sefunot*, 15, 5 (1971–81), pp. 105–33 (in Hebrew); Eliezer Bashan, "Societies for the Help of the Sick in the Communities of the Middle East," in *Homage to Abraham Spiegelman* (1979), pp. 209–20 (offprint, in Hebrew).

90 On these schools see, *inter alia*, Haim Bentov, "The Method of Teaching the Talmud in the *Yeshivot* of Salonika and Turkey," *Sefunot*, 13, 3 (1971–8), pp. 7–102 (in Hebrew); Jacob Geller, "The Economic Survival of the *Yeshivot* and *Talmudei Torah* in the Ottoman Empire," *Mimizrah Umi-maarav*, 1 (1974), pp. 167–221 (in Hebrew).

91 On this subject, see Abraham Shaul Amarillo, "The Great *Talmud Torah* Society in Salonika," *Sefunot*, 13, 3 (1971–8), pp. 275–308 (in Hebrew).

92 Azriel Shohat, "The Taxation System and Leadership in the Communities of Greece in the Sixteenth Century," *Sefunot*, 11, 1 (1971–8), p. 316 (in Hebrew).

93 Barnai, "Ottoman Jewry in the Seventeenth to Eighteenth Centuries," p. 497.

94 On this subject, see Jacob Barnai, *The Jews in Palestine in the Eighteenth Century under the Patronage of the Istanbul Committee of Officials for Palestine*, tr. from Hebrew by Naomi Goldblum (University of Alabama Press, Tuscaloosa, 1992).

95 Freidenreich, *Jews of Yugoslavia*, p. 16. In the same way, Mediterranean communities such as Ragusa, ruled by a consul collecting taxes for the Republic of Venice, did not follow the same organizational model as the Empire and adapted their structures to the local context.

96 Néhama, *Histoire des Israélites de Salonique*, vol. 2, p. 115.

97 Shohat, "Taxation System and Leadership," p. 305.

98 On these exemptions, see Meir Benayahu, "Ordinances of Safed for the Immunity from Taxation of Scholars and the Attempt at Repeal by Rabbi Yehuda Aberlin," *Sefunot*, 7 (1963), pp. 102–17 (in Hebrew); Joseph Hacker, "Historic-Halakhic and Social Analysis of the Payment of the Poll Tax by Palestinian Jewish Scholars in the Sixteenth Century," *Shalem*, 4 (1984), pp. 63–117 (in Hebrew); Néhama, *Histoire des Israélites de Salonique*, vol. 2, p. 117.

99 On the taxes see, *inter alia*, Abraham Danon, "Etude historique sur les impôts directs et indirects des communautés israélites en Turquie," *Revue des études juives*, 31 (1895), pp. 52–61; Simon Marcus, "Community Taxes and the Register of the Community Tax in Rhodes," *Sefunot*, 1 (1957), pp. 279–302 (in Hebrew); Shohat, "Taxation System and Leadership," p. 301–39.

100 Shohat, "Taxation System and Leadership," p. 307.

101 Gerber, *Jews of the Ottoman Empire*, pp. 36–7.

102 On this tax, see Hacker, "The Chief Rabbinate," pp. 236–43.

103 Shohat, "Taxation System and Leadership," p. 309.

104 Gerber, *Jews of the Ottoman Empire*, p. 37.

105 Danon, "Etude historique sur les impôts," p. 58.

106 Gerber, *Jews of the Ottoman Empire*, pp. 44–5.

107 Barnai, "Ottoman Jewry in the Seventeenth to Eighteenth Centuries," p. 495.

108 Ibid., p. 488.

109 Marcus, "Community Taxes" p. 279.

110 On the fires see, *inter alia*, Eliezer Bashan, "Fires and Earthquakes in Izmir in the Seventeenth to Nineteenth Centuries and a Document on the Accusation Directed against the Jews of Lighting the Fires," *Miqqedem Umiyyam*, 2 (1986), pp. 13–27 (in Hebrew).

111 Barnai, "On the History of the Jewish Community of Istanbul," pp. 62–3.

112 Ibid., p. 56.

113 Shohat, "Taxation System and Leadership," p. 317.

114 Néhama, *Histoire des Israélites de Salonique*, vol. 2, p. 116.

115 Marcus, "Community Taxes," p. 282.

116 Danon, "Etude historique sur les impôts," p. 56; Néhama, *Histoire des Israélites de Salonique*, vol. 2, p. 117.

117 Shohat, "Financial System and Leadership," p. 321.

118 Néhama, *Histoire des Israélites de Salonique*, vol. 2, p. 117.

119 Marcus, "Community Taxes," p. 287.

120 On this subject, see Danon, "La communauté juive de Salonique," pp. 219–20.

121 Ibid., pp. 209, 211.

122 Bornstein, "The Structure of Law-Courts," pp. 322–3.

123 Danon, "La communauté juive de Salonique," p. 229.

124 On this subject, see Yizhak Rafael Molho, "Anthology of Regulations in Ladino in Salonika," *Sefunot*, 2 (1958), pp. 26–60 (in Hebrew).

125 On this subject, see Michael Molho, "Regulations on the Location of Houses, Courtyards and Shops," *Sinai*, 14 (5–6) (1951), pp. 296–314 (in Hebrew).

126 On this subject, see Néhama, *Histoire des Israélites de Salonique*, vol. 3, p. 148.

127 On the family, see Hacker, "Natives of Spain in the Ottoman Empire," p. 476.

128 Barnai, "On the History of the Jewish Community of Istanbul," p. 59.

129 Yomtov Assis, "Crime and Violence in Spanish Jewish Society in the Thirteenth to Fourteenth Centuries," *Zion*, 50 (1985), pp. 221–40 (in Hebrew); Yomtov Assis, "Sexual Behaviour in Mediaeval Hispano-Jewish Society" in Ada Rapoport-Albert and Steven J. Zipperstein, eds, *Essays in Honour of Chimen Abramsky* (Weidenfeld & Nicolson, London, 1989), pp. 25–59.

130 Danon, "La communauté juive de Salonique," pp. 223–4.

131 Gerber, *Jews of the Ottoman Empire*, pp. 16–17.

132 Freidenreich, *Jews of Yugoslavia*, p. 12.

133 Haim Gerber, "On the History of the Jews in Istanbul in the Seventeenth to Eighteenth Centuries," *Peamim*, 12 (1982), p. 29 (in Hebrew).

134 Ibid., pp. 29–45; Gerber, "Jews in Adrianople," p. 50; Haim Gerber, "The Sharia Archives, the Court of Bursa, as a Source for the History of the Jews in the Town," *Miqqedem Umiyyam*, 1 (1981), pp. 31–7 (in Hebrew).

135 Epstein, *The Ottoman Jewish Communities*, pp. 19–52.

136 Eliezer Bashan, "Economic Association with non-Jews, the Principle and its Achievement," *Mahanayim*, 2 (1992), pp. 78–85 (in Hebrew).

137 Barnai, "Ottoman Jewry in the Seventeenth to Eighteenth Centuries," p. 489.

138 Ibid.

139 Ibid., p. 490.

140 See Joseph Hacker, "Superbe et désespoir," p. 293.

2 ECONOMY AND CULTURE

1 Mark Alan Epstein, *The Ottoman Jewish Communities and their Role in the Fifteenth and Sixteenth Centuries* (Klaus Schwarz, Freibourg, 1980), pp. 125–8. On Jewish tax farmers and collectors in the Ottoman Empire, see

Haim Gerber, *The Jews of the Ottoman Empire in the Sixteenth and Seventeenth Centuries: Economy and Society* (Zalman Shazar, Jerusalem, 1982), pp. 49–60 (in Hebrew).

2   For a discussion of the place of the Jews in the economy of Bursa, see Haim Gerber, "Jews in the Economic Life of the Anatolian City of Bursa in the Seventeenth Century," *Sefunot*, 16 (1980), pp. 235–72 (in Hebrew).

3   Avigdor Levy, *The Sephardim in the Ottoman Empire* (Darwin Press, Princeton, 1992), p. 27.

4   Daniel Goffman, *Izmir and the Levantine World, 1550–1650* (University of Washington Press, Seattle, 1990), pp. 87, 143.

5   Epstein, *The Ottoman Jewish Communities*, p. 89.

6   Ibid., pp. 83–93. For the Nasi family, see Cecil Roth, *Doña Gracia of the House of Nasi* (Jewish Publication Society of America, Philadelphia, 1948); Cecil Roth, *The House of Nasi: The Duke of Naxos* (Jewish Publication Society of America, Philadelphia, 1948); Paul Grunebaum-Ballin, *Joseph Naci, duc de Naxos* (Mouton, Paris, 1968).

7   Epstein, *The Ottoman Jewish Communities*, p. 112. For a discussion of the Jewish involvement with the Ottoman mint, see Samuel Lachman, "Jews in the Mints of Ottoman Turkey," *Shekel*, 21, 2 (1988), pp. 12–15.

8   See the discussion in Haim Gerber, "Enterprise and International Commerce in the Economic Activity of the Jews in the 16th–17th Centuries," *Zion*, 43 (1978), pp. 65–6 (in Hebrew); Haim Gerber, "Jews and Moneylending in the Ottoman Empire," *Jewish Quarterly Review*, 72 (1981), pp. 100–18; Haim Gerber, "Jews in the Economic Life," p. 245; Eliezer Bashan, "Jewish Moneylending in Constantinople and Smyrna during the 17th–18th Centuries as Reflected in the British Levant Company's Archives," in Aricl Toaff and Simon Schwarzfuchs, eds, *The Mediterranean and the Jews: Banking, Finance and International Trade (XVI–XVIII Centuries)* (Bar-Ilan University Press, Ramat Gan, 1989), pp. 57–73.

9   Levy, *The Sephardim*, p. 40.

10   Traian Stoianovich, "The Conquering Balkan Orthodox Merchant," *Journal of Economic History*, 20 (1960), p. 240.

11 Epstein, *The Ottoman Jewish Communities*, pp. 79–84. See also Bernard Lewis, "The Privilege granted by Mehmed II to his Physician," *Bulletin of the School of Oriental and African Studies*, 14 (1952), pp. 550–63.

12 For a discussion of these physicians, see Avram Galante, *Histoire des Juifs de Turquie*, reprint (Isis, Istanbul, [1985]), vol. 9, pp. 77–117; Uriel Heyd, "Moses Hamon, Chief Jewish Physician to Sultan Suleyman the Magnificent," *Oriens*, 16 (1963), pp. 152–70; Meir Benayahu, "The Court Doctor Moshe Benbanast and the Poem of Rabbi Judah Zarko on his Exile to Rhodes," *Sefunot*, 12 (1971–8), pp. 123–43 (in Hebrew); Jacob Barnai, "On the History of the Jewish Community of Istanbul in the Eighteenth Century," *Miqqedem Umiyyam*, 1 (1981), p. 57 (in Hebrew).

13 Levy, *The Sephardim*, p. 29; Walter Weiker, *Ottomans, Turks and the Jewish Polity: A History of the Jews of Turkey* (University Press of America/The Jerusalem Center for Public Affairs, Lanham/New York/London, 1992), p. 79.

14 Benjamin Braude, "The Rise and Fall of Salonika Woollens, 1500–1650: Technology Transfer and Western Competition," *Mediterranean Historical Review*, 6, 2 (1991), p. 200. The first book to treat the history of the Jewish textile industry in Salonika is I. S. Emmanuel, *Histoire de l'industrie des tissus des Israélites de Salonique* (Librairie Lipschutz, Paris, 1935).

15 Benjamin Braude, "International Competition and Domestic Cloth in the Ottoman Empire, 1500–1650: A Study in Undevelopment," *Review*, 2 (1979), p. 437.

16 Braude, "The Rise and Fall," pp. 224–8.

17 Joseph Néhama, "The Jews of Salonica in the Ottoman Period," in R. D. Barnett and W. M. Schwab, eds, *The Sephardi Heritage: The Western Sephardim* (Gibraltar Books, Grendon, Northants, 1989), vol. 2, p. 208.

18 Morris D. Goodblatt, *Jewish Life in Turkey in the XVIth Century* (Jewish Theological Seminary of America, New York, 1952), pp. 52–8.

19 Joseph Néhama, *Histoire des Israélites de Salonique* (Durlacher/Molho, Paris/Salonika, 1936), vol. 3, pp. 37–51; Snezhka Panova, "The Development of the Textile Industry in the Balkan Countries and the Role of the Jewish Population in the XVIth–XVIIth Centuries," *Annual*, 11 (1976), pp. 123–40.

20 See the discussion in Azriel Shohat, "The King's Cloth in Salonika," *Sefunot*, 12 (1971–8), pp. 169–88 (in Hebrew); Minna Rozen, "Contest and Rivalry in Mediterranean Maritime Commerce in the First Half of the Eighteenth Century: The Jews of Salonica and the European Presence," *Revue des études juives*, 147 (1988), p. 313, n14.

21 Braude, "The Rise and Fall," pp. 232–3.

22 Shmuel Avitsur, "Contribution to the History of the Woollen Textile Industry in Salonika," *Sefunot*, 12 (1971–8), p. 164 (in Hebrew).

23 Ibid., p. 160. Simon Schwarzfuchs, "Quand commença le déclin de l'industrie textile des Juifs de Salonique?" in Toaff and Schwarzfuchs, eds, *The Mediterranean and the Jews*, p. 220. For the debate on the dating of the decline of the industry, see ibid., pp. 215–35, and Braude, "International Competition;" Braude, "The Cloth Industry of Salonica in the Mediterranean Economy," *Peamim*, 15 (1983), pp. 82–95 (in Hebrew); Braude, "The Rise and Fall."

24 Braude, "International Competition," pp. 440–5.

25 See Simon Schwarzfuchs, "La Décadence de la Galilée juive du XVIe siècle et la crise du textile au Proche-Orient," *Revue des études juives*, 121 (1962), pp. 169–79.

26 Rozen, "Contest and Rivalry," p. 318; Schwarzfuchs, "Quand commença," p. 230.

27 Eliezer Bashan, "The Rise and Decline of the Sephardi Communities in the Levant – The Economic Aspects," in Barnett and Schwab, eds, *The Western Sephardim*, p. 360; Levy, *The Sephardim*, p. 25; Weiker, *Ottomans*, p. 38.

28 See the discussion of ethnic economic networks in Benjamin Braude, "Venture and Faith in the Commercial Life of the Ottoman Balkans, 1500–1650," *The International History Review*, 7 (1985), pp. 519–42. On links between different Jewish groups along the Mediterranean, see Minna Rozen, "The Fattoria – a Chapter in the History of Mediterranean Commerce in the Sixteenth and Seventeenth Centuries," *Miqqedem Umiyyam*, 1 (1981), pp. 104–10 (in Hebrew).

29 John R. Lampe and Marvin R. Jackson, *Balkan Economic History, 1550–1950* (Indiana University Press, Bloomington, 1982), p. 25.

30   Néhama, "The Jews of Salonica," p. 221.

31   Haim Gerber, "On the History of the Jews of Istanbul in the Seventeenth and Eighteenth Centuries," *Peamim*, 12 (1982), p. 36 (in Hebrew).

32   Lampe and Jackson, *Balkan Economic History*, p. 37.

33   Eliezer Bashan, "A Jewish Guild in Izmir at the Beginning of the Eighteenth Century," *Mimizrah Umimaarav*, 5 (1986), p. 156 (in Hebrew).

34   Haim Gerber, "Guilds in Seventeenth Century Anatolian Bursa," *Asian and African Studies*, 11 (1976), pp. 83–4.

35   Jacob Barnai, "Jewish Guilds in Turkey in the Sixteenth to Nineteenth Centuries," in Nahum Gross, ed., *Jews in Economic Life* (Zalman Shazar, Jerusalem, 1985), pp. 133–48 (in Hebrew).

36   For the study of one such guild, see Yizhak Rofeh, "Benevolent Society of the Boat-Owners in Constantinople," *Sefunot*, 10 (1966), pp. 621–32 (in Hebrew). For the survival of guilds and the ethnic division of labor, see the reproduction of contemporary documentation in Charles Issawi, *The Economic History of the Middle East 1800–1914* (University of Chicago Press, Chicago and London, 1975), pp. 114–25, and Jacob Barnai, "The Ottoman Empire, Seventeenth–Eighteenth Centuries," in Haim Beinart, ed., *The Sephardi Heritage* (Magnes Press, Jerusalem, 1992), p. 493 (in Hebrew).

37   See Hana Jacobson, "Marrano Immigrants from Portugal and their Role in the Industrial Development of the Ottoman Empire in the 16th Century," in Zvi Ankori, ed., *From Lisbon to Salonika and Constantinople: Annual Lectures on the Jews of Greece* (Tel-Aviv University, Tel-Aviv, 1988), pp. 27–51 (in Hebrew).

38   Meir Benayahu, "The Abravanel Family in Salonika," *Sefunot*, 12 (1971–5), p. 20 (in Hebrew); Bashan, "The Rise and Decline," pp. 350–1.

39   Goffman, *Izmir*, p. 79.

40   See among many other accounts the discussion in Marc Saperstein, "Martyrs, Merchants and Rabbis: Jewish Communal Conflict as Reflected in the Responsa on the Boycott of Ancona," *Jewish Social Studies*, 43, 3–4 (1981), pp. 215–28; Ruth Lamand, " 'The Ancona Boycott' – The Other Side of the Medallion," in Ankori, ed., *From Lisbon*, pp. 135–54 (in Hebrew).

41   Bashan, "The Rise and Decline," p. 351.

42   Zvi Loker, "Spanish and Portuguese Jews amongst the Southern Slavs – Their Settlement and Consolidation during the Sixteenth to Eighteenth Centuries," in Barnett and Schwab, eds, *The Western Sephardim*, p. 291.

43   Gilles Veinstein, "Une communauté ottomane: Les Juifs d'Avlonya (Valona) dans la deuxième moitié du XVIe siècle," in Gaetano Cozzi, ed., *Gli Ebrei e Venezia, secoli XIV–XVIII* (Edizioni Comunità, Milan, 1987), p. 785.

44   Jonathan Israel, *European Jewry in the Age of Mercantilism 1550–1750*, 2nd ed. (Clarendon Press, Oxford, 1989), p. 34.

45   Benjamin Arbel, "Venice and Jewish Merchants of Istanbul in the Sixteenth Century," in Toaff and Schwarzfuchs, eds, *The Mediterranean and the Jews*, p. 45.

46   Ibid., pp. 46–7.

47   For the latest discussion of the activities of this financier, see Benjamin Ravid, "An Autobiographical Memorandum by Daniel Rodriga, *Inventore* of the *Scala* of Spalato," in Toaff and Schwarzfuchs, eds, *The Mediterranean and the Jews*, pp. 189–213.

48   See the analysis of this phenomenon in Minna Rozen, "Strangers in a Strange Land: The Extraterritorial Status of the Jews in Italy and the Ottoman Empire in the Sixteenth to the Eighteenth Centuries," in Aron Rodrigue, ed., *Ottoman and Turkish Jewry: Community and Leadership*, (Indiana University Turkish Studies, Bloomington, 1992), pp. 123–66.

49   There is a very large literature on the causes of the decline of the Ottoman Empire. For one recent interpretation see the articles in Huri İslamoğlu-Inan, ed., *The Ottoman Empire and the World Economy* (Cambridge University Press / Editions de la Maison des Sciences de l'Homme, Cambridge/Paris, 1987).

50   Israel, *European Jewry*, pp. 113–14; Néhama, "The Jews of Salonica," p. 221.

51   See Stoianovich, "The Conquering Balkan Orthodox Merchant."

52   Jacob Barnai, "Portuguese Marranos in Izmir in the Seventeenth Century," in Menahem Stern, ed., *The Nation and its History* (Zalman Shazar, Jerusalem, 1983), pp. 289–98 (in Hebrew).

53   Minna Rozen, "Les Marchands juifs livournais à Tunis et le commerce avec Marseille à la fin du XVIIe siècle," *Michael*, 9 (1985), pp. 87–129.

54   Rozen, "Contest and Rivalry," pp. 323–4. For an overview of the activities of the Francos, see Jacob Barnai, "The Jews in the Ottoman Empire," in Shmuel Ettinger, ed., *History of Jews in Islamic Countries* (Zalman Shazar, Jerusalem, 1986), vol. 2, pp. 254–8.

55   See the discussion in Simon Schwarzfuchs, "The Salonika Scale: The Struggle between the French and Jewish Merchants," *Sefunot*, 15 (1971–8), pp. 77–102 (in Hebrew).

56   Rozen, "Contest and Rivalry," pp. 320–1.

57   Jean-Pierre Filippini, "Le Rôle des négociants et des banquiers juifs de Livourne dans le grand commerce international en Méditerranée au XVIIIe siècle," in Toaff and Schwarzfuchs, eds, *The Mediterranean and the Jews*, pp. 129–31.

58   Bashan, "A Jewish Guild," p. 165.

59   Goffman, *Izmir*, pp. 36–41, 63–4.

60   Goffman, *Izmir* pp. 64–5.

61   Bashan, "A Jewish Guild," p. 156; Goffman, *Izmir*, p. 89.

62   Goffman, *Izmir* pp. 87–8.

63   Ibid., p. 143.

64   Eliezer Bashan, "Fires and Earthquakes in Izmir in the Seventeenth to Nineteenth Centuries and a Document on an Accusation directed against the Jews of Lighting the Fires," *Miqqedem Umiyyam*, 2 (1986), p. 15.

65   Bashan, "A Jewish Guild," pp. 165–6.

66   Eliezer Bashan, "Contacts between Jews in Smyrna and the Levant Company of London in the Seventeenth and Eighteenth Centuries," *Transactions of the Jewish Historical Society of England*, 29 (1988), p. 57.

67   Ibid.

68   Bashan, "Jewish Moneylending," p. 66.

69   Troianovich, "The Conquering Balkan Orthodox Merchant," p. 299.

70   Ali İhsan Bağış, *Non-Muslims in Ottoman Commerce* (Turhan Kitabevi, Ankara, 1983), pp. 88–9 (in Turkish).

71   See Barnai, "On the History."

72   Gerber, "Jews in the Economic Life," pp. 237, 254.

73   Barnai, "On the History," pp. 59–63.

74   Snezhka Panova, "On the Social Differentiation of the Jewish Population in the Bulgarian Lands during the XVIth–XVIIIth Centuries," *Annual*, 12 (1977), p. 142.

75   Robert W. Olson, "Jews in the Ottoman Empire in the Light of New Documents," *Jewish Social Studies*, 41 (1979), pp. 75–88.

76   Moïse Franco, *Essai sur l'histoire des Israélites de l'Empire ottoman*, reprint (UISF, Paris, 1981), pp. 32–9; Salomon A. Rozanes, *History of the Jews of Turkey and of the Middle East* (Rav Kook Institute, Jerusalem, 1945), vol. 6, pp. 64–7 (in Hebrew).

77   Ibid.

78   On these conflicts, see the preceding chapter. See also Jean-Christophe Attias, *Le Commentaire biblique: Mordekhai Komtino ou l'herméneutique du dialogue* (Cerf, Paris, 1991).

79   Joseph Hacker, "The Intellectual Activity of the Jews of the Ottoman Empire during the Sixteenth and Seventeenth Centuries," in Isadore Twersky and Bernard Septimus, eds, *Jewish Thought in the Seventeenth Century* (Harvard University Press, Cambridge, Mass., and London, 1987), pp. 104–5.

80   Ibid., p. 105.

81   Ibid., pp. 105–7. For one such family, see Benayahu, "The Abravanel Family."

82   Roth, *Doña Gracia*, pp. 140–1; Levy, *The Sephardim*, p. 38.

83   For the Hamon family, see Heyd, "Moses Hamon."

84   Hacker, "Intellectual Activity," p. 106.

85   For Hebrew printing in the Ottoman Empire, see Abraham Yaari, *Hebrew Printing in the Middle East* (The Hebrew University, Jerusalem, 1936), (in Hebrew); Yaari, *Hebrew Printing in Constantinople* (Magnes Press, Jerusalem, 1967), (in Hebrew); Joseph Hacker, "Printing at Constantinople in the Sixteenth Century," *Areshet*, 5 (1972), pp. 457–93 (in Hebrew); Israel Mehlman, "Contribution to the History of Printing in Salonika," *Sefunot*, 13 (1971–8), pp. 215–72 (in Hebrew).

86   See Abraham Shaul Amarillo, "The Great *Talmud Torah* Society in Salonika," *Sefunot*, 13 (1971–8), pp. 275–308 (in Hebrew).

87   For a discussion of traditional Jewish education on the eve of the modern period, see Aron Rodrigue, *French Jews, Turkish Jews: The Alliance Israélite Universelle and the Politics of Jewish Schooling in Turkey, 1860–1925* (Indiana University Press, Bloomington and Indianapolis, 1990), pp. 35–8.

88   For a discussion of the *halakhic* activities of the Sephardim in this period, see H. J. Zimmels, "The Contribution of the Sephardim to the Responsa Literature till the Beginning of the Sixteenth Century," in Richard David Barnett, ed., *The Sephardi Heritage: Essays on the Historical and Cultural Contribution of the Jews of Spain and Portugal* (Valentine Mitchell, London, 1971), vol. 1, pp. 367–401.

89   Joseph Hacker, "R. Jacob Ibn Habib – On the Configuration of the Jewish Leadership in Salonika in the beginning of the 16th Century," in *Proceedings of the 6th World Congress of Jewish Studies* (World Union of Jewish Studies, Jerusalem, 1976), vol. 2, pp. 118–19 (in Hebrew).

90   See Michael Molho, "The Rabbi Samuel de Medina," *Sinai*, 41, 1 (1957), pp. 36–58 (in Hebrew).

91   See the fascinating biography by R. J. Zwi Werblowsky, *Joseph Caro, Lawyer and Mystic* (Oxford University Press, London, 1962).

92   On the *halakhic* activities of the Jews in Spain, see *inter alia* Avraham Grossman, "The Halakhic Creativity of Spanish Sages," in Beinart, ed., *The Sephardi Heritage*, pp. 150–73 (in Hebrew).

93   Hacker, "The Intellectual Activity," pp. 114–16.

94   Leah Bornstein-Makovetsky, "Structure, Organization and Spiritual Life of the Sephardi Communities in the Ottoman Empire from the Sixteenth to Eighteenth Centuries," in Barnett and Schwab, eds, *The Sephardi Heritage: The Western Sephardim*, vol. 2, p. 332.

95   Marc D. Angel, *Voices in Exile: A Study in Sephardic Intellectual History* (Ktav and Sephardic House, Hoboken, NJ, 1991), pp. 16–22; Moshe Idel, "Jewish Thought in Medieval Spain," in Beinart, ed., *The Sephardi Heritage*, pp. 208–16 (in Hebrew).

96   Bornstein-Makovetsky, "Structure, Organization," p. 332.

97   Yizhak R. Molho, "Moïse Barouh Almosnino (1518–1581)," *Tesoro de los Judíos Sefardíes*, 7 (1964), p. lvii.

98   Bornstein-Makovetsky, "Structure, Organization," p. 334.

99   Angel, *Voices in Exile*, p. 22. On Meir Ibn Gabbai, see Roland Goetschel, *Meir Ibn Gabbai: le discours de la Kabbale espagnole* (Peeters, Louvain, 1981).

100   On this ambiguity in some speculative approaches, see Shaul Regev, "The Rabbi Samuel de Medina," *Mehkerei Yerushalayim bemahshevet Yisrael*, 5 (1986), pp. 155–89 (in Hebrew).

101   On his life and thought, see Hava Tirosh-Rothschild, *Between Worlds: The Life and Thought of Rabbi David ben Judah Messer Leon* (SUNY Press, Albany, New York, 1991).

102   See Werblowsky, *Joseph Caro*.

103   Hacker, "The Intellectual Activity," p. 123.

104   Moshe Idel, "Religion, Thought and Attitudes: The Impact of the Expulsion on the Jews," in Elie Kedourie, ed., *Spain and the Jews: The Sephardi Experience, 1492 and After*, (Thames & Hudson, London, 1992), p. 131.

105   Ibid., p. 133.

106   Ibid., pp. 133–4.

107 On Jewish mysticism, among many other works by him, see Gershom G. Scholem, *Major Trends in Jewish Mysticism* (Shocken, New York, 1961); Scholem, *On the Kaballah and Its Symbolism* (Schocken, New York, 1965). For a different interpretation, see Moshe Idel, *Kabbalah: New Perspectives* (Yale University Press, New Haven, 1988).

108 See Pamela J. Dorn, "Change and Ideology: The Ethnomusicology of Turkish Jewry" (doctoral dissertation, Indiana University), 1991; Stanford J. Shaw, *The Jews of the Ottoman Empire and the Turkish Republic* (New York University Press, New York, 1991), p. 105.

109 For a discussion of the psychological state among the exiles and their descendants, see Joseph Hacker, "Superbe et désespoir: l'existence sociale et spirituelle des Juifs ibériques dans l'Empire ottoman," *Revue Historique*, 578 (1991), pp. 261–93.

110 Angel, *Voices in Exile*, pp. 11–16; Joseph Hacker, "Israel among the Nations in the Description of Rabbi Samuel of the Beit Ha-Levi of Salonica," *Zion*, 34, 1–2 (1969), p. 85 (in Hebrew).

111 Ibid., pp. 86–7.

112 On Jewish messianism, see Gershom G. Scholem, *The Messianic Idea in Judaism and Other Essays* (Schocken, New York, 1971). For Abravanel's messianism see *inter alia* Benzion Netanyahu, *Don Isaac Abravanel, Statesman and Philosopher*, 3rd edn (The Jewish Publication Society of America, Philadelphia, 1972) and Jean-Christophe Attias, *Isaac Abravanel, la mémoire et l'espérance* (Cerf, Paris, 1992).

113 Aryeh Shmuelevitz, "Capsali as a Source for Ottoman History, 1450–1523," *International Journal of Middle East Studies*, 9 (1978), pp. 339–41.

114 This work appeared in Sabbionetta in 1554. For Ha-Kohen's messianism, see Yosef Hayim Yerushalmi, "Messianic Impulses in Joseph Ha-Kohen," in Bernard D. Cooperman, ed., *Studies in Sixteenth Century Jewish Thought* (Harvard University Press, Cambridge, Mass., 1983), pp. 460–87.

115 See Yosef Hayim Yerushalmi, *A Jewish Classic in the Portuguese Language* (Calouste Gulbenkian, Lisbon, 1989), pp. 31–4.

116 Angel, *Voices in Exile*, p. 34.

117 See the works of Gershom G. Scholem, most notably *Major Trends* and *Sabbatai Sevi: The Mystical Messiah, 1626–1676* (Princeton University Press, Princeton, NJ, 1977). This interpretation has been most recently restated by Rachel Elior, "Messianic Expectations and Spiritualization of Religious Life in the Sixteenth Century," *Revue des études juives*, 145 (1986), pp. 35–49.

118 See most notably Idel, *Kabbalah* and "Religion, Thought and Attitudes."

119 Hacker, "The Intellectual Activity," pp. 131–3.

120 Levy, *The Sephardim*, p. 84. For the events surrounding the rise of Sabbetai Zevi, the classic study is to be found in Scholem, *Sabbatai Sevi*.

121 Goffman, *Izmir*, pp. 90–1.

122 On Eskapa and the Izmir community, see Jacob Barnai, "Rabbi Joseph Eskapa and the Rabbinate in Izmir," *Sefunot*, 18, 3 (1985), pp. 53–81 (in Hebrew).

123 This account of the life and activities of Zevi is based on Scholem, *Sabbatai Sevi*. The literature on Zevi is enormous. See, for example, the whole issue of *Sefunot*, 14 (1971–7) (in Hebrew) edited by Meir Benayahu which is devoted to Zevi and to Sabbateanism.

124 Galante, *Histoite*, vol. 8, pp. 224–47. See also Gershom G. Scholem, "Doenmeh," *Encyclopaedia Judaica*, vol. 6 (Jerusalem, Keter, 1972), pp. 148–52.

125 See Jacob Barnai, "Messianism and Leadership: The Sabbatean Movement and the Leadership of the Jewish Communities of the Ottoman Empire," in Rodrigue, ed., *Ottoman and Turkish Jewry*, pp. 167–82.

126 Ibid., pp. 174–9.

127 Ibid., p. 174.

128 See Elisheva Carlebach, *The Pursuit of Heresy: Rabbi Moshe Hagiz and the Sabbatian Controversy* (Columbia University Press, New York, 1990).

129 There is a large literature on this language. For a bibliography, see David Bunis, *Sephardic Studies: A Research Bibliography incorporating Judezmo Language, Literature and Folklore and Historical Background* (Garland, New York, 1981).

130 Yizhak R. Molho, "La Littérature judéo-espagnole en Turquie au premier siècle après les éxpulsions d'Espagne et du Portugal," *Tesoro de los Judíos Sefardíes*, 1 (1959), p. 18.

131 Ibid. See the discussion of the language in these Bibles in Haim Vidal Sephiha, *Le Ladino, judéo-espagnole calque: Deutéronome, Versions de Constantinople 1547 et Ferrare 1553* (Institut d'Etudes Hispaniques, Paris, 1973).

132 For a discussion of these two publics, see Yosef Hayim Yerushalmi, "Castilian, Portuguese, Ladino: The Literature in Vernacular Languages of Sephardi Jewry" in Zvi Ankori, ed., *In the Past and Today: Annual Lectures on Greek Jewry* (1977–1983), (Tel-Aviv University, Tel-Aviv, 1984), pp. 35–53 (in Hebrew).

133 Molho, "Moïse Barouh Almosnino," pp. lx–lxi; Michael Molho, *Literatura Sefardita de Oriente*, (CSIC/Instituto Arias Montano, Madrid/Barcelona, 1960), p. 140; Michael Molho, "R. Moses Almosnino, the Savior of the Community of Salonika in the Sixteenth Century," offprint from *Sinai*, 8 (1941), 12pp. (in Hebrew); Michael Molho, "R. Moses Almosnino, his Life, his Works," offprint from *Sinai*, 10 (1942), 23pp. (in Hebrew); Naftali Ben-Menahem, "Contribution to the Establishment of the Bibliography of R. Moses Almosnino," *Tesoro de los Judíos Sefardíes*, 5 (1962), pp. 126–8 (in Hebrew).

134 Molho, *Literatura*, pp. 140, 227; Isaac R. Molho, "La littérature judéo-espagnole," pp. 18–19.

135 See most notably the works of Haim Vidal Sephiha, *Le Ladino* and *Le Ladino (Judéo-espagnol calque): Structure et évolution d'une langue liturgique*, 2 vols (Association Vidas Largas, Paris, 1979); also *Le Judéo-espagnol* (Entente, Paris, 1986).

136 See the numerous examples to be found in catalogs such as Abraham Yaari, *Catalogue of Books in Judeo-Spanish* (The Hebrew University, Jerusalem, 1934), (in Hebrew); Henry V. Besso, *Ladino Books in the Library of Congress: A Bibliography* (Library of Congress, Washington, DC, 1963); and Aron Rodrigue, *Guide to the Ladino Materials in the Harvard College Library* (Harvard College Library, Cambridge, Mass., 1992). See the discussion in Isaac Jerusalmi, *From Ottoman Turkish to Ladino* (Ladino Books, Cincinnati, 1990), p. 36.

137 Charles A. Ferguson, "Diglossia," *Word*, 15 (1959) p. 336.

138 Yaari, *Catalogue*, p. 7.

139 Michael Molho, "The Sage Jacob Hulli, One of the Great Judeo-Spanish Writers, Author of the Meam Loez, his Family, his Life, his Times," *Tesoro de los Judíos Sefardíes*, 5 (1982), pp. 80–94 (in Hebrew); Michael Molho, *Le Meam Loez: Encyclopédie populaire du sépharadisme levantin* (Thessalonica, 1945), pp. 11–12.

140 Jerusalmi, *From Ottoman Turkish*, pp. 25–6; Molho, *Literatura*, pp. 140, 228, 230.

141 Molho, *Literatura*, pp. 230–1. See the section under "Ethics" in Yaari, *Catalogue*, pp. 28–37.

142 Molho, *Literatura*, p. 297.

143 Molho, *Le Meam Loez*, p. 15; Yaari, *Catalogue*, pp. 7–13. See also most recently Elena Romero, "Literary Creation in Prose of Sephardi Jewry," in Beinart, ed., *The Sephardi Heritage*, pp. 736–9. A romanized version of Houlli's work is in David Gonzalo Maeso and Pascal Recuero, eds, *Meam Loez, el gran comentario bíblico sefardí*, 4 vols (Editorial Gredos, Madrid, 1964–74).

144 Yerushalmi, "Castilian," pp. 37–42.

3 EASTERN SEPHARDI JEWRY IN THE ERA OF WESTERNIZATION

1 Jacob Katz, *Tradition and Crisis: Jewish Society at the End of the Middle Ages* (Schocken Books, New York, 1977), p. 214; Jacques Le Goff, *Histoire et mémoire* (Gallimard, Paris, 1988), p. 43.

2 S. N. Eisenstadt, *Tradition, Change and Modernity* (John Wiley & Sons, New York/London, 1973), p. 153; Katz, *Tradition and Crisis*, p. 214.

3 S. N. Eisenstadt, *Patterns of Modernity* (Frances Pinter, London, 1987), vol. 1, p. 5; Le Goff, *Histoire et mémoire*, p. 61.

4 Eisenstadt, *Tradition, Change and Modernity*, p. 259.

5 On this relation of forces, see Gustave von Grunebaum, *L'identité culturelle de l'Islam*, tr. R. Stuvéras (Gallimard, Paris, 1973), p. 13.

6   On the *Haskalah* in Central and Eastern Europe, see Jacob Katz, ed., *Toward Modernity: The European Jewish Model* (Transaction Books, New Brunswick/Oxford, 1987).

7   On this, see Pierre Rosanvallon, *L'État en France de 1798 à nos jours* (Seuil, Paris, 1990), pp. 100–10.

8   On the reinterpretation of modernity, see Dominique Schnapper, "The Jews and Political Modernity in France," in Eisenstadt, *Patterns of Modernity*, vol. 1, p. 158; I. M. Lapidus, "Islam and Modernity," ibid., vol. 2, p. 91.

9   On this subject, see C. E. Black, *The Dynamics of Modernization* (Harper & Row, New York, 1967), p. 50.

10 On this subject, see Jonathan Frankel and Steven J. Zipperstein, eds, *Assimilation and Community: The Jews in Nineteenth-Century Europe* (Cambridge University Press, Cambridge, 1992).

11 Halil İnalcık, "The Nature of Traditional Society: Turkey," in Halil İnalcık, *The Ottoman Empire: Conquest, Organization and Economy* (Collected Studies, Variorum Reprints, London, 1978), p. 62.

12 On modernization as an external impact, see Le Goff, *Histoire et mémoire*, pp. 84–5.

13 For the text of this rescript, see A. Schopoff, *Les Réformes et la protection des chrétiens en Turquie, 1673–1904* (Plon-Nourrit, Paris, 1904), pp. 17–24.

14 H. İnalcık, "Application of the Tanzimat and its Social Effects," in Halil İnalcık, *Ottoman Empire*, p. 4.

15 For the text, see Schopoff, *Les Réformes et la protection des chrétiens*, pp. 48–54.

16 For this latter law, cf. G. Young, *Corps de droit ottoman* (Clarendon Press, Oxford, 1905), vol. 2, pp. 226–9.

17 For a more detailed analysis of the reforms of the *Tanzimat* and their impact on non-Muslims, particularly the Jews, see Aron Rodrigue, *French Jews, Turkish Jews: The Alliance Israélite Universelle and the Politics of Jewish Schooling in Turkey, 1860–1925* (Indiana University Press, Bloomington/Indianapolis, 1990), pp. 28–35.

18 A. Ubicini and Pavet de Courteille, *Etat présent de l'Empire ottoman* (J. Dumoisne, Paris, 1876), p. 47. These figures are far from reliable.

19 Kemal H. Karpat, *Ottoman Population, 1830–1914: Demographic and Social Characteristics* (University of Wisconsin Press, Madison, 1985), p. 169. Jewish sources give almost double this figure, but here again it is necessary to be cautious: *Univers israélite* (hereafter UI), 49 (21 August, 1908), p. 710. The Ottoman statistics do not include Jews of foreign nationality.

20 On this period, see Esther Benbassa, "Haim Nahum Efendi, dernier Grand Rabbin de l'Empire ottoman (1908–1920): Son rôle politique et diplomatique" (unpublished doctoral dissertation, University of Paris-III, Paris, 1987), 2 vols. A revised version has been published as *Une diaspora sépharade en transition: Istanbul XIXe–XXe siècles* (Cerf, Paris, 1993).

21 Katz, *Tradition and Crisis*, p. 251; Jacob Katz, "The Jewish Response to Modernity in Western Europe," in Eisenstadt, *Patterns of Modernity*, vol. 1, p. 105.

22 Carter V. Findley, *Bureaucratic Reform in the Ottoman Empire: The Sublime Porte, 1789–1922* (Princeton University Press, Princeton, 1980), pp. 206–9; Carter V. Findley, "The Acid Test of Ottomanism: The Acceptance of Non-Muslims in the Late Ottoman Bureaucracy," in Benjamin Braude and Bernard Lewis, eds, *Christians and Jews in the Ottoman Empire: The Functioning of a Plural Society* (2 vols, Holmes & Meier, New York, 1982), vol. 1, pp. 339–68.

23 Avigdor Levy, *The Sephardim in the Ottoman Empire* (Darwin Press, Princeton, 1992), p. 111.

24 Ibid., p. 110.

25 Nasid Baylav, *The History of Pharmacy* (Yörük Matbaası, Istanbul, 1968), p. 219 (in Turkish).

26 Ibid., pp. 219–27.

27 Stanford Shaw and Ezel Kural Shaw, *History of the Ottoman Empire and Modern Turkey* (Cambridge University Press, Cambridge/New York, 1976–7), vol. 2, p. 113.

28 Barukh Mevorakh, "The Damascus Libel and the Activity of Jewry to end it," *Skira hodshit*, 27, 5 (1980), pp. 37–8 (in Hebrew).

29 Jonathan Frankel, "Crisis as a Factor in Modern Jewish Politics, 1840 and 1881–2," in Jehuda Reinharz, ed., *Living with Antisemitism: Modern Jewish Responses* (University Press of New England, Hanover/London, 1987), p. 54.

30 Rodrigue, *French Jews, Turkish Jews*, p. 13.

31 Ibid., p. 15.

32 For this report, written by Jacques-Isaac Altaras and Joseph Cohen, see Simon Schwarzfuchs, *Les Juifs d'Algérie et la France (1830–1855)* (Ben Zvi Institute, Jerusalem, 1981), pp. 67–190.

33 On this subject, see Huri İslamoğlu-İnan, ed., *The Ottoman Empire and the World Economy* (Cambridge University Press/Editions de la Maison des Sciences de l'Homme, Cambridge/Paris, 1987).

34 A. J. Sussnitzki, "Zur Gliederung wirtschaftslicher Arbeit nach Nationalitäten in der Türkei," *Archiv für Wirtschaftsforschung im Orient*, 2 (1917), pp. 382–407. For an English translation, see Charles Issawi, ed., *The Economic History of Turkey, 1800–1914* (University of Chicago Press, Chicago, 1980), pp. 114–25.

35 Rodrigue, *French Jews, Turkish Jews*, p. 40. For the biography of Albert Cohn, see Yuda Nehama, *A Happy Memory or the Biography of the Very Famous Scholar and Philanthropist Abraham Cohen Called Dr. Albert Cohn*, (n.p., Salonika, 1877; in Judeo-Spanish).

36 *Archives israélites* (hereafter AI), 17 (1856), p. 584.

37 For the actual circular, see UI, 11 (1855–6), pp. 342–4.

38 Simon Marcus, "The Beginnings of the Haskalah and the Upheavals in Educational Matters in Salonika," in *Salonika, Mother City in Israel;* (Center for Research into Salonikan Jewry, Jerusalem/Tel-Aviv, 1967), p. 67 (in Hebrew).

39 For the correspondence between I. Navon and N. Sokolow, see Central Zionist Archives (hereafter CZA), files A18/420 and K11/20/2.

40 Simon Marcus, "Contribution to the History of the Jews of Adrianople," *Sinai*, 29, 11–12 (1951), p. 339 (in Hebrew); for the correspondence between the two, see CZA, K11/20.

41 Black, *The Dynamics of Modernization*, p. 57.

42 Yuda Nehama, *Correspondence*, Bezez, Salonika, 1892/1893, [1944], 2 parts (in Hebrew).

43 Abraham Shaul Amarillo, "Benevolent Societies," *Sefunot*, 15, 5 (1971–81), p. 115.

44 A. Ubicini and Pavet de Courteille, *Etat présent de l'Empire ottoman* (J. Dumoisne, Paris, 1876), p. 205.

45 Moïse Franco, *Essai sur l'histoire des Israélites de l'Empire ottoman* (repr. UISF, Paris, 1981), pp. 161–6.

46 Ibid., pp. 164–5.

47 Avram Galante, *Histoire des Juifs de Turquie* (repr, Isis, Istanbul, [1985]), vol. 5, p. 12.

48 See the circular sent to the rabbis by the grand vizier: Franco, *Essai sur l'histoire des Israélites*, pp. 165–6.

49 *Archives of the Italian Jewish Community of Istanbul* (Istanbul), letter from the Legation of the Kingdom of Italy to the foreign Jewish community of the Spanish and Portuguese rite in Constantinople, signed M. Cerruti, 2 May, 1862.

50 Vicki Tamir, *Bulgaria and Her Jews: The History of a Dubious Symbiosis* (Sepher Hermon Press, New York, 1979), p. 136.

51 On Freemasonry in the Empire at this time, see Paul Dumont, "La Turquie dans les archives du Grand Orient de France: les Loges maçonniques d'obédience française à Istanbul du milieu du XIXe siècle à la veille de la Première Guerre mondiale," in Jean-Louis Bacqué-Grammont and Paul Dumont, eds, *Economie et sociétés dans l'Empire ottoman (fin du XVIIIe siècle-début du XXe siècle)* (Editions du CNRS, Paris, 1983), pp. 171–201; Paul Dumont, "La Franc-maçonnerie d'obédience française à Salonique au début du XXe siècle," *Turcica*, 16 (1984), pp. 65–94.

52 On the economy in the Ottoman Empire, see Issawi, *Economic History of Turkey*; Şevket Pamuk, *The Ottoman Empire and European Capitalism* (Cambridge University Press, Cambridge, 1987); Reşat Kasaba, *The Ottoman Empire and the World Economy* (SUNY Press, Albany, 1988).

53 On the activities of Abraham de Camondo, see Aron Rodrigue, "Abraham de Camondo of Istanbul: The Transformation of Jewish Philanthropy," in Frances Malino and David Sorkin, eds, *From East and West: Jews in a Changing Europe, 1750–1870* (Basil Blackwell, Oxford, 1990), pp. 46–56.

54 See Rodrigue, *French Jews, Turkish Jews*, pp. 8–17; Paul Dumont, "Jewish Communities in Turkey during the Last Decades of the Nineteenth Century in the Light of the Archives of the Alliance Israélite Universelle," in Braude and Lewis, eds, *Christians and Jews in the Ottoman Empire*, vol. 1, pp. 209–42.

55 On a dispute of this type, see Avner Levi, "*Shavat Aniim*: Social Cleavage, Class War and Leadership in the Sephardi Community – The Case of Izmir, 1847," in Aron Rodrigue, ed., *Ottoman and Turkish Jewry: Community and Leadership* (Indiana University Turkish Studies, Bloomington, 1992), pp. 183–202.

56 Rodrigue, *French Jews, Turkish Jews*, pp. 111–20.

57 Paul Dumont, "La Structure sociale de la communauté juive de Salonique à la fin du XIXe siècle," *Revue historique*, 263 (April–June 1980), pp. 378–80.

58 On this subject, see Esther Benbassa and Aron Rodrigue, "L'Artisanat juif en Turquie à la fin du XIXe siècle: l'Alliance israélite universelle et ses oeuvres d'apprentissage," *Turcica*, 17 (1985), pp. 113–26.

59 On this subject, see Esther Benbassa, "L'Éducation féminine en Orient: l'école de filles de l'Alliance israélite universelle à Galata, Istanbul (1879–1912)," *Histoire, economie et société*, 4 (1991), pp. 548, 559. See also the revised English version of this article, "Education for Jewish Girls in the East: A Portrait of the Galata School in Istanbul, 1872–1912," *Studies in Contemporary Jewry*, 9 (1993), pp. 163–73.

60 Dumont, "La structure sociale," pp. 362–3.

61 Donald Quataert, "Premières fumées d'usine," in Gilles Veinstein, ed., *Salonique 1850–1918: la "ville des Juifs" et le réveil des Balkans, Autrement*, vol. 12 (Paris, 1992), p. 177.

62 Ibid., p. 181; Dumont, "La structure sociale," pp. 352–3.

63 Quataert, "Premières fumées d'usine," pp. 184–5.

64   David Levi, "Jewish Activity in Commercial Life (or the History of Two Families)," in David Recanati, ed., *Memorial to Salonika* (Committee for the Publication of Books on the Salonika Community, Tel-Aviv, 1971–86), vol. 2, pp. 198–201 (in Hebrew).

65   Quataert, "Premières fumées d'usine," pp. 189–90.

66   Dumont, "La structure sociale," p. 375.

67   Michael Molho, "Trades of the Sea in Salonika," in Barukh Uziel, ed., *Salonikan Archives* (Centre for Research into Salonikan Jewry, Tel-Aviv, 1961), section A, pp. 53–4 (in Hebrew).

68   N. M. Gelber, "An Attempt to Internationalize Salonika," *Jewish Social Studies*, 17, 2 (1955), p. 116.

69   Alexandra Yerolympos, "La part du feu," in Veinstein, *Salonique 1850–1918*, p. 262.

70   Stanford J. Shaw, "The Population of Istanbul in the Nineteenth Century," *Türk Tarih Dergisi*, 32 (1979), p. 412.

71   Ibid.

72   Ibid.

73   *Archives de l'Alliance israélite universelle* (hereafter AAIU), Turkey II. C. 8, A. H. Navon, 15 January, 1900.

74   For general studies of the activities of the Alliance, see Narcisse Leven, *Cinquante ans d'histoire: l'alliance israélite universelle (1860–1910)*, 2 vols (Alcan and Guillaumin, Paris, 1911–20,); André Chouraqui, *Cent ans d'histoire: l'Alliance israélite universelle et la renaissance juive contemporaine (1860–1960)*, (PUF, Paris, 1965); Aron Rodrigue, *Images of Sephardi and Eastern Jewries in Transition. The Teachers of the Alliance Israélite Universelle, 1860–1939:* (University of Washington Press, Seattle, 1993).

75   Rodrigue, *French Jews, Turkish Jews*, p. 177.

76   *L'Indépendant*, 30 April, 1915.

77   For a work on the education of girls in the Alliance schools, see Benbassa, "L'éducation féminine," pp. 529–59.

78 Le Goff, *Histoire et mémoire*, p. 86.

79 Rodrigue, *Images*, pp. 50–1.

80 Ibid.

81 On the life of one of these Alliance teachers-cum-notables, see Esther Benbassa with Aron Rodrigue, *Une vie judéo-espagnole à l'Est: Gabriel Arié* (Cerf, Paris, 1992).

82 Tamir, *Bulgaria and Her Jews*, p. 108.

83 AAIU, France XVII. F.28, M. Fresco, annual report, 1904–5; *Bulletin de l'Alliance israélite universelle* (hereafter BAIU), 30 (1908), pp. 128–9.

84 AAIU, Turkey LIV. E., M. Fresco, letter received 27 April, 1906.

85 *Journal de Salonique*, 9 July, 1908.

86 See Aron Rodrigue, "The Alliance Israélite Universelle and the Attempt to Reform Rabbinical and Religious Instruction in Turkey," in Simon Schwarzfuchs, ed., *L'"Alliance" et les communautés du Bassin méditerranéen à la fin du XIXe siècle et son influence sur la situation sociale et culturelle* (Misgav Yerushalayim, Jerusalem, 1987), pp. liii–lxx.

87 For Turkey, see Rodrigue, *French Jews, Turkish Jews*, pp. 113–14.

88 A Jewish organization structured into Lodges and Chapters on the model of the Masonic orders. It was founded in the United States in 1843.

89 On Haim Nahum, see Esther Benbassa, *Haim Nahum: A Sephardic Chief Rabbi* (The University of Alabama Press, Tuscaloosa, 1995).

90 Eisenstadt, *Tradition, Change and Modernity*, p. 210.

91 Benbassa, *Haim Nahum passim;* Michael Molho, "Le Judaïsme grec en général et la communauté de Salonique an particulier entre les deux guerres mondiales," in *Homenaje a Millas-Vallicrosa* (CSIC, Barcelona, 1956), vol. 2, p. 89.

92 AAIU, Greece XVII. E. 202 C, J. Néhama, 2 January, 1919.

93 US Department of State, Greece, 1910–29, reel 17, 868.42/9, Robert E. Fernald to the Secretary of State, report prepared 21 November, 1927.

94 Rodrigue, *French Jews, Turkish Jews*, pp. 115–16.

95 Gabriel Arié, *The Jews of the Balkan States* ("Hamishpat" Publishers, Sofia, 1914 – lecture), p. 6 (in Judeo-Spanish).

96 On all these measures, cf. Leven, *Cinquante ans d'histoire*, vol. 1, pp. 93–111.

97 Harriet Pass Freidenreich, *The Jews of Yugoslavia: A Quest for Community* (The Jewish Publication Society of America, Philadelphia, 1979), pp. 30–1; Arié, *The Jews of the Balkan States*, pp. 6–9.

98 Freidenreich, *Jews of Yugoslavia*, p. 31.

99 By way of example, see AI, 13 (1 July, 1878), pp. 392–3, 426–7; BAIU, 1st half 1878, pp. 55–7; Leven, *Cinquante ans d'histoire*, vol. 1, pp. 200–32.

100 BAIU, 1st half 1878, pp. 57–8.

101 Freidenreich, *Jews of Yugoslavia*, p. 32.

102 Ibid., p. 33.

103 Ibid., tables 3 and 8, pp. 215, 219.

104 Ibid., p. 16.

105 Ibid., table 5, p. 216.

106 Ibid.

107 Yakir Aventov, "On Jewish Life in Salonika and in the Bosnian Provinces at the Beginning of the Twentieth Century," in Zvi Loker, ed., *History of the Jews of Yugoslavia* (Association of Immigrants from Yugoslavia, Jerusalem/Tel-Aviv/Haifa, 1991), vol. 2, p. 216 (in Hebrew).

108 Freidenreich, *Jews of Yugoslavia*, table 4, p. 215.

109 Zvi Loker, ed., *Encyclopaedia of Jewish Communities: Yugoslavia* (Yad Vashem, Jerusalem, 1988), p. 208 (in Hebrew).

110 Freidenreich, *Jews of Yugoslavia*, p. 19.

111 Ibid.

112 Ibid., p. 21.

113 *Central Archives of the History of the Jewish People* (hereafter CAHJP), P3 1100, H. Goldman to the Joint Distribution Committee, 27 February, 1919.

114 Freidenreich, *Jews of Yugoslavia*, p. 36.

115 Tamir, *Bulgaria and her Jews*, p. 99.

116 Saul Mézan, *Les Juifs espagnols en Bulgarie* ("Hamishpat" Publishers, Sofia, 1925), vol. 1, p. 67; Joseph Avramov, "A Few Facts from the History of the Bulgarian Jews," *Annual*, 22 (1987), p. 68.

117 For Eastern Rumelia, see the 1882 leaflet in A. Romano, Joseph Ben, Nissim Levy, eds, *Encyclopaedia of the Jewish Diaspora – Bulgarian Jewry* (Encyclopaedia of the Jewish Diaspora Editions, Jerusalem/Tel-Aviv, 1967), vol. 10, cols 65–6 (in Hebrew).

118 Ibid., col. 69; Haim Keshales, *History of the Jews of Bulgaria* (Davar, Tel-Aviv, 1969–73), vol. 2, pp. 211–34 (in Hebrew).

119 Mézan, *Les Juifs espagnols en Bulgarie*, p. 86.

120 N. M. Gelber, "Jewish Life in Bulgaria," *Jewish Social Studies*, 8 (1946), p. 107, table 1.

121 Ibid., p. 85.

122 Ibid., table 8, p. 118.

123 Astruc Kalev, "Data Concerning the Demographic Situation of the Bulgarian Jews, 1887–1940," *Annual*, 16 (1981), p. 90.

124 Mézan, *Les Juifs espagnols en Bulgarie*, p. 85.

125 Kalev, "Data Concerning the Demographic Situation of the Bulgarian Jews," pp. 91–2.

126 Rodrigue, *French Jews, Turkish Jews*, pp. 86–8.

127 Keshales, *History of the Jews of Bulgaria*, vol. 2, pp. 53–4.

128 Ibid., p. 62.

129 Ibid.

130 Ibid., p. 109; Gelber, "Jewish Life in Bulgaria," pp. 108–9.

131 Ibid., p. 109.

132 Ibid., p. 111.

133 Isaac Moscona, "On the Social Polarization of the Bulgarian Jews," *Annual*, 17 (1982), p. 102.

134 Gelber, "Jewish Life in Bulgaria," pp. 114–15; Keshales, *History of the Jews of Bulgaria*, vol. 2, pp. 65–6.

135 Moscona, "On the Social Polarization of the Bulgarian Jews," p. 100.

136 Ibid., p. 103.

137 Yerolympos, "La part du feu," p. 262. The Jewish population was higher before the Greek conquest and it declined in the course of the first year as a result of emigration, in particular to Ottoman areas. Michael Molho puts the Jewish population in 1912 at 80,000 souls: M. Molho, "Le Judaïsme grec en général," p. 75. On the other hand, N. K. Moutsopoulos suggests the figure of 65,000: N. K. Moutsopoulos, *Thessaloniki, 1900–1917* (Molho Publications, Thessaloniki, 1981), p. 23.

138 See, for example, the letter sent by an Alliance teacher to Paris at the time of the entry of the Greek troops: Rodrigue, *Images*, pp. 236–8.

139 On this subject, see Quataert, "Premières fumées d'usine," pp. 177–94.

140 Moutsopoulos, *Thessaloniki*, p. 23.

141 See Gelber, "An Attempt to Internationalize Salonica," pp. 105–20; Rena Molho, "The Jewish Community of Salonika and Its Incorporation into the Greek State," *Middle Eastern Studies*, 24, 4, (1988), pp. 391–4; Bernard Lory,

"1912, les Hellènes entrent dans la ville," in Veinstein, ed., *Salonique 1850–1918*, pp. 247–53; CZA, Z3/119, D. Florentin to F. M. Warburg, 17 December, 1912, 3 January, 1913 (there are several files on the subject in the Zionist Archives: Z3/479, 486–7, 519, 521); AAIU, Greece I. C.51, J. Néhama, 3 January, 1913; Ministry for Foreign Affairs, Paris (hereafter MAE), NS, Turkey, vol. 138, M. Bompard (Constantinople) to Paris, 17 March, 1918; ibid., P. Cambon (London) to S. Pichon, 3 April, 1913.

142 See AAIU, Greece II. C.53, J. Néhama, 11 February, 1919; M. Molho, "Le Judaïsme grec en général," pp. 85–6.

143 On this circumstantial support of the minority rights of the Jews, see Rena Molho, "Venizelos and the Jewish Community of Salonika," *Journal of the Hellenic Diaspora*, 13, 3–4 (1986), pp. 121–3.

144 On the fire and its consequences, see *inter alia*: *CAHJP*, P3 110, Hetty Goldman to the Joint Distribution Committee, 22 December, 1918; US Department of State, Greece, 1910–29, reel 18, 868.48/7, United States consulate to the Secretary of State, letters August–October, 1917; "Political and Spiritual Upheavals (1888–1922)" in Recanati, ed., *Memorial to Salonika*, vol. 1, pp. 207–9 (in Hebrew); Yerolympos, "La part du feu," pp. 262–3.

145 George Mavrogordatos, *The Stillborn Republic: Social Conditions and Party Strategies in Greece, 1922–1936* (University of California Press, Berkeley, 1983), p. 254.

146 Ibid., p. 186.

147 On the elections of 1915, see AAIU, Greece II. C.53, J. Néhama, 18 June, 1915. For an analysis of relations between the Jews and Venizelism, see Mavrogordatos, *Stillborn Republic*, pp. 227–61.

148 Mavrogordatos, *Stillborn Republic*, pp. 238–9.

149 Ibid. See also League of Nations, *Protection des minorités de langue, de race et de religion par la Société des Nations* (League of Nations, Geneva, 1927), p. 22.

150 US Department of State, Greece, 1910–29, reel 6, 868.00/465, Salonica, S. O'Donoghue to the Secretary of State, 17 December, 1923; *Paix et Droit*, 1 (January 1924), p. 8.

151 Mavrogordatos, *Stillborn Republic*, pp. 240–1; AAIU, Greece III. C. 55, J. Néhama, letters of 4 and 22 December, 1931; ibid., Greece III. C. 56, J. Néhama, 26 May, 1933.

152 CAHJP, Salonika 150, report, 7 February, 1930.

153 Ibid. See also *Paix et Droit*, 5 (May 1924), pp. 10–11; 7 (July 1924), pp. 2, 5; 1 (January 1926), p. 2; 5 (May 1926), p. 8; 6 (June 1926), p. 3.

154 US Department of State, Greece, 1910–29, reel 6, 868.00/478, Howard A. Bowman, 14 April, 1924.

155 CAHJP, Salonika 150, Jewish community to Leon Motzkin, 23 July, 1929.

156 AAIU, Greece XVIII. E. 202g, J. Néhama, 25 September, 1930.

157 Ibid., J. Néhama, letters of 2 August and 3 December, 1931.

158 AAIU, Greece XIX. E. 202i, J. Néhama, 2 June, 1936; M. Molho, "Le Judaïsme grec en général," p. 104.

159 M. Molho, "Le judaïsme grec en général," p. 92; AAIU, Greece XVIII. E. 202 F., J. Néhama, 19 August, 1924; CZA Z4/2724, S. Pazi of Keren Hayesod to the secretary general in London, 10 November, 1925.

160 US Department of State, Greece, 1910–29, reel 6, 868.00/457, Sidney O'Donoghue to the Department of State, 28 November, 1923.

161 M. Molho, "Le judaïsme grec en général," pp. 102–3.

162 Ibid.

163 Ibid.

164 The results of this census can be found in Stanford J. Shaw, *The Jews of the Ottoman Empire and the Turkish Republic* (New York University Press, New York, 1991), p. 285.

165 See the texts of the Treaty of Lausanne, clauses 38 to 44 in Jacob C. Hurewitz, ed., *The Middle East and North Africa in World Politics: A Documentary Record*, 2nd ed. (Yale University Press, New Haven, 1979), vol. 2, pp. 330–1.

166 See AAIU, Turkey II. C. 8, D. Fresco, 4 and 24 March, 1926; *Public Record Office* (hereafter PRO), FO 371/10866, R. C. Lindsay, 8 December, 1925; MAE, Levant 1918–40, Turkey, vol. 256, A. Brugère to A. Briand, 15 June, 1926; CZA Z4/2299, W. Senator to L. Stein, 21 March, 1926; *League of Nations*, Documents 1919–46, Minorities, Council Documents, C.185.1927 I(b), correspondence and reports attached to the memorandum by the Turkish government, 4 April, 1927.

167 Naphtali Nathan, "Notes on the Jews of Turkey," *The Jewish Journal of Sociology*, 16, 2 (1964), p. 173; *State Archives* (Jerusalem), 50/26, Ankara, I. Yanai, 12 July, 1953.

168 *Şalom*, 31 December 1986.

169 Cemil Koçak, "Private and Foreign Schools after the Tanzimat," in *From the Tanzimat to the Republic: Encyclopaedia of Turkey* (İletişim, Istanbul, 1985), vol. 2, p. 439 (in Turkish).

170 AAIU, Turkey II. C. 8, E. Nathan, 14 May, 1935.

171 For more details on the "nationalization" of Jewish education, see Rodrigue, *French Jews, Turkish Jews*, pp. 163–4.

172 US Department of State, Turkey 1930–44, reel 10, 867.4016 Jews/2, C. H. Sherrill to the Secretary of State, 20 December, 1932; ibid., Jews/3, W. Perry George to the Secretary of State, 13 December, 1932; ibid., Jews/7, C. A. Allen to the Secretary of State, 11 December, 1933; ibid., Jews/13, R. P. Skinner to the Secretary of State, 2 August, 1934. On Tekinalp, see Jacob M. Landau, *Tekinalp: Turkish Patriot, 1883–1961* (Nederlands Historisch-Archaeologish Institut te Istanbul, Leyden, 1984). See also AAIU, Turkey, II. C. 8, E. Nathan, 25 May, 1934, 13 June, 1934; ibid., Marcel Franco, 8 December, 1937; Çetin Yetkin, *The Jews in the Life of the Turkish State* (Afa Yayınları, Istanbul, 1992), pp. 243–6 (in Turkish).

173 AAIU, Turkey II. C. 8, V. Algranti, enclosure, received 13 May, 1929.

174 Rodrigue, *French Jews, Turkish Jews*, p. 162.

175 Adina Weiss Lieberles, "The Jewish Community of Turkey," in D. Elazar, H. P. Freidenreich, B. Hazzan, and A. W. Lieberles, eds, *The Balkan Jewish Communities* (Center for Jewish Community Studies of the Jerusalem Center for Public Affairs, University Press of America, Lanham/New York/London, 1984), p. 134.

176   Walter Weiker, *Ottomans, Turks and the Jewish Polity: A History of the Jews of Turkey* (The Jerusalem Center for Public Affairs, University Press of America, Lanham/New York/London, 1992), p. 285.

177   Tamir, *Bulgaria and Her Jews*, pp. 94–5.

178   Keshales, *History of the Jews of Bulgaria*, vol. 2, p. 221.

179   Freidenreich, *Jews of Yugoslavia*, p. 96.

180   On this subject, consult Benedict Anderson, *Imagined Communities: Reflections on the Origin and Spread of Nationalism* (Verso, London, 1983).

181   Homi K. Bhabha, ed., *Nation and Narration* (Routledge, London, 1990), p. 4.

182   Eisenstadt, *Tradition, Change and Modernity*, p. 211.

183   A popular religious movement, born in the second half of the eighteenth century in Eastern Europe, based on ecstasy, the cohesion of the group and a charismatic leadership, founded by the Ba'al Shem Tov (also called by the shortened form, the Besht).

184   Literally: the opponents, i.e. the opponents of Hasidism, a mostly Lithuanian movement born in the last decades of the eighteenth century. Its leader was the Vilna Gaon.

185   Marcus, "Contribution to the History of the Jews of Adrianople," p. 334.

186   *Bolitino de la sosyedad Dorshei Hahaskalah* [Bulletin of the Dorshei Hahaskalah Society] (State publishing house, Edirne, 5649/1889), pp. 3–4 (in Judeo-Spanish).

187   Ibid., pp. 4–5.

188   Ibid., p. 8.

189   On this society and its achievements, see *Selbst-Emancipation*, January 26, 1892, July 18, 1892.

190   AAIU, Turkey LXXIV, E, G. Arié, 20 May, 1895.

191   Yizhak R. Molho, "The Language of Truth Society, the First Association for the Oral Practice and Teaching of the Hebrew Language in Salonica at the

End of the Nineteenth Century," *Tesoro de los Judíos Sefardíes*, 9 (1966), pp. 106–8 (in Hebrew).

192 On this society, see AAIU, Greece I. G. 3, J. Néhama, received 13 January, 1903; David Benveniste, *The Jews of Salonika in the Modern Period* (Kiryat Sefer, Jerusalem, 1973), p. 141 (in Hebrew).

193 Israel Salvator, "Salomon Avraam Rozanes: Originator of the Historiography of the Bulgarian Jews (1860–1938)," *Annual*, 19 (1984), pp. 343–71.

194 Albert E. Kalderon, *Abraham Galante: A Biography* (Sepher Hermon Press, New York, 1983).

195 Franco, *Essai sur l'histoire des Israélites*, pp. 266–75; Abraham Elmaleh, "Judeo-Spanish Literature and the Press," *Hashiloah*, 26, 1 (1912), part 1, pp. 70–1 (in Hebrew).

196 Michael Molho, *Literatura Sefardita de Oriente* (CSIC, Instituto Arias Montano, Madrid/Barcelona, 1960), pp. 323–7; M. Molho, "Literature and Journalism," in *Salonika, Mother City in Israel*, p. 101 (in Hebrew).

197 Avner Levi, "Alexander Ben Ghiat and His Contribution to Journalism and Belles-lettres in Ladino," in Issachar Ben-Ami, ed., *The Heritage of Sephardi and Oriental Jews* (Magnes Press, Jerusalem, 1982), p. 212 (in Hebrew).

198 To get an idea, see Henry V. Besso, *Ladino Books in the Library of Congress: A Bibliography* (Library of Congress, Washington, DC, 1963).

199 Michael Molho, "Works in Judeo-Spanish Printed at Salonika," in *Salonika, Mother City in Israel*, p. 100 (in Hebrew); Elmaleh, "Judeo-Spanish Literature and the Press," pt 1, p. 70.

200 Franco, *Essai sur l'histoire des Israélites*, p. 276; Elmaleh, "Judeo-Spanish Literature and the Press," pt 1, p. 73.

201 Abraham Yaari, *Catalogue of Books in Judeo-Spanish* (The Hebrew University, Jerusalem, 1934), pp. 59–89 (in Hebrew).

202 On this subject, see Elena Romero, *El Teatro de los sefardíes orientales* (CSIC, Madrid, 1979), 3 vols.

203 M. Molho, *Literatura Sefardita de Oriente*, p. 301.

204 M. Molho, "Literature and Journalism," p. 101.

205 On this, see Moshe Attias, "Jacob Jona: The Wandering Popular Poet in Salonika," *Sefunot*, 15, 5 (1981), pp. 155–202 (in Hebrew).

206 Franco, *Essai sur l'histoire des Israélites*, pp. 278–9; Elmaleh, "Judeo-Spanish Literature and the Press," pt 2, pp. 255–6.

207 Levy, *The Sephardim in the Ottoman Empire*, pp. 100–1.

208 Israel Salvator, "La Presse périodique juive en ladino et en *ivrit* (hébreu) en Bulgarie," *Annual*, 1967, pp. 276–7 (French summary); Tamir, *Bulgaria and Her Jews*, pp. 109–10.

209 Freidenreich, *Jews of Yugoslavia*, p. 133; Loker, ed., *Encyclopaedia of Jewish Communities*, p. 215.

4 PATHS OF POLITICIZATION

1 On this subject, see Esther Benbassa, "Zionism in the Ottoman Empire at the End of the 19th and the Beginning of the 20th Century," *Studies in Zionism*, 11, 2 (1990), pp. 127–40.

2 On these Sephardi pre-Zionists, see David Benveniste and Haim Mizrahi, "Rabbi Yehudah Bibas and the Community of Corfu of his day," *Sefunot*, 2 (1958), pp. 303–31 (in Hebrew); Meir Benayahu, "New Facts about Yehudah Bibas," *Tesoro de los Judios sefardies*, 3 (1960), pp. 95–111 (in Hebrew); Yizhak R. Molho, "Trois sephardis, trois précurseurs de l'Etat juif: Moses Montefiore, Juda Bibas, Juda Alcalay," *Tesoro de los Judios sefardies*, 8 (1965), pp. xv–xxvii; Jacob Katz, *Jewish Emancipation and the Self-Emancipation* (The Jewish Publication Society of America, Philadelphia, 1986); Jennie Lebel, "'Longing for Jerusalem' – Rabbi Yehudah Alkalay, the Political and Communal Context of His Activity," *Peamim*, 40 (1989), pp. 21–48 (in Hebrew); Arie Morgenstern, "Between Rabbi Yehudah Bibas and an Emissary of the *Prushim* of Jerusalem," *Peamim*, 40 (1989), pp. 156–9 (in Hebrew).

3 See his letters (in French translation): AAIU, Bulgaria I. G. 1, July 12, August 17, and September 10, 1890 (date of receipt).

4 Zvi Loker, "H. G. Nahmias: His Efforts for a Nationalist Awakening among the Jews of Serbia," *Peamim*, 40 (1989), pp. 49–53 (in Hebrew).

5   Apart from the apologetic book by Yaakov Vinshel, *Marco Barukh* (Shak-mona, Jerusalem, 1981) (in Hebrew), reference can also be made to Sch. Gorelik, *Jüdische Köpfe* (Fritz Gurlitt, Berlin, 1920), pp. 40–6; Binyamin Yosef Arditti, "Y. M. Barukh and his Activity in Bulgaria," in *Aharon Ben-Yosef: The Man and his Work, Letters and Documents* (published by the Committee for the Book on Aharon Ben-Yosef, Tel-Aviv, 1953), pp. 159–69 (in Hebrew).

6   On this subject, see Marcel Caleb, "Bulgarian Jewry and its Zionist Move-ment," in *Aharon Ben-Yosef: The Man and his Work*, p. 139 (in Hebrew); Haim Keshales, *History of the Jews of Bulgaria* (5 vols, Davar, Tel-Aviv, 1969–73), vol. 2, p. 514 (in Hebrew).

7   See Esther Benbassa, *Une diaspora sépharade en transition: Istanbul XIXe–XXe siècles* (Cerf, Paris, 1993), pp. 152–5.

8   See, for example, *Selbst-Emancipation*, January 18, 1892, April 7, 1892.

9   *El Amigo del Puevlo*, April 15, 1894, March 1, 1895.

10 See a copy of this journal, copied *a posteriori*, unnumbered: CZA, F2/2; Keshales, *History of the Jews of Bulgaria*, vol. 2, p. 276.

11 Joseph Romano, A. Ben, Nissim Levy, eds., *Encyclopaedia of the Jewish Diaspora – Bulgarian Jewry* (Encyclopaedia of the Jewish Diaspora Editions, Jerusalem/Tel-Aviv, 1967), vol. 10, col. 78 (in Hebrew); Keshales, *History of the Jews of Bulgaria*, vol. 2, pp. 265–7; Jean-Marie Delmaire, "De Hibbat Zion au sionisme politique" (doctoral dissertation, University of Strasbourg-II, 1986), vol. 1, pp. 212–15 (the first two volume have been reprinted by the ANRT of Lille).

12 *El Amigo del Puevlo*, October 15, 1894, May 1, 1895, AAIU, Bulgaria I. G. 2, S. Danon, January 24, 1896.

13 On this settlement, see *inter alia*, *El Amigo del Puevlo*, August 13, 1896, August 29, 1896, January 22, 1897; *Die Welt*, June 4, 1897, 17 September, 1897.

14 Keshales, *History of the Jews of Bulgaria*, vol. 2, pp. 299–303.

15 On this subject see, *inter alia*, Neville J. Mandel, "Ottoman Policy and Restrictions on Jewish Settlement in Palestine, 1881–1908," pt 1, *Middle Eastern Studies*, 10, 3 (1974), pp. 312–32; Neville J. Mandel, "Ottoman

Practice as Regards Jewish Settlement in Palestine, 1881–1908," *Middle Eastern Studies*, 11, 1 (1975), pp. 33–46; Neville J. Mandel, "Turks, Arabs and Jewish Immigration into Palestine, 1882–1914," *St Antony's Papers*, 17 (1965), pp. 77–108.

16   On this subject, see Hana Wiener, "Zionist Policy in Turkey up to 1914," in Israel Kolatt, ed., *History of the Jewish Community in Palestine since 1882* (Israel Academy, Bialik Institute, Jerusalem, 1989), pp. 257–349 (in Hebrew).

17   On this subject, see Esther Benbassa, "Presse d'Istanbul et de Salonique au service du sionisme (1908–1914): les motifs d'une allégeance," *Revue historique*, 276/2, 560 (1986), pp. 337–65.

18   On this subject, see Esther Benbassa, "Zionism and the Politics of Coalitions in the Ottoman Jewish Communities in the Early Twentieth Century," in Aron Rodrigue, ed., *Ottoman and Turkish Jewry: Community and Leadership* (Indiana University Turkish Studies, Bloomington, 1992), pp. 225–51.

19   CZA, Z2/32, D. Wolffsohn to N. Leven, 21 February, 1911; ibid., J. Bigart and N. Leven to D. Wolffsohn, 3 March, 1911; ibid., D. Wolffsohn to N. Leven, 10 April, 1911.

20   See, for example, the anti-Zionist lampoon of the "Alliancist" group, which also had repercussions in the corridors of the state: David Fresco, *Le Sionisme* (Imprimerie Fresco, Istanbul, 1909).

21   CZA, Z3/8, V. Jacobson to the Zionist Central Office, 14 September, 1909.

22   Ibid., Z2/9, minutes of the meetings of the Press Committee from September 15, 1909 to October 8, 1910, signed N. Sokolow, S. Hochberg, V. Jabotinsky, and V. Jacobson; see also Aryeh Shmuelevitz, "The Hebrew Language Weeklies in Turkey: An Appeal to Revive a Concept of National Culture, in *Proceedings of the Conference on "The Foreign Language Press in Turkey"*, 16, 17, 18 May, 1984 (University of Istanbul Press, Istanbul, 1985), pp. 111–25.

23   On this subject, see Esther Benbassa, "Les Stratégies associatives dans la société juive ottomane (XIXe–XXe siècles)," *Revue d'histoire moderne et contemporaine*, 38, 2 (1991), pp. 295–312.

24   For this council's plan of action, cf. PRO, FO 371/417/47289, R. Webb to the Foreign Office, received 26 March, 1919.

25 *El Tiempo*, March 25, 1919.

26 CZA, Z4/1222 (1), I. Caleb to the Zionist Organization, December 28, 1919.

27 *La Nation*, 23 July, 1920; 12th Zionist Congress, 1921, *Organization Report*, p. 173.

28 CZA, Z4/888, M. Dizengoff to M. Ussishkin, T. Zlatopolski, I. A. Naiditch, 26 August, 1919.

29 12th Zionist Congress, *Organization Report*, 1921, p. 173.

30 CZA, Z4/888.

31 Ibid., Z4/2299, I. Caleb to the delegate of the League of Nations, April 4, 1922.

32 12th Zionist Congress, 1921, *Organization Report*, p. 63.

33 CZA, S6/487, Palestine Office to the Zionist leadership's Department of Emigration, 22 January, 1925.

34 Ibid., KKL5/6662, (T.) Weil to the KKL, 1934.

35 Ibid., S6/2555, General Union of Immigrants from the Near East in Palestine to the Jewish Agency, July 7, 1935; ibid., Jewish Agency to the Union, May 23, 1935; ibid., S6/3763, M. D. Gaon to the Jewish Agency, January 23, 1936.

36 CZA, S6/4767, H. Barlas to the Jewish Agency, September 17, 1942. On this subject, see ch. 5 below.

37 Zeev Vania Hadari, "National Solidarity and Rescue of Persecuted Jews," *Studies on the Holocaust Period*, 5 (1987), p. 263 (in Hebrew). See also Dalia Ofer, *Escaping the Holocaust: Illegal Immigration to the Land of Israel, 1939–1944* (Oxford University Press, New York/Oxford, 1990).

38 Yoav Gelber, "The Delegation in Istanbul at the Center of the Reaction to the Holocaust by the Jewish Settlement in Palestine," *Studies on the Holocaust Period*, 5 (1987), p. 265 (in Hebrew).

39 Ibid., p. 274.

40 CZA, S20/532, B. Khalfon, report, July 1950.

41 Ibid., S6/2555, Union of Immigrants from the Near East in Palestine to M. Tcherniak, 1 September, 1935; ibid., S6/1707, W. Senator to M. Shertok, 26 November, 1935.

42 Ibid., KH4B/1972, S. Dinar to the directorate of the Zionist Organization, 11 February, 1938; ibid., S32/493, M. Madjar, S. Dinar to the Joint Committee for Youth Affairs, 24 March, 1939; KKL5/9548, I. Tshernovitz, 16 July, 1939.

43 Hadari, "National Solidarity and Rescue of Persecuted Jews," p. 249.

44 CZA, S6/1710, A. B. to the Jewish Agency's Immigration Department.

45 Ibid., S6/1711, R. Caraco and A. Franco to Dr A. Lauterbach, September 3, 1945.

46 Ibid., S6/1956, B. Shamil to the Jewish Agency, September 3, 1946.

47 Ibid., Sh. V. A. to the Jewish Agency, May 28, 1946.

48 *Archives of the Makabi*, O. Litczis to H. Cazès, November 16, 1944. According to the file, the correspondence lasted until 1966.

49 CZA, S32/493, J. B. Eliezer to B. Benshalom, February 23, 1946.

50 Ibid., S6/1711, A. Ben-Yosef to the Immigration Department, March 16, 1946.

51 Ibid., A. A. Mayer to (H. Barlas), S6/1712, February 17, 1948.

52 *State Archives*, 2567/7, memorandum submitted by the Jewish Agency to the Committee on Palestine at UNO, 1947.

53 CZA, KH4/B/1971, report by J. Milbauer, March 27, 1950.

54 Ibid.

55 Yosef Ben Pinhas Uziel, "The Beginning of the Zionist Movement in Salonika – Memories," in Barukh Uziel, ed., *Salonikan Archives* (Centre for Research into Salonikan Jewry, Tel-Aviv, 1961), p. 36 (in Hebrew).

56 Asher Moissis, "The Zionist Movement in Salonika and in the other Towns of Greece," in David Recanati, ed., *Memorial to Salonika* (2 vols, Committee for the Publication of Books on the Salonika Community, Tel-Aviv, 1971– 86), vol. 1, p. 44 (in Judeo-Spanish).

57 AAIU, Greece I. G. 3, J. Barukh to Paris, received August 19, 1919.

58 George Mavrogordatos, *The Stillborn Republic: Social Conditions and Party Strategies in Greece, 1922–1936* (University of California Press, Berkeley, 1983), p. 256.

59 Ibid.

60 Haim A. Toledano, "L'Organisation Mizrahi," in Recanati, *Memorial to Salonika*, vol. 1, p. 53 (in French).

61 Mavrogordatos, *The Stillborn Republic*, pp. 255–6.

62 US Department of State, Greece 1910–1929, 868.00/276, reel 5, Leland B. Morris to the Department of State, December 31, 1921; 13th Zionist Congress, 1923, *Report of the Executive*, p. 257.

63 AAIU, Greece I. G. 3, J. Barukh, received August 19, 1919.

64 Yosef Uziel, "History of the Zionist Movement," in *Salonika, Mother City in Israel* (Centre for Research into Salonikan Jewry, Jerusalem/Tel-Aviv, 1967), p. 112 (in Hebrew); Abraham Sh. Recanati, "The Revisionist Zionists of Salonika," in Recanati, *Memorial to Salonika*, vol. 1, p. 56 (in Judeo-- Spanish).

65 Uziel, "Beginning of the Zionist Movement," p. 39 (in Hebrew); AAIU, Greece II. C. 53, J. Néhama, February 11, 1919.

66 AAIU, Greece I. G. 3, J. Néhama, April 17, 1917.

67 Shlomoh Reuven, "The Zionist Movement in Salonika," in Zvi Ankori, ed, *In the Past and Today: Annual Lectures on Greek Jewry (1977–1983)*, (University of Tel-Aviv, Tel-Aviv, 1984), p. 99 (in Hebrew).

68 13th Zionist Congress, 1923, *Report of the Executive*, p. 256.

69 16th Zionist Congress, 1929, *Report of the Executive*, p. 335.

70   Haim A. Toledano, "The Mizrachi Organisation in Salonika," in Recanati, *Memorial to Salonika*, vol. 1, pp. 423–54 (in Hebrew).

71   14th Zionist Congress, 1925, *Report of the Executive*, p. 346.

72   Ibid.

73   Reuven, "Zionist Movement in Salonika," p. 100; on the vicissitudes of this movement, see in particular, the testimony of its founder: Abraham Sh. Recanati, "The Revisionist Zionists in Salonika," in Recanati, *Memorial to Salonika*, vol. 1, pp. 463–99 (in Hebrew).

74   CAHJP, Salonika 51, Zionist Federation of Greece to the committee of the Union of Radical Zionists, 18 December, 1935; ibid., copy of an agreement between the General Zionist Federation, the *Mizrahi* organization *Torah Veavodah* ("Torah and Labor") and the Radical Zionist Union, 1936.

75   CZA, KH4B/2036; Hans Kohn, "Letters from Abroad: The New Regime in Greece," *Menorah* (May 1929), pp. 442–5.

76   CZA, KH4B/2044, enquiry into the state of Zionism in Greece, January 15, 1939.

77   Ibid., S5/2550, Dr A. Lauterbach to the Mizrachi movement, August 20, 1940.

78   CAHJP, Greece 1382, President of the Zionist Federation of Greece to Greenstein, attached to letter of February 6, 1945.

79   CZA, S25/5282, J. Tshernowitz to the Jewish Agency, visit July 9–23.

80   Ibid., KH4B/2052, report by A. Ami, 1953.

81   Menahem Shelah, "The Extermination of the Jews of Yugoslavia: The Communities in Serbia and in Croatia," *Peamim*, 27 (1986), p. 31 (in Hebrew).

82   Harriet Pass Freidenreich, *The Jews of Yugoslavia: A Quest for Community* (The Jewish Publication Society of America, Philadelphia, 1979), p. 170.

83   Ibid., p. 7.

84 Ibid., p. 163.

85 Yakir Aventov, "The First Steps of Zionism at the Beginning of the Twentieth Century in the Bosnian Provinces," in Zvi Loker, ed., *History of the Jews of Yugoslavia* (Association of Immigrants from Yugoslavia, Jerusalem/Tel-Aviv/Haifa, 1991), vol. 2, pp. 231–2 (in Hebrew).

86 Freidenreich, *Jews of Yugoslavia*, p. 154.

87 14th Zionist Congress, 1925, *Report of the Executive*, p. 350.

88 20th Zionist Congress, 1937, *Report of the Executive*, p. 130.

89 Freidenreich, *Jews of Yugoslavia*, p. 158.

90 Zvi Loker, ed., *Encyclopaedia of Jewish Communities: Yugoslavia* (Yad Vashem, Jerusalem, 1988), p. 52.

91 Freidenreich, *Jews of Yugoslavia*, p. 160.

92 Ibid., p. 166.

93 20th Zionist Congress, 1937, Report of the Executive, p. 130.

94 *Joint Distribution Committee* (hereafter JDC), file 157, Yugoslavia, 13 December, 1937, letter signed by the community leaders.

95 Loker, ed., *Encyclopaedia of Jewish Communities*, p. 17.

96 Freidenreich, *Jews of Yugoslavia*, p. 162.

97 Loker, ed., *Encyclopaedia of Jewish Communities*, p. 210; Freidenreich, *Jews of Yugoslavia*, p. 151; Yaakov Mastro, "The Community of Sarajevo between the two Wars," in Loker, ed., *History of the Jews of Yugoslavia*, vol. 2, p. 269 (in Hebrew).

98 CZA, Z4/2447 (1924).

99 Ibid., P. Romano and M. Cohen, September 27, 1923.

100 Ibid., Zionist executive to the political secretariat of the Zionist Organization in London, 24 June, 1924; ibid., M. Ussishkin to the Zionist Organization in London, December 1, 1924.

101   CZA, Z4/2447, 24 September, 1924.

102   Freidenreich, *Jews of Yugoslavia*, p. 149.

103   Ibid., p. 169.

104   Ibid., p. 167.

105   CZA, S25/5280, David Pardo, report, August 27, 1947.

106   Keshales, *History of the Jews of Bulgaria*, vol. 2, p. 321.

107   13th Zionist Congress, 1923, *Report of the Executive*, p. 248.

108   21st Zionist Congress, 1939, *Organization Report*, p. 132.

109   13th Zionist Congress, 1923, *Report of the Executive*, p. 249.

110   On this last point, see CZA, Z3/790, unsigned letter, 19 April, 1912.

111   Ibid., Z3/790, P. Romano, June 1912; Nikolai Tsvjatkov, "Education among the Bulgarian Jews towards the End of the 19th Century and the Beginning of the 20th Century," *Annual*, 15 (1980), p. 108; AAIU, Bulgaria V. B. 116, G. Arié, 22 May, 1913.

112   Keshales, *History of the Jews of Bulgaria*, vol. 2, pp. 339–40.

113   CZA, KH4/B/690, J. Halévi to Keren Hayesod, December 6, 1926.

114   13th Zionist Congress, 1923, *Report of the Executive*, p. 248.

115   Ibid.

116   CZA, S25/9279, report on Jewish affairs in Bulgaria, May 24, 1943.

117   Ibid., S25/5281, note on persecuted Jews by the Anglo-American Committee, March 21, 1946. On Jews during the communist regime, see Keshales, *History of the Jews of Bulgaria*, vol. 4 (in Hebrew).

118   Keshales, *History of the Jews of Bulgaria*, vol. 2, p. 326.

119   Ibid., p. 334.

120 Shlomoh Shealtiel, "The Foundation of the 'Poalei Zion' Party in Bulgaria and its Organ 'Probuda' (1910–1912)" (unpublished MA thesis), Tel-Aviv University, 1988, 2 vols. (in Hebrew); see also Keshales, *History of the Jews of Bulgaria*, vol. 2, p. 402.

121 For historical accounts of the Revisionist movement, see *Archives of the Jabotinsky Institute*, 17G, J. Yossifof, n.d.; there are other undated typewritten documents in this file, as well as a letter addressed to Dr Schechtman, dated 20 July, 1962, with an illegible signature. See also Joseph B. Schechtman and Yehudah Benari, *History of the Revisionist Movement* (Hadar, Tel-Aviv, 1970), vol. 1, pp. 359–61.

122 18th Zionist Congress, 1933, *Report of the Executive*, p. 140.

123 Keshales, *History of the Jews of Bulgaria*, vol. 2, p. 411.

124 Ibid., p. 342.

125 Ibid., p. 307.

126 Ibid., p. 341.

127 16th Zionist Congress, 1929, *Report of the Executive*, p. 320.

128 Keshales, *History of the Jews of Bulgaria*, vol. 2, pp. 309, 312.

129 Abraham A. Benaroya, "Beginnings of the Socialist Movement among the Jews of Salonika," in Recanati, *Memorial to Salonika*, vol. 1, p. 309 (in Hebrew). Among the most recent articles on developments in the movement, see Paul Dumont, "Une organisation socialiste ottomane: la Fédération ouvrière de Salonique (1908–1912)," *Etudes balkaniques*, 1 (1975), pp. 76–88; Paul Dumont, "La Fédération socialiste ouvrière de Salonique à l'époque des guerres balkaniques," *East European Quarterly*, 14, 4 (1980), pp. 383–410; George B. Leon, *The Greek Socialist Movement and the First World War: The Road to Unity* (East European Quarterly, Boulder, Colorado, 1976); Georges Haupt and Paul Dumont, *Socialist Movements in the Ottoman Empire* (tr. from French by Tuğrul Artunkal; Gözlem Yayınları, Istanbul, 1977; in Turkish).

130 Abraham A. Benaroya, "A Note on 'The Socialist Federation of Saloniki,' " *Jewish Social Studies*, 11 (1949), p. 72. Benaroya's memoirs were published in 1931 in the Greek journal *Tahidramos* ("Mercury") of Salonika.

131 Dumont, "La Fédération socialiste ouvrière," p. 383.

132 Ibid., p. 391.

133 Benaroya, "Beginnings of the Socialist Movement," p. 320.

134 Ibid.

135 Joshua Starr, "The Socialist Federation of Salonika," *Jewish Social Studies*, 7 (1945), p. 334.

136 On socialism and communism in Bulgaria, see Keshales, *History of the Jews of Bulgaria*, vol. 2, pp. 255–64.

137 On this subject, read Moshe Mosek, "The Struggle for the Defence of the Jews of Bulgaria after the Liberation," in Benjamin Pinkus, ed, *East European Jewry: From the Holocaust to the Redemption, 1944–1948* (Ben-Gurion University of the Negev, Beersheva, 1987), pp. 188–215 (in Hebrew).

138 Freidenreich, *Jews of Yugoslavia*, p. 178.

139 Uziel, "Beginning of the Zionist Movement," p. 39.

5 THE END OF THE JUDEO-SPANISH BALKANS: THE HOLOCAUST AND MIGRATIONS

1 For a discussion, see Bernard Lewis, *Semites and Anti-Semites: An Inquiry into Conflict and Prejudice* (W. W. Norton, New York and London, 1986).

2 See Jacob Barnai, " 'Blood Libels' in the Ottoman Empire of the Fifteenth to the Nineteenth Centuries," in Shmuel Almog, ed., *Antisemitism through the Ages* (Pergamon Press, Oxford and New York, 1988), pp. 189–94.

3 Ibid., p. 191.

4 For a detailed study of one blood libel incident, see Esther Benbassa, "Le Procès des sonneurs de tocsin: Une accusation calomnieuse de meurtre rituel à Izmir en 1901" in Abraham Haim, ed., *Society and Community: Proceedings of the Second International Congress for Research of the Sephardi and Oriental Jewish Heritage* (Misgav Yerushalayim, Jerusalem, 1991), pp. 35–53.

5 AAIU, Greece, I. C. 2, Community of Candia, May 26, 1873, June 2, 1873.

6 See AAIU, Greece I. C. 6, I. C. 7, I. C. 8, letters from Corfu to the Central Committee of the Alliance, 1891–3.

7 AAIU, Bulgaria I. C. 4, Gabriel Arié, June 30, 1891, September 11, 1891, November 27, 1891, and all of the dossier of Bulgaria I. C. 5, 1891–1892. See also Vicki Tamir, *Bulgaria and Her Jews: The History of a Dubious Symbiosis* (Sepher Hermon Press, New York, 1979), pp. 116–17.

8 See the long list of antisemitic pamphlets published in Bulgaria during this period in David Benvenisti, "The Unfavorable Conditions for the Dissemination of Antisemitic Propaganda in Bulgaria (1891–1903)," *Annual*, 15 (1980), pp. 177–220.

9 US Department of State, Greece, 1910–1929, reel 17, 868.4016/47, Salonika, S. O'Donoghue to Secretary of State, 19 December, 1923; ibid., reel 6, 868.00/464, S. O'Donoghue to Secretary of State, 26 December, 1926.

10 AAIU, Greece II. C. 53, David Matalon, letters dated March 4, May 12, May 27, 1925.

11 George Mavrogordatos, *The Stillborn Republic: Social Conditions and Party Strategies in Greece, 1922–1936* (University of California Press, Berkeley, 1983), p. 255; Michael Molho, "Le Judaïsme grec en general et la communauté juive de Salonique en particulier entre les deux guerres mondiales," in *Homenaje a Millas-Vallicrosa* (CSIC, Barcelona, 1956), vol. 2, p. 99.

12 Ibid., pp. 99–100; AAIU, Greece III. C. 56, Joseph Néhama, June 26, 1931, July 2, 1931.

13 AAIU, Greece III. C. 55, Joseph Néhama, April 18, 1932.

14 AAIU, Greece III. C. 56, Joseph Néhama, April 1, 1937.

15 See Aron Rodrigue, *French Jews, Turkish Jews: The Alliance Israélite Universelle and the Politics of Jewish Schooling in Turkey, 1860–1925* (Indiana University Press, Bloomington and Indianapolis, 1990), p. 162. See also *Paix et Droit*, 8, 5 (May 1928), pp. 1–3.

16 Ibid. See also Stanford J. Shaw, *Turkey and the Holocaust: Turkey's Role in Rescuing Turkish and European Jewry from Nazi Persecution, 1933–1945* (New York University Press, New York, 1993), p. 35.

17 AAIU, Turkey I. C. 4, J. Panigel, June 29, 1923.

18 See for example *Paix et Droit*, 10 (December 1930), pp. 1–3; 3 (March 1931), p. 12; *Le Judaïsme Séphardi*, 4, 25 (January 1, 1935), p. 12; 4, 28 (April 1, 1935), p. 52.

19 See also AAIU, Turkey II. C. 8, Elie Nathan, 25 May, 1934. See also AAIU, Fonds Georges Leven, France I. A. 4bis, Boite 3, Nathan [1939]. For some of the criticism in the press, and the Jewish responses to it, see Çetin Yetkin, *The Jews in the Life of the Turkish State* (Afa Yayınları, Istanbul, 1992), pp. 244–6 (in Turkish).

20 For these, see *inter alia* AAIU, Turkey II. C. 8, A. Benveniste, September 22, 1927 (includes numerous newspaper clippings).

21 Law no. 2510, dated June 14, 1934 which appeared in the Turkish *Official Journal*, no. 2733, in AAIU, Turkey XXXI, E., E. Nathan, August 1934.

22 *Le Judaïsme Séphardi*, 29–30 (May–June 1935), p. 88; Stanford J. Shaw, *The Jews of the Ottoman Empire and the Turkish Republic* (New York University Press, New York, 1991), p. 253; Stanford J. Shaw, *Turkey*, pp. 14–15.

23 The episode is widely reported in consular reports which also have clippings from the Turkish press. See, for example, US Department of State, Turkey, 1930–1944, reel 10, 867.4016 Jews/9, R. P. Skinner to Secretary of State, 29 June, 1934; ibid., 867.4016 Jews/11, R. P. Skinner to Secretary of State, 16 June, 1934; ibid., 867.4016 Jews/8, Secretary of State to US Ambassador, Ankara, 27 July, 1934; Auswärtiges Amt, Inland II, T120, reel 4270, K1567/K386979–82, Istanbul consulate to Berlin, 18 July, 1934. For a study of these events, see Avner Levi, "The Anti-Jewish Pogrom in Thrace, 1934," *Peamim*, 20 (1984), pp. 111–32 (in Hebrew).

24 See, for example, the report in Auswärtiges Amt, Inland II, T120, reel 4365, K867/K220168–73, Ankara Embassy to Berlin, 1 February, 1938.

25 See the discussion in R. J. Crampton, *A Short History of Modern Bulgaria* (Cambridge University Press, Cambridge and New York, 1987), pp. 93–9.

26 AAIU, Bulgaria I. C. 30, Gabriel Arié, 28 November, 1923; ibid., Bulgaria V. B. 118, Gabriel Arié, 2 February, 1924.

27 US Department of State, Bulgaria, 1910–1944, reel 12, 874.4016/45, R. Atherton to Secretary of State, 4 April, 1939; ibid., 874.4016/41,

R. Atherton to Secretary of State, 3 May, 1939. See also Frederick B. Chary, *The Bulgarian Jews and the Final Solution 1940–1944* (University of Pittsburgh Press, Pittsburgh, 1972), pp. 7–8.

28 Harriett Pass Freidenreich, *The Jews of Yugoslavia: A Quest for Community* (The Jewish Publication Society of America, Philadelphia, 1979), pp. 172, 177.

29 Ibid., p. 184.

30 Ibid., pp. 188–9.

31 Ibid., pp. 183–4.

32 Menachem Shelah, "Belgrade," in Israel Gutman, ed., *Encyclopedia of the Holocaust* (Macmillan New York and London, 1990), vol. 1, p. 169.

33 Christopher R. Browning, *Fateful Months: Essays on the Emergence of the Final Solution* (Holmes and Meier, New York and London, 1985), pp. 47–9.

34 Ibid., pp. 50–5. On the *Wehrmacht*'s behavior, see Mark Mazower, "Military Violence and National Socialist Values: The *Wehrmacht* in Greece 1941–1944," *Past and Present*, 134 (1992), pp. 129–58.

35 Browning, *Fateful Months*, p. 71.

36 Ibid., pp. 76–85. See also Menachem Shelah, "Sajmiste: An Extermination Camp in Serbia," *Holocaust and Genocide Studies*, 2 (1987), pp. 243–60.

37 For the best study of Greece during the Second World War, see Mark Mazower, *Inside Hitler's Greece: The Experience of Occupation, 1941–44* (Yale University Press, New Haven and London, 1993).

38 CZA S25/6282, minutes of the Jewish community of Salonika, list dated November 11, 1945. See also Leni Yahil, *The Holocaust: The Fate of European Jewry* (Oxford University Press, New York and Oxford, 1990), p. 409. The number 49,000 is given in Michael Molho and Joseph Néhama, *In Memoriam: Hommage aux victimes juives des Nazis en Grèce* (N. Nicolaidès, Salonika, 1948), vol. 1, p. 1.

39 Ibid., p. 31. On the persecution of the Jews of Greece, see Daniel Carpi, "The Jews of Greece during the Holocaust (1941-1943)," in Zvi Ankori, ed., *In the Past and Today: Annual Lectures on Greek Jewry, (1977–1983)* (Tel-Aviv

University, Tel-Aviv, 1984), pp. 107–35 (in Hebrew), and Steven Bowman, "Jews in Wartime in Greece," *Jewish Social Studies*, 48 (1986), pp. 45–62.

40   Molho and Néhama, *In Memoriam*, vol. 1, pp. 34–7.

41   Ibid., pp. 47–51.

42   Ibid., pp. 54–5.

43   See "Episodes of the Holocaust," in Barukh Uziel, ed., *Salonikan Archives* (Center for Research into Salonikan Jewry, Tel-Aviv, 1961), fascicule A, p. 81 (in Hebrew).

44   Molho and Néhama, *In Memoriam*, vol. 1, pp. 60–71.

45   Yahil, *The Holocaust*, p. 412.

46   For a discussion of the attitude of the Church leaders, see Steven B. Bowman, "Greek Jews and Christians during World War II," in Yehuda Bauer et al., eds., *Remembering the Future: Working Papers and Addenda. Jews and Christians during and after the Holocaust* (Pergamon Press, Oxford, 1989), vol. 1, pp. 215–23.

47   Steven Bowman, "Greece," in Gutman, *Encyclopedia of the Holocaust*, vol. 2, p. 614.

48   Yahil, *The Holocaust*, p. 413.

49   Around 650 Jews served in the Resistance. See Mazower, *Inside Hitler's Greece*, p. 260.

50   Yahil, *The Holocaust*, pp. 414–16.

51   See Haim Avni, *Spain, the Jews, and Franco* (The Jewish Publication Society, Philadelphia, 1982), p. 32.

52   Auswärtiges Amt, Inland II, T120, reel 4353, Juden in Griechenland, E421210, K211500, H322493, Consul Schoenberg to Berlin, 15 March, 1943.

53   The list containing the names of the Spanish citizens deported to Bergen-Belsen and then taken to Spain is in Auswärtiges Amt, Inland II, T120, reel 4662, Juden in Griechenland, K348338–43, unsigned list, 31 July, 1943. This episode is discussed fully in Avni, *Spain, the Jews, and Franco*, pp. 147–56.

There is extensive documentation over the "foreign" Jews of Salonika in the archives of the German Foreign Ministry.

54 Yahil, *The Holocaust*, p. 416; Jonathan Steinberg, *All or Nothing: The Axis and the Holocaust 1941–1943* (Routledge, London, 1990), pp. 99–100. See also Joseph Rochlitz, ed., "Excerpts from the Salonika Diary of Lucillo Merci (February–August 1943)," *Yad Vashem Studies*, 18 (1987), pp. 293–323.

55 Yahil, *The Holocaust*, p. 414. Others give slightly different figures. See Molho and Néhama, *In Memoriam*, vol. 1, p. 94, and Daniel Carpi, "Nuovi documenti per la storia dell'Olocausto in Grecia: L'attegiamento degli Italiani," *Michael*, 7 (1981), p. 142.

56 Steven B. Bowman, "Thrace," in Gutman, *Encyclopedia of the Holocaust*, vol. 4, p. 1,465. For a memoir by a survivor of the deportation from Didymotikhon, see Marco Nahon, *Birkenau* (University of Alabama Press, Tuscaloosa, Alabama, 1989).

57 The best discussion of this is in Steinberg, *All or Nothing*.

58 See ibid., pp. 52–84. See also Daniel Carpi, "The Rescue of Jews in the Italian Zone of Occupied Croatia," in Israel Gutman and Efraim Zuroff, eds., *Rescue Attempts during the Holocaust: Proceedings of the Second Yad Vashem International Historical Conference* (Yad Vashem, Jerusalem, 1977), pp. 465–525; Menachem Shelah, *Blood Account: The Rescue of Croatian Jews by the Italians* (Sifriyat Poalim, Tel-Aviv, 1986), (in Hebrew).

59 Steinberg, *All or Nothing*, pp. 101–2, 153.

60 Steven B. Bowman, "Athens," in Gutman, *Encyclopedia of the Holocaust*, vol. 1, p. 104.

61 Ibid. See also Molho and Néhama, *In Memoriam*, vol. 2, pp. 17–18.

62 Ibid., pp. 28–30.

63 Steven B. Bowman, "Athens," in Gutman, *Encyclopedia of the Holocaust*, vol. 1, p. 105; Molho and Néhama, *In Memoriam*, vol. 2, pp. 50–1.

64 Molho and Néhama, *In Memoriam*, vol. 2, pp. 58–60.

65 Ibid., p. 53.

66 Molho and Néhama, *In Memoriam*, vol. 2, pp. 70–1, 76.

67 Yahil, *The Holocaust*, p. 421.

68 CZA S25/5282, undated list prepared by the Central Board of the Jewish Communities of Greece [1946?]. Dina Porat gives similar numbers in "The Jews of Greece – An Example of the Link between Conscience and Rescue during the Period of the Holocaust," *Dapim Leheker Tkufat Hashoah*, 8 (1990), p. 123 (in Hebrew). See also Yizhak Kerem, "The Attempts to Save the Jews of Greece during World War II," *Peamim*, 27 (1986), p. 77 (in Hebrew).

69 Porat, "The Jews of Greece," p. 123.

70 CZA S25/5282, undated list prepared by the Central Board of the Jewish Communities of Greece [1946?]. The number for Athens is from Yizhak Kerem, "Greece – The Postwar Period," in Gutman, *Encyclopedia of the Holocaust*, vol. 2, p. 616.

The Jewish population of Greece before and after the Holocaust

Region	Situation in 1940	Numbers deported	Situation in 1947	Situation in June 1959
Thrace	2,852	2,692	74	38
Macedonia	62,800	51,162	2,309	1,410
Thessaly	2,727	405	1,831	856
Continental Greece	3,825	1,780	5,100	2,669
Peloponnese	337	90	152	37
Epirus	2,584	2,384	238	115
Islands	4,825	4,060	667	135
Total	79,950	62,573	10,371	5,260

These figures are from Molcho and Néhama, *In Memoriam*, vol. 2, p. 326. They are somewhat different from the ones referred to above. Nevertheless, they give an idea of the losses according to region.

71 Menachem Shelah, "Sarajevo," in Gutman, *Encyclopedia of the Holocaust*, vol. 4, p. 1,327.

72 Ibid. See also Shelah, "Croatia," in Gutman, *Encyclopedia of the Holocaust*, vol. 1, pp. 323–8; the accounts in Shelah, *Blood Account*, and Steinberg, *All or Nothing*, passim. For extensive treatment of the Holocaust in Yugoslavia, see Zvi Loker, ed., *Encyclopedia of Jewish Communities: Yugoslavia* (Yad Vashem, Jerusalem, 1988) (in Hebrew); Menahem Shelah, ed., *History of the Holocaust: Yugoslavia* (Yad Vashem, Jerusalem, 1990) (in Hebrew).

73 *Jewish losses in Yugoslavia during the Holocaust*

Region	Number of Jews before the war	Number of Jews dead during the Holocaust	Percentage of losses
Serbia	12,500	11,000	88
Banat	4,200	3,800	92.8
Croatia, Slavonia	25,000	20,000	80
Batchka, Barania	16,000	13,500	84.4
Bosnia-Herzegovina	14,000	10,000	71.5
Macedonia	7,762	6,982	90
Slovenia	1,500	1,300	86
Other	1,280	630	48
Total	82,242	62,242	82

Source: Shelah, "The Extermination," p. 59.

74 Chary, *The Bulgarian Jews*, p. 29.

75 Ibid., p. 17.

76 Ibid., p. 36.

77 Vicki Tamir, *Bulgaria and Her Jews*, pp. 169–73; Jacqueline Soferman, "Anti-Jewish Legislation in Bulgaria, 1940–1942, and the Reactions that it Engendered," *Peamim*, 27 (1986), pp. 143–68 (in Hebrew).

78 Avraham Ben-Yakov, "Bulgaria," in Gutman, *Encyclopedia of the Holocaust*, vol. 1, p. 266. A translation into English of the law is in US Department of State, Bulgaria, 1910–44, reel 17, 874.4016/55, unsigned (Sofia) to Secretary of State, 28 February, 1941.

79 US Department of State, Bulgaria, 1910–44, reel 17, 874.4016/56, unsigned report (Sofia) to Secretary of State, received on 17 April, 1941; Tamir, *Bulgaria and Her Jews*, pp. 176–7.

80 For one such region, see Jenny Lebel, "The Extermination of the Jews of Yugoslavia: The Communities of Macedonia, Pirot and Kossovo," *Peamim*, 27 (1986), pp. 62–74 (in Hebrew).

81 Chary, *The Bulgarian Jews*, p. 52.

82 Ibid., pp. 54–68; CZA S25/9279, Jewish Affairs – Legal and Political Status, 24 May, 1943.

83 Yahil, *The Holocaust*, p. 580.

84 Chary, *The Bulgarian Jews*, pp. 48–9.

85 Ibid., p. 80; Nissan Oren, "The Bulgarian Exception: A Reassessment of the Salvation of the Jewish Community," *Yad Vashem Studies*, 7 (1968), p. 95.

86 Chary, *The Bulgarian Jews*, pp. 101–22.

87 Ibid., p. 122.

88 Ibid., pp. 122–8. See also Aleksander Matkovski, "The Destruction of Macedonian Jewry in 1943," *Yad Vashem Studies*, 3 (1959), pp. 203–58. Most of Aleksander Matkovski's book, *A History of the Jews in Macedonia* (Skopje, Macedonian Review Editions, 1982), is devoted to the period of the Holocaust.

89 Chary, *The Bulgarian Jews*, pp. 86–7.

90 Ibid., p. 90.

91 Ibid., p. 91; Haim Keshales, *History of the Jews of Bulgaria* (Davar, Tel-Aviv, 1971), vol. 3, pp. 92–4 (in Hebrew).

92 Chary, *The Bulgarian Jews*, p. 92.

93 Ibid., pp. 92–6.

94 Ibid., pp. 96–100.

95 Ibid., pp. 129–38.

96 Ibid., pp. 149–50.

97 CZA S25/9279, Bulgaria, Jewish Affairs – Legal and Political Status, 22 December, 1943.

98 Ben-Yakov, "Bulgaria," in Gutman, *Encyclopedia of the Holocaust*, vol. 1, p. 270.

99 Shaw, *The Jews of the Ottoman Empire*, p. 252; *Turkey*, pp. 4–14.

100 CZA S25/6308, laws of 1941. See the text of the law in Shaw, *Turkey*, pp. 261–3.

101 See Dalia Ofer, *Escaping the Holocaust: Illegal Immigration to the Land of Israel, 1939–1944* (Oxford University Press, New York and London, 1990), p. 320.

102 Ibid., pp. 147–66.

103 Ibid., pp. 94–5.

104 Rıdvan Akar, *The Capital Tax: An Example of Anti-Minority Politics in the Era of One Party Rule* (Belge Yayınları, Istanbui, 1992), p. 84 (in Turkish). Also cited in Auswärtiges Amt, Inland II, T120, reel 4665, Judenfrage in der Türkei 1938–1943, K1509/K347889-K348082, J. Seiler to Rademacher, 14 October, 1942.

105 AAIU, Fonds Georges Leven, France I. A. 4bis, Boite 3, Elie Nathan [1939]. See also Shaw, *Turkey*, p. 48.

106 Ibid.

107 CZA C10434, note prepared by Haim Barlas and sent to the Turkish authorities, 15 December, 1943. See also Shaw, *Turkey*, p. 124.

108 Yetkin, *Jews*, p. 84

109 See Shaw, *Turkey*, pp. 60-254.

110 See CZA C10434, US Ambassador Steinhardt to Haim Barlas, 9 February, 1944. Standford J. Shaw gives an overly positive interpretation while

Christopher Browning, basing himself on German sources, presents a negative picture. See Shaw, *Turkey*, pp. 124–7, and Christopher Browning, *The Final Solution and the German Foreign Office* (Holmes and Meier, New York and London, 1978), pp. 155–6.

111 The list of names and of places of birth in Serge Klarsfeld, *Le Mémorial de la déportation des Juifs de France* (Paris, 1978) makes this amply clear.

112 On the atmosphere during the war period, and on the treatment of the Jews, see Avner Levi, "The Jews of Turkey on the eve of World War II and during the War," *Peamim*, 29 (1986), pp. 32–47 (in Hebrew).

113 CZA S25/3150, A. A. to M. Shertok, 10 August, 1940.

114 Akar, *The Capital Tax*, p. 12.

115 Ibid.

116 CZA S25/3152, E. Epstein to M. Shertok, November 16, 1941; CZA S25/3150, E. Epstein to M. Shertok, 6 June, 1942; Auswärtiges Amt, Inland II, T120, reel 4665, Judenfrage in der Türkei, K1509/K347889-K348082, collection of caricatures sent by the Ankara Embassy to Berlin on November 4, 1942. See the samples reproduced in Akar, *The Capital Tax*.

117 PRO, FO 371/30031/R5813, Ankara Embassy to London, June 4, 1941. See also Levi, *The Jews of Turkey*, p. 43.

118 Auswärtiges Amt, Inland II AB, T120, reel 4665, Judenfrage in der Türkei, K1509/K347889-K348082, J. Seiler to Rademacher, October 14, 1942; Akar, *The Capital Tax*, p. 83.

119 Ibid., p. 83.

120 Ibid., pp. 114–17.

121 CZA S25/3150, E. Epstein to M. Shertok, June 6, 1942.

122 Akar, *The Capital Tax*, p. 46.

123 Faik Ökte, *The Disaster of the Wealth Tax* (Nebioğlu Yayınları, Istanbul, 1951), pp. 47–9 (in Turkish).

124 Akar, *The Capital Tax*, pp. 54–8.

125 Rıdvan Akar, "The Capital Tax," *Ekonomik Panorama*, April 24, 1988 (in Turkish). The same numbers are to be found in an article in the London *Times*, reported in CZA S25/3152, September 12, 1943.

126 Akar, *The Capital Tax*, p. 62.

127 Akar, *The Capital Tax*, pp. 62–5. See MAE, Vichy, Levant, Guerre 1939–1945, vol. 134, G. Bergery to P. Laval, February 12, 1943; US Department of State, Turkey 1930–1944, reel 31, 867.512/239, Ankara (unsigned) to Secretary of State, June 22, 1943; PRO, FO 37400–37401, correspondence of Sir Hugh Knatchbull-Hugessen with London, January–October 1943. It is a striking paradox of Vichy foreign policy that the same regime which effectively deemancipated the Jews of France, and handed over "foreign Jews" to the Germans, did not balk at financially helping Jews in Turkey who had French citizenship and who were subject to the Capital Tax under the category of "alien." The French Embassy gave loans to all French citizens in Turkey to pay the assessments, and also intervened with the authorities to obtain reductions in the sums requested. In the list of 80 French self-employed citizens and French businesses that the Embassy helped, eight were Jews or owned by Jews. Five out of 38 French employees subject to the tax were also Jews, and were also helped. See MAE, Vichy, Levant, Guerre 1939–1945, vol. 134, Bergery, September 22, 1943.

128 Ökte, *The Disaster*, p. 157; Akar, *The Capital Tax*, p. 71.

129 CZA S75/1812, lecture by Yizhak Ben Zvi, October 18, 1943.

130 Akar, *The Capital Tax*, pp. 77–8.

131 CZA S32/493, unsigned report, 1947; CZA S20/532, B. Khalfon to Jerusalem, 1950.

132 Joseph Néhama, "The Jews of Salonika," p. 240.

133 Raymond Renard, *Sepharad: le monde et la langue judéo-espagnole des Séphardim* (Annales universitaires de Mons, Mons, 1966), p. 78.

134 KemalKarpat, "The Migratory Movements of Jews in the Ottoman Empire," *Cathedra*, 51 (1989), pp. 78–92 (in Hebrew).

135 CZA, Z4/354, I. Caleb to M. Zolotarevsky, 12 July, 1926.

136 Renard, *Sepharad: le monde et la langue*, p. 99.

137 Annie Benveniste, *Le Bosphore à la Roquette: la communauté judéo-espagnole à Paris (1914–1940)* (L'Harmattan, Paris, 1989), p. 70.

138 JDC, Turkey 1051, E. Resnik to J. Hyman, 27 March, 1944.

139 Néhama, "The Jews of Salonika," p. 279.

140 Imre Ferenczi, *International Migrations* (National Bureau of Economic Research, New York, 1929), vol. 1, pp. 489, 491, quoted by Walter Weiker, *Ottomans, Turks and the Jewish Polity: A History of the Jews of Turkey* (The Jerusalem Center for Public Affairs, University Press of America, Lanham/New York/London, 1992), pp. 268–9.

141 David De Sola Pool, "The Levantine Jews in the United States," *The American Jewish Year Book*, 15 (1913), p. 209.

142 N. K. Moutsopoulos, *Thessaloniki, 1900–1917* (Molho Publications, Thessaloniki, 1981), p. 55.

143 Marc D. Angel, *The Jews of Rhodes: The History of a Sephardic Community*, 2nd edn (Sepher Hermon Press, New York, 1980), pp. 103–9; Eliezer Bashan, "Emigration from Salonica to Palestine in the Sixteenth to Eighteenth Centuries" in Zvi Ankori, ed., *In the Past and Today: Annual Lectures on Greek Jewry (1977–1983)* (University of Tel-Aviv, Tel-Aviv, 1984), pp. 73–83 (in Hebrew); Jacob Barnai, "On the History of Relations between the Jews of Izmir and Those of Palestine in the Seventeenth to Eighteenth Centuries," *Shalem*, 5 (1987), pp. 98–102 (in Hebrew).

144 Joseph Hacker, "Spanish Jewry's Relations with Palestine between 1391 and 1492," *Shalem*, 1 (1974), pp. 105–56 (in Hebrew).

145 CZA, Z4/354, I. Caleb to M. Zolotarevsky, July 12, 1926

146 Ibid., Z4/3263, D. Pardo to the Zionist Executive in London, July 17, 1934; ibid., S6/4767, H. Barlas to the Jewish Agency, September 17, 1942; ibid., S6/3435, Palestine Office to the Workers' Council, November 20, 1943; ibid., S32/493, A. Levinski to B. Benshalom, March 3, 1943; Archives of the

Labor and Pioneer Movement, Lavon Institute, IV 104/89, report addressed to the Union of Immigrants from Turkey in Palestine, June 11, 1943; MAE, Vichy, Levant, Guerre, G. Bergery to P. Laval, March 9, 1943.

147 CZA, S6/1426, report of the meeting of the Union of Immigrants from Turkey in Palestine, May 6, 1944.

148 Ibid., S6/2555, Union of Immigrants from Turkey in Palestine to M. Tcherniak, 1 September, 1935; ibid., Union of Immigrants from Turkey in Palestine to the Jewish Agency, 7 September, 1935; ibid., S6/1171, lecture by H. Barlas on the position regarding emigration from Turkey, October 26, 1942.

149 Ibid., S6/1709-1, Immigration Department (Jerusalem) to Immigration Department (Haifa), August 1, 1943.

150 CZA, S6/3435, Palestine Office to the Workers' Council, November 20, 1943.

151 Ibid., S32/493, A. Levinski to B. Benshalom, March 3, 1944.

152 Ibid.

153 Archives of the Haganah, 14/641, Menashe report, July 19, 1949.

154 Ibid.

155 CZA, KH4/B/1971, B. Benshalom to D. Packer and A. Serper, October 30, 1950.

156 State Archives, 2397/24, the acting representative of Israel to A. Levavi in Ankara, May 13, 1953.

157 CZA, S32/493, report of an investigation (1947).

158 State Archives, 2397/24, the acting representative of Israel to A. Levavi in Ankara, May 13, 1953.

159 Stanford J. Shaw, *The Jews of the Ottoman Empire and the Turkish Republic* (New York University Press, New York, 1991), p. 285.

160 AAIU, Greece, I. G. 3, J. Néhama, 3 December 1931; Greece III. C. 55, May 17, 1932, May 26, 1932; Greece III. C. 56, January 2, 1933.

161 Asher Moïssis, "The Zionist Movement in Salonika and in the Other Towns of Greece," in David Recanati, ed., *Memorial to Salonika* (Committee for the

Publication of Books on the Salonika Community, Tel-Aviv, 1971–86), vol. 1, p. 46 (in Judeo-Spanish).

162   AAIU, Greece III. C. 55, J. Néhama, 26 May, 1932.

163   Yizhak R. Molho, *Salonika Sailors in Israel* (n.p., Jerusalem, 1951), p. 61 (in Hebrew).

164   20th Zionist Congress, 1937, *Report of the Executive*, p. 103.

165   For illegal emigration from Yugoslavia, see Menahem Shelah, "There is no Room in the aeroplanes . . .," in Anita Shapira, ed., *Illegal Immigration*, (Am Oved, Tel-Aviv, 1990), pp. 165–86 (in Hebrew); and from Bulgaria: Shlomoh Shealtiel, "Dr B. Confino to A. Epstein, two men – one route," in Shapira, ed., *Illegal Immigration*, pp. 61–86 (in Hebrew).

166   CZA, S25/5282, report on the Jews of Athens, January 4, 1945; ibid., KH4B/2045, Robert Raphael to the President of the Zionist Federation of Greece, February 6, 1945.

167   Ibid., S25/5282, report from J. Tchernowitz to the Jewish Agency, visit July 9–23, 1945.

168   B. Gil, *Pages of Immigration: Thirty Years of Immigration to Israel, 1919–1949* (Jewish Agency, Jerusalem, 1950), p. 28 (in Hebrew).

169   "After the Holocaust," in Recanati, ed., *Memorial to Salonika*, vol. 1, p. 270 (in Hebrew).

170   Harriet Pass Freidenreich, *The Jews of Yugoslavia: A Quest for Community* (The Jewish Publication Society of America, Philadelphia, 1979), p. 193.

171   Ibid.

172   Gil, *Pages of Immigration*, p. 28.

173   CZA, S25/5281, note on the Jews of Bulgaria, submitted to the Anglo-American Committee by the Sephardi delegation, March 21, 1946.

174   Ibid.

175   Mosheh Mosek, "The Struggle for the Defence of the Jews of Bulgaria after the Liberation," in Benjamin Pinkus, ed., *East European Jewry: From the Holocaust to the Redemption, 1944–1948* (Ben-Gurion University of the Negev, Beersheva, 1987), pp. 204–5 (in Hebrew).

176   Gil, *Pages of Immigration*, p. 28.

177   Tamir, *Bulgaria and Her Jews*, p. 230; Yvette Anavi, "Short Review of the History of the Sephardi Jews of Bulgaria," *Los Muestros*, 7 (July 1992), p. 10 (in Judeo-Spanish); this last source gives the figure of 7,676 for the year 1951.

Emigration to Palestine, later Israel

Country of origin	1919–23	1924–31	1932–8	1939–45	1946–15.5.48	15.5.48–31.12.49	Total
Bulgaria	328	1,209	1,121	3,220	1,179	35,089	42,146
Greece	158	815	5,651	1,161	982	1,540	10,307
Turkey	478	1,303	2,179	4,196	121	30,657	38,934
Yugoslavia	145	154	640	858	147	6,596	8,540
Total	1,109	3,481	9,591	9,435	2,429	73,882	99,927

Source: Gil, *Pages of Immigration*, p. 28.

178   Walter Weiker, *The Unseen Israelis: The Jews from Turkey in Israel* (The Jerusalem Center for Public Affairs, University Press of America, Lanham/New York/London, 1988), p. 127.

CONCLUSION

1   On this subject, see Ismar Schorsch, "The Myth of Sephardic Supremacy," *Leo Baeck Institute Year Book*, 34 (1989), pp. 47–66.

2   On these names, read David Bunis, "The Language of the Judeo-Spanish – Historical Study," in Haim Beinart, ed., *Sephardi Heritage* (Magnes Press, Jerusalem, 1992), pp. 694–713 (in Hebrew).

3   Very few documents mention this. See, for example, Jacques Biélinsky, *Journal 1940–1942: un journaliste juif à Paris sous l'Occupation* (edited by Renée Poznanski, Cerf, Paris, 1992), pp. 90, 141; José Papo, *En attendant l'aurore: activité de la communauté séphardite de Paris pendant l'Occupation, 1940–1945* (n.p., Paris, April 1945).

4   Walter Weiker, *Ottomans, Turks and the Jewish Polity: A History of the Jews of Turkey* (The Jerusalem Center for Public Affairs, University Press of America, Lanham/New York /London, 1992), p. 303.

5   Walter E. Weiker, *The Unseen Israelis: The Jews from Turkey in Israel* (The Jerusalem Center for Public Affairs, University Press of America, Lanham/Mayland 1988), p. 127.

Archival Sources

The Archives listed below were the ones that allowed us to conduct research for this book.

Archives de l'Alliance Israélite Universelle (AAIU), Paris
Archives de la Marine, Vincennes
Archives du Ministère de la Guerre, Vincennes
Archives du Ministère des Affaires Etrangères (MAE), Paris
Archives of Hashomer Hazair, Givat Haviva
Archives of the Hagana, Tel Aviv
Archives of the Italian Jewish Community, Istanbul
Archives of the Jabotinsky Institute, Tel Aviv
Archives of the Labour and Pioneer Movement, Lavon Institute, Tel Aviv
Archives of the Macabi Organization, Ramat Gan
Auswärtiges Amt, Bonn (microfilm in National Archives, USA)
Central Archives for the History of the Jewish People (CAHJP), Jerusalem
Central Zionist Archives (CZA), Jerusalem
Joint Distribution Committee (JDC), New York
League of Nations, Documents 1919-46, Minorities, Council Documents
Public Record Office (PRO), London
State Archives, Jerusalem
U.S. Department of State, National Archives, Washington, D.C.

Newspapers and Periodicals

Aksion, Salonika
La Alborada, Sarajevo
El Amigo del Puevlo, Belgrade, Sofia, Ruse
Archives Israélites (AI), Paris
L'Aurore, Istanbul, Cairo
Avanti, Salonika
El Avenir, Salonika
Bolitino de la Sosyedad Dorshei Hahaskalah, Edirne
Bolitino del Konsistorio Sentral de Bulgaria, Sofia
La Boz de la Verdad, Edirne
La Boz del Puevlo, Izmir
La Boz del Puevlo, Salonika
La Boz de Oriente, Istanbul
La Boz de Turkiye, Istanbul
La Buena Esperansa, Izmir
Bulletin Semestriel de l'Alliance Israélite Universelle (BAIU), Paris
El Burlon, Salonika
Carmel, Philippopoli
El Dia, Philippopoli
Djurnal del Lavorador, Salonika
La Epoka, Salonika
La Esperansa, Salonika
Haherut, Jerusalem
Hamenora, Istanbul
Hamevasser, Istanbul

Haolam, Cologne, Vilna, Odessa
Haor, Jerusalem
Hapoel Hazair, Jaffa
Hashiloah, Odessa, Warsaw, Berlin, Krakow, Jerusalem
Havazelet, Jerusalem
Hazevi, Jerusalem
İkdam, Istanbul
L'Indépendant, Salonika
Le Jeune Turc, Istanbul
Jevrejski Glas, Sarajevo
Jewish Chronicle, London
The Jewish World, London
Le Journal de Salonique, Salonika
Le Journal d'Orient, Istanbul
Le Judaïsme Séphardi, Paris, London
El Judio, Istanbul
El Jugueton, Salonika
Karmi, Pressburg
Karmi Sheli, Vienna, Belgrade
El Koreo de Viena, Vienna
El Liberal, Salonika
Lloyd Ottoman, Istanbul
La Luz, Sofia
El Mesajero, Salonika
El Meseret, Izmir
Le Moniteur Oriental, Istanbul
La Nasion, Salonika
La Nation, Istanbul
Paix et Droit, Paris
Le Progrès, Salonika
Puerta del Oriente, Izmir
El Puevlo, Salonika
La Revista Popular, Salonika
Şalom, Istanbul
Selbst-Emancipation, Vienna
La Solidaredad Ovradera, Salonika
Stamboul, Istanbul
Takvim-i Vekayi, Istanbul
Tasvir-i Efkâr, Istanbul
El Telegrafo, Istanbul
Tevhid-i Efkâr, Istanbul
El Tiempo, Istanbul

La Tribuna Libera, Salonika
La Turquie, Istanbul
Univers Israélite (UI), Paris
La Vara, Cairo
La Vera Luz, Istanbul
La Verdad, Salonika
La Verdad, Sofia
Die Welt, Vienna, Cologne, Berlin

Select Bibliography

The following updated bibliography consists of books and articles cited in the notes, and of works which are important both for this book and for the history of Sephardim. Articles in edited volumes have not been listed here separately, but are cited in full in the notes.

Abitbol, Michel, Galit Hassan-Rokem, and Yom Tov Assis, eds. *Society and Culture: Sephardi Jews after the Expulsion*. Jerusalem: Misgav Yerushalayim, 1997.

Aharon Ben-Yosef: The Man and His Work, Letters and Documents. Tel Aviv: Committee for the Book on Aharon Ben-Yosef, 1953. (in Hebrew)

Akar, Rıdvan. "The Capital Tax." *Ekonomik Panorama*, 24 April 1988. (in Turkish)

————. *The Capital Tax: An Example of Anti-Minority Politics in the Era of One Party Rule*. Istanbul: Belge Yayınları, 1992. (in Turkish)

Aktar, Ayhan. "The Capital Tax and Istanbul." *Toplum ve Bilim*, 71 (winter 1996), pp. 97–149. (in Turkish)

————. "Economic Nationalism in Turkey: The Formative Years, 1912–1925." *Boğaziçi Journal*, 10, no. 1-2 (1996), pp. 263–90.

————. "How to Interpret the Jewish Incidents in Thrace." *Tarih ve Toplum*, 155 (Nov. 1996), pp. 45–56. (in Turkish)

————. "The Politics of Turkicization in the First Years of the Republic." *Tarih ve Toplum*, 156 (Dec. 1996), pp. 4–18. (in Turkish)

Albert, Phyllis, and Frances Malino, eds. *Essays in Modern Jewish History: A Tribute to Ben Halpern*. Rutherford: Fairleigh Dickinson University Press, 1982.

Alcalá, Angel, ed. *Judíos, Sefarditas, Conversos: La Expulsión de 1492 y sus consecuensias. Ponencias del Congreso Internacional celebrado en Nueva York en noviembre de 1992*. Valladolid: Ambito, 1995.

Almog, Shmuel, ed. *Antisemitism through the Ages.* Oxford: Pergamon Press, 1988.

Almog, Shmuel, Israel Bartal, Michael Graetz, et al., eds. *Transition and Change in Modern Jewish History: Essays Presented in Honour of Shmuel Ettinger.* Jerusalem: Zalman Shazar, 1987. (in Hebrew)

Amarillo, Abraham Shaul. "Benevolent Societies." *Sefunot*, 15, no. 5 (1971–81), pp. 105–33. (in Hebrew)

————. "The Great *Talmud Torah* Society in Salonika." *Sefunot*, 13, no. 3 (1971–78), pp. 275–308. (in Hebrew)

Anavi, Yvette. "Short Review of the History of the Sephardi Jews of Bulgaria." *Los Muestros*, 7 (July 1992), pp. 9–10. (in Judeo-Spanish)

Anderson, Benedict. *Imagined Communities: Reflections on the Origin and Spread of Nationalism.* London: Verso, 1983.

Angel, Marc D. *The Jews of Rhodes: The History of a Sephardic Community.* 2d ed. New York: Sepher Hermon Press, 1980.

————. *Voices in Exile: A Study in Sephardic Intellectual History.* Hoboken, New Jersey: Ktav and Sephardic House, 1991.

Ankori, Zvi. *An Encounter through History: Jews and Greeks and Their Relations through the Ages.* Tel Aviv: Tel Aviv University, 1984. (in Hebrew)

————, ed. *From Lisbon to Salonika and Constantinople: Annual Lectures on the Jews of Greece.* Tel Aviv: Tel Aviv University, 1988. (in Hebrew)

————, ed. *In the Past and Today: Annual Lectures on Greek Jewry (1977–1983).* Tel Aviv: Tel Aviv University, 1984. (in Hebrew)

Arditti, Binyamin Yosef. *Antisemitic Literature in Bulgaria: Bibliography.* Holon: n.p., 1972. (in Hebrew)

————. *The Jews of Bulgaria during the Period of the Nazi Regime.* Holon: n.p. [1962?]. (in Hebrew)

Arié, Gabriel. *The Jews of the Balkan States.* Sofia: "Hamishpat" Publishers, 1914. (in Judeo-Spanish)

Ashtor, Eliyahu. *The Jews of Moslem Spain.* 3 vols. Philadelphia: The Jewish Publication Society of America, 1973–79.

Aslanov, Leon. "Some Problems of Demographic Investigations on the Life and Development of the Jewish Population in the People's Republic of Bulgaria." *Annual*, 14 (1979), pp. 183–88.

Assis, YomTov. "Crime and Violence in Spanish Jewish Society in the Thirteenth to Fourteenth Centuries." *Zion*, 50 (1985), pp. 221–40. (in Hebrew)

————. *The Golden Age of Aragonese Jewry: Community and Society in the Crown of Aragon, 1213–1327.* London: Vallentine Mitchell, 1997.

————. *Jewish Economy in the Medieval Crown of Aragon, 1213–1327: Money and Power.* Leiden: E. J. Brill, 1997.

————. "The Papal Inquisition and Aragonese Jewry in the Early Fourteenth Century." *Medieval Studies*, 49 (1987), pp. 391–410.

Assouline, Pierre. *Le Dernier des Camondo.* Paris: Gallimard, 1997.

Astruc, Kalev. "Data Concerning the Demographic Situation of the Bulgarian Jews." *Annual*, 16 (1981), pp. 85–96.

Asuero, Pablo Martín. "La Imagen española de los judíos otomanos (1790–1907)." *Miscelánea de Estudios Arabes y Hebráicos*, 45 (1996), pp. 135–47.

Attal, Robert. *Les Juifs de Grèce: Bibliographie*. Jerusalem: Ben Zvi Institute and The Hebrew University, 1984.

Attias, Jean-Christophe. *Le Commentaire biblique: Mordekhai Komtino ou l'herméneutique du dialogue*. Paris: Cerf, 1991.

——. *Isaac Abravanel, la mémoire et l'espérance*. Paris: Cerf, 1992.

Attias, Jean-Christophe, and Esther Benbassa. *Dictionnaire de civilisation juive*. Paris: Larousse, 1997.

Attias, Moshe. "Jacob Jona: The Wandering Popular Poet in Salonika." *Sefunot*, 15, no. 5 (1981), pp. 155–202. (in Hebrew)

Avitsur, Shmuel. "Contribution to the History of the Woolen Textile Industry in Salonika." *Sefunot*, 12 (1971–78), pp. 147–68. (in Hebrew)

Avni, Haim. *Argentina and the Jews: A History of Jewish Immigration*. Tr. Gila Brand. Tuscaloosa: University of Alabama Press, 1991.

——. *Spain, the Jews, and Franco*. Philadelphia: The Jewish Publication Society of America, 1982.

Avramov, Joseph. "A Few Facts from the History of the Bulgarian Jews." *Annual*, 22 (1987), pp. 61–69.

Bacqué-Grammont, Jean-Louis, and Paul Dumont, eds. *Economie et sociétés dans l'Empire ottoman (fin du XVIIIe-début du XXe siècle)*. Paris: Editions du CNRS, 1983.

Baer, Gabriel. "The Administrative, Economic and Social Functions of Turkish Guilds." *International Journal of Middle East Studies*, 1, no. 1 (1970), pp. 28–50.

Baer, Yitshak. *A History of the Jews in Christian Spain*. Tr. L. Schoffman. 2 vols. Philadelphia: The Jewish Publication Society of America, 1978.

Bağış, Ali İhsan. *Non-Muslims in Ottoman Commerce*. Ankara: Turhan Kitabevi, 1983. (in Turkish)

Baker, Derek, ed. *Religious Motivation: Biographical and Sociological Problems for the Church Historian*. Oxford: Basil Blackwell, 1978.

Bali, Rifat N. "Antisemitism in Turkey during the Republican Period." *Felsefelogos*, March 1998: 65–96. (in Turkish)

——. "Cevat Rifat Atilhan: His Life, His Publications, and His Thought." Part 1. *Tarih ve Toplum*, 175 (July 1998), pp. 15–24. (in Turkish)

——. "The Debates on the Capital Tax." *Tarih ve Toplum*, 165 (Sept. 1997), pp. 47–59. (in Turkish)

——. "The Fire of Hasköy (13 March 1908)." *Tarih ve Toplum*, 159 (March 1997), pp. 21–24. (in Turkish)

——. "The Jewish Contribution to Turkish Literature in the Republican Period." *Varlık*, March 1997: 48–51. (in Turkish)

———. "A Jewish Economic and Social Welfare Organization: The Small Loan Association." *Tarih ve Toplum*, 160 (April 1997) 45–54. (in Turkish)

———. "A Jewish Organization for Solidarity and Mutual Help: The Grand Lodge of the Eleventh District of B'nai B'rith, Its History, and Its Periodical *Hamenora*." *Müteferrika*, 8–9 (spring-summer 1996), pp. 41–60. (in Turkish)

———. "Official Ideology and Non-Muslim Citizens." *Birikim*, 105–6 (Jan.-Feb. 1998), pp. 170–76. (in Turkish)

———. "A Racist Association: The Turkish Association against Zionism." *Toplumsal Tarih*, 29 (May 1996), pp. 32–36. (in Turkish)

———. "The Turkish Nationalism of the Jews." *Birikim*, 102 (Nov. 1997), pp. 47–53. (in Turkish)

———. "The Welfare Party and the Jews of Turkey." *Birikim*, 91 (Nov. 1996), pp. 74–87. (in Turkish)

Barnai, Jacob. "Christian Messianism and the Portuguese Marranos: The Emergence of Sabbateanism in Smyrna." *Jewish History*, 7 (1993), pp. 119–24.

———. "The Congregations in Izmir in the Seventeenth Century." *Peamim*, 48 (1991), pp. 66–84. (in Hebrew)

———. *The Jews in Palestine in the Eighteenth Century under the Patronage of the Istanbul Committee of Officials for Palestine*. Tr. Naomi Goldblum. Tuscaloosa: University of Alabama Press, 1992.

———. "On the History of Relations between the Jews of Izmir and Those of Palestine in the Seventeenth and Eighteenth Centuries." *Shalem*, 5 (1987), pp. 95–114. (in Hebrew)

———. "On the History of the Jewish Community of Istanbul in the Eighteenth Century." *Miqqedem Umiyyam*, 1 (1981), pp. 53–66. (in Hebrew)

———. "The Origins of the Jewish Community of Izmir in the Ottoman Period." *Peamim*, 12 (1982), pp. 47–58. (in Hebrew)

———. "Orthodox Historiography and the Sabbatean Movement." *Yahadut Zemaneynu*, 9 (1995), pp. 19–44. (in Hebrew)

———. "The Outbreak of Sabbateanism: The Eastern European Factor." *The Journal of Jewish Thought and Philosophy*, 4 (1994), pp. 171–83.

———. "Rabbi Joseph Eskapa and the Rabbinate in Izmir." *Sefunot*, 18, no. 3 (1985), pp. 53–81. (in Hebrew)

———. "The Status of the Chief Rabbinate in Jerusalem in the Ottoman Period." *Cathedra*, 13 (1980), pp. 47–69. (in Hebrew)

Barnai, Jacob, and Haim Gerber. "Jewish Guilds in Constantinople at the End of the Eighteenth Century." *Michael*, 7 (1981), pp. 206–26. (in Hebrew)

———. *The Jews of Izmir in the Nineteenth Century*. Jerusalem: Misgav Yerushalayim, 1985. (in Hebrew)

Barnett, Richard David, ed. *The Sephardi Heritage*. Vol. I, *Essays on the Historical and Cultural Contribution of the Jews of Spain and Portugal*. London: Vallentine Mitchell, 1971.

Barnett, Richard David, and W. M. Schwab, eds. *The Sephardi Heritage.* Vol. II, *The Western Sephardim.* Grendon, Northants: Gilbraltar Books, 1989.

Baron, Salo W. *A Social and Religious History of the Jews.* 18 vols. New York and Philadelphia: Columbia University Press and The Jewish Publication Society of America, 1957–83.

Barquín López, Amelia. *Edición y estudio de doce novelas aljamiadas sefardíes de principios del siglo XX.* N.p.: Universidad del País Vasco, n.d.

Basco, Santiago, and Adela Rubio. *El Cal Aragón: Los Judíos aragoneses en Salónica.* Saragossa: Ibercaja, 1995.

Bashan, Eliezer. "Contacts between Jews in Smyrna and the Levant Company of London in the Seventeenth and Eighteenth Centuries." *Transactions of the Jewish Historical Society of England,* 29 (1988), pp. 53–73.

———. "Economic Association with Non-Jews: The Principle and Its Achievement." *Mahanayim,* 2 (1992), pp. 78–85. (in Hebrew)

———. "Fires and Earthquakes in Izmir in the Seventeenth through Nineteenth Centuries and a Document on the Accusation Directed against the Jews of Lighting the Fires." *Miqqedem Umiyyam,* 2 (1986), pp. 13–27. (in Hebrew)

———. "A Jewish Guild in Izmir at the Beginning of the Eighteenth Century." *Mimizrah Umimaarav,* 5 (1986), pp. 155–72. (in Hebrew)

———. "Jewish Interpreters in British Consular Service in the Middle East in the Years 1581–1825." *Sefunot,* 6, no. 21 (1993), pp. 41–69. (in Hebrew)

———. "The Position of the Salonikan Rabbis in the Sixteenth to the Eighteenth Centuries in the Dispute Relating to the Influence of a Wealthy Minority on Public Life." *Mimizrah Umimaarav,* 2 (1980), pp. 27–52. (in Hebrew)

———. "Societies for the Help of the Sick in the Communities of the Middle East." In *Homage to Abraham Spiegelman,* N.p., 1979, pp. 209–20.

Battesti-Pelegrin, Jeanne, ed. *"Qu'un sang impur . . .": Les Conversos et le pouvoir en Espagne à la fin du Moyen Age, Actes du 2e Colloque d'Aix-en-Provence, 18–20 novembre 1994.* Aix-en-Provence: n.p., 1997.

Bat Ye'or. *The Dhimmi: Jews and Christians under Islam.* Tr. David Maisel, Paul Fenton, and David Littman. Rutherford: Fairleigh Dickinson University Press, 1985.

Bauer, Yehuda, et al. *Remembering the Future: Working Papers and Addenda. Jews and Christians during and after the Holocaust.* 3 vols. Oxford: Pergamon Press, 1989.

Baylav, Nasid. *The History of Pharmacy.* Istanbul: Yörük Matbaası, 1968. (in Turkish)

Beinart, Haim. *Conversos on Trial: The Inquisition in Ciudad Real.* Jerusalem: Magnes Press, 1981.

———. *The Expulsion from Spain.* Jerusalem: Magnes Press, 1994. (in Hebrew)

———, ed. *The Sephardi Legacy.* 2 vols. Jerusalem: Magnes Press, 1992.

Ben-Ami, Issachar, ed. *The Heritage of Sephardi and Oriental Jews.* Jerusalem: Magnes Press, 1982. (in Hebrew)

Benardete, Mair Jose. *Hispanic Culture and Character of the Sephardic Jews.* New York: Hispanic Institute in the United States, 1953.

Benaroya, Abraham. *Hopes and Disappointments*. Athens: Stokhastis, 1989. (in Greek)

———. "A Note on 'The Socialist Federation of Saloniki.'" *Jewish Social Studies*, 11 (1949), pp. 69–72.

Benayahu, Meir. "The Abravanel Family in Salonika." *Sefunot*, 12 (1971–75), pp. 9–69. (in Hebrew)

———. "The Court Doctor Moshe Benbanast and the Poem of Rabbi Judah Zarko on His Exile to Rhodes." *Sefunot*, 12 (1971–78), pp. 123–43. (in Hebrew)

———. "Facts about the Jews of Spain in the First Century of Their Settlement in Turkey." *Sinai*, 14, no. 3–4 (1951), pp. 181–207. (in Hebrew)

———. "The Great Fires in Izmir and Adrianople." *Reshumot*, 2 (1946), pp. 1–12. (in Hebrew)

———. "New Facts about Yehudah Bibas." *Tesoro de los Judíos Sefardíes*, 3 (1960), pp. 95–111. (in Hebrew)

———. "Ordinances of Safed for the Immunity from Taxation of Scholars and the Attempt at Repeal by Rabbi Yehuda Aberlin." *Sefunot*, 7 (1963), pp. 102–17. (in Hebrew)

Benbassa, Esther. "Comment être non-musulman en terre d'islam." *L'Histoire*, 134 (1990), pp. 86–91.

———. *Une Diaspora sépharade en transition: Istanbul XIXe–XXe siècles*. Paris: Cerf, 1993.

———. "L'Education féminine en Orient: L'Ecole de filles de l'Alliance israélite universelle à Galata, Istanbul (1879–1912)." *Histoire, Economie et Société*, 4 (1991), pp. 529–59.

———. "Education for Jewish Girls in the East: A Portrait of the Galata School in Istanbul, 1872–1912." *Studies in Contemporary Jewry*, 9 (1993), pp. 163–73.

———. "L'Expulsion des Juifs d'Espagne." *L'Histoire*, 154 (1992), pp. 24–31.

———. "Haim Nahum Effendi, dernier Grand Rabbin de l'Empire ottoman (1908–1920): Son Rôle politique et diplomatique." Unpublished doctorat d'état thesis, 2 vols., Université de Paris III, 1987.

———. "Israël face à lui-même: Judaïsme occidental et judaïsme ottoman (19e–20e siècles)." *Pardès*, 7 (1988), pp. 105–29.

———. "Presse d'Istanbul et de Salonique au service du sionisme (1908–1914): Les Motifs d'une allégeance." *Revue Historique*, 276/2, no. 560 (1986), pp. 337–65.

———. "Le Sionisme dans l'Empire ottoman à l'aube du 20e siècle." *Vingtième Siècle: Revue d'Histoire*, 24 (Oct.-Dec. 1989), pp. 69–80.

———. "Le Sionisme et la politique des alliances dans les communautés juives ottomanes (début du XXe siècle)." *Revue des Etudes Juives*, 150, no. 1-2 (1991), pp. 107–31.

———. "Les Stratégies associatives dans la société juive ottomane (XIXe–XXe siècles)." *Revue d'Histoire Moderne et Contemporaine*, 38, no. 2 (1991), pp. 295–312.

———. "Zionism in the Ottoman Empire at the End of the Nineteenth and the Beginning of the Twentieth Century." *Studies in Zionism*, 11, no. 2 (1990), pp. 127–40.

———, ed. *Haim Nahum: A Sephardic Chief Rabbi in Politics, 1892–1923*. Tr. Myriam Kochan. Tuscaloosa: University of Alabama Press, 1995.

———, ed. *Mémoires juives d'Espagne et du Portugal*. Paris: Publisud, 1996.

———, ed. *Transmission et passages en monde juif*. Paris: Publisud, 1997.

Benbassa, Esther, and Aron Rodrigue. "L'Artisanat juif en Turquie à la fin du XIXe siè-cle: L'Alliance israélite universelle et ses oeuvres d'apprentissage." *Turcica*, 17 (1985), pp. 113–26.

———, eds. *A Sephardi Life in Southeastern Europe: Gabriel Arié*. Seattle: University of Washington Press, 1998.

Benezra, Nissim M. *Une Enfance juive à Istanbul (1911–1929)*. Istanbul: Isis, 1996.

Ben-Menahem, Naftali. "Contribution to the Establishment of the Bibliography of R. Moses Almosnino." *Tesoro de los Judíos Sefardíes*, 5 (1962), pp. 126–28. (in Hebrew)

Bentov, Haim. "The Method of Teaching the Talmud in the *Yeshivot* of Salonika and Turkey." *Sefunot*, 13, no. 3 (1971–78), pp. 7–102. (in Hebrew)

Benveniste, Annie. *Le Bosphore à la Roquette: La Communauté judéo-espagnole à Paris (1914–1940)*. Paris: L'Harmattan, 1989.

Benveniste, David. *The Jews of Salonika in the Modern Period*. Jerusalem: Kiryat Sefer, 1973. (in Hebrew)

Benveniste, David, and Haim Mizrahi. "Rabbi Yehudah Bibas and the Community of Corfu of His Day." *Sefunot*, 2 (1958), pp. 303–31. (in Hebrew)

Benvenisti, David. "'El Pueblo,' the First Jewish Marxist Newspaper in Bulgaria (1902–1903)." *Annual*, 13 (1978), pp. 209–38.

———. "The Unfavorable Conditions for the Dissemination of Antisemitic Propaganda in Bulgaria (1891–1903)." *Annual*, 15 (1980), pp. 177–220.

Besso, Henry V. *Ladino Books in the Library of Congress: A Bibliography*. Washington, D.C.: Library of Congress, 1963.

Bhabha, Homi K., ed. *Nation and Narration*. London: Routledge, 1990.

Biélinsky, Jacques. *Journal 1940–1942: Un Journaliste juif à Paris sous l'Occupation*. Ed. Renée Poznanski. Paris: Cerf, 1992.

Birnbaum, Pierre, ed. *Histoire politique des Juifs de France: Entre universalisme et particu-larisme*. Paris: Presses de la Fondation Nationale des Sciences Politiques, 1990.

Birnbaum, Pierre, and Ira Katznelson, eds. *Paths of Emancipation: Jews, States and Citizenship*. Princeton: Princeton University Press, 1995.

Blacke, C. E. *The Dynamics of Modernization*. New York: Harper and Row, 1967.

Bodian, Miriam. *Hebrews of the Portuguese Nation: Conversos and Community in Early Modern Amsterdam*. Bloomington: Indiana University Press, 1997.

Bora, Siren. *History of the Jews of Izmir, 1908–1923*. Istanbul: Gözlem, 1995. (in Turkish)

Bornstein[-Makovetsky], Leah. "The Leadership of the Jewish Communities in the Middle East from the Fifteenth to the Eighteenth Century." Unpublished doctoral thesis, Hebrew University of Jerusalem, 1978. (in Hebrew)

———. "The Remnants of the Rabbinical Tribunal of Balat in Istanbul (1839)." *Sefunot*, 19, no. 4 (1989), pp. 53–122.

———. "The Structure of Law Courts in the Sixteenth and Seventeenth Centuries in the Communities of the Ottoman Empire, as Portrayed in Rabbinical Literature." Paper presented at the International Conference on Jewish Communities in Muslim Lands, Jerusalem, n.d. [197?].

Bosworth, C. E., et al., eds. *Essays in Honor of Bernard Lewis: The Islamic World*. Princeton: Darwin Press, 1989.

Bowman, Steven. "Jews in Wartime in Greece." *Jewish Social Studies*, 48 (1986), pp. 45–62.

———. *The Jews of Byzantium, 1204–1453*. Tuscaloosa: University of Alabama Press, 1985.

Braude, Benjamin. "The Cloth Industry of Salonika in the Mediterranean Economy." *Peamim*, 15 (1983), pp. 82–95. (in Hebrew)

———. "International Competition and Domestic Cloth in the Ottoman Empire, 1500–1650: A Study in Undevelopment." *Review*, 2 (1979), pp. 437–51.

———. "The Rise and Fall of Salonica Woolens, 1500–1650: Technology Transfer and Western Competition." *Mediterranean Historical Review*, 6, no. 2 (1991), pp. 216–36.

———. "Venture and Faith in the Commercial Life of the Ottoman Balkans, 1500–1650." *International History Review*, 7 (1985), pp. 519–42.

Braude, Benjamin, and Bernard Lewis, eds. *Christians and Jews in the Ottoman Empire: The Functioning of a Plural Society*. 2 vols. New York: Holmes and Meier, 1982.

Browning, Christopher R. *Fateful Months: Essays on the Emergence of the Final Solution*. New York: Holmes and Meier, 1985.

———. *The Final Solution and the German Foreign Office*. New York: Holmes and Meier, 1978.

Bunis, David. *Sephardic Studies: A Research Bibliography Incorporating Judezmo Language, Literature and Folklore and Historical Background*. New York: Garland, 1981.

Capsali, Elijah. *Seder Eliyahu Zuta ("The Little Order of Elijah")*. Ed. Shlomo Simonsohn, Meir Benayahu, and Aryeh Shmuelevitz. 2 vols. Jerusalem: Ben Zvi Institute, 1975–77. (in Hebrew)

Carlebach, Elisheva. *The Pursuit of Heresy: Rabbi Moshe Hagiz and the Sabbatean Controversy*. New York: Columbia University Press, 1990.

Caro Baroja, Julio. *Inquisición, brujería y criptojudaismo*. Barcelona: Galaxia Gutenberg, 1996.

Carpi, Daniel. "Nuovi Documenti per la storia dell'Olocausto in Grecia: L'Attegiamento degli Italiani." *Michael*, 7 (1981), pp. 119–200.

———, ed. *Italian Diplomatic Documents on the History of the Holocaust in Greece (1941–1943)*. Tel Aviv: Tel Aviv University, Diaspora Research Institute, 1999.

Castro, Americo. *La Realidad histórica de España*. Mexico, D.F.: Biblioteca Porrúa, 1954.

Chary, Frederick B. *The Bulgarian Jews and the Final Solution, 1940–1944*. Pittsburgh: University of Pittsburgh Press, 1972.

Chazan, Robert. "The Barcelona 'Disputation' of 1263: Christian Missionizing and Jewish Response." *Speculum*, 52 (1977), pp. 824–42.

———. *Church, State, and Jew in the Middle Ages*. New York: Behrman House, 1980.

———. *Daggers of Faith: Thirteenth-Century Christian Missionizing and Jewish Response*. Berkeley and Los Angeles: University of California Press, 1989.

Chouraqui, André. *Histoire des Juifs en Afrique du Nord*. Paris: Hachette, 1985.

Cohen, Amnon. *Jewish Life under Islam: Jerusalem in the Sixteenth Century*. Cambridge, Mass.: Harvard University Press, 1984.

Cohen, Amnon, and Bernard Lewis. *Population and Revenue in the Towns of Palestine in the Sixteenth Century*. Princeton: Princeton University Press, 1978.

Cohen, David. "The Policy of 'Final Solution' of the Jewish Problem in Bulgaria and Its Failure as Revealed by German Documents." *Annual*, 18 (1983), pp. 81–110.

Cohen, Hayim J. *The Jews of the Middle East, 1860–1972*. New York: John Wiley, 1973.

Cohen, Jeremy. *The Friars and the Jews: The Evolution of Medieval Anti-Judaism*. Ithaca: Cornell University Press, 1982.

Cohen, Rivka. *Constantinople, Salonika, Patras: Community and Supra-Community Organization of Greek Jewry under Ottoman Rule, 15th–16th Centuries*. Tel Aviv: Tel Aviv University, 1984. (in Hebrew)

Colbert, J.-B. *Lettres, Instructions et Mémoires*. 7 vols. Ed. P. Clément. Paris: Imprimerie Impériale, 1861–73.

Constantopoulou, Photini, and Thanos Veremis, eds. *Documents on the History of Greek Jews: Records from the Historical Archives of the Ministry of Foreign Affairs*. Athens: Kastaniotis, 1998.

Cooperman, Bernard D., ed. *Studies in Sixteenth-Century Jewish Thought*. Cambridge, Mass.: Harvard University Center for Jewish Studies, 1983.

Copsidas, Kostis. *Les Juifs de Thessalonique à travers les cartes postales, 1886–1917*. Salonika: n.p., 1989.

Cozzi, Gaetano, ed. *Gli Ebrei e Venezia, secoli XIV–XVIII*. Milan: Edizioni Comunità, 1987.

Crampton, R. J. *A Short History of Modern Bulgaria*. Cambridge: Cambridge University Press, 1987.

Dalven, Rae. *The Jews of Ioannina*. Philadelphia: Cadmus Press, 1990.

Danon, Abraham. "La Communauté juive de Salonique au XVIe siècle." *Revue des Etudes Juives*, 40 (1900), pp. 206–30; ibid., 41 (1900), pp. 98–117, 250–65.

———. "Documents Relating to the History of the Karaites in European Turkey." *Jewish Quarterly Review*, 17, no. 2 (1926), pp. 165–322.

———. "Etude historique sur les impôts directs et indirects des communautés israélites en Turquie." *Revue des Etudes Juives*, 31 (1895), pp. 52–61.

———. *Etudes sabbatiennes*. Paris: Durlacher, 1910.

———. "The Karaites in European Turkey." *Jewish Quarterly Review*, 15, no. 3 (Jan. 1925), pp. 285–360.

Davison, Roderic H. *Reform in the Ottoman Empire, 1856–1876*. Princeton: Princeton University Press, 1963.

———. "Turkish Attitudes concerning Christian-Muslim Equality in the Nineteenth Century." *American Historical Review*, 59 (1954), pp. 844–64.

Delmaire, Jean-Marie. "De Hibbat Zion au sionisme politique." 2 vols. Doctorat d'etat thesis, Université de Strasbourg II, 1986. (printed by the ANRT, Lille)

Deshen, Shlomo, and Walter P. Zenner, eds. *Jewish Societies in the Middle East: Community, Culture and Authority*. Washington, D.C.: University Press of America, 1982.

Detcheverry, A. *Histoire des Israélites de Bordeaux*. Bordeaux: Balarac Jeune, 1850.

Díaz Más, Paloma. *The Jews from Spain*. Chicago: University of Chicago Press, 1992.

Dorn, Pamela J. "Change and Ideology: The Ethnomusicology of Turkish Jewry." Unpublished doctoral dissertation, Indiana University, Bloomington, 1991.

Dumont, Paul. "La Condition juive en Turquie à la fin du XIXe siècle." *Nouveaux Cahiers*, 57 (1979), pp. 25–38.

———. "La Fédération socialiste ouvrière de Salonique à l'époque des guerres balkaniques." *East European Quarterly*, 14, no. 4 (1980), pp. 383–410.

———. "Une Organisation socialiste ottomane: La Fédération ouvrière de Salonique (1908–1912)." *Etudes Balkaniques*, 1 (1975), pp. 76–88.

———. "Une Source pour l'étude des communautés juives en Turquie: Les Archives de l'Alliance Israélite Universelle." *Journal Asiatique*, 267 (1979), pp. 101–35.

———. "La Structure sociale de la communauté juive de Salonique à la fin du dix-neuvième siècle." *Revue Historique*, 263 (1980), pp. 351–93.

Edwards, John H. *The Jews in Christian Europe, 1400–1700*. London: Routledge, 1991.

———. "Religious Belief and Social Conformity: The 'Converso' Problem in Late-Medieval Cordoba." *Transactions of the Royal Historical Society*, 5th ser., no. 31 (1981), pp. 115–28.

Efthymiou, Maria. *Jews and Christians in the Southeastern Islands of the Aegean Sea under Ottoman Rule*. Athens: Trokhalia, 1992. (in Greek)

Ehrenpreis, Mordekhai. *Between East and West*. Reprint. Tel Aviv: Sigalit, 1986. (in Hebrew)

Eisenstadt, S. N. *Patterns of Modernity*. 2 vols. London: Frances Pinter, 1987.

———. *Tradition, Change, and Modernity*. New York: John Wiley, 1973.

Elazar, D., H. Freidenreich, B. Hazzan, and A. W. Lieberles, eds. *The Balkan Jewish Communities*. Lanham, Maryland, and New York: University Press of America and The Jerusalem Center for Public Affairs, 1984.

Elior, Rachel. "Messianic Expectations and Spiritualization of Religious Life in the Sixteenth Century." *Revue des Etudes Juives*, 145 (1986), pp. 25–49.

Elmaleh, Abraham. "Judeo-Spanish Literature and the Press." Parts 1 and 2. *Hashiloah*, 26, no. 1 (1912), pp. 67–73, 253–60. (in Hebrew)

Emecen, Feridun M. *A Forgotten Community: The Jews of Manisa*. Istanbul: Eren, 1997. (in Turkish)

Emmanuel, I. S. *Histoire de l'industrie des tissus des Israélites de Salonique*. Paris: Librairie Lipschutz, 1935.

Encyclopaedia Judaica. 17 vols. Jerusalem: Keter, 1972.

Epstein, Mark Alan. *The Ottoman Jewish Communities and Their Role in the Fifteenth and Sixteenth Centuries*. Fribourg: Klaus Schwarz, 1980.

Ercan, Yavuz. "The Juridical, Internal, and Economic Situation of Non-Muslims in Turkey in the Fifteenth and Sixteenth Centuries." *Belleten*, 48, no. 188 (Sept. 1983), pp. 1119–49. (in Turkish)

Escamilla-Colin, Michèle. *Crimes et châtiments dans l'Espagne inquisitoriale*. 2 vols. Paris: Berg International, 1992.

Eshkenazy, Eli. "Economy, Way of Life and Culture of the Jews in the Balkan Peninsula during the XVIIIth Century." *Annual*, 6 (1971), pp. 151–78.

———. "The Jews in the Balkan Peninsula during the XVIIIth Century: Life, Economy and Culture." *Annual*, 8 (1973), pp. 75–94.

Ettinger, Shmuel, ed. *History of the Jews in Islamic Countries.* 3 vols. Jerusalem: Zalman Shazar, 1981–86. (in Hebrew)

Eventov, Yakir. *History of the Jews of Yugoslavia.* Tel Aviv: Union of Yugoslav Immigrants in Israel, 1971. (in Hebrew)

Farhi, David. "The Jews of Salonika in the Young Turk Revolution." *Sefunot*, 15 (1971–81), pp. 135–52. (in Hebrew)

Fattal, Antoine. *Le Statut légal des non-musulmans en pays d'islam.* Beirut: Imprimerie Catholique, 1958.

Feilchenfeld, A. "Anfang und Blütezeit der Portugiesengemeinde in Hamburg." *Zeitschrift des Vereins für Hamburgische Geschichte*, 10 (1899), pp. 199–240.

Ferguson, Charles A. "Diglossia." *Word*, 15 (1959), pp. 325–40.

Findley, Carter V. *Bureaucratic Reform in the Ottoman Empire: The Sublime Porte, 1789–1922.* Princeton: Princeton University Press, 1980.

Franco, Moïse. *Essai sur l'histoire des Israélites de l'Empire ottoman.* Reprint. Paris: UISF, 1981.

Frankel, Jonathan, and Steven J. Zipperstein, eds. *Assimilation and Community: The Jews in Nineteenth-Century Europe.* Cambridge: Cambridge University Press, 1992.

Freidenreich, Harriet Pass. *The Jews of Yugoslavia: A Quest for Community.* Philadelphia: The Jewish Publication Society of America, 1979.

Fresco, David. *Le Sionisme.* Istanbul: Imprimerie Fresco, 1909.

From the Tanzimat to the Republic: Encyclopaedia of Turkey. 6 vols. Istanbul: İletişim Yayınları, 1985. (in Turkish)

Galante, Avram. *Histoire des Juifs de Turquie.* 9 vols. Reprint. Istanbul: Isis, 1985.

Gampel, Benjamin, ed. *Crisis and Creativity in the Sephardic world, 1391–1648.* New York: Columbia University Press, 1997.

Gaon, Moshe David. *La Presse en judéo-espagnol: Bibliographie.* Jerusalem: Hebrew University Press, 1965. (in Hebrew)

Gelber, N. M. "An Attempt to Internationalize Salonika." *Jewish Social Studies*, 17, no. 2 (1955), pp. 105–20.

———. "Jewish Life in Bulgaria." *Jewish Social Studies*, 8 (1946), pp. 103–26.

Gelber, Yoav. "The Delegation in Istanbul at the Center of the Reaction to the Holocaust by the Jewish Settlement in Palestine." *Studies on the Holocaust Period*, 5 (1987), pp. 265–76. (in Hebrew)

Geller, Jacob. "The Economic Survival of the *Yeshivot* and *Talmudei Torah* in the Ottoman Empire." *Mimizrah Umimaarav*, 1 (1974), pp. 167–221. (in Hebrew)

Gerber, Haim. "Enterprise and International Commerce in the Economic Activity of the Jews in the Sixteenth and Seventeenth Centuries." *Zion*, 43 (1978), pp. 38–67. (in Hebrew)

————."Guilds in Seventeenth-Century Anatolian Bursa." *Asian and African Studies*, 11 (1976), pp. 59–86.

————. "Jews and Moneylending in the Ottoman Empire." *Jewish Quarterly Review*, 72 (1981), pp. 100–118.

————. "The Jews in Adrianople in the Sixteenth to Seventeenth Centuries." *Sefunot*, 3, no. 18 (1985), pp. 35–52. (in Hebrew)

————. "Jews in the Economic Life of the Anatolian City of Bursa in the Seventeenth Century." *Sefunot*, 16 (1980), pp. 235–72. (in Hebrew)

————. *The Jews of the Ottoman Empire in the Sixteenth and Seventeenth Centuries: Economy and Society*. Jerusalem: Zalman Shazar, 1982. (in Hebrew)

————. "On the History of the Jews in Istanbul in the Seventeenth and Eighteenth Centuries." *Peamim*, 12 (1982), pp. 27–46. (in Hebrew)

————. "The Sharia Archives, the Court of Bursa, as a Source for the History of the Jews in the Town." *Miqqedem Umiyyam*, 1 (1981), pp. 31–37. (in Hebrew)

Gerber, Jane S. *Jewish Society in Fez, 1450–1700: Studies in Communal and Economic Life*. Leiden: E. J. Brill, 1980.

————. *The Jews of Spain: A History of the Sephardic Experience*. New York: The Free Press, 1992.

Gerson, Frederick, and Anthony Percival, eds. *Cultural Marginality in the Western Mediterranean*. Toronto: New Aurora Editions, 1990.

Gil, B. *Pages of Immigration: Thirty Years of Immigration to Israel, 1919–1949*. Jerusalem: Jewish Agency, 1950. (in Hebrew)

Ginio, Eyal. "The Jews of Istanbul in the Quest for a National Identity in the Light of the Ladino Press." *Yahadut Zemaneynu*, 10 (1996), pp. 115–37.

Goetschel, Roland, ed. *1492: L'Expulsion des Juifs d'Espagne*. Paris: Maisonneuve et Larose, 1996.

————. *Isaac Abravanel: Conseiller des princes et philosophe (1437–1508)*. Paris: Albin Michel, 1996.

Goffman, Daniel. *Izmir and the Levantine World, 1550–1650*. Seattle: University of Washington Press, 1990.

Goldberg, Harvey E., ed. *Sephardi and Middle Eastern Jewries: History and Culture in the Modern Era*. Bloomington: Indiana University Press, 1996.

Goodblatt, Morris D. *Jewish Life in Turkey in the XVIth Century*. New York: Jewish Theological Seminary of America, 1952.

Gorelik, S. *Jüdische Köpfe*. Berlin: Fritz Gurlitt, 1920.

Griffe, Elie. *Le Languedoc cathare et l'Inquisition (1229–1329)*. Paris: Letouzey et Ané, 1980.

Gross, Nahum, ed. *Jews in Economic Life*. Jerusalem: Zalman Shazar, 1985. (in Hebrew)

von Grunebaum, Gustav. *Modern Islam: The Search for Cultural Identity*. Berkeley and Los Angeles: University of California Press, 1962.

Grunebaum-Ballin, Paul. *Joseph Naci, duc de Naxos*. Paris: Mouton, 1968.

Gutman, Israel, ed. *Encyclopedia of the Holocaust*. 4 vols. London: Macmillan, 1990.

Gutman, Israel, and Efraim Zuroff, eds. *Rescue Attempts during the Holocaust: Proceedings of the Second Yad Vashem International Historical Conference.* Jerusalem: Yad Vashem, 1977.

Hacker, Joseph. "The Chief Rabbinate in the Ottoman Empire in the Fifteenth and Sixteenth Centuries." *Zion*, 49, no. 3 (1984), pp. 225–63. (in Hebrew)

———. "The Despair of Redemption and the Messianic Expectation in the Writings of Rabbi Shlomo of the House of Halevi of Salonika." *Tarbiz*, 39, no. 2 (1970), pp. 195–213. (in Hebrew)

———. "Historic-Halakhic and Social Analysis of the Payment of the Poll Tax by Palestinian Jewish Scholars in the Sixteenth Century." *Shalem*, 4 (1984), pp. 63–117. (in Hebrew)

———. "Israel among the Nations in the Description of Rabbi Samuel of the Beit ha-Levi of Salonika." *Zion*, 34, no. 1-2 (1969), pp. 43–89. (in Hebrew)

———. "The Jewish Society of Salonika in the Fifteenth and Sixteenth Centuries: A Chapter in the History of Jewish Society in the Ottoman Empire." Unpublished doctoral thesis, Hebrew University of Jerusalem, 1978. (in Hebrew)

———. "Printing at Constantinople in the Sixteenth Century." *Areshet*, 5 (1972), pp. 457–93. (in Hebrew)

———. "Spanish Jewry's Relations with Palestine between 1391 and 1492." *Shalem*, 1 (1974), pp. 105–56. (in Hebrew)

———. "Superbe et désespoir: L'Existence sociale et sprituelle des Juifs ibériques dans l'Empire ottoman." *Revue Historique*, 578 (Apr.-June 1991), pp. 261–93.

Hacohen, Dov. "The Hebrew Press in Izmir." *Kiryat Hasefer*, 64, no. 4 (1992), pp. 1403–23. (in Hebrew)

Hadari, Zeev Vania. "National Solidarity and Rescue of Persecuted Jews." *Studies on the Holocaust Period* 5 (1987), pp. 249–63. (in Hebrew)

———. *Second Exodus: The Full Story of Jewish Illegal Immigration to Palestine, 1945–1948.* London: Vallentine Mitchell, 1991.

Haim, Abraham, ed. *Society and Community: Proceedings of the Second International Congress for Research of the Sephardi and Oriental Jewish Heritage.* Jerusalem: Misgav Yerushalayim, 1991.

Haliczer, S. "The Castilian Urban Patriciate and the Jewish Expulsion of 1480–1492." *American Historical Review*, 78 (1973), pp. 35–58.

Haskell, Guy H. *From Sofia to Jaffa: The Jews of Bulgaria and Israel.* Detroit: Wayne State University Press, 1994.

Haupt, George, and Paul Dumont. *Socialist Movements in the Ottoman Empire.* Tr. Tuğrul Artunkal. Istanbul: Gözlem Yayınları, 1977. (in Turkish)

Herculano, A. *History of the Origin and Establishment of the Inquisition in Portugal.* Tr. J. C. Branner. New York: Ktav, 1972.

Hertzberg, Arthur. *The French Enlightenment and the Jews.* New York: Columbia University Press, 1968.

Hertzig, Arno, and Saskia Rodhe, eds. *Die Juden in Hamburg 1590 bis 1990.* Hamburg: Dölling und Galitz Verlag, 1991.

Heyd, Uriel. "The Jewish Communities of Istanbul in the Seventeenth Century." *Oriens,* 6 (1953), pp. 299–314.

———. "Moses Hamon, Chief Jewish Physician to Sultan Suleyman the Magnificent." *Oriens,* 16 (1963), pp. 152–70.

Hillgarth, J. N. *The Spanish Kingdoms.* 2 vols. Oxford: Clarendon Press, 1976–78.

Hirschberg, H. Z. *A History of the Jews in North Africa.* 2 vols. Leiden: E. J. Brill, 1974–81.

Homenaje a Millas-Vallicrosa. 2 vols. Barcelona: CSIC, 1956.

Hurewitz, Jacob C., ed. *The Middle East and North Africa in World Politics: A Documentary Record.* 2 vols. 2d ed. New Haven: Yale University Press, 1975–79.

Hyamson, Albert M. "The Damascus Affair of 1840." *Transactions of the Jewish Historical Society of England,* 16 (1945–51), pp. 47–71.

Idel, Moshe. *Kabbalah: New Perspectives.* New Haven: Yale University Press, 1988.

Ilel, Joseph. "The Participation of the Bulgarian Jews in the Wars of 1885, 1912–1913 and 1915–1918." *Annual,* 22 (1987), pp. 121–76.

İnalcık, Halil. *The Ottoman Empire: The Classical Age, 1300–1600.* Tr. N. Itzkowitz and C. Imber. London: Weidenfeld and Nicolson, 1973.

———. *The Ottoman Empire: Conquest, Organization and Economy, Collected Studies.* London: Variorum Reprints, 1978.

İslamoğlu-İnan, Huri, ed. *The Ottoman Empire and the World Economy.* Cambridge and Paris: Cambridge University Press and Editions de la Maison des Sciences de l'Homme, 1987.

Israel, Jonathan I. "A Conflict of Empires: Spain and the Netherlands, 1618–1648." *Past and Present,* 76 (1977), pp. 34–47.

———. "The Economic Contribution of Dutch Sephardi Jewry to Holland's Golden Age, 1595–1713." *Tijdschrift voor Geschiedenis,* 96 (1983), pp. 505–36.

———. *European Jewry in the Age of Mercantilism, 1550–1750.* 2d ed. Oxford: Clarendon Press, 1989.

Issawi, Charles. *The Economic History of the Middle East, 1800–1914.* Chicago: University of Chicago Press, 1975.

———, ed. *The Economic History of Turkey, 1800–1914.* Chicago: University of Chicago Press, 1980.

Istanbul à la jonction des cultures balkaniques, méditerranéennes, slaves et orientales, aux XVIe–XIXe siècles. Bucharest: AIESEE, 1977.

Jabotinsky, Zeev. *Correspondence, 1898–1914.* Ed. Daniel Carpi and Moshe Halevy. Jerusalem: Jabotinsky Institute in Israel, Hasifriya Haziyonit, 1992. (in Hebrew)

Jacobson, Hanna. *Jews in the Trade Routes and the Silver Mines of Macedonia: The Jewish Communities of Serres and Sidrokapisi in the Fifteenth and Sixteenth Centuries.* Tel Aviv: Tel Aviv University, 1984. (in Hebrew)

Jelavich, Charles, and Barbara Jelavich. *The Establishment of the Balkan National States, 1804–1920.* Seattle: University of Washington Press, 1977.

Jerusalmi, Isaac. *From Ottoman Turkish to Ladino*. Cincinnati: Ladino Books, 1990.

Os Judeus Portugueses entre os Descobrimentos e a Diáspora: Catalogue of the Exhibition at the Calouste Gulbenkian Foundation in Lisbon between 21 June and 4 September 1994. Lisbon: Fundaçao Calouste Gulbenkian, 1994.

Juhasz, Esther, ed. *Sephardi Jews in the Ottoman Empire: Aspects of Material Culture.* Jerusalem: Musée d'Israël, 1990.

Kalderon, Albert E. *Abraham Galante: A Biography*. New York: Sepher Hermon Press, 1983.

Kalev, Astruc. "Data Concerning the Demographic Situation of the Bulgarian Jews." *Annual*, 16 (1981), pp. 85–96.

Kamen, Henry. "The Mediterranean and the Expulsion of Spanish Jews in 1492." *Past and Present*, 119 (1988), pp. 30–55.

———. *The Spanish Inquisition: A Historical Revision*. New Haven: Yale University Press, 1998.

Kaplan, Yosef. *From Christianity to Judaism: The Story of Isaac Orobio de Castro*. Tr. R. Loewe. Oxford: Oxford University Press, 1989.

Karabatak, Halûk. "The Events of 1934 in Thrace and the Jews." *Tarih ve Toplum*, 146 (Feb. 1996), pp. 4–16. (in Turkish)

Karmi, Ilan. *The Jewish Community of Istanbul in the Nineteenth Century: Social, Legal and Administrative Transformations*. Istanbul: Isis, 1996.

Karpat, Kemal H. "The Migratory Movements of Jews in the Ottoman Empire." *Cathedra*, 51 (1989), pp. 78–92. (in Hebrew)

———. *Ottoman Population, 1830–1914: Demographic and Social Characteristics*. Madison: University of Wisconsin Press, 1985.

Kasaba, Reşat. *The Ottoman Empire and the World Economy*. Albany: SUNY Press, 1988.

Kastoryano, Riva. "Du millet à la communauté: Les Juifs de Turquie." *Pardès*, 15 (1992), pp. 137–58.

———. "L'Intégration politique par l'extérieur: La Communauté juive de Turquie." *Revue Française de Science Politique*, 42, no. 5 (Oct. 1992), pp. 786–801.

Katz, Jacob. *Jewish Emancipation and Self-Emancipation*. Philadelphia: The Jewish Publication Society of America, 1986.

———. *Tradition and Crisis: Jewish Society at the End of the Middle Ages*. New York: Schocken Books, 1977.

———, ed. *Toward Modernity: The European Jewish Model*. New Brunswick: Transaction, 1987.

Kečkemet, Duško. *Jews in the History of Split*. N.p., 1972. (in Serbo-Croatian)

Kedourie, Elie, ed. *Spain and the Jews: The Sephardi Experience, 1492 and After*. London: Thames and Hudson, 1992.

Kellenbenz, H. *Sephardim an der unteren Elbe*. Wiesbaden: F. Steiner, 1958.

Kerem, Yizhak. "The Attempts to Save the Jews of Greece during World War II." *Peamim*, 27 (1986), pp. 77–109. (in Hebrew)

———. "The Greek-Jewish Theater in Judeo-Spanish, ca. 1880–1940." *Journal of Modern Greek Studies*, 14 (1996), pp. 31–45.

Keshales, Haim. *History of the Jews of Bulgaria*. 5 vols. Tel Aviv: Davar, 1969–73. (in Hebrew)

Klarsfeld, Serge. *Le Mémorial de la déportation des Juifs de France*. Paris: Klarsfeld, 1978.

Kohen, David, and Ljuben Zlatarov. "German Documents about the Bulgarian Jews' Deportation Policy and Its Failure." *Annual*, 17 (1982), pp. 303–30.

Kolatt, Israel, ed. *History of the Jewish Community in Palestine since 1882*. Jerusalem: Israel Academy, Bialik Institute, 1989. (in Hebrew)

Kriegel, Maurice. *Les Juifs à la fin du Moyen Age dans l'Europe méditerranéenne*. Paris: Hachette, 1979.

———. "La Prise d'une décision: L'Expulsion des Juifs d'Espagne en 1492." *Revue Historique*, 260, no. 527 (1978), pp. 49–90.

Lachman, Samuel. "Jews in the Mints of Ottoman Turkey." *Shekel*, 21, no. 2 (1988), pp. 12–15.

Lampe, John R., and Marvin R. Jackson. *Balkan Economic History, 1550–1950*. Bloomington: Indiana University Press, 1982.

Landau, Jacob M. *Tekinalp: Turkish Patriot, 1883–1961*. Leiden: Nederlands Historisch-Archaeologisch Instituut te Istanbul, 1984.

Laqueur, Walter. *A History of Zionism*. New York: Schocken, 1972.

Laskier, Michael M. *The Alliance Israélite Universelle and the Jewish Communities of Morocco, 1862–1962*. Albany: SUNY Press, 1983.

League of Nations. *Protection des minorités de langue, de race et de religion par la Société des Nations*. Geneva: League of Nations, 1927.

Lebel, Jenny. "The Extermination of the Jews of Yugoslavia: The Communities of Macedonia, Pirot, and Kosovo." *Peamim*, 27 (1986), pp. 62–74. (in Hebrew)

———. "'Longing for Jerusalem': Rabbi Judah Alcalay, the Political and Communal Context of His Activity." *Peamim*, 40 (1989), pp. 21–48. (in Hebrew)

Le Goff, Jacques. *Histoire et mémoire*. Paris: Gallimard, 1988.

Leibovici, Sarah, ed. *Chronique des Juifs de Tétouan (1860–1896)*. Paris: Maisonneuve et Larose, 1984.

———, ed. *Mosaïques de notre mémoire: Les Judéo–Espagnols du Maroc*. Paris: UISF, 1982.

Leon, George B. *The Greek Socialist Movement and the First World War: The Road to Unity*. Boulder, Colo.: East European Quarterly, 1976.

Leroy, Béatrice. *L'Aventure sépharade: De la péninsule ibérique à la Diaspora*. Paris: Albin Michel, 1986.

———. *Les Edits d'expulsion des Juifs: 1394, 1492, 1496, 1501*. Biarritz: Atlantica, 1998.

———. *L'Espagne des Torquemada: Catholiques, Juifs et convertis au XVe siècle*. Paris: Maisonneuve et Larose, 1995.

———. *L'Expulsion des Juifs d'Espagne*. Paris: Berg International, 1990.

———. *Les Juifs dans l'Espagne chrétienne avant 1492*. Paris: Albin Michel, 1993.

Leven, Narcisse. *Cinquante ans d'histoire: L'Alliance israélite universelle (1860–1910).* 2 vols. Paris: Alcan et Guillaumin, 1911–21.

Levi, Avner. "The Anti-Jewish Pogrom in Thrace, 1934." *Peamim,* 20 (1984), pp. 111–32. (in Hebrew)

———. *The Jews in the Turkish Republic.* Adapted by Rifat N. Bali. Istanbul: İletişim, 1992. (in Turkish)

———. "The Jews of Turkey on the Eve of World War II and during the War." *Peamim,* 29 (1986), pp. 32–47. (in Hebrew)

Levy, Avigdor. *The Sephardim in the Ottoman Empire.* Princeton: Darwin Press, 1992.

———, ed. *The Jews of the Ottoman Empire.* Princeton: Darwin Press, 1994.

Levy, Moritz. *Die Sephardim in Bosnien.* Sarajevo: A. Kajon, 1911.

Lewis, Bernard. *The Emergence of Modern Turkey.* 2d ed. Oxford: Oxford University Press, 1968.

———. *The Jews of Islam.* Princeton: Princeton University Press, 1984.

———. "The Privilege Granted by Mehmed II to His Physician." *Bulletin of the School of Oriental and African Studies,* 14 (1952), pp. 550–63.

———. *Semites and Antisemites: An Inquiry into Conflict and Prejudice.* New York: W. W. Norton, 1986.

Liakos, Antonis. *The Socialist Workers Organization of Thessaloniki (Federation) and Socialist Youth.* Thessaloniki: Paratiritis, 1985. (in Greek)

Loker, Zvi. "H. G. Nahmias: His Efforts for a Nationalist Awakening among the Jews of Serbia." *Peamim,* 40 (1989), pp. 49–53. (in Hebrew)

———. "Le Rabbin Juda ben Salomon Hay Alcalay et l'Alliance Israélite Universelle à propos des ses lettres inédites." *Revue des Etudes Juives,* 144, nos. 1-3 (1985), pp. 127–44.

———, ed. *Encyclopaedia of Jewish Communities: Yugoslavia.* Jerusalem: Yad Vashem, 1988. (in Hebrew)

———, ed. *History of the Jews of Yugoslavia.* 2 vols. Jerusalem, Tel Aviv and Haifa: Association of Immigrants from Yugoslavia, 1991. (in Hebrew)

Lowry, Heath. "Portrait of a City: The Population and Topography of Ottoman Selânik (Thessaloniki) in the Year 1478." *Diptykha,* 2 (1980–81), pp. 254–92.

MacKay, Angus. "The Hispanic-Converso Predicament." *Transactions of the Royal Historical Society,* 5th ser., 35 (1985), pp. 159–79.

———. "Popular Movements and Pogroms in Fifteenth-Century Castile." *Past and Present,* 55 (1972), pp. 33–67.

Maeso Gonzalo, David, and Pascal Recuero, eds. *Meam Loez, el gran comentario bíblico sefardí.* 4 vols. Madrid: Editorial Gredos, 1969–74.

Malino, Frances, and David Sorkin, eds. *From East and West: Jews in a Changing Europe, 1750–1870.* Oxford: Basil Blackwell, 1990.

Mallet, Laurent. "Caricatures of Jews in the Periodical 'Caricature' (1936–1948)." *Toplumsal Tarih,* 34 (1996), pp. 26–33. (in Turkish)

Malvezin, Théodore. *Histoire des Juifs à Bordeaux.* Bordeaux: Lefebvre, 1875.

Mandel, Neville J. "Ottoman Policy and Restrictions on Jewish Settlement in Palestine, 1881–1908." *Middle Eastern Studies*, 10, no. 3 (1974), pp. 312–32.

———. "Ottoman Practice as Regards Jewish Settlement in Palestine, 1881–1908." *Middle Eastern Studies*, 11, no. 1 (Jan. 1975), pp. 33–46.

———. "Turks, Arabs and Jewish Immigration into Palestine, 1882–1914." *St. Antony's Papers*, 17 (1965), pp. 77–108.

Mann, Vivian B., ed. *A Tale of Two Cities: Jewish Life in Frankfurt and Istanbul, 1750–1850.* New York: The Jewish Museum, 1982.

Mantran, Robert. *L'Empire ottoman du XVIe au XVIIIe siècle: Administration, économie, société.* London: Variorum Reprints, 1984.

———, ed. *Histoire de l'Empire ottoman.* Paris: Fayard, 1989.

Marcus, Simon. "Community Taxes and the Register of the Community Tax in Rhodes." *Sefunot*, 1 (1957), pp. 279–302. (in Hebrew)

———. "Contribution to the History of the Jews of Adrianople." *Sinai*, 29, nos. 7-8, 11-12 (1951), pp. 7–23, 318–44; ibid., 45, no. 13 (1959), pp. 376–86. (in Hebrew)

———. "The First Gueron Rabbis in Adrianople." *Sinai*, 35, no. 3 (1954), pp. 187–98. (in Hebrew)

———. "The History of the Rabbis of the Gueron Family of Adrianople." *Sinai*, 7-8 (1947), pp. 48–63. (in Hebrew)

Matkovski, Aleksander. "The Destruction of Macedonian Jewry in 1943." *Yad Vashem Studies*, 3 (1959), pp. 203–58.

———. *A History of the Jews in Macedonia.* Skopje: Macedonian Review Editions, 1982.

Mavrogordatos, George. *The Stillborn Republic: Social Conditions and Party Strategies in Greece, 1922–1936.* Berkeley and Los Angeles: University of California Press, 1983.

Mazower, Mark. *Inside Hitler's Greece: The Experience of Occupation, 1941–44.* New Haven: Yale University Press, 1993.

———. "Military Violence and National Socialist Values: The *Wehrmacht* in Greece, 1941–1944." *Past and Present*, 134 (1992), pp. 129–58.

———. "Salonica between East and West, 1860–1912." *Dialogos*, 1 (1994), pp. 104–27.

Méchoulan, Henry. *Amsterdam au temps de Spinoza: Argent et liberté.* Paris: PUF, 1990.

———. *Etre Juif à Amsterdam au temps de Spinoza.* Paris: Albin Michel, 1991.

———. "The Jewish Community of Amsterdam in the Seventeenth Century." *Peamim*, 48 (1991), pp. 104–16. (in Hebrew)

———, ed. *Les Juifs d'Espagne: Histoire d'une diaspora, 1492–1992.* Paris: Liana Levi, 1992.

Mehlman, Israel. "Contribution to the History of Printing in Salonika." *Sefunot*, 13 (1971–78), pp. 215–72. (in Hebrew)

Melammed, Renée Levine. *Heretics or Daughters of Israel? The Crypto-Jewish Women of Castile.* Oxford: Oxford University Press, 1999.

Mevorakh, Barukh. "The Damascus Libel and the Activity of Jewry to End It." *Skira Hodshit*, 27, no. 5 (1980), pp. 37–42. (in Hebrew)

———. "The Role of the Damascus Libel in the Development of the Jewish Press in the Years 1840–1846." *Zion*, 23-24 (1958–59), pp. 47–65. (in Hebrew)

Meyuhas, Ginio Alisa, ed. *Jews, Christians, and Muslims in the Mediterranean World after 1492.* London: Frank Cass, 1992.

Mézan, Saul. *Les Juifs espagnols en Bulgarie.* Sofia: Imprimerie Hamishpat, 1925.

Milano, Attilo. *Storia degli Ebrei italiani nel Levante.* Florence: n.p., 1959.

Molho, Michael. *Contribution to the History of Salonika.* Thessaloniki: Akuaroni and Behar, 5692/1932. (in Judeo-Spanish)

———. *Literatura Sefardita de Oriente.* Madrid, Barcelona: CSIC, Instituto Arias Montano, 1960.

———. *Le Meam Loez, encyclopédie populaire du sépharadisme levantin.* Thessaloniki: n.p., 1945.

———. "R. Moses Almosnino: His Life, His Works." *Sinai,* 10 (1942). Offprint, 23 pages. (in Hebrew)

———. "R. Moses Almosnino, the Savior of the Community of Salonika in the Sixteenth Century." *Sinai,* 8 (1941). Offprint, 12 pages. (in Hebrew)

———. "The Rabbi Samuel de Medina." *Sinai,* 41, no. 1 (1957), pp. 36–58. (in Hebrew)

———. "Regulations on the Renting of Houses, Courtyards, and Shops." *Sinai,* 14, no. 5-6 (1951), pp. 296–314. (in Hebrew)

———. "The Sage Jacob Houlli, One of the Great Judeo-Spanish Writers, Author of the *Meam Loez*: His Family, His Life, His Times." *Tesoro de los Judíos Sefardíes,* 5 (1962), pp. 80–94.

Molho, Michael, and Joseph Néhama. *In Memoriam: Hommage aux victimes juives des Nazis en Grèce.* 2 vols. Thessaloniki: Salonique, 1948. (2d ed. 1988)

Molho, Rena. "The Jewish Community of Salonika and Its Incorporation into the Greek State." *Middle Eastern Studies,* 24, no. 4 (1988), pp. 291–403.

———. "Les Juifs de Salonique, 1856–1919: Une Communauté hors norme." Unpublished doctoral thesis, Université des Sciences Humaines de Strasbourg, 1997.

———. "Popular Antisemitism and State Policy in Salonika during the City's Annexation to Greece." *Jewish Social Studies,* 50, no. 3-4 (summer-fall 1988–93), pp. 253–64.

———. "Salonique après 1912: Les Propagandes étrangères et la communauté juive." *Revue Historique,* 581 (1992), pp. 127–40.

———. "Venizelos and the Jewish Community of Salonika." *Journal of the Hellenic Diaspora,* 13, no. 3-4 (1986), pp. 113–23.

Molho, Yizhak R. "Anthology of Regulations in Ladino in Salonika." *Sefunot,* 2 (1958), pp. 26–60. (in Hebrew)

———. "The Community of Salonika in the Seventeenth Century." *Tesoro de los Judíos Sefardíes,* 2 (1959), pp. 31–42. (in Hebrew)

———. "*The Language of Truth* Society, the First Association for the Oral Practice and Teaching of the Hebrew Language in Salonika at the End of the Nineteenth Century." *Tesoro de los Judíos Sefardíes,* 9 (1966), pp. 106–8. (in Hebrew)

———. "La Littérature judéo-espagnole en Turquie au premier siècle après les expulsions d'Espagne et du Portugal." *Tesoro de los Judíos Sefardíes,* 1 (1959), pp. 15–53.

————. "Moise Barouh Almosnino (1518–1581)." *Tesoro de los Judíos Sefardíes*, 7 (1964), pp. xlix–lxviii.

————. *Salonika Sailors in Israel*. Jerusalem: n.p., 1951. (in Hebrew)

————. "Trois séphardis, trois précurseurs de l'Etat juif: Moses Montefiore, Juda Bibas, Juda Alcalay." *Tesoro de los Judíos Sefardíes*, 8 (1965), pp. xv–xxvii.

Morgenstern, Arie. "Between Rabbi Judah Bibas and an Emissary of the *Prushim* of Jerusalem." *Peamim*, 40 (1989), pp. 156–59. (in Hebrew)

Moscona, Isaac. "On Some Historic Moments of Judaism in Bulgaria and in Balkan Lands." Unpublished manuscript. Sofia: 1980. (in Judeo-Spanish)

————. "On the Social Polarization of the Bulgarian Jews." *Annual*, 17 (1982), pp. 99–113.

Moutsopoulos, N. K. *Thessaloniki, 1900–1917*. Thessaloniki: Molho Publications, 1981.

Nahmias, Berri. *Cry for Tomorrow*. Athens: Katkos, 1989. (in Greek)

Nahon, Gérard. "Inscriptions funéraires hébraïques et juives à Bidache, Labastide-Clairence (Basses-Pyrénées) et Peyrehorade (Landes)." *Revue des Etudes Juives*, 127-28 (1968–69), pp. 347–75.

————. *Métropoles et périphéries séfarades d'Occident*. Paris: Cerf, 1993.

————. *Les "Nations" juives portugaises du sud-ouest de la France (1648–1791): Documents*. Paris: Fondation C. Gulbenkian, 1981.

Nahon, Marco. *Birkenau*. Tuscaloosa: University of Alabama Press, 1989.

Nahum, Henri. *Juifs de Smyrne, XIXe–XXe siècle*. Paris: Aubier, 1997.

Nathan, Naphtali. "Notes on the Jews of Turkey." *Jewish Journal of Sociology*, 16, no. 2 (1964), pp. 172–89.

Natsaris, Marcel. *Chronicle, 1941–1945*. Thessaloniki: Ets Haim, 1991. (in Greek)

Néhama, Joseph. *Histoire des Israélites de Salonique*. 7 vols. Paris and Thessaloniki: Durlacher and Molho, 1935–78.

Nehama, Yuda. *Correspondence*. 2 vols. Thessaloniki: Bezez, 1844–92. (in Hebrew)

————. *A Happy Memory; or, The Biography of the Very Famous Scholar and Philanthropist Abraham Cohen, Called Dr. Albert Cohn*. Thessaloniki: n.p., 1877. (in Judeo-Spanish)

Netanyahu, Benzion. *Don Isaac Abravanel, Statesman and Philosopher*. 3d ed. Philadelphia: The Jewish Publication Society of America, 1972.

————. *The Marranos of Spain from the Late XIVth to the Late XVIth Century according to Contemporary Hebrew Sources*. New York: American Academy for Jewish Research, 1966.

————. *The Origins of the Inquisition in Fifteenth-Century Spain*. New York: Random House, 1995.

Nirenberg, David. *Communities of Violence: Persecution of Minorities in the Middle Ages*. Princeton: Princeton University Press, 1996.

Novitch, Myriam. "End of Macedonia and Thrace Jewish Communities." *Tesoro de los Judíos Sefardíes*, 4 (1961), pp. liv–lvi.

Ofer, Dalia. *Escaping the Holocaust: Illegal Immigration to the Land of Israel, 1939–1944*. Oxford: Oxford University Press, 1990.

Ökte, Faik. *The Disaster of the Wealth Tax*. Istanbul: Nebioğlu Yayınları, 1951. (in Turkish)

Oliver, Khaim. *We Were Saved: How the Jews in Bulgaria Were Kept from the Death Camps.* Tr. V. Izmirliev. Sofia: Sofia-Press, 1978.

Olson, Robert W. "Jews in the Ottoman Empire in Light of New Documents." *Tarih Enstitüsü Dergisi*, 7-8 (1976-77), pp. 119-44.

———. "Jews in the Ottoman Empire in the Light of New Documents." *Jewish Social Studies*, 41 (1979), pp. 75-88.

Oren, Nissan. "The Bulgarian Exception: A Reassessment of the Salvation of the Jewish Community." *Yad Vashem Studies*, 7 (1968), pp. 83-106.

Oschlies, Wolf. *Bulgarien, Land ohne Antisemitismus.* Erlangen: Ner-Tamid-Verlag, 1976.

Palmor, Sarah. "A Zionist Appeal in Rumania, 1881." *Arkhiyon*, 5 (1991), pp. 36-48. (in Hebrew)

Pamuk, Şevket. *The Ottoman Empire and European Capitalism.* Cambridge: Cambridge University Press, 1987.

Panova, Snezhka. "L'Activité économique des Juifs dans les Balkans aux XVIe et XVIIe siècles." *Annual*, 1 (1966), pp. 195-96. (summary in French)

———. "The Development of the Textile Industry in the Balkan Countries and the Role of the Jewish Population in the XVIth-XVIIth Centuries." *Annual*, 11 (1976), pp. 123-40.

———. "On the Social Differentiation of the Jewish Population in the Bulgarian Lands during the XVIth-XVIIIth Centuries." *Annual*, 12 (1977), pp. 135-45.

Papo, José. *En attendant l'aurore: Activité de la communauté séphardite de Paris pendant l'Occupation, 1940-1945.* Paris: n.p., 1945.

Perahia, Leon. *Mazal: Recollections of Death Camps (1943-1945).* Thessaloniki: n.p., 1990. (in Greek)

Peters, Edward. *Heresy and Authority in Medieval Europe.* Philadelphia: University of Pennsylvania Press, 1980.

———. *Inquisition.* New York: The Free Press, 1988.

Pierron, Bernard. *Juifs et chrétiens de la Grèce moderne.* Paris: L'Harmattan, 1996.

Pinkus, Benjamin, ed. *East European Jewry: From the Holocaust to the Redemption, 1944-1948.* Beer-Sheva: Ben-Gurion University of the Negev, 1987. (in Hebrew)

Pinto, Avram. *The Jews of Sarajevo and of Bosnia-Herzegovina.* Sarajevo: Veselin Maslesa, 1987. (in Serbo-Croatian)

Plaut, Joshua Eli. *Greek Jewry in the Twentieth Century, 1913-1983: Patterns of Jewish Survival in the Greek Provinces before and after the Holocaust.* Madison and London: Fairleigh Dickinson University Press and Associated University Presses, 1996.

Polk, William R., and Richard L. Chambers, eds. *Beginnings of Modernization in the Middle East: The Nineteenth Century.* Chicago: University of Chicago Press, 1968.

Porat, Dina. "The Jews of Greece: An Example of the Link between Conscience and Rescue during the Period of the Holocaust." *Dapim Leheker Tkufat Hashoa*, 8 (1990), pp. 123-34. (in Hebrew)

Proceedings of the Conference on "The Foreign Language Press in Turkey," 16-18 May 1984. Istanbul: Istanbul University Press, 1985.

Proceedings of the Eighth World Congress of Jewish Studies. Division B. Jerusalem: World Union of Jewish Studies, 1982.

Proceedings of the Ninth World Congress of Jewish Studies. Vol. III. Jerusalem: World Union of Jewish Studies, 1986.

Proceedings of the Sixth World Congress of Jewish Studies. Vol. II. Jerusalem: World Union of Jewish Studies, 1972.

Pullan, Brian. *The Jews of Europe and the Inquisition of Venice, 1560–1670.* Oxford: Basil Blackwell, 1983.

Rapoport-Albert, Ada, and Steven J. Zipperstein, eds. *Essays in Honour of Chimen Abramsky.* London: Weidenfeld and Nicholson, 1989.

Recanati, David, ed. *Memorial to Salonika.* 2 vols. Tel Aviv: Committee for the Publication of Books on the Salonika Community, 1971–86. (in Hebrew, Judeo-Spanish, and French)

Regev, Shaul. "The Rabbi Samuel de Medina." *Mehkerei Yerushalayim bemahshevet Yisrael,* 5 (1986), pp. 155–89. (in Hebrew)

Reinharz, Jehuda, ed. *Living with Antisemitism: Modern Jewish Responses.* Hanover: University Press of New England, 1987.

Renard, Raymond. *Sepharad: Le Monde et la langue judéo-espagnole des Séphardim.* Mons: Annales Universitaires de Mons, 1966.

Révah, I. S. "Les Marranes." *Revue des Etudes Juives,* 118 (1959–60), pp. 29–77.

Rivlin, Braha, ed. *Encyclopaedia of Jewish Communities: Greece.* Jerusalem: Yad Vashem, 1998. (in Hebrew)

Rochlitz, Joseph. "Excerpts from the Salonika Diary of Lucillo Merci (February-August 1943)." *Yad Vashem Studies,* 18 (1987), pp. 293–323.

Rodrigue, Aron. "'Difference and Tolerance' in the Ottoman Empire." Interview by Nancy Reynolds. *Stanford Humanities Review,* 5 (fall 1995), pp. 81–92.

———. *French Jews, Turkish Jews: The Alliance Israélite Universelle and the Politics of Jewish Schooling in Turkey.* Bloomington: Indiana University Press, 1990.

———. *Images of Sephardi and Eastern Jewries in Transition, 1860–1939: The Teachers of the Alliance Israélite Universelle.* Seattle: University of Washington Press, 1993.

———. "Jewish Society in a Thracian Town: The Alliance Israélite Universelle in Demotica, 1897–1924." *Jewish Social Studies,* 45, no. 3-4 (1983), pp. 263–86.

———, ed. *Guide to the Ladino Materials in the Harvard College Library.* Cambridge, Mass.: Harvard College Library, 1992.

———, ed. *Ottoman and Turkish Jewry: Community and Leadership.* Indiana University Turkish Studies Series. Bloomington: Indiana University Press, 1992.

Rofeh, Yizhak. "Benevolent Society of the Boat Owners in Constantinople." *Sefunot,* 10 (1966), pp. 621–32. (in Hebrew)

Romano, A., and Lévy (Buko) Nissim Ben Joseph, eds. *Encyclopaedia of the Jewish Diaspora: Bulgarian Jewry.* Vol. X. Jerusalem and Tel Aviv: Encyclopaedia of the Jewish Diaspora Editions, 1967. (in Hebrew)

Romano, Jasa. *Jews of Yugoslavia, 1941–1945.* Belgrade: Savez Jevrejskih Opstina Jugoslavije, 1980. (in Serbo-Croatian)

Romero, Elena. *La Creación literaria en lengua sefardí*. Madrid: Editorial MAPFRE, 1992.

————. *El Teatro de los sefardíes orientales*. 3 vols. Madrid: CSIC, 1979.

Rosa, Jacob da Silva. "Additions to 'The Catalogue of Judeo-Spanish Books' of A. Yaari." *Kiryat Sefer*, 13 (Apr. 1936), pp. 131–37. (in Hebrew)

Rosanvallon, Pierre. *L'État en France de 1789 à nos jours*. Paris: Seuil, 1990.

Roth, Cecil. *Doña Gracia of the House of Nasi*. Philadelphia: The Jewish Publication Society of America, 1948.

————. *The House of Nasi: The Duke of Naxos*. Philadelphia: The Jewish Publication Society of America, 1948.

————. "Neue Kunde von der Marranen-Gemeinde in Hamburg." *Zeitschrift für die Geschichte der Juden in Deutschland*, 2 (1930), pp. 228–36.

Roth, Norman Denis. *Conversos, Inquisition and the Expulsion of the Jews of Spain*. Madison: University of Wisconsin Press, 1995.

Rozanes, Salomon A. *History of the Jews of Turkey and of the Middle East*. 6 vols. Tel Aviv and Sofia: Devir, Rav Kook Institute, Husijatin, 1907–45. (in Hebrew)

Rozen, Minna. "The Activities of Influential Jews at the Sultan's Court in Istanbul in Support of the Jewish Settlement of Jerusalem in the Seventeenth Century." *Michael*, 43 (1982), pp. 394–430. (in Hebrew)

————. "Contest and Rivalry in Mediterranean Maritime Commerce in the First Half of the Eighteenth Century: The Jews of Salonica and the European Presence." *Revue des Etudes Juives*, 147 (1988), pp. 309–52.

————. "The Fattoria: A Chapter in the History of Mediterranean Commerce in the Sixteenth and Seventeenth Centuries." *Miqqedem Umiyyam*, 1 (1981), pp. 104–10. (in Hebrew)

————. *Hasköy Cemetery: Typology of Stones*. Tel Aviv and Philadelphia: Diaspora Research Institute, Tel Aviv University, and Center for Judaic Studies, University of Pennsylvania, 1994.

————. "The Livornese Jewish Merchants in Tunis and the Commerce with Marseilles at the End of the Seventeenth Century." *Michael*, 9 (1985), pp. 87–129. (in Hebrew)

————, ed. *The Days of the Crescent: Contributions to the History of the Jews of the Ottoman Empire*. Tel Aviv: Tel Aviv University, 1996. (in Hebrew)

Ruckhaberle, Dieter, and Christiane Ziesecke, eds. *Rettung der bulgarischen Juden, 1943: Eine Dokumentation*. Berlin: Publica, 1984.

Sachar, Howard Morley. *Farewell España: The World of the Sephardim Remembered*. New York: Knopf, 1994.

Salonika, Mother City in Israel. Jerusalem and Tel Aviv: Center for Research into Salonikan Jewry, 1967. (in Hebrew)

Salvator, Israel. "La Presse périodique juive en ladino et en *ivrit* (hébreu) en Bulgarie." *Annual*, 2 (1967), pp. 276–77. (summary in French)

————. "Salomon Avraam Rozanes, Originator of the Historiography of the Bulgarian Jews (1860–1938)." *Annual*, 19 (1984), pp. 343–71.

Saperstein, Marc. "Martyrs, Merchants and Rabbis: Jewish Communal Conflict as

Reflected in the Responsa on the Boycott of Ancona." *Jewish Social Studies*, 43, no. 3-4 (1981), pp. 215–28.

Schama, Simon. *The Embarrassment of Riches*. New York: Knopf, 1987.

Schaub, Jean-Frédéric. *Les Juifs du roi d'Espagne, Oran, 1509–1669*. Paris: Hachette, 1999.

Schechtman, Joseph B., and Benari, Yehuda. *History of the Revisionist Movement*. Vol. I. Tel Aviv: Hadar, 1970. (in Hebrew)

Schevil, Ferdinand. *A History of the Balkans*. New York: Dorset Press, 1991.

Scholem, Gershom G. *Major Trends in Jewish Mysticism*. New York: Schocken, 1961.

———. *The Messianic Idea in Judaism and Other Essays*. New York: Schocken, 1971.

———. *On the Kaballah and Its Symbolism*. New York: Schocken, 1965.

———. *Sabbatai Sevi: The Mystical Messiah, 1626–1676*. Princeton: Princeton University Press, 1977.

Schopoff, A. *Les Réformes et la protection des Chrétiens en Turquie, 1673–1904*. Paris: Plon-Nourrit, 1904.

Schorsch, Ismar. "The Myth of Sephardic Supremacy." *Leo Baeck Institute Year Book*, 34 (1989), pp. 47–66.

Schwarzfuchs, Simon. "La Décadence de la Galilée juive du XVIe siècle et la crise du textile au Proche-Orient." *Revue des Etudes Juives*, 121 (1962), pp. 169–79.

———. *Les Juifs d'Algérie et la France (1830–1855)*. Jerusalem: Ben Zvi Institute, 1981.

———. "The Salonika Scale: The Struggle between the French and Jewish Merchants." *Sefunot*, 15 (1971–78), pp. 77–102. (in Hebrew)

———, ed. *L'"Alliance" et les communautés du bassin méditerranéen à la fin du XIXe siècle et son influence sur la situation sociale et culturelle*. Jerusalem: Misgav Yerushalayim, 1987.

Şeni, Nora, and Sophie Le Tarnec. *Les Camondos ou l'éclipse d'une fortune*. Arles: Actes Sud, 1997.

Sephiha, Haim Vidal. *L'Agonie des Judéo-Espagnols*. Paris: Entente, 1977.

———. *Le Judéo-espagnol*. Paris: Entente, 1986.

———. *Le Ladino, judéo-espagnol calque: Deutéronome, versions de Constantinople 1547 et Ferrare 1553*. Paris: Institut d'Etudes Hispaniques, 1973.

———. *Le Ladino (judéo-espagnol calque): Structure et évolution d'une langue liturgique*. 2 vols. Paris: Association Vidas Largas, 1979.

Sevilla-Sharon, Moshe. *The Jews of Turkey*. Istanbul: İletişim Yayınları, 1992. (in Turkish)

Shapira, Anita, ed. *Illegal Immigration*. Tel Aviv: Am Oved, 1990. (in Hebrew)

Shaw, Stanford J. *The Jews of the Ottoman Empire and the Turkish Republic*. New York: New York University Press, 1991.

———. "The Population of Istanbul in the Nineteenth Century." *Türk Tarih Dergisi*, 32 (1979), pp. 403–14.

———. *Turkey and the Holocaust: Turkey's Role in Rescuing Turkish and European Jewry from Nazi Persecution, 1933–1945*. New York: New York University Press, 1993.

Shaw, Stanford J., and Ezel Kural Shaw. *History of the Ottoman Empire and Modern Turkey*. 2 vols. Cambridge: Cambridge University Press, 1976–77.

Shealtiel, Shlomo. "The Foundation of the Poalei Zion Party in Bulgaria and Her Organ *Probuda* (1910–1912)." Unpublished M.A. thesis, Tel Aviv University, 1988. (in Hebrew)

Shelah, Menahem. *Blood Account: The Rescue of Croatian Jews by the Italians.* Tel Aviv: Sifriyat Poalim, 1986. (in Hebrew)

———. "The Extermination of the Jews of Yugoslavia: The Communities in Serbia and in Croatia." *Peamim*, 27 (1986). (in Hebrew)

———. "Sajmiste: An Extermination Camp in Serbia." *Holocaust and Genocide Studies*, 2 (1987), pp. 243–60.

———, ed. *History of the Holocaust: Yugoslavia.* Jerusalem: Yad Vashem, 1990. (in Hebrew)

Shmuelevitz, Aryeh. "Capsali as a Source for Ottoman History, 1450–1523." *International Journal of Middle East Studies*, 9 (1978), pp. 339–41.

———. *The Jews of the Ottoman Empire in the Late Fifteenth and Sixteenth Centuries: Administrative, Economic, Legal, and Social Relations as Reflected in the Responsa.* Leiden: E. J. Brill, 1984.

Shneidman, Jerome L. "Jews as Royal Bailiffs in Thirteenth-Century Aragon." *Historia Judaica*, 19 (1957), pp. 55–66.

Shohat, Azriel. "The King's Cloth in Salonika." *Sefunot*, 12 (1971–78), pp. 169–88. (in Hebrew)

———. "Notes on the Communal Organization of the Jews in the Ottoman Empire in the Sixteenth Century." *Miqqedem Umiyyam*, 1 (1981), pp. 133–37. (in Hebrew)

———. "The Taxation System and Leadership in the Communities of Greece in the Sixteenth Century." *Sefunot*, 11, no. 1 (1971–78), pp. 301–39. (in Hebrew)

Sicroff, Albert A. *Les Controverses des statuts de pureté de sang en Espagne du XVe au XVIIe siècle.* Paris: Didier, 1960.

———. "The Marranos—Forced Converts or Apostates?" *Midstream*, 12 (1966), pp. 71–75.

Soferman, Jacqueline. "Anti-Jewish Legislation in Bulgaria, 1940–1942, and the Reactions That It Engendered." *Peamim*, 27 (1986), pp. 143–68. (in Hebrew)

Sokolow, Nahum. *History of Zionism, 1600–1918.* 2 vols. London: Longmans, Green, 1919.

Stanellos, Leonidas. *The Jewish Quarter of Corfu: History, Urbanism.* Athens: Central Committee of Jewish Communities of Greece, 1991. (in Greek)

Starr, Joshua. "The Socialist Federation of Salonica." *Jewish Social Studies*, 7 (1945), pp. 323–36.

Steinberg, Jonathan. *All or Nothing: The Axis and the Holocaust, 1941–1943.* London: Routledge, 1990.

Stern, Menahem, ed. *The Nation and Its History.* Jerusalem: Zalman Shazar, 1983. (in Hebrew)

Stillman, Norman. *Sephardi Religious Responses to Modernity.* London: Harwood, 1996.

Stillman, Norman, and Yedida Stillman. *From Iberia to Diaspora: Studies in Sephardic History and Culture.* Leiden: E. J. Brill, 1999.

Stillman, Yedida, and George Zucker, eds. *New Horizons in Sephardic Studies.* Albany: SUNY Press, 1993.

Stoianovich, Traian. "The Conquering Balkan Orthodox Merchant." *Journal of Economic History*, 20 (1960), pp. 234–313.

Studemund-Halévy, Michael. *Die Sefardien in Hamburg: Zur Geschichte einer Minderheit.* 2 vols. Hamburg: Buske, 1994–97.

Szajkowski, Zosa. "Trade Relations of the Marranos in France with the Iberian Peninsula in the Sixteenth and Seventeenth Centuries." *Jewish Quarterly Review*, 50 (1959–60), pp. 69–78.

Tadić, Jorjo. *The Jews in Dubrovnik up to the Mid-Seventeenth Century.* Sarajevo: La Benevolencia, 1937. (in Serbo-Croatian)

Tamir, Vicki. *Bulgaria and Her Jews: The History of a Dubious Symbiosis.* New York: Sepher Hermon Press, 1979.

Tavares, M. J. Pimenta Ferro. *Os Judeus em Portugal no século xv.* 2 vols. Lisbon: Universidad Nova de Lisboa, 1982–84.

Tirosh-Rothschild, Hava. *Between Worlds: The Life and Thought of Rabbi David ben Judah Messer Leon.* Albany: SUNY Press, 1991.

Toaff, Ariel, and Simon Schwarzfuchs, eds. *The Mediterranean and the Jews: Banking, Finance and International Trade (XVIth–XVIIIth Centuries).* Ramat Gan: Bar-Ilan University Press, 1989.

Toprak, Zafer. "The Role Played by the Government and the Republican People's Party in the Events of Thrace." *Toplumsal Tarih*, 34 (Oct. 1996), pp. 19–25. (in Turkish)

Tousimis, Georgios. "The Absence of a Chief Rabbi within the Jewish Community of Salonika in the Interwar Period and Its Consequences." *History*, 2 (1990), pp. 109–20. (in Greek)

Trigano, Shmuel, ed. *La Société juive à travers l'histoire.* 4 vols. Paris: Fayard, 1992–93.

Tritton, A. S. *The Caliphs and Their Non-Muslim Subjects: A Critical Study of the Covenant of Umar.* London: Humphrey Milford, 1930.

Tsur, Yaron. "France and the Jews of Tunisia: The Policy of the French Authorities toward the Jews and the Activities of the Jewish Elites during the Period of Transition from an Independent Muslim State to the Colonial Regime, 1873–1888." Unpublished doctoral thesis, Hebrew University of Jerusalem, 1988. (in Hebrew)

Tsvjatkov, Nikolai. "Education among the Bulgarian Jews towards the end of the 19th Century and the Beginning of the 20th Century." *Annual*, 15 (1980), pp. 103–14.

Twersky, Isadore, and Bernard Septimus, eds. *Jewish Thought in the Seventeenth Century.* Cambridge, Mass.: Harvard University Press, 1987.

Ubicini, A., and Pavet de Courteille. *Etat présent de l'Empire ottoman.* Paris: J. Dumoisne, 1876.

Uziel, Barukh, ed. *Salonikan Archives.* Tel Aviv: Center for Research into Salonikan Jewry, 1961. (in Hebrew)

Uziel, Yosef ben Pinhas. *The White Tower: The Life of the Jews of Salonika.* N.p.: The Institute for Research on Salonikan Jewry, n.d. (in Hebrew)

Vasiley, Kuncho. "The Idea about the Equality of the Nations in the Bulgarian National Liberation Revolution and the Bulgarian Jews." *Annual*, 13 (1978), pp. 15–27.

Veinstein, Gilles. "Sur la draperie juive de Salonique (XVIe–XVIIe siècles)." *Revue du Monde Musulman et de la Méditerranée*, 66 (1992), pp. 55–62.

———, ed. *Salonique, 1850–1918: La "Ville des Juifs" et le réveil des Balkans*. Paris: Autrement, 1992.

Vinshel, Yaakov. *Marco Barukh*. Jerusalem: Shakmona, 1981. (in Hebrew)

Weiker, Walter. *Ottomans, Turks and the Jewish Polity: A History of the Jews of Turkey*. Lanham and New York: University Press of America and The Jerusalem Center for Public Affairs, 1992.

———. *The Unseen Israelis: The Jews from Turkey in Israel*. Lanham and New York: University Press of America and The Jerusalem Center for Public Affairs, 1988.

Weill, Georges. "Emancipation et humanisme: Le Discours idéologique de l'Alliance Israélite Universelle au XIXᵉ siècle." *Nouveaux Cahiers*, 52 (1978), pp. 1–20.

Werblowsky, R. J. Zwi. *Joseph Caro, Lawyer and Mystic*. Oxford: Oxford University Press, 1982.

Wolff, Philip. "The 1391 Pogroms in Spain: Social Crisis or Not?" *Past and Present*, 50 (1971), pp. 4–18.

Yaari, Abraham. *Catalogue of Books in Judeo-Spanish*. Jerusalem: Hebrew University, 1934. (in Hebrew)

———. *Hebrew Printing in Constantinople*. Jerusalem: Magnes Press, 1967. (in Hebrew)

———. *Hebrew Printing in the Middle East*. Jerusalem: Hebrew University, 1936. (in Hebrew)

Yahil, Leni. *The Holocaust: The Fate of European Jewry*. Oxford: Oxford University Press, 1990.

Yerushalmi, Yosef Hayim. *From Spanish Court to Italian Ghetto: Isaac Cardoso, a Study in Seventeenth-Century Marranism and Jewish Apologetics*. 3 vols. 2d ed. New York: Columbia University Press, 1971.

———. "The Inquisition and the Jews of France in the Time of Bernard Gui," *Harvard Theological Review*, 63 (1970), pp. 317–76.

———. *A Jewish Classic in the Portuguese Language*. 2 vols. Lisbon: Fundaçao Calouste Gulbenkian, 1989.

———. *The Lisbon Massacre of 1506 and the Royal Image in the Shebet Yehudah*. Cincinnati: Hebrew Union College, Jewish Institute of Religion, 1976.

———. *Sefardica: Essais sur l'histoire des Juifs, des Marranes et des Nouveaux-Chrétiens d'origine hispano-portugaise*. Paris: Chandeigne, 1998.

———. *Zakhor: Jewish History and Jewish Memory*. Seattle: University of Washington Press, 1982.

Yetkin, Çetin. *The Jews in the Life of the Turkish State*. Istanbul: Afa Yayınları, 1992. (in Turkish)

Young, G. *Corps de droit ottoman*. 2 vols. Oxford: Clarendon Press, 1905.

Zafrani, Haim. *Juifs d'Andalousie et du Maghreb*. Paris: Maisonneuve et Larose, 1996.

———. *Mille ans de vie juive au Maroc: Histoire et culture, religion et magie*. Paris: Maisonneuve et Larose, 1983.

Index of Names and Places

Aba, Isaac Judah, 63
Abdulhamid II (sultan of Ottoman Empire), 71, 121–2
Abenaish, Salomon, 14
Abner of Burgos, xxxi
Aboab, Isaac, 63
Abravanel, Isaac, xxx, xxxiii, xxxvi, 55
Abravanel family, 43
Abud, Nissim Moses, 64
Aciman family, 48
Acre, 34
Adrianople see Edirne
Africa, 185; see also North Africa
Alatun family, 49
Albala, Jacques, 167
Albania, 9, 58
Albo, Joseph, xxxiii
Aleichem, Shalom, 111
Aleppo, xx, 15, 46
Alexandria, xx
Alexandropolis (Dedeağaç), 176
Alfonso of Valladolid, xxxi
Alfonso V, xxxiii
Alfonso VI, xxviii
Algeria, lii, liii, 74
Ali, Mohammed (viceroy of Egypt), 73
Alkabez, Shlomoh Ha-Levi, 54
Alkalay, Judah, 117
Alkalay family, 92
Allatini, Moïse, 76–7
Allatini family, 81
Almosnino, Moses Barukh, 52, 53, 55, 61

Amaragi, Isaac, 63
Americas, xix, 43, 98; see also United States
Amsterdam xviii, xix, xliii, xlvii–xlviii, l, li, lii, 47
Anatolia, 5, 6, 20, 97; see also Turkey
Ancona, xliv, xlv, 9, 43
Al-Andalus, xxvi
Andalusia, xxxvii
Ankara, 163, 202n
Antwerp, xlviii, l
Aquinas, Thomas, 53
Aragon, xxvi, xxvii, xxix, xxx, xxxi, xxxiii, xxxiv
Arama, Meir, 52
Arditi, Benjamin, 153
Argentina, 185
Arguete, Isaac, 63
Arié family, 48
Arta, 14, 171
Asa, Abraham, 63
Asch, Sholem, 111
Asher, Jacob ben, 50
Ashkenazi, Isaac Luria, 54
Ashkenazi, Salomon, 38
Asia Minor, xix, xx, 5, 43, 45, 47
Askale, 183
Asseo, Chief Rabbi David, 102
Athens, 166, 167, 168, 169, 170–2, 202n
Atilhan, Cevat Rifat, 162
Auschwitz–Birkenau, 168, 169, 171
Austria, 69

Austria-Hungary, 25, 66, 67, 79, 91–2, 143, 164
Avigdor, Chief Rabbi Jacob, 77–8

Ba'al Shem Tov, 238n
Balat (Jewish district in Istanbul), 183
Banat, 257n
Barcelona, xxxi
Barlas, Haim, 180
Baron de Hirsch (district in Salonika), 168
Barrientos, Fray Lope de, xxxiv
Barukh, Iako, 177
Barukh, Marco, 118, 119–20
Barzilai, Chief Rabbi Eliahu, 170–1
Basel, 117, 135
Batchka, Barania, 257n
Bavaria, 5
Baviera, La (Jewish district in Sofia), 5
Bayezid II (sultan of Ottoman Empire), 7, 8
Bayonne, xlv, xlvi, xlvii
Beckerle, Adolf, 175
Beirut, 81
Beit Ha-Levi, Salomon Le-, 52, 55
Beit Ha-Levi family, 49
Beit Hanan, 190
Bejerano, Chief Rabbi Haim, 102
Belev, Aleksandur, 163, 174–7, 178
Belgian Congo, 185
Belgium, 185
Belgrade, 9, 25, 33, 89–90, 91–2, 144, 147, 149, 165, 189
Ben Banvenest family, 49
Benaroya, Abraham, 155, 156
Benveniste, Abraham, xxxiii
Benveniste, Chief Rabbi Haim, 57
Benveniste, Raphael Isaac Meir, 63
Berav, Rabbi Jacob, 51, 56
Bergen-Belsen, 169
Berlin, 90, 177
Bessarabia, 130
Bibas, Judah, 117
Bitola see Monastir
Bordeaux xvi, xvii, xlv, xlvi, xlvii, xlix
Boris III (king of Bulgaria), 173, 176, 177, 178
Bosnia, xix, 42, 81, 113, 146–7, 164, 172
Bosnia-Herzegovina, 66, 67, 90, 143, 165, 257n
Brazil, xlviii, li
Brunner, Alois, 167
Buda, 6, 16, 43
Bulgaria, xix, xxi, xxii, 5, 9, 48, 66, 67, 68, 78, 85, 88, 90, 92–5, 104, 109,
113, 116–20, 123, 130, 133, 135, 141, 144, 148, 149, 150–7, 160, 161, 163, 165, 166, 168, 173–9, 180, 183, 184, 185, 189–90, 191, 196, 197, 265n
Bursa, 9, 33, 37, 42, 48, 132, 202n
Byzantine Empire, 17
Byzantium, 1

Cairo, xx, 15, 57
Calabria, 16
Camondo, Abraham de, 77–8, 79–80
Camondo family, 77, 80
Campbell (Jewish district in Salonika), 141, 142, 143, 161, 188
Canada, 185
Çanakkale (Dardanelles), 162–3
Candia, 160
Cantacuzenus, Michael, 37
Capsali, Chief Rabbi Moses, 14–15
Capsali, Elijah, 7–8, 55
Carlsbad, 148
Carmona, Bekhor Isaac, 48–9
Carmona, Elia, 111
Carmona family, 48
Caro, Joseph, 52, 53, 54, 61, 193
Cartagena, Alonso de, xxxiv, xxxv
Castile, xxvi, xxvii, xix, xxx, xxxii–xxxiv, 20, 30
Castro, Orobio de, xlviii
Catalonia, xxxi, lii, 16
Cathars, xxx
Cavalla, 81
Cazès, Moïse, 111
Cemal, Pasha, 122
Central Europe, xix, 119, 179
Ceylon, xlviii
Chmielnicki, 56, 57
Christiani, Pablo, xxxi
Cidellus (Josef Ferruziel), xxviii
Cohen, Isaac, 141
Cohen, Moïse see Tekinalp, Munis
Cohn, Albert, 75, 76, 77, 78
Colbert, xlvii
Constantinople, 1, 4, 5, 14
Cordoba, xxxii, xxxiii
Cordova, 16
Cordovero, Moses, 54
Corfu, 14, 135, 160, 171
Corinth, 41
Costa, Uriel da, 1
Covo, Judah, 40
Crémieux, Adolphe, 73, 110
Crete, 45, 55
Croatia, 90, 143, 146, 164, 165, 172–3, 257n
Croissy, Colbert de, xlvii

Cuba, 185
Cvetkovich-Machek, 164
Cyprus, 6

Dalmatia, 9, 42–4, 165, 170, 172
Damascus, xx, 15, 34, 70, 72, 159–60
Damaskinos (Archbishop of Athens), 168
Dannecker, Theodor, 175
Danon, Abraham, 76, 107
Dardanelles *see* Çanakkale
Dax, xlv, xlvi
Dedeağaç *see* Alexandropolis
Demotica *see* Didhimotikhon
d'Espina, Alonso, xxxiv
Díaz, Fernand, xxxv, xxxiv
Didhimotikhon (Demotica), 169
Dizengoff, Meir, 130
Dobrudja, 173, 174
Dubrovnik *see* Ragusa
Dulcino, 58
Dumas, Alexandre, 111
Dupnitsa, 176
Duran, Rabbi Simon ben Semah, lii

Eastern Europe, xix, 25, 50, 106, 107, 114, 119, 120, 122
Eastern Rumelia, 66, 90, 93
Ecija, xxxii
Edirne (Adrianople), xix, 4, 5, 6, 9, 13, 16, 39, 40, 41, 42, 49, 50, 51, 52, 54, 58, 59, 63, 76, 83, 101, 106, 107, 117, 132, 162–3, 202n
Egypt, 1, 27, 37
Ehrenpriess, Chief Rabbi Marcus, 151
Eichmann, Karl Adolf, 167, 168, 175
Elnekave, David, 113
England *see* Great Britain
Epirus, 14, 166, 256n
Epstein, Isaac, 77, 135
Ercole II, Duke, xliii
Eskapa, Joseph, 57
Europe xxvi, xviii, xlix, lii, 4, 34, 38, 44–5, 46–7, 60, 72, 73, 74, 80, 98, 184, 189, 191, 197

Ferdinand of Aragon, xxxv
Ferrara, xliii, 60
Ferrer, Vicente, xxxii
Ferruziel, Josef (Cidellus), xxvii
Fertile Crescent, xviii, 5
Fez, liii, 16
Filov, Bogdan, 174
Florentin, David, 113, 125, 138
Fonseca, Daniel de, 38
Formon, Zadik Ben Yosef, 61

France, xxx, xxxi, xxxv, xxxvii, xliv, xlv, xlvi, xlvii, 4, 45, 46, 47, 55, 68, 69, 74, 79, 88–9, 95, 122, 148, 176, 178, 180, 185, 261n
Franco, Marcel, 162
Frankfurt, 166
Fresco, David, 113
Frumkin, Abraham, 108

Gabay, Isaac, 113
Gabay, Yehezkiel, 113
Gabay family, 48
Gabbai, Meir Ibn, 53
Gabrovski, Petur, 163, 174, 177, 178
Galante, Abraham, 109
Gallipoli, 58
Gaza, 10
Geloso, Carlo, 170
Genadios (Archbishop of Salonika), 168
Genoa, 5
Germany, xliv, xlv, li, lii, 4, 5, 74, 79, 90, 162–4, 180, 181, 184, 173–4
Ghiat, Alexander Ben, 110, 111
Gibraltar, 46
Givat Brenner, 133
Givat Brenner, 133
Golenic, 146
Gorna Dzhumaya, 176
Graetz, Heinrich, 110
Granada, xxv, xxvi, xxxi, li, 14, 38
Great Britain, xxx, xxxviii, 39, 40, 41, 45, 46–7, 57, 69, 73, 79, 95, 179
Greece, xix, xxii, 65, 66, 68, 81, 85, 89, 95, 96–101, 104, 130, 134–43, 154–6, 160, 162–3, 166–72, 174, 178, 184, 185, 189, 190, 191, 197, 256n, 265n
Grotius, Hugo, xlix
Gueron, Joseph, 174
Gumulcine *see* Komotini
Gurion, David Ben, 152, 155
Guttmacher, Eliyahu, 117

Haarlem, xlvii
Habib, Jacob Ibn, 52–3
Habib, Levi Ben, 51, 52
Hagiz, Rabbi Moses, 59
Haidar, 171
Haifa, 138, 188
Ha-Kohen, Abraham, 63
Ha-Kohen, Joseph, 55, 110
Halevi, Rabbi Benjamin Meir, 5
Halevi, Don Samuel, xxix
Halevi, Salomon, xxxiv
Halevy, Joseph, 76, 107
Halevy, Saadi Bezalel, 76, 113, 125

Hamburg, xliv, xlviii, l, xlviii, xlix, 117, 135
Hamon, Joseph, 14, 38
Hamon, Moses, 14, 38
Hamon family, 49
Handali, Esther, 38
Hartuv, 120
Hasköy (Jewish district in Istanbul), 5
Hasson, Albert, 167
Hayon, Vita, 147
Hazan, Aharon de Yosef, 113
Henry II, xliv
Henry III, xxxii
Henry IV, xxxv
Herzl, Theodor, 122
Hirsch, Baron de, 168
Holland, 25, 45, 47
Hulli, Rabbi Jacob ben Meir, 62–3, 64
Hungary, 4, 90

Iakova, Violeta, 175
Iberian peninsula, 6, 7, 49–50, 52, 60, 195, 196; *see also* Portugal; Spain
India, xlviii
Ioannina, 14, 171
Iran, 83, 195
Isabella, xxxv
Israel, xx–xxi, xxiii, 16–17, 112, 151, 157, 185–91, 197; *see also* Palestine
Israel, Menasseh ben, l
Istanbul, xix, 5, 6, 9, 10, 11–12, 13, 14–15, 16, 17, 20, 22–3, 25–8, 32, 33, 37, 38, 39, 42, 46, 47, 48, 49, 50, 54, 58, 60, 61, 63, 64, 71, 73, 75, 77, 78, 80, 81, 82, 83–4, 85, 87, 88, 101, 103, 107, 108, 110, 112, 117, 118, 121, 124–5, 127–8, 130–1, 132, 135, 160, 163, 179, 180, 183, 185, 202n
Italy, xliii, xliv, xlix, lii, 5, 12, 16, 25, 34, 37, 40, 42–3, 45, 50, 53, 54, 55, 60, 95, 148, 163, 165, 166, 169, 170–2, 185, 187, 189
Izmir (Smyrna), xix, 10, 17, 23–4, 37, 41, 42, 46, 47, 49, 50, 57, 59, 63, 75, 82, 83–4, 101, 108, 110, 112, 132, 133, 160, 185

Jabotinsky, Vladimir, 124, 140–1, 191
Jacobo of Gaeta, 38
Jacobson, Victor, 121
Jaffa, 122
James I, xxviii, xxx
James II, xxxi
Jasenovac, 172
Jerusalem, xx, 8, 10, 15, 27, 49, 51, 54, 57, 59, 75, 112, 120, 122, 148, 149

John I, xxxi
John II, xxxiv, xxxviii
Jona, Jacob, 111

Kalisher, Zvi Hirsch, 117
Karageorgevitch, Alexander, 90
Kavala, 176
Kaya, Şükrü, 181
Kfar Shitin, 190
Kirklareli, 162–3
Kishinev, 168
Kiustendil, 177
Komotini (Gümülcine), 176
Konya, 202n
Köprülü, Grand Vizir Ahmed, 58
Koretz, Chief Rabbi Zvi, 167, 168, 171
Kouffinas, Moshe, 189

Labastide-Clairence, xlv
La Guardia, xxxvi
Lamia, 5
Lapapa, Chief Rabbi Aaron, 57
Larissa, 39, 135, 171, 202n
Latin America, 185, 189
Leghorn, 16
Leipzig, 47
Leon, David Ben Judah Messer, 53
Levi, Buko, 177
ha-Levi, Zerahiah, xxxiii
Levy, Sam, 113
Lichtheim, Richard, 124
Lisbon, xxxix
Livorno, 44, 46, 47, 77
Logothetopoulos, Konstantinos, 166
Lom, 176
London xviii, xix, li, lii, 127, 130
Lorki, Joshua, xxxiii
Louis XIV, xlvi
Low Countries, 8
Lukov, Hristo, 175
Lull, Ramon, xxxi
Lunel, 4
Lusitanus, Amatus, 53
Lyons, 185

Macedonia, xix, 9, 42, 66, 81, 89, 90, 91–2, 99, 145, 154, 161, 163, 165, 166, 168, 173, 174, 175–6, 178, 185, 256n, 257n
Madrid, 61
Maghreb, xix, 16; *see also* North Africa
Magriso, Isaac, 63, 64
Mahmud II (sultan of Ottoman Empire), 48, 68
Maimonides, 53, 107
Majorca, xxviii

Malchi, Esperanza, 38
Mantua, xliii
Manuel I, King, xxxviii
Mapu, Abraham, 113
Marseilles, 185
Martínez, Ferrant, xxxii
Martini, Raymundus, xxi
Medici, Marie de, xlvi
Medina, Samuel de, 52
Mehmed II (sultan of Ottoman Empire), 5, 14, 38
Meir, Chief Rabbi Jacob, 135
Mendelssohn, Moses, 113
Mendes, Alvaro *see* Yaesh, Salomon Ibn
Mendes, Doña Gracia, 14, 16, 49; *see also* Nasi, Doña Gracia
Menton, Ratti, 72
Merci, Lucillo, 169
Merten, Dr. Max, 167
Mesopotamia, 149, 195
Metaxas, Ioannis, 137, 141, 142, 161
Mexico, 185
Milan, 10
Mitrani, Barukh ben Yizhak, 76, 106, 117
Mitrani, Rahamim Menahem, 63
Mizrahi, Chief Rabbi Elijah, 14–15, 27
Modiano family, 81
Molho, Michael, 109
Molho, Salomon, 55
Molho, Solomon, xli
Molière, 111
Monastir (Bitola), 9, 17, 33, 41, 91–2, 145, 176, 185, 202n
Montefiore, Sir Moses, 73, 75, 110
Montenegro, 90
Montpellier, 4
Morocco, xxvi, liii, liv, 16, 46, 83, 169, 185
Morpurgo family, 81
Muhammad, Prophet, 3
Munk, Salomon, 73
Mytilene, Duke of, 14

Nachmanides, Moses, xxxi
Nahmias, David, 50
Nahmias, H. G., 118
Nahmias, Samuel, 50
Nahum, Chief Rabbi Haim, 19, 24, 86–7, 126
Naples, lii, 10
Nasi, Don Joseph (Joào Mendes, Duke of Naxos), 14, 37, 43, 49, 193
Nasi, Doña Gracia, 43, 193; see also Mendes, Doña Gracia
Nathan of Gaza, 57

Navarre, lii
Navon, Elie Isaac, 76
Naxos, Duke of *see* Nasi, Don Joseph
Néhama, Joseph, 109, 185
Néhama, Yuda, 76, 106, 107
Netherlands, xliv, xlv, xlvi, l
New York, xix, 185
Nicopolis, 5, 9, 52, 202n
Niego, Elsa, 162
North Africa xvii, lii–liv, 1, 13, 16, 83, 85, 88, 149, 190, 191, 195
Nuremberg, 5

Odessa, 133
Ohri, 16
Olympos, 81
Orestias, 169
Osijek, 144
Ottolenghi, Moses Jacob, 77

Pakuda, Bahya Ibn, 61
Palestine, 1, 10, 15, 25, 27, 28, 54, 56, 66, 98, 113, 116, 117, 120, 121–2, 125, 128–34, 137, 138, 140, 141, 142, 145, 146, 148, 149, 152, 178, 179, 180, 185, 186–91, 265n; *see also* Israel
Panitsa, Liliana, 177
Papanastassiou, Alexander, 98
Papo, Eliezer, 63
Paris, xlv, 69, 76, 85, 138, 141, 149, 185, 196
Paul III, Pope, xliii
Paul IV, Pope, xliii
Pavelich, Ante, 172
Pedro the Cruel, xxix
Peloponnese, 256n
Perahia, Reuven Isaac, 118
Perez, Isaac Leib, 111
Perfet, Rabbi Isaac bar Sheshet, lii
Pesaro, 43
Peshev, Dimitur, 177
Peter the Great, 68
Peyrehorade, xlv, lxi n81
Philippopolis (Plovdiv), 5, 9, 94, 95, 120, 152, 176
Philippson, Ludwig, 113
Pires, Diego, xli
Pirot, 176
Pleven, 39
Plovdiv *see* Philippopolis
Poland, xxvii, lii–liii, 37, 43, 56, 177
Pontremoli, Raphael Hiya, 63
Portugal xviii, 8, 14, 16, 42, 52; New Christians in, xxxix–xliii
Preveza, 171

Prévost, Abbé, 111
Primo, Rabbi Samuel, 59
Provence, lii, 8

Rab, 172
Radigales, Sebastian Romero, 169
Ragusa (Dubrovnik), 9, 43, 44
Rallis, Ioannia, 166, 168
Recanati, Abraham, 138, 140–1
Reuveni, David, xlii, 55
Rhodes, 6, 28–9, 39, 41, 171, 180, 185
Rhodesia, 185
Richelieu, xlv, lxi n81
Rosales, Jacob, lii
Rothschild, Alphonse de, 75, 77
Rothschild family, 73, 110
Roti, Jacob, lii
Rotterdam, xlvii
Rouen, xlv, xlvi
Rovigo, Abraham, 59
Rozanes, Salomon 109
Rumania, 90, 130, 168, 173, 178, 179
Rumeli, 43, 45
Ruppin, Arthur, 124
Ruse, 94, 95, 175
Russia *see* Soviet Union

Saban, Chief Rabbi Rafael, 102
Safed, xix, 6, 10, 13, 15, 39–40, 49, 51,
    52, 54, 56
Saias family, 81
Saint-Pierre, Bernardin de, 111
Sajmiste, 165–6
Salonika, xix, xxi, xxii, xxiii, 5, 6, 8, 9,
    10, 12, 15, 16, 17, 20–2, 25–6, 28–9,
    30, 39–41, 42, 43, 45, 56, 49–50, 51,
    52, 53, 54, 56, 58, 61, 63, 66, 76, 77,
    78, 81–2, 83–4, 85–6, 87, 96–101,
    104, 108–9, 111, 112–13, 114, 117,
    125, 126, 129, 130, 133, 134–43, 145,
    148, 154–5, 157, 158, 160, 161,
    166–70, 171, 172, 184–5, 186, 188–9,
    197, 202n
Saltiel, Saby, 166, 167
Samakov, 48
Santa Fé, Jérónimo de, xxxiii
Santa Marća, Pablo de, xxxiv
Saraçoğlu, Şükrü, 182
Saragossa, xxxi
Sarajevo, xix, 9, 25–6, 33, 43, 66, 91–2,
    144, 145, 146, 147, 148, 149, 172,
    202n
Sarmiento, Pedro, xxxiv
Sava River, 165
Saydam, Refik, 180
Scholem, Gershom, 56

Seattle, 185
Segovia, xxxv
Selim I (sultan of Ottoman Empire), 38
Selim II (sultan of Ottoman Empire), 37
Selim III (sultan of Ottoman Empire),
    68
Semlin *see* Zemun
Seneor, Abraham, xxx, xxxiii, xxxvi
Seville, xxvi, xxxii, xxxv, xxxvi
Serbia, xix, 42, 66, 68, 81, 89–90, 91–2,
    163, 164–6, 174, 176, 257n
Serbs, Croats, and Slovenes, Kingdom
    of, 90, 143–4, 165
Serres, 176
Shakespeare, 111
Shaki, Haim Isaac, 64
Shalem, Moses Emanuel, 63
Shalem, Shlomoh, 111
Shalom family, 92
Shealtiel, 14
Sherezli, Israel, 112
Shtip, 176
Shumla (Shumen), 83
Sicily, li, 16, 39
Silva, Duarte de, l
Siroz, 202n
Sivas, 202n
Sivrihisar, 183
Skopje (Uskub), 9, 41, 91, 176, 202n
Slovenia, 165, 257n
Smyrna *see* Izmir
Sofia, 5, 6, 9, 43, 84, 93–4, 95–6, 161,
    163, 173, 175, 176, 177, 202n
Sofulu *see* Souflion
Sokolow, Nahum, 76
Soncino, Eliezer Gershon, 50, 60
Souflion (Sofulu), 169
South Africa, 185
Soviet Union, 121, 165, 175, 181
Spain, xviii, 4, 7, 12–13, 20, 28, 30, 32,
    37, 38, 39, 169, 185, 186, 192–3, 194;
    Jews in, xxvi–xxxix
Spalato (Split), 9, 44
Spinoza, Baruch, l
Stambolisky, Aleksandŭr, 163
Stefan (Metropolitan of Sofia), 177
Steinhardt, Laurence, 180
Sterodimos, Dr Speros, 170
Strasbourg, 77
Stroop, Jürgen, 171
Struma, 179, 181
Sue, Eugène, 111, 113
Suleiman the Magnificent (sultan of
    Ottoman Empire), 26, 37, 38
Switzerland, 189
Syria, 27, 73, 149

Tadzher, Leon, 175
Taitazak, Joseph, 51, 52, 53
Talavera, Fray Hernando de, xxxv
Tangier, xix, 16
Taragano, Alberto, 111
Tekinalp, Munis (Moïse Cohen), 103, 162
Tel-Aviv, 130, 138, 188
Tetuan, xix, 16, 83
Thessaly, 256n
Thrace, xix, 99, 162–3, 165, 166, 174, 175–6, 178, 185, 256n
Tiberias, 49
Tito, Marshal, 149
Tokat, 202n
Toledo, xxxii, xxxiv, 16
Toledo, Abraham de, 63
Torrès family, 81
El Transito, xxix
Treblinka, 176
Trikala, 39, 171, 202n
Tripoli, xx
Tsolakoglu, Georgios, 166
Tunis, 16, 46
Tunisia, lii, liv, 46
Turkey, xxi, xxii, 4, 8, 24, 55, 58, 85, 89, 95, 98, 101–4, 109, 114, 121–34, 137, 157, 159–60, 161–3, 179–84, 185, 186–8, 190, 191, 194, 195, 196, 197, 261n, 265n

Uganda, 152
Ukraine, 130
Ülkümen, Selahettin, 180
United States, 16, 44–5, 178, 185, 186, 189
Urbino, xliii
Uskub *see* Skopje
Usque, Abraham, xliii
Usque, Samuel, 8
Ussishkin, Menhamen, 148–9
Ustasha, 172
Uziel, Rafael, 113
Uziel, Salomon, 167

Valencia, xxviii, xxxii
Valladolid, xxxiii, xxxv, 20
Valona, 9, 17, 43, 53
Vechiarelli, 170
Venice, xliv, 5, 9, 10, 42, 43–4, 45, 47, 52, 53
Venizelos, Eleutherios, 97–9, 136, 137–8, 161
Verga, Salomon Ibn, 110
Vidin, 9, 43
Vienna, 81, 112, 119, 144, 147, 149, 167, 176
Vilna Gaon, 238n
Vital, Hayyim, 54
Vojvodina, 90, 143, 146, 164
Volos, 83, 135, 155, 171, 189
Vratsa, 160

Weizmann, Chaim, 178
Western Europe, xxx, xliv, lii, 16, 48, 64, 106; Marannos in, xlii–lii
Wilson, Woodrow, 127
Wise, Stephen, 178
Wisliceny, Dieter, 167, 171

Xanthi, 176

Yaavez, Rabbi Joseph, 55
Yaesh, Salomon Ibn (Alvaro Mendes), 43
Yahya, Jacob ben David Ibn, 51
Yehuda, Eliezer Ben, 76
Yugoslavia, xxi, 89, 90, 91–2, 104, 113, 143–50, 154, 157, 163–4, 170, 172–3, 174, 178, 184, 185, 189, 191, 196, 197, 265n

Zagreb, 144, 146, 147, 148, 172
Zamboni, Guelfo, 169
Zarfati, Rabbi Isaac, 4
Zemun (Semlin), 165–6
Zevi, Sabbetai, 57–9
Zimra, David Ibn Abi, 51
Zur Mosheh, 189
Zvi, Yizhak Ben, 155

Subject Index

acculturation
  Ashkenazim 90
  extent 105
  Haskalah 108
  linguistic 92, 114
  obstacles 115
  pre-Zionism 119
  Sephardim 91
aggadic texts 52–3
aid, mutual 25
Alliance Israélite Universelle 73, 78,
  82–9
  Bulgaria 93, 94, 150
  Jewish emancipation 90
  nationalization 104
  state interventions 100
  Turkey 102
  Zionism 119, 122, 124–5, 126–7,
  138, 150
Albigensian Crusade xxx, xxxv
Almohade invasion xxvi
antisemitism 159–64
  Bulgaria 93, 94, 104, 118, 190
  Italian-occupied Greece 171
  rise of 139
  Salonika, under Greek rule 96, 97,
  98, 101, 104: and Zionism 135,
  141, 142
  Turkey 132, 134, 181, 183, 184
  virulence 137
  Yugoslavia 92
Aristotelianism 53
arsenal tax 28
Ashkenazim 195

communal conflicts 12, 15
community structures 16
emigration 189
Haskalah 108
ideological trends 106
nation-states 90–1
politicization: pre-Zionism 117;
  Sephardism 147, 148, 149;
  Zionism 124–5, 143, 144
prestige 191
Sarajevo 172
assimilationism 115
asylum, Turkey 179
autonomy 16–26
  in Bulgaria 93
  communal legislation 30
  of Jewish community xxvii, xxviii,
  xxxi
  Zionism 127

banditry 45
bankers 79
berurei averot 30–1
Betar 138, 141
Bibliothèque israélite society 109
bills of exchange 42
birth rate 91, 92
Black Death xxxi
blood-libel accusations xxxi, xxxv
Bnei Mizrahi 141
Bnei Mizrahi-Brit Trumpeldor 141
bourgeoisie
  Alliance Israélite Universelle 82
  Turkish 103

Bulgarian language   94, 119, 156
Bulgarization   119

Calvinists   xlvii
cartels   42
Castilian law   16, 30
censorship   31
centralization   xxvii, xxxvi
 and autonomy   18
 and Chief Rabbis   24
 and congregations   23
challenges   34
Chief Rabbis   24
 fee for right to   27
 pre-Zionism   119
 role   70
 Turkey   104
 Zionism   124, 127, 129, 130
Chmielnicki massacres   56–7
Christianity   xxv, xlvii, xlviii, liv
Christians   xxviii
civil rights   90
civil service   94
clandestinity and Zionism   130–4
class conflict   xxxii
cloth tax   40, 41
commerce. *See* trade
Committee of Officials [Istanbul]   25
communism   137, 156–7, 158
 and Zionism   145
concessions   28
conflicts, communal   11–16, 17
congregations
 finances   26
 organization into   17, 20, 21, 23, 24
continuity, intergenerational   13
Convention of Valladolid   xxxiii
conversion   xxv, xxxi–xxxv, xxxvii,
  xxxviii, xxxix, xlviii
 forced   xl, xli, xliii, xlv
convivencia   xxix–xxx, xxxvii
cooperatives   95
Counter-Reformation   xlv
Court, imperial   38
courtier class   xxvi, xxvii, xxviii, xxix,
  xxxii, xxxiv
creativity, literary   110–15
crypto-Jews   xxxiv
crypto-Judaism   xxxix, xl, xli
culture *see* intellectual life

Dagger of Faith, (Martini)   xxxi
Damascus Affair   72–3, 74, 159
death rate   91, 93
Decree of Expulsion   xxxvi, xxxvii, xl,
  xlii, xlvi

decrees *see* law and order
demographic growth   91, 93
deportations
 Bulgaria   175, 176–8
 communal conflicts   11, 12
 German-occupied Greece   168, 169
 Ottoman Empire   5–6
 Turkey   180
desertion   187
dhimma and *dhimmis*
 cessation   123
 community structure   18
 living quarters   32
 Ottoman Empire   2, 3
 poll tax   26
 state legislation   29
 Turkey   188
 Westernization   69
 and Zionism   137
didactic works   112
diglossia   62
diplomacy   38
discrimination
 Turkey   103, 181
 see also antisemitism
Disputation of Tortosa   xxxiii
doctors
 numbers, Bulgaria   95
 power and influence   38
documents, payments for   28
Dönmes   182
Dorshei Leshon Ever society   108
drama, works of   111
dress   32
Dutch West India Company   xlviii
duties, exceptional   28
dwellings   33

economic profile of Jews
 Bulgaria   94
 Ottoman Empire   6
 Salonika   100–1
 Sarajevo   92
economy. *See also* trade
 Ottoman Empire   36–49
 Salonika   161
Edict of Expulsion   xxxix
education
 Alliance Israélite Universelle   83–9
 autonomy   24–5
 Bulgaria   93–4, 118–19: socialism
  156
 élites, role of   75–8
 Haskalah   106, 108
 literary creativity   112
 nationalization   104

postwar 187
priority 50–1
Salonika, under Greek rule 97, 100
secularization 91–2
Turkey 102–3
Westernization 71–2
élites
pre-Zionism 119
role of 72–82: declining 103
Tanzimat 70
teachers, liaison with 85
Zionism 122, 123, 138
emigration xxxix, xl, xliii, lii, 184–91
entrepreneurship 45
ethics literature 63
ethnic-religious communities 17, 18
excommunication 19, 20
for non-payment of tax 29
executive council 21–2
lay leadership 22–3
exegesis 52
Expulsion xxx, xxxvii, xxxviii, xxxix, li
expulsions xxv, xlvi, li

fascism
Croatia 172
emergence 163
Greece 170
and Zionism 141
Ferrara Bible xlv
finances, communal 26–9
fire, Salonika (1917) 97–8, 100, 136, 139
Fortalitium Fidei (d'Espina) xxxv
Fourth Lateran Council xxx
Francos
Alliance Israélite Universelle 83
customs 34
élites 74–5, 76, 77–9, 81
impact 46
French language
Alliance Israélite Universelle 84, 88
and bourgeoisie 82
curtailment, Turkey 102
and Judeo-Spanish language 114
and Sephardi distinctiveness 89
Talmud Torah 86
frontier changes 65–7

gabelle 28
Gallicization 88
German language 91
girls *see* women and girls

"golden age" myth 193
graduates 71–2
Greek language 97, 100
guilds 33, 41–2

halakhah 51–2
conflicts 49
emphasis on 56
popularity 60
Hamburg Bank lii
harassment 162, 163
by Germans 167
in Turkey 181
see also antisemitism
harem, imperial 38
Hashomer Hazair 141, 145, 146, 149, 153
Haskalah 106–9, 193
Alliance Israélite Universelle 83
pre-Zionism 120
hazakah 31
Hebrew language 108, 109
Hebrew rabbinical culture 49–55
Hebrew script 60
Hehaluz 133
Hehaluz Turkiah 133
heresy xxxv, xxxvi, xxxviii, xl, xli
Herzlian Zionism
Bulgaria 116
Palestine 117
Hibat Zion movement 118, 119, 120
historical literature 110
Hitahdut 128
homiletics 52
Huguenots li

Imperial Court 38
independent workers 95
indigo 40
industrial infrastructure 81
inflation
impact 44–5
postwar 100
Inquisition xxx, xxxv, xxxvi, xxxvii, xl, xli, xlii, xliv, xlv, xlix li
Portuguese xli, xlvi, liv
intellectual life 49
Hebrew rabbinical culture 49–55
literary creativity 110–15
religious Judeo-Spanish literature 60–4
Sabbatean explosion 55–60
internal dynamics, Westernization 106
Haskalah and science of Judaism 106–9

internal dynamics (*continued*)
    literary creativity   110–15
international commerce
    Bulgaria   95
    Sephardim   42–4
international economy   44–9
Islam *see* Muslims and Islam

janissaries
    cloth tax   40, 41
    and *sarrafs*   37, 48
    upkeep costs   44
journalists   113
    antisemitism   162
    see also newspapers
Judaism   xlix
    science of   106–9
Judeo-Spanish language   51, 92, 94,
    105, 196–7
    Israel   198
    Nazism   159
    Westernization   114
Judeo-Spanish literature   110–11
    rise of   60–4

Kabbala   53–4
    and messianism   56, 59
Kadimah society   109
Karaites
    communal conflicts   15
    community structures   16
    Ottoman Empire, arrival in   5, 6
Kemalism   183
    and Zionism   131
"king's cloth"   40

Ladino   61, 62, 63
language   liii, liv
law and order   xxvi–xxvii, 29–34
    anti-Jewish sentiment   90, 174,
    178
    autonomy   18–19
    Salonika, under Greek rule   97, 99
    Turkey   181, 182
    Westernization   70
libraries   49, 50
literacy   51
literature   49–50
    creativity   110–15
    Judeo-Spanish, rise of   60–4
    philosophical and scientific questions
    53
    responsa   51–2, 61
living conditions   91
living quarters   32–3, 162
loan banks   95

Makabi gymnastic society   128
Marranism   xxxiv, xxxvi, xl–xli, xlii
Marranos   xxxiv, xli, xlii, liii
    communal conflicts   14
    community structure   24
    in Western Europe   xlii–lii
    international commerce   42–3, 45
    literature   53, 61, 64
    Ottoman Empire, arrival in   8
    reintegration   52
marriages   97
Marxism   156, 157
maskilim
    Haskalah   106–7, 109: pre-Zionism
    120
    schools   76, 78
    teachers, liaison with   85
Meam Loez   62, 63–4
mercantile capitalism   li
messianism   xli, 55–6, 59–60
    pre-Zionists   120
    Zevi   57–8, 59
middle class
    Alliance Israélite Universelle   84
    emigration   187
    expansion   80
    French influence   88
    Salonika   82
    Turkish   101
    Zionism   124
middleman role
    decline of   103
    international trade   46, 47
military service   69, 100, 187
mint   37
Mizrahi movement   139–40, 153
modernity and modernization   66–7, 68
    and Jewish nationalism   109
    Salonika   97
moneylenders   37
monogamy   32
multinationalism, Yugoslavian   147
music   54
Muslims and Islam   xxv, xxvi, xxviii,
    lii, liv, 1, 2–3, 102
    deportations   5
    law and order   18
    living quarters   32–3
    middle class   101
Mustarabi   15
mysticism   53, 59
myths, Sephardim historiography
    192–4

nation-states
    emergence   65–6, 67

Sephardim, response to   89–105
nationalism
  Bulgarian   118, 119
  exclusives   131
  Greek   136
  and *Haskalah*   109
  receptivity to   89
  secularization   92
  Sephardism   148
  Turkish   104
  and Zionism   129, 154
Nazism   159, 164
  Greece   166, 167, 170–1
  Turkey   181
Neemanei Zion society   132, 133
New Christians   xxxiv–xxxviii, xl, xlii,
    xliv, xlvii, li
  of Portugal   xxxviii–xlii
newspapers   73–4
  antisemitism   161, 162, 166
  Haskalah movement   106, 107
  pre-Zionism   120
  role of   110, 111, 112–13
  socialism   155, 156
  Zionism   122, 124, 125–6, 139, 142:
    Bulgaria   153

open politicization   87
ordinances *see* law and order
Ottoman Empire   xlii, lii, liv
  arrival in   1–10
  economy   36–49
  Westernization   68–72

papacy   xliii
  of Portugal   xxxviii–xliii
Pastoureaux (Shepherd's Crusade)
    xxxi
patriarchal family   32
pauperization *see* poverty
Pentateuch, translation   60–1
persecution   xxx, xxxix, xliii,
    payments to avoid   27
philosophical inquiry   53
physicians *see* doctors
piracy   45
plays   111
Poalei Zion   150, 152
poetry   111
  religious   63
pogroms   xxxii, xxxiii, xxxix, lii
politicization   116–17
  education   89
  open   87
  pre-Zionist actors   117–21
  Sephardism   143–50

socialist options   154–8
  Zionists   121–34: in Bulgaria
    150–4; in Greece   134–43
poll tax   3, 7
  abolition   69
  and autonomy   18, 26
  "kings cloth"   40
poverty
  Bulgaria   95–6
  extent   28, 187
  Macedonia   92
  Salonika   82
power, access to   87
pre-Zionism   116–21
prestige of Jews   191, 197
printing presses   50
proletariat   81–2
proportional representation   127
prostitution   33–4
protection of Jews
  from antisemitism   160
  Ottoman Empire   2, 3, 44
publishing   50, 112
Pugio Fidei (Martini)   xxxi

Rabbanites   5, 6
rabbinical culture   49–55, 56
  Judeo-Spanish literature   62–3, 64
rabbis
  community structures   23
  pre-Zionism   119
  see also Chief of Rabbis
Rashi script   60, 166
re-Christianization   xxx, xxxii
Reconquista   xxv, xxvi, xxvii, xxviii,
    xxx–xxxi
Reformation   li
regulations *see* law and order
religious law *see halakhah*
rents   28
repatriation   168
  to Spain   169
resistance movement
  Bulgaria   173
  Greece   171
responsa literature   51–2, 61
Revisionism   145–6, 150, 152–3
  Sephardim, awareness of   190–1
riots   xxix, xxxi, xxxii, xxxiv, xxxv,
    xxxix
  antisemitic   159, 160
ritual murder accusations   159–60
Romaniots
  communal conflicts   11–12, 14, 15
  community structures   16, 19, 20
  intellectual life   49

Romaniots (*continued*)
  Ottoman Empire, arrival in   5, 6, 7
  tax farming   37
royal alliance   xxvi, xxvii, xxviii, xxix, xxx, xxxii, xxxvi, xxxvii
ruling class, Ottoman Empire   1–2

Sabbateanism
  explosion of   55–60
  repercussions   62
salt tax   28
sarrafs   37, 48
Saturdays   99, 140
schools *see* education
scientific inquiry   53
self-perception, Jews'   123, 144
separation, marital   31
Serbo-Croat language   92
  curriculum, introduction to   91
Sfat Emet society   108–9
shekel   151
Shepherd's Crusade (Pastoureaux) xxxi
slaves   xxxviii, 33
socialism   137, 154–8
  and Zionism   141, 145, 150, 152
socialization
  Alliance Israélite Universelle   86
  nationalism and Zionism   154
songs   111
state agencies   95
state service   71
structures, community   16–26
Struma incident   179, 181
sumptuary regulations   32
Sundays   99, 139, 140, 161

Talmud Torah   25, 50
  Alliance Israélite Universelle   86
  Westernization   77
  Zionism   135
Tanzimat   68–9, 70, 71
tax collection   6, 12, 15, 37, 48
tax exemption   11, 26, 29
taxation   xxvii, xxviii, xxix, xxxiii, xxxvi, 26–9
  internal   97
  Ottoman Empire   1, 2, 3, 7, 10: and autonomy   18, 26; community structures   21; revenue   48
  Turkey   182–4, 186
  and Zionism   134
  see also poll tax
teachers   85

textile manufacture
  guilds   42
  Sephardim   39–41
theaters   111
Thirty Years War   xlvi
timar system   44
tobacco industry crisis   100
trade   xxvi, xliv, xlii, xliii, xliv, xlvii, xlviii, xlix, l, li, lii
trades unions   154–5
transport system
  Salonika   188–9
  and volume of trade   79
Turkicization   72, 102–3, 134
Turkish citizenship   180
Turkish language   102–3, 162

upper class   88
upward mobility   80
Ustasha regime   172
usufruct of real estate   31

Venizelism   98–9
visas, Turkey   179

Wattasid dynasty   lii
Westernization
  impact   65–7
  internal dynamic: *Haskalah* and science of Judaism   106–9; literary creativity   110–15
  Ottoman Empire   68–72
  Sephardim   89–105
  strategies: Alliance Israélite Universelle   83–9; élites, role of 72–82
  and Zionism   126
widows   31
Wissenschaft movement   107
women and girls
  Bulgarian illiteracy   94
  education   51, 84, 85: teachers 85
  harems   38
  socialization   154
  tertiary sector employment   80
wool   39, 40–1, 46
Workers' Socialist Federation   154–6, 158

xenophobia, Turkish   101, 163, 181, 182, 183

Young Turks   71, 72
  open politicization   87

Turkicization process   102
Zionism   121, 134

Zionism and Zionists   116, 157–8
  Bulgaria   150–4
  and emigration   186, 188–9

Greece   134–43
Ottoman Empire   121–34
  and Sephardism   144–6, 147–50,
    191
  and socialism   156, 157
Zohar   54, 56